Envisioning Legality

Envisioning Legality: Law, Culture and Representation brings together leading scholars working at the intersection of law, representation, and visual culture. Its wager is that the cultural representations which hold us in their thrall – from *Game of Thrones* to *The Dark Knight*, *The Oprah Winfrey Show* to *The Wire*, war photography to Inuit cinema – not only represent law, but constitute the ocular and spectacular fabric of legality itself. The essays in this volume explore the economies of looking, questions of genre that determine audience response, the affective perspective of the spectator, and their psychic investments, as modes of representational legality in which law is performed or enforced, and legal subjects affectively constituted. In so doing they shed new light on key concerns of critical legal scholarship, including law's capacity to redress past wrongs, recognise and combat injustices, and orient our communities in relation to uncertain futures. *Envisioning Legality* thereby presents a Cultural Legal Studies that provides the means for envisioning and reimagining law, legality and justice in a global, mediated world.

Timothy D. Peters is a Senior Lecturer at USC Law School, University of the Sunshine Coast, Queensland, Australia.

Karen Crawley is a Lecturer at Griffith Law School, Griffith University, Queensland, Australia.

Envisioning Legality

Law, Culture and Representation

Edited by Timothy D. Peters
and Karen Crawley

Routledge
Taylor & Francis Group
LONDON AND NEW YORK

First published 2018
by Routledge

2 Park Square, Milton Park, Abingdon, Oxfordshire OX14 4RN
52 Vanderbilt Avenue, New York, NY 10017

Routledge is an imprint of the Taylor & Francis Group, an informa business

First issued in paperback 2019

British Library Cataloguing-in-Publication Data
A catalogue record for this book is available from the British Library

Library of Congress Cataloging-in-Publication Data
Names: Peters, Timothy D., editor. | Crawley, Karen, editor.
Title: Envisioning legality : law, culture and representation / edited by Timothy D. Peters and Karen Crawley.
Description: Abingdon, Oxon ; New York, NY : Routledge, 2018. | Includes bibliographical references and index.
Identifiers: LCCN 2017027140 | ISBN 9781138123762 (hbk)
Subjects: LCSH: Law and literature. | Law in motion pictures. | Law on television. | Culture and law. | Sociological jurisprudence.
Classification: LCC PN56.L33 E58 2018 | DDC 809/.933554—dc23
LC record available at https://lccn.loc.gov/2017027140

ISBN: 978-1-138-12376-2 (hbk)
ISBN: 978-0-367-23256-6 (pbk)

Typeset in Galliard
by Apex CoVantage, LLC

Contents

Figures

Contributors

Book editors

Dr Timothy D. Peters

Senior Lecturer, USC Law School, University of the Sunshine Coast, Queensland, Australia

Dr Peters is a Senior Lecturer at the USC Law School, University of the Sunshine Coast, an Adjunct Research Fellow at the Law Futures Centre, Griffith University and is President of the Law, Literature and the Humanities Association of Australasia. He holds an LLB, a Bachelor of Commerce and a PhD from Griffith University, where he was a lecturer from 2011 to 2017. His research explores the intersections of legal theory, theology and popular culture and he is currently completing a book manuscript for Edinburgh University Press with the working title *A Theological Jurisprudence of Popular Cinema: Superheroes, Science Fictions and Fantasies of Modern Law*. Timothy was a Managing Editor of the *Griffith Law Review* (2012–2017) and Secretary of both the Law, Literature and Humanities Association of Australasia (2009–2016) and Law and Society Association of Australia and New Zealand (2006–2016).

Dr Karen Crawley

Lecturer, Griffith Law School, Griffith University, Queensland, Australia

Karen Crawley is a lecturer at the Griffith Law School and a Managing Editor of the *Australian Feminist Law Journal*. She researches at the intersections of law and aesthetics, drawing on literary theory, visual culture and critical theory. She is a graduate of the University of Sydney, with Honours in English Literature and Law, and did her postgraduate study at McGill University (LLM and PhD). She serves on the board of the Law, Literature and Humanities Association of Australasia.

Book contributors

Dr Edwin Bikundo

Senior Lecturer, Griffith Law School, Griffith University, Queensland, Australia

Edwin Bikundo is a Senior Lecturer at the Griffith University School of Law. He has teaching and research interests in International and Comparative Law as well as Legal Theory. A recent aspect of this research is: "Carl Schmitt as a Subject and Object of International Criminal Law: Ethical Judgment in Extremis" published in *The International Criminal Law Review* (2016): 216–236. Before joining Griffith University, he was a doctoral student and then a sessional member of the Law Faculty at the University of Sydney. Prior to that he studied at the University of Pune in India, Utrecht University in the Netherlands and at the Kenya School of Law. Edwin also practised as an Advocate of the High Court of Kenya and taught at the Faculty of Law at the University of Nairobi and the Faculty of Arts at Egerton University in Kenya.

Associate Professor Penny Crofts

Faculty of Law, University of Technology, Sydney, Australia

Penny Crofts is Associate Professor in the Faculty of Law at the University of Technology, Sydney. She conducts interdisciplinary research into the criminal law, drawing on historical, literary, philosophical and empirical materials to critically investigate its models of culpability and enforcement. She is the author of *Wickedness and Crime: Laws of Homicide and Malice* (London: Routledge, 2013).

Professor Bonnie Honig

Brown University, Providence, RI, USA and American Bar Foundation, Chicago, USA

Bonnie Honig is Nancy Duke Lewis Professor at Brown University in the departments of Modern Culture and Media (MCM) and Political Science. She is also Affiliate Research Professor at the American Bar Foundation, Chicago. Her most recent books are *Antigone, Interrupted* (Cambridge: Cambridge University Press, 2013) and *Public Things: Democracy in Disrepair* (Oxford: Oxford University Press, 2017). She can be reached at bonnie_honig@brown.edu

Professor Rebecca Johnson

Faculty of Law, University of Victoria, British Columbia, Canada

Rebecca Johnson is Professor at the Faculty of Law at the University of Victoria, Canada, and Associate Director of the Indigenous Law Research Unit. Her work centres the place of the cultural imaginary in the legal order. She has written on such topics as same-sex family formation, colonialism, judicial dissent, affect and emotion, mothers and babies in prison, cinematic violence, the Western, and Inuit cinema. She has co-edited a special issue of the *Canadian Journal of Women and the Law* on 'Law, Film, and Feminism,' and is currently working on the implementation of the Truth and Reconciliation Commission's findings in legal education.

Professor William P. MacNeil

Dean & Head, School of Law & Justice, Southern Cross University, New South Wales & Queensland, Australia

Professor MacNeil is Dean & Head, School of Law & Justice, Southern Cross University, where he holds The Honourable John Dowd Chair in Law. His most recent book, *Novel Judgements: Legal Theory as Fiction* (Abingdon, Oxon: Routledge, 2012), won the Penny Pether Prize for Scholarship in Law, Literature and the Humanities, 2013. MacNeil is currently at work on a study of the jurisprudence of science fiction, fantasy and horror, and is the series editor for Edinburgh Critical Studies in Law, Literature and the Humanities. As of 2017, Professor William MacNeil is the Chair of the Council of Australian Law Deans (CALD). He can be reached at william.macneil@scu.edu.au

Professor Desmond Manderson

Australian National University, Canberra, Australia

Desmond Manderson is a professor at The Australian National University. From 2002 to 2011, he was Canada Research Chair in Law and Discourse at McGill University, and Australian Research Council Future Fellow at ANU College of Law and Humanities Research Centre from 2012 to 2015. His most recent book was *Kangaroo Courts and the Rule of Law: The Legacy of Modernism* (London: Routledge, 2012). He is currently completing *Just in Time: Law in the Visual Arts,* a major research project funded by the fellowship scheme. The ARC's support for the essay in this collection is gratefully acknowledged.

Associate Professor Kieran Tranter

Griffith Law School, Griffith University, Queensland, Australia

Kieran Tranter is Associate Professor at the Griffith Law School. He researches law, technology and the future, with a particular focus on the law and culture of digital and autonomous disruption. He has published widely on issues of law and technology, including science fiction's jurisprudence of technology, the law's relationship with cultures of automobility, and how law responds to technological change. He has served as Managing Editor of the *Griffith Law Review* and is on the Advisory Board for the *Journal of Law, Culture and the Humanities.*

Professor Alison Young

School of Social & Political Sciences, University of Melbourne, Australia

Alison Young is the Francine V. McNiff Professor of Criminology in the School of Social and Political Sciences at the University of Melbourne. She has an LLB (Hons) from Edinburgh University and a Masters and PhD in Criminology from Cambridge University. She is the author of *Street Art World* (London: Reaktion Press, 2016), *Street Art, Public City: Law, Crime and the Urban Imagination* (London: Routledge, 2014), *The Scene of Violence: Cinema, Crime, Affect* (London: Glasshouse, 2010), *Street/Studio: From Street to Studio* (Fishermans Bend, Victoria: Thames & Hudson, 2010), *Judging the Image: Art, Value, Law* (London: Routledge, 2005) and *Imagining Crime:*

Textual Outlaws and Criminal Conversations (London: Sage Publications, 1996), as well as numerous articles on the intersections of law, crime and culture. Her key research areas are law, art and public culture; cinema and crime; and image studies generally. She is an Honorary Professor in the Law School at City University, London, and an Adjunct Professor in the School of Law, Griffith University, and has been a visiting fellow at Westminster University, Birkbeck College, Hong Kong University, New York University and the Australian National University. She is completing an ARC Discovery Project on the reception of street art in the cultural field, focusing upon its transformative potential in urban space.

Acknowledgements

This collection arose out of a symposium organised under the auspices of the Griffith Law School and the Socio-Legal Research Centre (now the Law Futures Centre) at Griffith University in 2012 entitled "Representational Legality: Reading Culture, Thinking Law." The symposium was supported by grants from both the Griffith Law School Research Support Scheme and the Griffith Social and Behavioural Research College Funding Support Scheme. We would like to thank all the participants in the Representational Legality symposium for their significant engagement with each other and each of the papers presented: Professor Maria Aristodemou, Dr Edwin Bikundo, Associate Professor Penny Crofts, Professor Bonnie Honig, Professor Rebecca Johnson, Professor William MacNeil, Professor Desmond Manderson and Associate Professor Kieran Tranter. We would also like to thank Professor Brad Sherman, Carol Ballard, Madonna Adcock and the Socio-Legal Research Centre for their support and assistance in organising and running the symposium. Thanks also go to Chanel Vasilj and Jessica Armao for their excellent research assistance in the early stages of the book project.

Thanks to Routledge for agreeing to publish the collection, and in particular to Colin Perrin, Laura Muir and Hannah Lovelock for their support and immense patience as the collection came to life.

Grateful acknowledgment is made for the permission to reproduce the images in Chapter 7, "Trench, trail, screen: scenes from the scopic regime of sovereignty":

- The Estate of the late Frances Antoinette Mooy and the State Library of NSW: Frank Hurley, *Battle-Scarred Sentinels* (1917)
- The Estate of the late Frances Antoinette Mooy and the National Film and Sound Archives Australia: *Dawn (or Morning) at Passchendaele* (1917)
- Rightsmith: Still from Damien Parer, *Kokoda Front Line!* (Cinesound Review, No. 0568, 1942).

Chapter 5, "Machiavellian fantasy and the game of laws: rex, sex and lex in George R. R. Martin's *A Song of Ice and Fire*" appeared in an earlier form as William MacNeil, "Machiavellian Fantasy and the Game of Laws" *Critical Quarterly* 57(1) (2015): 34–48 and we gratefully acknowledge the permission provided by John Wiley & Sons for the chapter's inclusion here.

Finally, we extend our most grateful thanks to Professor William MacNeil who has provided extensive support for us both in relation to this project but more generally as academic and intellectual mentor, Dean extraordinaire, pop culture guru and loving friend. Bill co-hosted and chaired the Representational Legality symposium and provided significant advice, input and encouragement in relation to the project as a whole. *Envisioning Legality* would not have been possible without him.

Chapter 1

Introduction: 'representational legality'

Karen Crawley and Timothy D. Peters

Lawful imaginings in cultural legal studies

This collection arose from an invitation to scholars of Cultural Legal Studies to focus on the representational nature of legality in the age of spectacle and global visual media. It is an era that Richard Sherwin has termed 'the neo-Baroque,' in which representations proliferate, churning through fictional and factual genres seamlessly, producing a never-ending combination of visual texts for consumption.[1] This overwhelming flood of representations may seem to splinter or fracture representations of law and its relationship to values such as justice or truth. But this is to miss how deeply law is implicated in questions of representation – through the doubling and repetition that brings life before it. The chapters in this collection understand that law is *constituted* through its envisioning, forming and figuring in cultural texts as much as juridical institutions. These representations are not simply imaginations or representations of law that is elsewhere operative (in juridical texts, institutions and officers), but indicate the ocular and spectacular fabric of legality itself. The economies of looking, the questions of genre that determine audience response, the affective perspective of the spectator, and their psychic investments – these are sites of representational legality, modes in which law is performed or enforced or has effects, and legal subjects experience its affect.[2] Representational legality is what binds us together and constitutes the *nomos* in which we live.[3]

1 Richard Sherwin, *Visualising Law in the Age of the Digital Baroque: Arabesques and Entanglements* (London and New York: Routledge, 2011).
2 On affect, see: Alison Young, *The Scene of Violence: Cinema, Crime, Affect* (London: Routledge, 2010); Ruth Buchanan and Rebecca Johnson, "Strange Encounters: Exploring Law and Film in the Affective Register," in Austin Sarat, ed., *Studies in Law, Politics and Society: A Special Symposium Issue on Law and Film*, Vol. 46 (Bradford: Emerald, 2009), 33; Anne Hickey-Moody and Peta Malins, eds, *Deleuzian Encounters: Studies in Contemporary Social Issues* (New York: Palgrave, 2008); Sara Ahmed, *The Cultural Politics of Emotion* (Edinburgh: Edinburgh University Press, 2004); Eve Kosofsky Sedgwick, *Touching Feeling: Affect, Pedagogy, Performativity* (Durham, NC: Duke University Press, 2003).
3 See Robert Cover, "Foreword: *Nomos* and Narrative," *Harvard Law Review* 4 (1983): 12–19.

Recent collections have showcased Cultural Legal Studies as a burgeoning field of humanist and interdisciplinary scholarship.[4] It has been developed by humanities scholars trained in literature, philosophy, art history and film studies applying their methods to law – methods influenced by semiology, deconstruction and psychoanalysis, among other hermeneutical frameworks. Unlike the facticity and ethnography of the socio-legal, Cultural Legal scholars share an interest in the workings of representations, how they signify and create normative worlds,[5] and how they function as the 'alter-egos of law,' 'the very material through which the legal institution becomes juridical.'[6] In law and literature, as in law and film, imagination and narrative do not simply create stories or myths in the world, but effectively make the entire world seem like a story; life and myth converge.[7] As Austin Sarat and Thomas Kearns wrote, '(w)e have internalized law's meanings and its representations of us so much that our own purposes and understandings can no longer be extricated from them.'[8] The force of law and the possibilities of justice are bound up in the stories or narratives we tell ourselves. Art's images and literature's narratives are central to these stories: they are vital to law's origin, meaning and legitimacy. Law cannot be separated out from the cultural texts that envision and constitute it – to separate out law and literature, for instance, is to impoverish both, reducing literature to a supplement or corrective to law.[9] Desmond Manderson's emphasis on literature's incompletion, its pluralism, its excesses of signification and its interpretative openness reminds us that justice is not an ideal so much as an experience or a process.[10] The dynamic process that occurs when a person engages with a cultural form shapes the meaning,

4 Cassandra Sharp and Marett Leiboff, eds, *Cultural Legal Studies: Law's Popular Cultures and the Metamorphosis of Law* (London: Routledge, 2016); Austin Sarat, Lawrence Douglas and Martha Umphrey, eds, *Law on the Screen* (Stanford, CA: Stanford University Press, 2005); Austin Sarat, ed., *Imagining Legality: Where Law Meets Popular Culture* (Tuscaloosa: University of Alabama Press, 2011); Peter Robson and Jessica Silbey, eds, *Law and Justice on the Small Screen* (London: Hart Publishing, 2012); Leslie J. Moran et al., eds, *Law's Moving Image* (London: Cavendish, 2004); Richard Sherwin, ed., *Popular Culture and Law* (Aldershot: Ashgate, 2006); M.D.A. Freeman, ed., *Law and Popular Culture* (Oxford: Oxford University Press, 2005); Guy Osborn and Steve Greenfield, *Readings in Law and Popular Culture* (London and New York: Routledge, 2006).

5 Marett Leiboff and Cassandra Sharp, "Cultural Legal Studies and Law's Popular Cultures," in Sharp and Leiboff, eds, *Cultural Legal Studies*, 9–12.

6 Peter Rush and Andrew Kenyon, "Alter Egos: The Mise-en-Scène," in Andrew Kenyon and Peter Rush, eds, *Aesthetics of Law and Culture: Texts, Images, Screens – Studies in Law, Politics and Society, Volume 34* (Emerald Group Publishing Limited, 2004), 3.

7 James Boyd White, *The Legal Imagination* (Chicago: University of Chicago Press, 1985).

8 Austin Sarat and Thomas R. Kearns, "Editorial Introduction," in Austin Sarat and Thomas R. Kearns, eds, *The Rhetoric of Law* (Ann Arbor: University of Michigan Press, 1994), 12–13.

9 See, for instance, Desmond Manderson, *Kangaroo Courts and the Rule of Law: The Legacy of Modernism* (London: Routledge, 2012) and Wai Chee Dimock, *Residues of Justice: Literature, Law and Philosophy* (Berkeley, Los Angeles and London: University of California Press, 1996).

10 See Manderson, *Kangaroo Courts.*

possibilities and limitations of our thinking about law and justice, which becomes, in Wendy Adam's words, 'a means rather than an end, an experiential pursuit rather than a definitive outcome, a way of discussing and dealing with the full range of diversity and normative complexity.'[11]

Cultural Legal Studies' focus on the texts of popular culture – and the wonders of alternative spaces, images and worlds – reflects the centrality of the imagination (and its appropriation) to the operation and effectiveness of law and legality. The chapters in this collection thus take as their focus the connections between the image, imagination and ways of seeing that are embedded in and circulate through our interactions with cultural texts. Over the past decade, this critical movement has embraced ever-more 'non-academic' cultural texts, from graphic novels to video games to street art,[12] and explicitly refused the distinction between low and high culture,[13] investing in works of popular culture – its love of myth and superheroes, its traffic in images of crimes, villains and rulers[14] – by inquiring into, for instance, 'the ways in which television and film portrayals of law speak to, and provoke, particular anxieties about law and desires for particular kinds of legality.'[15] Scholars have paid attention to the experience of reading literature, or watching film, or encountering an image, asking how these texts invite particular modes of engagement, engender certain perspectives, privilege

11 Wendy Adams, *Popular Culture and Legal Pluralism* (Melbourne: Taylor & Francis, 2016), 26.

12 For example, on graphic novels, see: Jason Bainbridge " 'This is the Authority. This Planet is Under Our Protection' – An Exegesis of Superheroes' Interrogations of Law," *Law Culture and the Humanities* 3:3 (2007): 455; Thomas Giddens, "Navigating the Looking Glass: Severing the Lawyer's Head in Arkham Asylum," *Griffith Law Review* 24:3 (2015): 395; on video games, see: Ashley Pearson and Kieran Tranter, "Code, Nintendo's Super Mario and Digital Legality," *International Journal for the Semiotics of Law* 28:4 (2015): 825; Michael Barnett and Cassandra Sharp, "The Moral Choice of inFAMOUS: Law and Morality in Video Games," *Griffith Law Review* 24:3 (2015): 482; on street art, see: Alison Young, *Street Art, Public City: Law, Crime and Urban Imagination* (London: Routledge, 2013); Karen Crawley, "Beyond the War on Graffiti: The Right to Visual Expression in Urban Spaces," *Griffith Journal of Law and Human Dignity Special Art Issue* (2015): 85–107.

13 Austin Sarat, "What Popular Culture Does for, and to, Law: An Introduction," in Austin Sarat, ed., *Imagining Legality: Where Law Meets Popular Culture* (Tuscaloosa: University of Alabama Press, 2011); Richard Sherwin, *When Law Goes Pop: The Vanishing Line between Law and Popular Culture* (Chicago: University of Chicago Press, 2000); Austin Sarat and Austin Kearns, eds, *Law in the Domains of Culture* (Ann Arbor: University of Michigan Press, 1998); William MacNeil, *Lex Populi: The Jurisprudence of Popular Culture* (Stanford, CA: Stanford University Press, 2007).

14 Leiboff and Sharp even define it in terms of popular culture. Leiboff and Sharp, "Cultural Legal Studies," 5.

15 Sarat, "What Popular Culture Does for, and to, Law," 6. For example, Sarat, "Imagining the Law of the Father: Loss, Dread and Mourning in the Sweet Hereafter", *Law and Society Review* 34 (2000), 5–46; Desmond Manderson, "Trust Us Justice: 24, Popular Culture, and the Law," in Sarat, ed. *Imagining Legality*, 22–52; Naomi Mezey, "Law's Visual Afterlife: Violence, Popular Culture, and Translation Theory," in Sarat, ed., *Imagining Legality*, 65–99.

certain readings and undermine others. Questions of iconography, theatricality, style, form, perspective, framing and genre come to the forefront of the analysis. In particular, scholarship on law and the visual has theorised the complex relationship between visual orders and legal subjectivity.[16] Law on the one hand is iconophobic – anxious about the seductive power of what Jean Baudrillard calls 'the evil demon'[17] of images – yet constituted by, and deeply invested in, a regime of images. As Costas Douzinas and Lynda Nead write in their seminal collection *Law and the Image* in 1999, '(l)aw's force depends partly on the inscription on the soul of a regime of images.'[18] This scholarship has shown how images cannot be analysed in the same way as texts: they are persuasive, non-linear, sequential and cumulative, convey meaning through associative logic, and are rapidly intelligible in a way that text is not. The realm of the image is the realm of the unconscious, the fabric of our imaginaries.

So questions of the image go to the law's effect and affect as a realm of power and meaning for legal subjects, a subject that is deeply implicated in the psychic dimension of legality. For as psychoanalytic jurisprudes have long emphasised, social or political explanations of law's force are only of limited relevance in understanding '*the visual effects of the law*, for . . . its dogmatic ability to hit the tender spot . . . cannot be accounted for by the ordinary means of observation.'[19] As William MacNeil's jurisprudential readings show us, the task of critique is not one of 'unmasking' law's ideology, the power lurking behind the Real politics of its reason, but of seeking to understand how legality itself is informed by desire or *jouissance*.[20] Ideology, fantasy and unconscious desire operate within and underneath the law, not outside of, or outside the processes of, representation. Edward Mussawir has suggested that we view law, like film, as 'an image-assemblage' through which 'affectivity, subjectivity, and perceptivity are distributed.'[21] At stake is not simply a technical understanding of the processes of image construction and interpretation that make up the workings of legality. The call is not

16 See, for example, Costas Douzinas and Lynda Nead, eds, *Law and the Image: The Authority of Art and the Aesthetics of Law* (Chicago and London: University of Chicago Press, 1999); Sherwin, *When Law Goes Pop*; Sherwin, *Visualizing Law*; Peter Goodrich, *Legal Emblems and the Art of Law:* Obiter Depicta *as the Vision of Governance* (New York: Cambridge University Press, 2014); Anne Wagner and Richard Sherwin, eds, *Law, Culture and Visual Studies* (New York: Sprinter, 2014).

17 Jean Baudrillard, *The Evil Demon of Images*, trans. Paul Patton and Paul Foss (Sydney: Power Institute of Fine Arts, 1987).

18 Costas Douzinas and Lynda Nead, "Introduction: Law and Aesthetics," in Douzinas and Nead, eds, *Law and the Image*, 4. See also Peter Goodrich, *Legal Emblems*, xvii–xix.

19 Pierre Legendre, "The Dogmatic Value of Aesthetics," *Parallax* 14:4 (2008): 10.

20 MacNeil, *Lex Populi*, 10. See also William MacNeil, *Novel Judgements: Legal Theory as Fiction* (London: Routledge, 2012) and Daniel Hourigan, *Law and Enjoyment: Power, Pleasure and Psychoanalysis* (London: Routledge, 2015).

21 Edward Mussawir, "The Cinematics of Jurisprudence: Scenes of Law's Moving Image," *Law and Literature* 17:1 (2005): 132.

simply for visual literacy, but the development of a 'visual jurisprudence'[22] that seeks to harmonise the aesthetic and the ethical, and to articulate the possibilities of justice in, through and beyond law.

The law is both constituted by, and operative through, representations – from the subject taken on legal personality through its *persona* or mask before the law, to the procedural logic of institutional law in modernity in which the legal subject is *represented* by the lawyer or judicial office before the law. The complexity of modern law, the rituals and processes that constitute the operations of court systems and the level of expertise needed to navigate them, all but require the subject to have an expert representative acting on their behalf. In the traditional fare of law and literature, law and film, and law and television, this representative aspect of legal systems was a standard focus of analysis – the depiction of legal actors (lawyers, prosecutors, judges), trials and court scenes. But these depictions, particularly in film and television, also tend to show the corruptibility of the law, and certainly of lawyers, with their tendency towards showboating and treating the law as a 'game' to be 'played' (think *Boston Legal* or *Suits*). Such depictions of law encompass a sense of dishonesty to the practices employed by lawyers, and frequently convey the notion that what is important is not the 'facts' to which the law will be applied, but the nature of the *presentation* of those facts, and the emotional responses they engender in litigants, witnesses and jury members. As Sherwin's work emphasises, this is one of the ways in which the over-saturation of images and visual narratives influences lawyers' use of images and narratives in court.[23] This aspect of the manipulation of representations by lawyers – presenting the facts not as they are, but telling a particular story – points also to the anxiety posed by images and their proliferation – the concern about whether images can be trusted, whether they present any sense of truth or fact or whether they simply form part of the 'truthiness' and emotional response of our 'post-truth' era.[24] What's more, however, is that the very focus of the law, with its specifically *limited* vision (structured around what can be admitted to law by the rules of evidence and the specific cases that can be brought before the court) is what creates the space for dishonesty, privileging the representation over facts, truth or justice.[25] The law itself operates only in relation to what can be represented to it, structuring itself as *reliant* on representations that do not

22 Richard Sherwin, "Visual Jurisprudence," *New York Law School Law Review* (2012–2013): 11–39.

23 Sherwin, *When Law Goes Pop* and *Visualizing Law*.

24 On 'truthiness,' see the discussion in Crawley and Manderson below. On the label of 'post-truth' applied to the Trump era, and the fallacy of seeing this as a new phenomenon, see Rune Møller Stahl and Bue Rübner Hansen, "The Fallacy of Post-Truth," *Jacobin* (12 December 2016): https://www.jacobinmag.com/2016/12/post-truth-fake-news-trump-clinton-election-russia

25 For discussions of law's vision in this collection, see the contributions from Crofts and Peters below. For an account of law's structuring of vision, see Goodrich, *Legal Emblems*.

simply represent but construct the world. But this returns us to the point that not only must the subject be represented to law, but the law only recognises the legal person, the *persona,* the mask of representation.[26] Not only can the subject not speak to law directly, only through a representative, but the law itself cannot speak but through representations.

This representational structure of the law, then, reflects a conceptual shift from law to legality. Legality refers to not just the operation of law but the pervasiveness and prevalence of legal forms in political, social and economic spheres, the subjection of domains of life to a knowledge structured by legal concepts, practices and methods, and the colonisation of disciplinary modes of life by juridical forms. These developments have been theorised before as the operation of biopolitics, 'the deep juridification that intertwines life with power.'[27] But biopolitics too operates through representation. For Agamben, biopolitics encompasses the law's capturing of life through 'the condition of being included through an exclusion.'[28] This structure of inclusion via exclusion is the traditional form of representation – the representation is that which stands in for and gains significance in relation to the original or referent it represents. It is this process via which life is represented to law. The law never applies to the facts or to life, but only to the representations of life presented to it. This dynamic, of course, brings into question the nature of that representation – and what representational legality recognises is that representations themselves operate independently of any original or referent, or even *without* a referent. This is to understand the representational nature of law not in regards to its ability to represent an original other, but rather as a material process itself that forms the basis of legality or legalities. Representational legality is the mode through which the political lives in, acts in, shapes, resources, and hurts the real and imaginary spaces that we live in.

The traditional view of representation – of that which stands in for or refers to an original or referent – reduces it to mere mimesis, as an object that is more or less related to that which is being represented and assessed based on its accuracy or lack thereof. But as contemporary scholarship on art and culture insists, art's force and political effectivity is not a function of its transmission of a message (semantic content), and therefore mere semiology is not enough; encountering art is a process.[29] The representational process (and not the object of

26 See Peter Goodrich, *Languages of Law: From Logics of Memory to Nomadic Masks* (London: Weidenfeld and Nicolson, 1990) and Connal Parsley, "The Mask and Agamben: the Transitional Juridical Technics of Legal Relation," *Law Text Culture* 14 (2010): 12–39.

27 Matthew Stone, Illan Wall and Costas Douzinas, "Introduction: Law, Politics and the Political," in Matthew Stone, Illan Wall and Costas Douzinas, eds, *New Critical Legal Thinking: Law and the Political* (London: Birkbeck Law Press, 2014), 2.

28 Giorgio Agamben, *Homo Sacer: Sovereign Power and Bare Life* (Stanford, CA: Stanford University Press, 1998), 22.

29 See further, Georges Didi-Huberman, *Confronting Images*, trans. John Goodman (University Park: Pennsylvania State University Press, 2005).

representation) is a kind of generative, performative speech that has effects in the world.[30] To participate in representational legality is not to receive a message from the law, but to have a juridical experience or encounter within the dynamic process by which cultural forms iterate and circulate in different contexts, stagings, enactments and framings. An understanding of re-presentation thus also goes to the modes of production and consumption of cultural texts – the materiality of representations as they are borne out of conditions of reproducibility: not only from the bodily capacity for voice and gesture, but out of machines, institutions and networks of transmission (the printer, the camera, the internet). The emergence of Cultural Legal Studies as a field cannot be divorced from the conditions of cultural production that have yielded a convergent visual culture (US-dominated, but with an interesting diaspora); its explanatory power and commercial viability is bound to the potential of a global appeal to a shared experience of a particular text or film.

Overview of this collection: multiple legalities

The shift in Cultural Legal Studies towards a cultural understanding of law has had a necessarily pluralising effect on how we think of law, because it views the making and interpreting of law as an ongoing social dialogue, not merely the product of specialised institutions. It positions citizens as part of and not just subject to law. This pluralising enables us to speak more easily of the multiple legalities at work: how legality and vision work together through cultural forms that preserve ambivalence; how scopic regimes – particular constellations of visual forms in time – inaugurate and solidify sovereign relationships between authority and legal subjects; how confessional legality undermines the traditional legal distinction between public and private in order to stabilise truth and discipline the self; how a kind of legality works outside of law in the lawful lawlessness of emergency powers. The essays in this collection invite us to think of the future of legality – the transition from modern to digital legality and the interplay of life and the archive – and the related question of the future of the human, with the coming of climate change the resurgence of a natural law, a law of post-politics that insists on the complex symbiosis between nature and human, or the alterity of another culture's envisioning of law. They attempt to think of legality beyond the space of critiquing corrupt and fallible law, and wonder how we might locate the basis of legality in community, trust and solidarity rather than in the top-down imposition of power.

30 See further, J.L. Austin, *How to Do Things with Words* (Cambridge, MA: Harvard University Press, 1955); Jacques Derrida, "Force of Law: The Mystical Foundation of Authority," trans. Mary Quaintance, *Cardozo Law Review* 11 (1990): 920–1045; Judith Butler, *Excitable Speech: A Politics of the Performative* (New York: Routledge, 1997); Marianne Constable, *Our Word is Our Bond: How Legal Speech Acts* (Stanford, CA: Stanford University Press, 2014).

The book is thematically divided into three sections. The first Part, 'Spectacles of law and justice,' analyses texts of speculative fiction – fantasy, science fiction, superheroes – not as straightforward representations of law, lawyers or legal institutions, but as ways of envisioning legality otherwise, both in terms of visual renderings of alternate worlds or possibilities as well as the imaginative refraction and estrangement of law itself. As such, the texts under analysis are not simply flights of fancy or utopian/dystopian visions of the future, but meditations on and mediations of our current times. For example, in 'I, archive: envisioning and programming digital legality from Syfy's *Caprica*,' Kieran Tranter is concerned with the transition from modern legality, which mediates life and law through text and violence, to digital legality, which operates according to a different schematics, bypassing the human that read and judged. If modern legality represents life in the archive, reconstructs it through reading, and subjects it to discipline and judgement, then digital legality, with its features of speed, binarism and automatism, Tranter argues, transforms these concepts of 'text,' life and violence. Through a reading of *Caprica,* the short-lived and commercially unsuccessful television sequel to *Battlestar Galactica,* Tranter sets out the challenge for legal theory: *not* to resist digital legality but to learn to program it. *Caprica*, he argues, envisions the decline of modern legality, showing events moving too quickly for the bumbling modern lawyer, and the process of archiving and retrieval of material files and texts. At the same time, the full-body duplicate avatars of *Caprica* gesture beyond modernity's reduction of life to text, and the division between subjects and objects it assumes; the avatars become life that learns, reflects and survives, and operate between real and virtual worlds. Tranter locates the possibility for justice in digital legality in an interruption in time, a pause or blink moment, in which the human object of the system finds means to intrude into the techno-totality of code.

Like Tranter, Penny Crofts is concerned with the potential of science fiction's speculative projections to force us to reimagine the relationship between law, justice, and time. In 'Don't blink: monstrous justice and the Weeping Angels of *Doctor Who*,' Crofts explores the suggestive similarity between the most terrifying villains in *Doctor Who*, the Weeping Angels, and the statue of justice that can be found in courtrooms around the world, Justicia. Both are figured as females carved in stone. Justicia is frequently depicted as blind, unable to be swayed by worldly concerns, and thus those to whom she metes justice are unobserved. In an inversion of this relationship, the Weeping Angels dispense their otherworldly 'justice' only when unobserved – whenever their victims are not looking, the Angels approach them and send them to another, unfamiliar time. These villains unsettle the television viewer by interpellating the viewer's own act of seeing, and the inhuman injunction not to blink. The monstrousness or 'rendering strange' of Justicia in the Weeping Angels allows Crofts to argue that justice is that which transgresses law, time and human finitude, and to remind us that the justice law offers, promises or threatens may horrify.

Timothy D. Peters focuses on Nolan's reimagining of the Batman story in *The Dark Knight Trilogy* (2005–2012), and locates in the transformation of

Harvey Dent from heroic lawyer to the villain Two-Face a critique of the traditional role of the vigilante-superhero, who seeks a retributive justice when the law fails to deliver. This traditional figure, like Dent, asks us to 'trust' him, and undermines the ocular vision of modern legality, in which justice must be concerned with process and substance, ends and means, with both being done and being seen to be done. Batman's response to Dent, Peters argues, reflects neither the traditional superhero enactment of justice outside of fallible or corruptible law, nor the messianism of Superman, for instance, who acts beyond the law to save us from it. In taking the blame for Dent's murders, Nolan's Batman does not act in either savior or vigilante mode, but offers an alternative theological vision of legality, which founds a community based on trust and hope. Rather than viewing Batman's action as the promulgation of an ideological lie that undergirds the repressive response to crime, Peters' Christological reading understands Batman as operating according to a different vision of legality, one that foregrounds trust and faith as the foundation of community. Nolan's Batman is not a heroic or messianic saviour figure of judgement that asks us to trust him, or who seeks better justice in the form of vengeance and punishment. Rather he is a figure who is more interested in forgiveness and solidarity, and in trusting others to do good.

William MacNeil's chapter, 'Machiavellian fantasy and the game of laws: rex, sex and lex in George R.R. Martin's *A Song of Ice and Fire*,' performs a jurisprudential reading of the most popular cultural text of the moment in both its novelistic and televisual forms. Looking beyond its expert deployment of the tropes (and fanbase) of the genres of fantasy, history and horror, MacNeil zeroes in on the legality of Westeros, which, despite its immoral power politics, is replete with juridical processes, institutions and concepts with its rules, hierarchies, and the transgressions of the same. But this socio-legal analysis does not suffice to understand the legality of Westeros, which is not pre-modern but rather post-modern – the novel's shifting narratorial perspectives, a formal demonstration of the collapse of metanarratives – and post-ideological: the character of Littlefinger can stand in for the ambitious prince whose only imperative is that of survival. In Daenerys's emancipatory army and Jon Snow's legality of right, MacNeil finds a politics of the law, combusting and deconstructing notions of sovereignty and the social, and gesturing towards a law of post-politics that embraces a new relationship between nature and humanity. This immanent higher law of humanity and nature's symbiosis is realised in the relationship between Daenerys and her dragons: cooperative, interactive and interdependent, forged by an organic bond that turns on reciprocal advantage rather than unilateral exploitation.

The second Part, 'Juridical spectators,' explores not so much the content of the texts under consideration (photographic, filmic and televisual), but their mode of operation – that is, focusing on *how* representations work rather than *what* is represented. For example, Alison Young's interrogation of Quentin Tarantino's *Inglourious Basterds* focuses specifically on the *form* of the representation of violence in the film. Young asks not 'How is violence depicted in the film?'

but 'How does the image of violence work?' and 'How do we watch it?'[31] She tracks three different critical responses to Tarantino's film – extravagant praise, severe denigration and a process of undercutting one by the other (praised tempered with criticism, critique countered with commendation) – as evidencing its refusal to provide the viewer with any other subject-position than ambivalence to the extreme violence depicted. Young's analysis of Tarantino's cinematography reveals the way in which the domain of images of World War II and the Holocaust are culturally legislated, with acceptable depictions requiring the solemnity and seriousness of testimony (think Spielberg's *Schindler's List*), rather than the 'fantastical' images of violence in *Inglourious Basterds.* Such responses, as Young points out, result in the outlawing of the imaginary in favour of documentary and a desire for certainty embedded in dominant narratives and genres. That is, we demand that certain stories be told in certain ways and for the image to produce meanings that accord with our cultural understandings and the way 'in which we make sense of everyday life'. The importance of ambiguous and ambivalent texts such as *Inglourious Basterds* is that they remind us that

> cultural texts must be read with openness to uncertainty, contestation and dispute. Meaning is not singular; interpretations may be multiple; and the task of cultural analysis is to put legality and vision into an oscillating relation mediated through the cinematic form.[32]

Whereas Young's analysis of Tarantino's 'war film' identifies the way in which culture legislates the acceptable telling – and visual depicting – of historical or historically situated narratives of war and genocide, Desmond Manderson's chapter identifies the way in which such acceptable forms of visual genre have changed over time. He does this through an analysis of the photographic depictions of war and their embedded 'scopic regimes'. Australian photographer Frank Hurley's constructed composites of World War I invoke a temporal *pastness*, a romantic determinateness of war as something that has already occurred and a transcendence to which the viewer must submit. Damien Parer's World War II documentary *Kokoda Front Line* actively engages the viewer, directly interpellating the Australian citizen to 'do their part' in a continuous present. However, as Manderson shows, the scopic regime that has dominated since the Vietnam War has been one of technological mastery, showing not the pain and suffering of those that fight for their country, but rather a dramatic distance and a 'bomb's eye view,' capturing rather than understanding nature in an 'ever-present *potential*'. Manderson's analysis reveals how the construction of these images in accordance with their different scopic regimes goes not to their *meaning* but to

31 Alison Young, "Ambivalence and the Spectatorship of Violence: Viewing Inglourious Basterds," Chapter 6, 122 below.
32 Young, "Ambivalence," Chapter 6, 138 below.

their *governance* and the way in which this governance of images constitutes the relationship between sovereignty and responsibility.

Karen Crawley and Desmond Manderson's chapter then moves from the scopic regime of the image to the televisual depiction of the relation between media star and their audience as a mode of confessional participation by the viewer-spectators. Whereas Manderson's analysis of the photograph notes Roland Barthes' claim that there is something 'necessarily real' about the photograph,[33] he and Crawley turn to the issue of truth in autobiographical narrative or memoir, and then the way in which therapeutic talk-show mirrors a similar relation to truth. By analysing the scandal over James Frey's *A Million Little Pieces* in relation to Oprah Winfrey and her Book Club, Crawley and Manderson are able to reveal the operation of the logic of confession today. The memoir is clearly a genre of confession, but what is more interesting is the way in which *The Oprah Winfrey Show* was constructed specifically on this logic of confession, with Oprah as the sovereign/priest to whom individuals would confess and find redemption and forgiveness. Running through this analysis is the 'double helix'[34] of confession and its juridical structure: the external, public dimension pertaining to the *content* of confession, which reaffirms prevailing social ideology (Oprah's instrumental reading of books for their 'conventional wisdom about being and becoming'); and the internal, *affective* dimension which 'disciplines the bodies and souls' of individuals (Oprah as arbiter of truth and feeling for her viewers). Frey's fabrication of the truth, however, as the authors demonstrate, revealed the logic of confession operating in Oprah's show – one which Oprah herself could not escape. Oprah's response, by re-interviewing Frey on the show, involved only a more overt operation of the logic of confession, one which makes specific use of the televisual form – looking directly into the camera and engaging the *viewer* as confessor.

The third Part of the collection, 'Scenes of legality,' analyses specific imagined scenes of legality from a variety of cultural positions (US, Germany, Canada) and the way in which these cultural texts envision – but also constitute – the forming, sustaining and critique of political and legal communities. Bonnie Honig's chapter continues her sustained interrogation and interruption of Sophocles' *Antigone* and Antigonean texts,[35] with an analysis of the tension between the political genres of tragedy and melodrama. In contrast to legal studies' love of tragedy as the genre for exploring legal subjectivity and law's demands, Honig argues that melodrama focuses on *affect* and thus the 'affective life of law.'[36] Through an analysis of the 1978 omnibus film *Germany in Autumn* (in particular, Rainer Werner Fassbinder's

33 Roland Barthes, *Camera Lucida* (New York: Farrar, Straus & Giroux, 1981).

34 Karen Crawley and Desmond Manderson, "The Confessor: Oprah Winfrey, James Frey, and the Logic of Confession," Chapter 8, 162 below.

35 See Bonnie Honig, *Antigone, Interrupted* (Cambridge: Cambridge University Press, 2013).

36 A phrase she borrows from Ravit Reichman, see Ravit Reichman, *The Affective Life of Law: Legal Modernism and the Literary Imagination* (Stanford, CA: Stanford University Press, 2009).

contribution to it) and Lars von Trier's *Dogville* (2003), she argues that melodrama is the 'genre that explores, and tries to work through, the impasses into which we are thrust by law.'[37] Honig compares the general aspects of classical tragedy and catastrophe (as a mode of ethical witnessing and fidelity to the event) as the main strategy of *Germany in Autumn* to the melodrama of Fassbinder's contribution, which 'self-consciously aestheticises' and provides a frame 'through which to explore despair.'[38] In Fassbinder's sequence, he is contained within his Munich apartment, shouting, impotent and eventually lying naked on the floor. Honig argues that Fassbinder's 'melodramatic self-absorption and collapse' is a 'dramatization of the effects on citizens of the state's expansion of its power' that gives an affective response to new forms of violence. Fassbinder's invocation of the rule of law in this scene, is thus not sober, principled and reasoned but 'the only recourse for those caught in an overheated political crisis' and a demonstration of 'the way in which law and lawful lawlessness (emergency powers) consume those who live in their ambit.'[39]

Edwin Bikundo also examines the tensions and paradoxes of 'lawful lawlessness' through an analysis of another text that crosses between the genres of tragedy and melodrama: David's Simon's US television series, *The Wire* (2002–2008). Drawing on the work of Giorgio Agamben, Bikundo places as central to the series the relation between law and life and that which binds the two together. The depictions in *The Wire* of the city of Baltimore as the main 'character,' is built on an intentional blurring of reality and fiction in a form of visual and narrative realism – Simon's series casts real individuals to 'play themselves' in a desire to show 'the faces and voices of the real city.'[40] Bikundo's analysis focuses on season 3 and the apparent legalisation of drugs in 'Hamsterdam,' which he argues is a visual representation of both Agamben's 'state of exception' – a space where the law is in force without significance (here literally marked off with white flags and where the police agree not to take action against the drug trade) – but also the 'carnival' and its inversion of roles (the police bus customers to Hamsterdam and the criminals investigate a murder). Bikundo argues that both the 'realism' of *The Wire* and its depiction of the 'state of exception' represent a much more significant foundation of legality: the Faustian pact that clarifies the relation between 'necessity' and 'agency'. Such a pact is what police sergeant Buni Colvin presents to his superiors when trying to explain and justify Hamsterdam and which, Bikundo argues, undergirds the very basis of law and legality today.

Honig's turn to melodrama as a way of unpacking the affective life of law, and Bikundo's exploration of visual realism as a means of legality, is taken in a different direction by Rebecca Johnson. Whereas Honig analyses the visually

37 Bonnie Honig, "Legal Unconsciousness: Tragedy and Melodrama in the Wake of Terror," Chapter 9, 194 below.

38 Honig, "Legal Unconsciousness," Chapter 9, 199 below.

39 Honig, "Legal Unconsciousness," Chapter 9, 207 below.

40 David Simons, quoted in Edwin Bikundo, "Mephistopheles in Hamsterdam: Carnival and the State of Exception in HBO's *The Wire*," Chapter 10, 211–212 below.

discomforting aspects of the body on display, and Bikundo the challenges of re-presentation of the city of Baltimore, Johnson examines the visual discomfort (at least to the Western viewer) of Inuit cinema. The affective life of law for Johnson operates in terms of the affect of storytelling as the means not just of communicating law, but of the law itself. In her analysis of *Atanarjuat* (2001) and *Before Tomorrow* (2008), Johnson focuses on the haptic visual qualities of the cinematography – significantly slower pacing, expansive shots and the distinctly non-verbal registers which invite the viewer to feel and be present in the communities and spaces depicted. But Johnson's analysis also identifies the way in which the films do not simply 'show' or 'represent' law, but envision 'both life and law in a particular way' and invite the 'audience to experience that life/law'.[41] This analysis encourages both the western viewer to engage the films as law and as structuring 'a rich space for us to imagine living deeply within another legal order'.[42] Johnson's reading of *Before Tomorrow* in particular, points to the challenge for the western viewer – our desire is to apportion guilt and responsibility, but the stronger reading of the film 'invites us, through its deployment of both story and haptic visuality to experience ways of living, rather than ways of dying'.[43]

Each of these contributions undertakes not only an analysis of a cultural text, its meaning and content, but the process, experience and encounter of that text as a mode of critical Cultural Legal Studies. In 2007, MacNeil observed that culture had replaced critique as 'not only *le mot juste* but also the fulcrum of millennial legal studies.'[44] But critique is and has always been a significant part of Cultural Legal Studies, as this collection makes clear – critique, understood as a practice that not so much arrives at judgement, but suspends it and renders it anew. As each of our contributors demonstrate, Cultural Legal Studies, in analysing the different modes of 'representational legality,' engages in a *practice* of critique rather than a judgement – a questioning of our sure ways of knowing and seeing. The role of critique in Cultural Legal Studies is therefore to disarticulate the series of connections made by the currently dominant forms of power expressed and articulated in our visual cultures, and to instead create a new set of connections, new constellations of visual legality, and a distinct openness to possibilities of law and legality not otherwise available. It is in this sense that Cultural Legal Studies engages in an envisioning of legality and justice 'otherwise'.

But not only is Cultural Legal Studies important in terms of the avenues of critique and critical encounter that it articulates. For it *also* operates as a modality for pedagogy – for both teaching and learning the law. While the sophistication of its approach, and its significant engagement with jurisprudence and critical

41 Rebecca Johnson, "Intercultural Cinema and the (Re)Envisioning of Law: Exploring Life, Death and Law in *Atanarjuat* and *Before Tomorrow*," Chapter 11, 234 below.

42 Johnson, "Intercultural Cinema," Chapter 11, 238 below.

43 Johnson, "Intercultural Cinema," Chapter 11, 248 below.

44 MacNeil, *Lex Populi*, 7.

theory, may at times prove challenging in the context of the reductive approach to legal curricula being experienced by law schools, the analysis of cultural texts that are broadly known (and actively engaged, observed and consumed by the community) opens up lines of discussion and debate not restricted to the scholar. Cultural Legal Studies is an activity for scholars and students of law alike, one that acknowledges their shared role as cultural jurists. For many of our contributors, and particularly those who have had an association with the Griffith Law School, this has involved teaching Cultural Legal Studies courses such as Legal Fictions: Representations of Law in Cinema, Literature and Philosophy, and Cultural Legal Studies: Critical Encounters between Law and Popular Culture. This teaching uses cultural artifacts not as a means of explaining a particular legal principle or an esoteric concept of jurisprudence, but as the very space in which our students live the law. This form of teaching, which challenges students to think the law and legal theory where they live, and in the spaces in which they think and engage, is one which seeks to make cultural legal scholars of our students, so that the means of analysis thus undertaken is not restricted to the classroom but does actually operate in the community. In this sense, Cultural Legal Studies makes it possible for the next generation of scholars, lawyers and judges to envision legality.

Bibliography

Adams, Wendy. *Popular Culture and Legal Pluralism.* Melbourne: Taylor & Francis, 2016.

Agamben, Giorgio. *Homo Sacer: Sovereign Power and Bare Life.* Stanford, CA: Stanford University Press, 1998.

Ahmed, Sara. *The Cultural Politics of Emotion.* Edinburgh: Edinburgh University Press, 2004.

Austin, J.L. *How to Do Things with Words.* Cambridge, MA: Harvard University Press, 1955.

Bainbridge, Jason. "'This is the Authority. This Planet is Under Our Protection' – An Exegesis of Superheroes' Interrogations of Law." *Law Culture and the Humanities* 3:3 (2007): 455–476.

Barnett, Michael, and Cassandra Sharp. "The Moral Choice of in*FAMOUS:* Law and Morality in Video Games." *Griffith Law Review* 24:3 (2015): 482–499.

Barthes, Roland. *Camera Lucida.* New York: Farrar, Straus & Giroux, 1981.

Baudrillard, Jean. *The Evil Demon of Images,* translated by Paul Patton and Paul Foss. Sydney: Power Institute of Fine Arts, 1987.

Buchanan, Ruth and Rebecca Johnson. "Strange Encounters: Exploring Law and Film in the Affective Register." In *Studies in Law, Politics and Society: A Special Symposium Issue on Law and Film,* Vol. 46, edited by Austin Sarat, 33–60. Bradford: Emerald, 2009.

Butler, Judith. *Excitable Speech: A Politics of the Performative.* New York: Routledge, 1997.

Constable, Marianne. *Our Word is Our Bond: How Legal Speech Acts.* Stanford, CA: Stanford University Press, 2014.

Cover, Robert. "Foreword: *Nomos* and Narrative." *Harvard Law Review* 4 (1983): 12–19.

Crawley, Karen. "Beyond the War on Graffiti: The Right to Visual Expression in Urban Spaces." *Griffith Journal of Law and Human Dignity*, Special Art Issue (2015): 85–107.

Derrida, Jacques. "Force of Law: The Mystical Foundation of Authority", translated by Mary Quaintance. *Cardozo Law Review* 11 (1990): 920–1045.

Didi-Huberman, Georges. *Confronting Images*, translated by John Goodman. University Park: Pennsylvania State University Press, 2005.

Dimock, Wai Chee. *Residues of Justice: Literature, Law and Philosophy*. Berkeley, Los Angeles and London: University of California Press, 1996.

Douzinas, Costas and Lynda Nead. "Introduction: Law and Aesthetics." In *Law and the Image: The Authority of Art and the Aesthetics of Law*, edited by Douzinas and Nead, 1–18. Chicago and London: University of Chicago Press, 1999.

Douzinas, Costas and Lynda Nead, eds. *Law and the Image: The Authority of Art and the Aesthetics of Law*. Chicago and London: University of Chicago Press, 1999.

Freeman, Michael D.A., ed. *Law and Popular Culture*. Oxford: Oxford University Press, 2005.

Giddens, Thomas. "Navigating the Looking Glass: Severing the Lawyer's Head in *Arkham Asylum*." *Griffith Law Review* 24:3 (2015): 395–417.

Goodrich, Peter. *Languages of Law: From Logics of Memory to Nomadic Masks*. London: Weidenfeld and Nicolson, 1990.

Goodrich, Peter. *Legal Emblems and the Art of Law:* Obiter Depicta *as the Vision of Governance*. New York: Cambridge University Press, 2014.

Hickey-Moody, Anne, and Peta Malins, eds. *Deleuzian Encounters: Studies in Contemporary Social Issues*. New York: Palgrave, 2008.

Honig, Bonnie. *Antigone, Interrupted*. Cambridge: Cambridge University Press, 2013.

Hourigan, Daniel. *Law and Enjoyment: Power, Pleasure and Psychoanalysis*. London: Routledge, 2015.

Legendre, Pierre. "The Dogmatic Value of Aesthetics." *Parallax* 14:4 (2008): 10–17.

Leiboff, Marett and Cassandra Sharp. "Cultural Legal Studies and Law's Popular Cultures." In *Cultural Legal Studies: Law's Popular Cultures and the Metamorphosis of Law*, edited by Sharp and Leiboff, 3–28. London: Routledge, 2016.

MacNeil, William. *Lex Populi: The Jurisprudence of Popular Culture*. Stanford, CA: Stanford University Press, 2007.

MacNeil, William. *Novel Judgements: Legal Theory as Fiction*. London: Routledge, 2012.

Manderson, Desmond. *Kangaroo Courts and the Rule of Law: The Legacy of Modernism*. London: Routledge, 2012.

Manderson Desmond. "Trust Us Justice: *24*, Popular Culture, and the Law." In *Imagining Legality: Where Law Meets Popular Culture*, edited by Austin Sarat, 22–52. Tuscaloosa: University of Alabama Press, 2011, 22–52.

Mezey, Naomi. "Law's Visual Afterlife: Violence, Popular Culture, and Translation Theory." In *Imagining Legality: Where Law Meets Popular Culture*, edited by Austin Sarat, 65–99. Tuscaloosa: University of Alabama Press, 2011.

Moran, Leslie J., Emma Sandon, Elena Loizidou and Ian Christie, eds. *Law's Moving Image*. London: Cavendish, 2004.

Mussawir, Edward. "The Cinematics of Jurisprudence: Scenes of Law's Moving Image." *Law and Literature* 17:1 (2005): 131–152.

Osborn, Guy and Steve Greenfield. *Readings in Law and Popular Culture*. London and New York: Routledge, 2006.

Parsley, Connal. "The Mask and Agamben: the Transitional Juridical Technics of Legal Relation." *Law Text Culture* 14 (2010): 12–39.

Pearson, Ashley and Kieran Tranter. "Code, Nintendo's Super Mario and Digital Legality." *International Journal for the Semiotics of Law* 28:4 (2015): 825–842.

Reichman, Ravit. *The Affective Life of Law: Legal Modernism and the Literary Imagination*. Stanford, CA: Stanford University Press, 2009.

Robson, Peter and Jessica Silbey, eds. *Law and Justice on the Small Screen*. London: Hart Publishing, 2012.

Rush, Peter and Andrew Kenyon. "Alter Egos: The Mise-en-Scène." In *Aesthetics of Law and Culture: Texts, Images, Screens – Studies in Law, Politics and Society, Volume 34*, edited by Andrew Kenyon and Peter Rush, 1–30. Emerald Group Publishing Limited, 2004.

Sarat, Austin. "Imagining the Law of the Father: Loss, Dread and Mourning in *The Sweet Hereafter*." *Law and Society Review* 34 (2000): 5–46.

Sarat, Austin, ed. *Imagining Legality: Where Law Meets Popular Culture*. Tuscaloosa: University of Alabama Press, 2011.

Sarat, Austin. "What Popular Culture Does for, and to, Law: An Introduction." In *Imagining Legality: Where Law Meets Popular Culture*, edited by Austin Sarat, 1–21. Tuscaloosa: University of Alabama Press, 2011.

Sarat, Austin and Thomas R. Kearns. "Editorial Introduction." In *The Rhetoric of Law*, edited by Austin Sarat and Thomas R. Kearns, 1–27. Ann Arbor: University of Michigan Press, 1994.

Sarat, Austin and Thomas R. Kearns, eds. *Law in the Domains of Culture*. Ann Arbor: University of Michigan Press, 1998.

Sarat, Austin, Lawrence Douglas and Martha Umphrey, eds. *Law on the Screen*. Stanford, CA: Stanford University Press, 2005.

Sedgwick, Eve Kosofsky. *Touching Feeling: Affect, Pedagogy, Performativity*. Durham, NC: Duke University Press, 2003.

Sharp, Cassandra and Marett Leiboff, eds. *Cultural Legal Studies: Law's Popular Cultures and the Metamorphosis of Law*. London: Routledge, 2016.

Sherwin, Richard, ed. *Popular Culture and Law*. Aldershot: Ashgate, 2006.

Sherwin, Richard. "Visual Jurisprudence." *New York Law School Law Review* (2012–2013): 11–39.

Sherwin, Richard. *Visualizing Law in the Age of the Digital Baroque: Arabesques and Entanglements*. London and New York: Routledge, 2011.

Sherwin, Richard. *When Law Goes Pop: The Vanishing Line between Law and Popular Culture*. Chicago: University of Chicago Press, 2000.

Stahl, Rune Møller and Hansen, Bue Rübner. "The Fallacy of Post-Truth." *Jacobin* (12 December 2016). Available at: www.jacobinmag.com/2016/12/post-truth-fake-news-trump-clinton-election-russia

Stone, Matthew, Illan Wall and Costas Douzinas. "Introduction: Law, Politics and the Political." In *New Critical Legal Thinking: Law and the Political*, edited by Matthew Stone, Illan Wall and Costas Douzinas, 1–12. London: Birkbeck Law Press, 2014.

Wagner, Anne and Richard Sherwin, eds. *Law, Culture and Visual Studies*. New York: Sprinter, 2014.

White, James Boyd. *The Legal Imagination*. Chicago: University of Chicago Press, 1985.
Young, Alison. *The Scene of Violence: Cinema, Crime, Affect*. London: Routledge, 2010.
Young, Alison. *Street Art, Public City: Law, Crime and Urban Imagination*. London: Routledge, 2013.

Part I

Spectacles of law and justice

Chapter 2

I, archive: envisioning and programming digital legality from Syfy's *Caprica*

*Kieran Tranter**

Introduction

What form of life can be envisioned for digital legality? Paper and text has provided the technical medium for positivism, sovereignty and the biopolitical *nomos* of modern legality. Within modern legality it is routine and normal for life to be represented in the archive, caught in files, reconstructed through reading and subject to discipline and judgment. Life and law were mediated by text and violence. But digital legality with its features of speed, binarism and automatism changes the established categories of 'life', 'law', 'text' and 'violence.' This leads both to the utopian dream of an escape from the text and the known violence of modern legality and the dystopian demise of value (what travels under the rubric 'human'), leaving barely imagined forms of inhuman violence within the techno-totality of code. The question for legal theory is not how to resist digital legality, but the complicit and technical question of how to program it.

This chapter is an exercise in envisioning and programming digital legality. It does so through Syfy's short-lived series *Caprica* (2010). *Caprica*, a pre-sequel to the academically popular *Battlestar Galactica* (2003–2010), was ordinary television, but good science fiction (s/f). The conventions of 'quality' television lie in character, dialogue and plot twists and *Caprica* had little to commend it on these criteria, but its science fictionality was good. *Caprica*'s worth is as a representation of the transitions to digital legality and it is from its schematics that the possibility of programming emerges.

This chapter is in two parts. The first part considers *Caprica* as envisioning digital legality. This has three sections. The first section reviews the show, its relation to its celebrated predecessor and its less than quality attributes. The second section sets out how *Caprica* envisions the demise of modern legality. Unusual for s/f, *Caprica* had a lawyer as a lead character and with him a continual set of representations of modern legality. These were always behind. Events moved too quickly for the lawyer and his modern law. The third section focuses on *Caprica*'s

* I would like to thank the editors and reviewers for their comments and Rod Meyer for his research assistance. Faults and errors remain mine.

animation of the archive. This was *Caprica*'s redeeming s/f premise. However, the archive was hard to know, unpredictable, and its face and tears were simulations. The unengaging irrelevance of modern law and the inhuman avatar of the archive envision features of digital legality – both its challenge to modern law and its features of speed, binarism and automatism.

The second part considers the programming of digital legality. Faced with the inhumanness of digital legality, what architecture might stabilise the disconnected concepts of life, law, text and violence? Rights were modern legality's problematic solution to the extraction from and imposition onto human life. Rights provided pause movements in which the human object of the legal system could participate in processes. For digital legality, the issue is how to program its speedy, hybrid automation to pause and require something more than a toggle-like binary yes or no. In pausing, there becomes the space for the analogue. In digital legality, pause and the possibility of the analogue exception, reconnects *zoe* to the system.

Envisioning digital legality in the machinations and the machines of *Caprica*

This part envisions digital legality through Syfy's *Caprica* (2010). It involves three complementary sections. The first section introduces *Caprica* through consideration of its relation to *Battlestar Galactica* and its less than quality attributes. The second section shows how *Caprica* represents the demise of modern legality through the bumbling character of Adama and the terminal representation of law and order. The third section maps how *Caprica* envisions the essential features of modern law's digital successor in its animation of the archive.

Caprica as television

Caprica was not a success.[1] Cancelled without the final five episodes of its first season being broadcast on US television,[2] it was a victim of its predecessor's success. *Caprica* occurs in the same universe as Syfy's critically and commercially successful reimagining of *Battlestar Galactica* (2003–2010).[3] That show, with its mix of space opera action, tension, character development and philosophical intrigue, was not only Syfy's most successful self-commissioned show but also founded a library of aca-fan commentary; including five edited volumes.[4] *Battlestar Galactica* began

1 Ronald D. Moore, David Eick, Jane Espenson and Kevin Murphy, *Caprica* (Universal Cable Productions, Syfy, 2010).

2 Maureen Ryan (2010) " 'Caprica' is Cancelled by Syfy," http://www.aoltv.com/2010/10/27/caprica-canceled (accessed August 26, 2015).

3 Ronald D. Moore and David Eick, *Battlestar Galactica* (David Eick Productions, Sci-Fi Channel, 2003–2010).

4 Richard Hatch, *So Say We All: An Unauthorised Collection of Thoughts and Opinions on Battlestar Gallactica* (Ben Bella Books, 2006); Tiffany Potter and C. W. Marshall, *Cylons in*

with an end – the nuclear destruction of the twelve human colonies/planets by the returning robotic life-forms the Cylons. It told a survival story of escaped refugees fleeing from and fighting the Cylons who turned out to be less malignant robots and more fleshy 'people' as the series progressed through its four seasons. *Battlestar Galactica* was grand, even in its grounded everyday episodes. Set on spaceships within a backdrop of a seemingly empty universe, it also told a meta-narrative of repetition and divine purpose.[5] It engaged because it showed the grubby, often irrational political and personal tensions within rulers and the ruled; but it did so within a space opera mega-text.[6] 'Heavy' episodes could be lightened by *Star Wars*-inspired space battles climaxing in heroism and tension-breaking explosions. *Caprica* continued the 'heavy' focus of personalities, conflict and personal pain but without the balancing features of *Battlestar Galactica*.

Caprica can be summarised quickly. It was a prequel that was supposed to tell the backstory of Battlestar Galactica – of how the humans invented the Cylons and how the Cylons rebelled in the First Cylon war. It did not get that far. The 18 episodes that were made show the invention and dissemination of the Cylons and the various 'seeds' for their revolution. Within this story-arc the focus was on the lives of two families on the planet Caprica, the Adamas and the Graystones. The Adamas were an immigrant family from the planet Tauron very much modelled on US stereotypes of Sicilian immigrants during the 20th century. Dark featured and subject to the racist taunts of 'Dirt Eaters', the Adamas predominantly interacted within the Tauron immigrant conclave. Within this family, the show focuses on Joseph Adama (Esai Morales) who had become a lawyer working mostly for clients from the Tauron community and particularly members of the mafia-like organised crime in that community, the Ha'la'tha. The other lead Adama was Joseph's brother Sam (Sash Roiz), who was a Ha'la'tha enforcer. In contrast to the Adamas, there were the corporate elites of the Graystones. Daniel Graystone (Eric Stoltz) is presented as a Bill Gates/Steve Jobs/Mark Zuckerberg digital pioneer and corporate heavyweight. Graystone and his blonde surgeon wife inhabited a world of money and power. The premise that puts these two worlds together was a terrorist attack on a train. The attack kills Adama's wife Shannon and his daughter Tamara (Genevieve Buechner) and the Graystones'

America: Critical Studies in Battlestar Gallactica (Continuum, 2008); Jason T. Eberl, *Battlestar Galactica and Philosophy: Knowledge Here Begins Out There* (Blackwell, 2008); Josef Steiff and Tristam D. Tamplin, *Battlestar Galactica and Philosophy: Mission Accomplished or Mission Frakked Up?* (Open Court, 2008); Roz Kaveney and Jennifer Stoy, *Battlestar Galactica: Investigating Flesh, Spirit and Steel* (I. B. Tauris, 2010).

5 Jim Casey, "All This Has Happened Before:" Repetition, Reimagination and Eternal Return," in *Cylons in America: Critical Studies in Battlestar Gallactica*, ed. Tiffany Potter and C. W. Marshall (Continuum, 2008), 237.

6 Laura King and John Hutnyk, "The Eighteenth Brumaire of Gaius Baltar: Colonialism Reimagined in Battlestar Gallactica," in *Breaching the Colonial Contract: Anti-Colonialism in the United States and Canada*, ed. Arlo Kempf (Springer, 2009), 237.

daughter Zoe (Alessandra Torresani).[7] As the narrative unfolded it turns out that the attack was sponsored by the militant monolithic cult (STO – Solders of the One) and Zoe Graystone was one of the terrorists.[8]

While this ensemble of characters and conflicts suggests an intriguing show, *Caprica* did not live up to expectations. A succession of television shows from *M*A*S*H*[9] (1972–1983), *Twin Peaks* (1990–1991),[10] *The Sopranos* (1999–2007)[11] and *Buffy the Vampire Slayer* (1997–2003)[12] have been singled out as 'quality.'[13] *Battlestar Galactica* is often included in such quality lists.[14] While the notion of 'quality television' is contested,[15] identified traits have included a strong central creative presence,[16] narrative genre-blending,[17] 'engaging-ness'[18] and more traditional film/lit crit criteria of character, narrative and aesthetics.[19] *Caprica* seemed to have ticked some of these. In terms of creative presence, *Caprica* continued the same creative team behind *Battlestar Galactica*, including lead showrunner Ronald D. Moore and award-winning television script writer Jane Espenson. It manifested a *Buffy the Vampire Slayer*-inspired genre blending with s/f, retrofuturism and family drama mixed in its mega-text. Yet it was not engaging, either to the audience, as brutally evidenced in its struggle to attract

7 Ronald D. Moore, David Eick, Jane Espenson and Kevin Murphy, "Caprica," *Caprica*, pilot, directed by Jeffrey Reiner (Universal Cable Productions, Syfy, 2010).
8 Ronald D. Moore, David Eick, Jane Espenson and Kevin Murphy, "Rebirth," *Caprica*, season 1, episode 3, directed by Jonas Pate (Universal Cable Productions, Syfy, 2010).
9 Larry Gelbart, *M*A*S*H* (20th Century Fox Television, CBS, 1972–1983).
10 Mark Frost and David Lynch, *Twin Peaks* (Lynch/Frost Productions, ABC, 1990–1991).
11 David Chase, *The Sopranos* (Chase Films, HBO, 1999–2007).
12 Joss Whedon, *Buffy the Vampire Slayer* (Mutant Enemy, 20th Century Fox, 1998–2003).
13 Sarah Cardwell, "Is Quality Television Any Good? Generic Distinctions, Evaluations and the Troubling Matter of Critical Judgement" in *Quality TV: Contemporary American Television and Beyond*, ed. Janet McCabe and Kim Akass (I. B. Tauris, 2011), 25; Robert J. Thompson, *Television's Second Golden Age: From Hill Street Blues to ER* (Continuum, 1996), 59–74.
14 Jennifer Stoy, "Of Great Zeitgeist and Bad Faith: An Introduction to Battlestar Galactica" in *Battlestar Galactica: Investigating Flesh, Spirit and Steel*, ed. Roz Kaveney and Jennifer Stoy (I. B. Tauris, 2010), 1–2.
15 See Charlotte Brunsdon, *Screen Tastes: Soap Opera to Satellite Dishes* (Routledge, 1997), 105–147; Dorothy Collins Swanson, *The Stories of Viewers for Quality Television: From Grassroots to Prime Time* (Syracuse University Press, 2000), 44; Christine Geraghty, "Aesthetics and Quality in Popular Television Drama," 6 *International Journal of Cultural Studies* 25 (2003), 31.
16 Matt Hills, *Triumph of a Time Lord: Regenerating Doctor Who in the Twenty-First Century* (I. B. Tauris, 2010), 26.
17 Robin Nelson, "Quality TV Drama: Estimations and Influences Through Time and Space" in *Quality TV: Contemporary American Television and Beyond*, ed. Janet McCabe and Kim Akass (I. B. Tauris, 2011), 46; Thompson, "Televsion's Second Golden Age," 15.
18 Cardwell, "Is Quality Television Any Good?" 31.
19 Geraghty, "Aesthetics and Quality," 34–35; Jonathan Bignell, "Seeing and Knowing: Reflexivity and Quality" in *Quality TV: Contemporary American Television and Beyond*, ed. Janet McCabe and Kim Akass (I. B. Tauris, 2011).

US ratings, or to the Syfy execs that dumped the show mid-season. This lack of engaging-ness can be seen directly in its characterisation, narrative and aesthetics.

The characters, especially Adama and Graystone, failed to connect. Any audience connection that might have been generated towards these two middle-aged men from the deaths of their family members quickly evaporated as the unappealing nature of their personalities unfolded. Adama was a passive blitherer; Graystone an egotistical psychotic. As the episodes progressed and more miseries, often of their own creation, were piled onto these two men, their anguish, pain and tears just floated by. Flawed characters such as Tony Soprano engage because of complexity, because, in Soprano's case, of his capacities for violence and care.[20] The leads of *Battlestar Galactica* were deeply flawed and complex; they engaged not because they always made the 'right' decision, but because there was a depth of feeling and a sense of purpose.[21] *Caprica*'s leads lacked this depth; they were neither tarnished heroes nor likable villains.

This continued to the macro and micro narratives of Caprica. The macro-narrative held few surprises. The Cylons were to be created and then would rebel. The first visual of the Cylon prototype, U-87, in Graystone's laboratory revealed it to be the first-generation Cylon centurion battle robots from *Battlestar Galactica*, the very robots which in that show rebelled and decimated humanity.[22] The inevitability of the Cylon revolution was further entrenched intra-text by the late season revelations that the Cylons were divinely inspired.[23] This locked-in-fate diminished the human characters to pawns fulfilling a cosmically ordained plan. As a result its scripts were uninspiring. Absent was the wit evident in scripts associated with celebrated showrunners like Joss Whedon. Instead, there were mumbled statements of affection or pain, or mundane quips about consumer goods.[24]

This blandness of script was not the problem with the aesthetics of the show. The aesthetics were confused. Retrofuturism in television s/f can work and Whedon's *Firefly* (2002)[25] stands as testimony to this,[26] but there was too much

20 Brenton J. Malin, *American Masculinity Under Clinton: Popular Media and the Nineties "Crisis of Masculinity"* (Peter Lang, 2005), 173–174.

21 Kieran Tranter, "Frakking Toasters and Jurisprudences of Technology: The Exception, the Subject and Techné in *Battlestar Gallactica*," 19 *Law and Literature Review* 45 (2007).

22 Moore et al., "Caprica."

23 Ronald D. Moore, David Eick, Jane Espenson and Kevin Murphy, "Things We Lock Away," *Caprica*, season 1, episode 13, directed by Tim Hunter (Universal Cable Productions, Syfy, 2010).

24 Daniel Graystone: 'And right now, I don't need a cell phone that will check my mail and wipe my ass! I need a cell phone that works.' Ronald D. Moore, David Eick, Jane Espenson and Kevin Murphy, "End of Line," *Caprica*, season 1, episode 10, directed by Roxann Dawson (Universal Cable Productions, Syfy, 2010).

25 Joss Whedon, *Firefly* (Mutant Enemy, 20th Century Fox, 2002).

26 Lorna Jowett, "Back to the Future: Retrofuturism, Cyberpunk, and Humanity in Firefly and Serenity," in *Investigating Firefly and Serenity: Science Fiction on the Frontier*, ed. Rhonda V. Wilcox and Tanya R. Cochran (I. B. Tauris 101, 2010).

disconnect and inconsistency with *Caprica*. The pilot established a 1950s modernist aesthetic that seemed to dissipate; the clothes, cars and domestic spaces got more 2010 as the season progressed. The cityscape scenes of an ultramodern glass and concrete metropolis with CGI Hellenistic statutes grafted into the architecture jarred. While the 1930s gangster aesthetic of the intra-text MMORPG 'New Cap City' worked, as did the steam-punk touchscreen paper, the purpose behind all these traces of the past was unclear.

In short, despite gesturing towards quality television, *Caprica* has not featured on any lists. Which presents an obvious issue: why write about *Caprica* at all?[27] Television is still a frontier for cultural legal studies and the work that has been done has focused on either 'quality'[28] or shows that involve representations of the law and lawyering.[29] It is the latter that immediately makes *Caprica* worthy of study. *Caprica* is unique for a cultural legal studies audience in that it is the first s/f since Frederik Pohl's and Cyril M. Kornbluth's little-known *Gladiator-at-Law* (1955)[30] to feature a lawyer as a principal protagonist.[31] S/f in print and on screen is full of heroes, military, political and religious leaders, scientists and many everymen/women/aliens/robots thrust into a challenging galaxy,[32] but not many lawyers.[33] This absence of the lawyer from s/f has some connection with s/f's mega-text. Definitions of s/f are many and there has developed a small academic literature dedicated to keeping track of the many definitions.[34] However, consistently travelling along with such notions as 'estrangement,'[35] 'formulaic'[36] and 'future'[37] has

27 Steven Kapica has examined *Caprica* with its hybridity of virtual and real as a site for the rethinking legal personhood. Steven Kapica, " 'I Don't Feel Like a Copy': Poshuman Legal Personhood and *Caprica*," 23 *Griffith Law Review* 612 (2014).

28 William P. MacNeil, " 'You Slay Me!' Buffy as Jurisprude of Desire," 24 *Cardozo Law Review* 2421 (2003); Tranter, "Frakking Toasters."

29 Stephen Gillers, "Taking LA Law More Seriously," 98 *Yale Law Journal* 1607 (1989); Robert E. Rosen, "Ethical Soap: LA Law and the Privileging of Character," 43 *University of Miami Law Review* 1227 (1989).

30 Frederick Pohl and C. M. Kornbluth, *Gladiator-at-Law* (Pan Books, 1955/1964).

31 Mitchell Travis and Kieran Tranter "Interrogating Absence: The Lawyer in Science Fiction," 21 *International Journal of the Legal Profession* 23 (2014), 33.

32 Per Schedle, *Androids, Humanoids, and Other Science Fiction Monsters* (New York University Press, 1993).

33 Paul R. Joseph, "Science Fiction," in *Prime Time Law: Fictional Television as Legal Narrative*, ed. Robert M. Jarvis and Paul R Joseph (Carolina Academic Press, 1998), 156–157.

34 Gary K. Wolfe, *Critical Terms for Science Fiction and Fantasy: A Glossary and Guide to Scholarship* (Greenwood Press, 1986), 109–111; Paul Kincaid, "On the Origins of the Genre," 44 *Extrapolation* 409 (2003), 417. See review of the literature, Mitchell Travis, "Making Space: Law and Science Fiction," 23 *Law and Literature* 241 (2011), 242–247.

35 Darko Suvin, "Metamorphoses of Science Fiction; On the Poetics and History of a Literary Genre," (Yale University Press, 1979), 4.

36 Damien Broderick, *Reading by Starlight: Postmodern Science Fiction* (Routledge, 1995), 155.

37 Isaac Asimov, "Introduction: The First Century of Science Fiction" in "Isaac Asimov Presents: The Best Science Fiction of the Nineteenth Century," *Knightsbridge* 9 (1981), 12.

always been an emphasis on science, technology and technological-driven change concepts that were important for the founding editors of the genre.[38] S/f is where technological society dreams its futures.[39] Law and technology make consistent yet uneasy bedfellows. There is much writing, thinking and consternation about law and technology[40] and much of this arises from each seeing the other as an*other*.[41] As Barton Beebe showed in his excellent account of lawyers' attempted engagement with pioneer space technology after Sputnik, law wants to rule technology, while technology continually escapes law.[42] Law's *outside-ness* to technology and technology's *outside-ness* to law probably goes some way to explaining the under representation of lawyers in s/f.

However, it is precisely this connection between law and technology in the character of Joseph Adama that makes *Caprica* worthy of further thought.[43] Through Adama, *Caprica* projects a law and its lawyering whose epoch is ending. It represents how modern law's technological substratum of paper, writing and interpretation means it is unable to cope with the speed, hybridity and automation of the digital.

The demise of modern legality

Adama bumbled through the 18 episodes of *Caprica*, never the master of his circumstances. He was not Perry Mason, heroically solving crimes for his white middle-class clients[44] and he was no Atticus Finch, presented by Harper Lee as the moral rock for his community.[45] Adama's brother was a henchman for organised crime and Adama was a professional henchman for the same syndicate. It is in this capacity that he was introduced in the pilot doing his 'law work' of bribing a judge and delivering an ultimatum to a politician.[46] Adama comes across as the anti-Atticus. He was not white middle-class and not from the ruling elite. He was

38 See John W. Campbell, quoted in Peter Nicholls et al., *The Encyclopaedia of Science Fiction: An Illustrated A to Z* (Granada, 1979), 159.
39 Kieran Tranter, "The Speculative Jurisdiction: The Science Fictionality of Law and Technology," 20 *Griffith Law Review* 817 (2011), 820; Istvan Csicsery-Ronay, *The Seven Beauties of Science Fiction* (Wesleyan University Press, 2008), 2–3.
40 Kieran Tranter, "The Law and Technology Enterprise: Uncovering the Template to Legal Scholarship on Technology," 3 *Law, Innovation and Technology* 31 (2011).
41 Kieran Tranter, "Terrors in the Text: Technology – Law – Future," 13 *Law and Critique* 75 (2002).
42 Barton Beebe, "Law's Empire and the Final Frontier: Legalizing the Future in the Earlyorpus Juris Spatialis," 108 *Yale Law Review* 1737 (1999).
43 Travis and Tranter, "Interrogating Absence," 26.
44 Steven D. Stark, "Law on Television: Perry Mason Meets Sonny Crockett: The History of Lawyers and the Police as Television Heros," 42 *University of Miami Law Review* 229 (1986), 249–250.
45 Paula Baron, "The Emperor's New Clothes: From Atticus Finch to Denny Crane," in *Alternative Perspectives on Lawyers and Legal Ethics: Reimagining the Profession*, ed. Reid Mortensen, Francesca Bartlett and Kieran Tranter (Routledge, 2011), 89.
46 Moore et al., "Caprica."

corrupt and a poor father. Incapacitated by grief, Adama neglects his surviving young son, Willie Adama (Sina Najafi). Willie falls in with his uncle who showed much greater affection[47] and this leads to Willie sustaining a fatal injury.[48] Adama was also not an Atticus-like stoic widower cherishing memories of his deceased wife. Rather he ends up in bed with his associate Evelyn (Teryl Rothery). In this seduction, he was characteristically passive.[49] The passivity extends to his power plays. He half-heartedly plots between the Ha'la'tha and Graystone but nothing comes of his machinations. In the episode 'Gravedancing' he instructs his brother to kill Graystone's wife in an act of *lex talionis*, only to spend the remainder of the episode frantically calling and texting Sam to relent.[50]

In *Caprica*'s presentation of Adama there is an envisioning of modern legality disrupted by the digital. He was visualised onscreen with the mundane props of modern lawyering. In the pilot Adama asked to borrow from a court clerk a pencil (which he keeps)[51] and in the few images of him engaging professionally with Evelyn, paper files were view. He carried a briefcase. While he is not shown Atticus-like advocating in court, he is shown in 'professional' settings seated behind a desk with papers advising the Ha'la'tha on investment decisions and operating as the Ha'la'tha's representative within Graystone Industries. These are the sites and signs of the lawyer of modern legality,[52] the familiar objects that allowed for the creation and management of text on paper and the physical sites where text creation and management were valued and concentrated. Modern legality was manifested by a medium of paper and associated technologies of paper management.[53] These technologies were the hard apparatuses of cardboard folders, books, pads, pens and typewriter keyboards and the associated soft technologies of files and folders. Through these lawyers participated in the great archive documenting, storing and remembering human life. Extract Ronald Dworkin's jurisprudence from its liberalism and what is left is an affirmation of the great archive of law; of texts upon texts; and the lawyer-role as one of an archive spider spinning new texts threaded from volumes upon volumes of past texts.[54]

47 Ronald D. Moore, David Eick, Jane Espenson and Kevin Murphy, "Reins of a Waterfall," *Caprica*, season 1, episode 4, directed by Ronald D. Moore (Universal Cable Productions, Syfy, 2010).

48 Ronald D. Moore, David Eick, Jane Espenson and Kevin Murphy, "Here be Dragons," *Caprica*, season 1, episode 18, directed by Michael Nankin (Universal Cable Productions, Syfy, 2010).

49 Ronald D. Moore, David Eick, Jane Espenson and Kevin Murphy, "False Labor," *Caprica*, season 1, episode 14, directed by John Dahl (Universal Cable Productions, Syfy, 2010).

50 Ronald D. Moore, David Eick, Jane Espenson and Kevin Murphy, "Gravedancing," *Caprica*, season 1, episode 5, directed by Michael Watkins (Universal Cable Productions, Syfy, 2010).

51 Moore et al., "Caprica."

52 Douglas E. Litowitiz, "Has Technology Improved the Practice of Law," 21 *Journal of the Legal Profession* 51 (1997).

53 Cornelia Vismann, *Files: Law and Media Technology* (Stanford University Press, 2008); Marco Wan, "The Unwritten Law of Files," 22 *Law and Literature* 199 (2010), 203–204.

54 Ronald Dworkin, *Taking Rights Seriously* (Harvard University Press, 1977). See also Ashley Pearson and Kieran Tranter, "Code, Nintendo's *Super Mario* and Digital Legality," 28 *International Journal for the Semiotics of Law* 825 (2015).

But the lawyer of modern legality was not just an archivist or librarian.[55] The lawyer, notwithstanding Dworkin's literary metaphors,[56] was not a creative artist trying to glimpse the truth of the world.[57] The recording, text-producing functions had a purpose, and that purpose was a 'doing in the world', a changing of the future. The life represented in the archive was known and ordered so as to be imposed back onto life. Private and public law-making in modern legality – from private contracts and wills to trust deeds and articles of association, to the routine policy guidelines issued by an administrating agency to Acts of Parliament that have all the symbolism of sovereign law – existed to control the future. All this paper was generated to have an impact; to direct and manage humans. For Lon Fuller this function of law – to impose some predictability onto the future – was the essence of modern law.[58] Modern legality was, quite simply, modern.[59] Reason and will met in the present to control the future.

What this means is that modern legality was a feedback system. The tools to extract life to text and then to archive were complemented by a series of counter mechanisms to thread back from archive to text to life. This is the violence of modern law; of law as a textual practice that goes on to change life. There is a certain truth surrounding the gangster lawyer of Adama; his bribing, his delivering threats and his digging up of dirt to discredit and manipulate his client's enemies. Twentieth-century jurisprudence reacted against the crude violence of earlier command theories of law. For H. L. A. Hart, law and lawyering should be seen as something more than the 'gunman analogy.'[60] However, as critics continually observed, the lawyer in modern legality, with her skills in text, manipulation and hierarchical conduct, was a paid bully.[61] The lawyer generated texts to be fed into enforcement machines, and these enforcement machines, through 'acceptance'[62] and when needed violence, changed lives. At the most extreme, the lawyer is an obvious participant in biopolitical governance; creating the paper whereby children are removed from parents and individuals become quarantined in time and space. Giorgio Agamben's focus on the camp and the exception revealed how in modern legality there was a precarious distinction between *bios*, the lawful life of the citizen in community and *zoe* the animalistic life animating the human body; with the ever possibility of the setting aside of *bios* leaving *zoe*

55 On these tensions, see Katherine Biber, "Evidence from the Archive: Implementing the *Court Information Act* in NSW," 33 *Sydney Law Review* 575 (2011).
56 Ronald Dworkin, "Law as Literature," in *The Politics of Interpretation*, ed. W. J. T. Mitchell (University of Chicago Press, 1982).
57 Martin Heidegger, "The Question Concerning Technology," in *The Question Concerning Technology and Other Essays* (Harper and Row, 1977), 5–11.
58 Lon L. Fuller, *The Morality of Law*, rev. edn (Yale University Press, 1969), 39–41.
59 Max Weber and Guenther Roth, *Economy and Society: An Outline of Interpretive Sociology* (University of California Press, 1968), 848.
60 H. L. A. Hart, *The Concept of Law* (Clarendon Press, 1961), 21–24.
61 Edward A. Dauer and Arthur Allen Leff, "Law as Friend: Correspondence," 86 *Yale Law Journal* 573 (1976).
62 Hart, *The Concept of Law*, 111–112.

exposed to thanatological mechanisms.[63] But in a less extreme way, modern lawyer's text-producing activities changed lives. Emptied of their specific content, the law writing of private law – contracts, wills, deeds, articles of association, settlements and court orders – are all the same. They affect how resources are to be distributed in the future and in this distribution the potentiality of lives. Adama's proximity to gangster violence in *Caprica* rendered explicit this necessary violence of modern law. That in modern law it is difficult to categorically distinguish the violence of the gunman from the violence of law enforcement.[64]

While Adama's association with certain textual practices *and with* gangster violence projects him as a representative of modern legality, *Caprica* does something more. There is something wrong with the envisioning of this legality in *Caprica*. In Adama's slow bumbling-ness there is a suggestion that modern legality is out of time. Beyond Adama the visuals of modern law were slow and corrupt. Law and order seemed to be dissipating in the world of *Caprica*. Corruption was tolerated, the Ha'la'tha seemed to operate openly. Adama's bribing of the judge was presented as routine and common. The various factions of the STO operated with impunity. The homeland security force, the GDD, was forever chasing crimes but not busting the terror cells. Repeatedly, the residual query from viewing an episode is 'where are the police?' Graystone was complicit in the murder of employees of a rival company[65] and a business competitor died in Graystone's house under questionable circumstances,[66] yet there were no police investigations. A STO faction bungled an attack on an airport, shot guards and engaged in a car chase; but they were not apprehended.[67] A teenage girl was kept hostage in an attic of her teacher's house in comfortable suburbia, yet she is not reported missing nor do neighbours report her shouts from the boarded-up windows.[68] In the world of *Caprica* modern law was not working. Adama passively cannot keep up with the speed of change around him; just as the GDD seem unable to prevent the violence of a not-so-secret terrorist organisation. In *Caprica* modern legality appeared tragic. It came across as sad and slow. What was being screened was an end; the end of law as it has been known.

Caprica is clear in its diagnosis of modern law's terminality. The materiality of the middle-aged lawyer and old enforcement institutions of paper and violence were being challenged. This comes to the redeeming science fictionality of *Caprica*. It has been suggested that good s/f should have an engaging *idea*; there should a central speculative projection of how a technological, economic, social

63 Giorgio Agamben *Homo Sacer: Sovereign Power and Bare Life* (Stanford University Press. 1998), 181–188.

64 William P. MacNeil, *Lex Populi: The Jurisprudence of Popular Culture* (Stanford University Press, 2007), 54.

65 Moore et al., "Caprica."

66 Moore et al. "Things We Lock Away."

67 Ronald D. Moore, David Eick, Jane Espenson and Kevin Murphy, "Retribution," *Caprica*, season 1, episode 12, directed by Jonas Pate (Universal Cable Productions, Syfy, 2010).

68 Moore et al., "Things We Lock Away."

or environmental change can reimagine culture, politics, society and/or identity.[69] *Caprica*'s engaging premise was not the tired s/f backstory of malignant robots, but its sophisticated projection of digitality and the archive.[70]

The digital and the archive

Caprica's premise of digitality and the archive went beyond s/f's established conceptions of computers, networks and the digital of the cyberpunk subgenre. Cyberpunk for all its drugs, cyborgs and silicone presented conservative narratives of wheeling and dealing within a 'new' cyber frontier.[71] *Caprica* did something different. The key invention that drives the show is Zoe Graystone's divinely inspired development of a program that can recreate an individual's personality within the virtual world. Coupled with the technology developed by her father that allowed full body duplicate avatars; that is, copying a person's body and face so that an avatar could look physically identical to the person's real-world body, the 'avatar program' generated a digital copy of the person. It created an avatar that looked, thought, remembered and felt that they were the real person. As a good s/f premise this fantasy was cloaked in plausibility.[72] The program constructed the digital duplicate through mining the digital archive for traces of a person's life. Social media, government, corporate and social databases and cloud repositories provided the big data that Zoe's program merged into an accurate personality construct. In s/f computers and artificial intelligence have often developed or acquired personality and in cyberpunk protagonists often escaped the 'meat' and merged with the network. The usual image for this transfer was a single physical moment in time when a brain-sucking, nefarious-looking helmet is placed on a head. *Caprica*'s success is that it does it better in its mundane-ness. Its 'digital doubles' emerge from the archive in a process that is highly familiar yet disturbingly different.

It is highly familiar because the construction of avatars that represent an individual and opens that individual through the representation to the violence of modern law *is exactly what modern legality has always done*. The moment writing entered the law, the textual avatar was born. Life was extracted. For the modern lawyer in private practice material facts were noted, summaries of meetings made, file notes compiled, correspondence kept, forms filled and witnesses, experts and other statements drafted. Representations of life were caught in text and ordered in files. For operators of the biopolitical machine of modern governance this capturing, recording, noting, documenting and archiving of life were the entire *raison d'etre*. The operation of the avatar program in *Caprica* in seeking out

69 Csicsery-Ronay, *The Seven Beauties of Science Fiction*, 47.

70 Kirsten Strayer, "Reinventing the Inhumans: Avatar's Cylons, and *Homo Sapiens* in Contemporary Science-Fiction Television Series," 38 *Literature/Film Quarterly* 194 (2010), 197.

71 Karen Cadora, "Feminist Cyberpunk," 22 *Science Fiction Studies* 357 (1995), 365; Carl Freedman, *Critical Theory and Science Fiction* (Wesleyan University Press, 2000), 196.

72 Suvin, *Metamorphoses*, 64–65.

'evidence' and then organising that evidence to give a 'picture' or 'account' of a person represents modern legality's established processes of extracting from the life-world to generate a textual avatar.

But it is highly unfamiliar because the digital avatar of *Caprica* did not passively wait within a file for a human decision maker to actively engage with it. The textual avatar of modern legality was obviously an object; the file on a desk or archived in a cabinet. There was materiality to the textual avatar and that meant that there was ontological clarity. Files were things; humans were agents. A file's movement and its activity in the world were through human doing. They were tools through which 'man' made 'his' world. However, in *Caprica*, the men, Graystone and Adama, were not masters of their worlds. They were always playing catch-up with their daughters' avatars. Graystone, having glimpsed the Zoe avatar within a virtual world attempts to 'resurrect' her by downloading her into the Cylon prototype.[73] In this shell she stays hidden from him resisting cajoling to manifest herself.[74] Then when the prototype is destroyed she further runs from him into the virtual worlds.[75] Adama's daughter's avatar, shocked into virtual life by a ham-fisted application of the program by Graystone also runs from her father.[76] Lost within the networks, the Tamara avatar finds a place within the 'New Cap City' MMORPG and grows up.[77] The Zoe avatar and the Tamara avatar were not the sixteen-year-old girls that died in the terrorist train bombing. They identify yet differentiated their digital selves from their deceased fleshly manifestations.[78] The data escaped control of the real. They were not passive; the unchanging snapshot reflection of a life. Nor were they cartoon puppets – as was Graystone's attempt to reverse engineer the avatar program by creating a very accommodating digital double of his wife.[79] The Zoe and Tamara avatars had purpose, and expressed care and anger. They were not 'simulacra and simulation'; ethereal inhabitants of an unreal data-sphere.[80] Virtual-world theorists claim a virtue in MMORPGs as safe play spaces.[81] The real is enriched through the creative play in the virtual. In this conceptualising, the virtual and real remain separated by a digital divide. Cross-over points – real to virtual currency exchanges and account sales – are specific and limited. However, in *Caprica* the boundaries of the virtual and the real

73 Moore et al., "Caprica."

74 Ronald D. Moore, David Eick, Jane Espenson and Kevin Murphy, "Ghost in the Machine," *Caprica*, season 1, episode 9, directed by Wayne Rose (Universal Cable Productions, Syfy, 2010).

75 Ronald D. Moore, David Eick, Jane Espenson and Kevin Murphy, "Unvanquished," *Caprica*, season 1, episode 11, directed by Eric Stoltz (Universal Cable Productions, Syfy, 2010).

76 Moore et al., "Caprica"; Moore et al., "End of Line."

77 Moore et al., "Ghosts in the Machine."

78 Moore et al., "Things We Lock Away."

79 Moore et al., "False Labor."

80 Jean Baudrillard, *Simulacra and Simulation* (University of Michigan Press, 1994).

81 Edward Castronova, "The Right Way to Play," 49 *New York Law School Law Review* 185 (2004).

are in dispute. The working of the avatar program on the archive of the girl's lives has become *life* that learns, reflects and evolves. Rosi Braidotti disputes Agamben's characterisation of *zoe* as animalistic and less than human, something that must be negated so that more than bare life can flourish.[82] She presents *zoe* more positively as generative, as 'the endless vitality of life as continuous becoming.'[83] It is life envisioned by Braidotti's *zoe* that is shown by the avatars in *Caprica* 'code into soul' Graystone calls it.[84] Furthermore, as is manifest in the final episode, the generative possibilities of the digital lives of the avatars, results in them returning to the real through downloads into robot chassis.[85] The overall vision from *Caprica* was that 'life' in the real and virtual became a single hybridity.

It is these characteristics of speed, autonomy and hybridity of the digital that *Caprica* identifies as the challenges to modern legality. The digital is changing the medium of law; changing how legal data moves and changing the role of human agency in law.[86] The file-dwelling textual avatar of modern legality has been digitalised; become an assemblage of zeros and ones that can be effortlessly transported, analysed, copied and changed.[87] With this the materiality of modern legality is in decline. Within law spaces the metal filing cabinet, the brief case, the libraries and the file vault are being replaced by a single smart touchscreen device.[88] The clack of the typewriter and the phosphorescent flash of the photocopier, the sounds and sights of the mechanisation of modern legality's paper medium are in decline as interactive icons and Wi-Fi silently create, organise and move legal data.[89] *Caprica*'s representations of living avatars and slow, sad modern legality envisions the beginnings of digital legality and its emerging features of speed, autonomy and hybridity. It is these features of speed, autonomy and hybridity of digital legality that need to be considered in the programming of digital legality.

The schematics and programming of digital legality

This part, drawing upon the identified features of speed, autonomy and hybridity, begins to consider the programming of digital legality. First, the schematics of digital legality are considered and in particular the *inhuman* nature of digital

82 Rosi Braidotti, *Transpositions: On Nomadic Ethics* (Polity Press, 2006), 210.
83 Braidotti, *Transpositions*, 41.
84 Moore et al., " Unvanquished."
85 Ronald D. Moore, David Eick, Jane Espenson and Kevin Murphy, "Apotheosis," *Caprica*, season 1, episode 19, directed by Jonas Pate (Universal Cable Productions, Syfy, 2010).
86 Pearson and Tranter, "Code, Nintendo's *Super Mario* and Digital Legality."
87 Maarten Henket, "Digital Hercules?" 17 *International Journal for the Semiotics of Law* 277 (2004), 285–288.
88 Frederick S. Ury, "Atticus Finch and the Future of the Legal Profession," 18 *Southwest Journal of International Law* 225 (2011), 226–227.
89 Anja Oskamp and Arno R. Lodder, "Introduction: Law, Information, Technology, and Artificial Intelligence," in *Information Technology and Lawyers*, ed. Arno R. Lodder and Anja Oskamp (Springer, 2005).

legality will be emphasised. Second is a consideration of what architecture might stabilise the now atomised concepts of life, law, text and violence. Rights were modern legality's problematic solution to the extraction from and imposition onto human life. Rights provided pause movements in which the human object of the legal system could participate in processes. For digital legality the issue is how to program its speedy, hybrid automation to pause and require something more than a toggle-like binary yes or no. In pausing, there becomes the space for the analogue. In digital legality, pause and the possibility of the analogue exception reconnects *zoe* to the system.

Schematics of digital legality

The schematics of modern law are well known and in that well known-ness probably overlooked. As discussed in the previous part, modern law amounts to a complex set of techniques and flow-rules that had two directions. The first direction started with 'life' that was transformed into 'text' and the text was filed within the great archive. The second direction was from great archive to 'text' (which was then archived) and then to 'life.' The first direction involved the 'violence' of interpretation; of recording and extracting from the life-world.[90] The second direction involved a 'real' violence of enforcement mechanisms. Each transition within modern legality was mediated by humans. That did not mean that humans had freedom in an absolute sense to determine how to effect these transitions. The institutions, roles and rules of modern law provided formal structures establishing who and how and when and in what form, these transitions were to be effected. The law actor of modern law could rightly be seen as a cyborg; their participation in modern legality was technologically mediated by the techniques and rules of the 'legal system'[91] and the physical tools of text creation and management. Even in modern legality, some sort of pre-technological, 100% organic and natural human agency was in the distant past. However, to say that the stages of modern legality were human-mediated is to say that the key processing work of investigation, interpretation and decision was centred in the human, aided and abetted by the prosthetic paper memory of text and archive.[92] This explains the anxieties for modern law of the danger of inappropriate subjectivity within law actors and the various ways to account, and limit, 'interpretation.'[93] This schematic of modern law is provided in Figure 2.1.

90 Jacques Derrida, "Force of the Law: The Mystical Foundations of Authority," in *Deconstruction and the Possibility of Justice*, ed. Drucilla Cornell, Michel Rogerfield and David Gray Carlson (Routledge, 1992), 6–17.

91 Joseph Raz, *The Concept of a Legal System* (Clarendon Press, 1980).

92 Peter Goodrich, *Languages of Law: From Logics of Memory to Nomadic Masks* (Weidenfeld and Nicolson, 1990).

93 Alan C. Hutchinson, "A Postmodern Hart: Taking Rules Sceptically," 58 *Modern Law Review* 788 (1995).

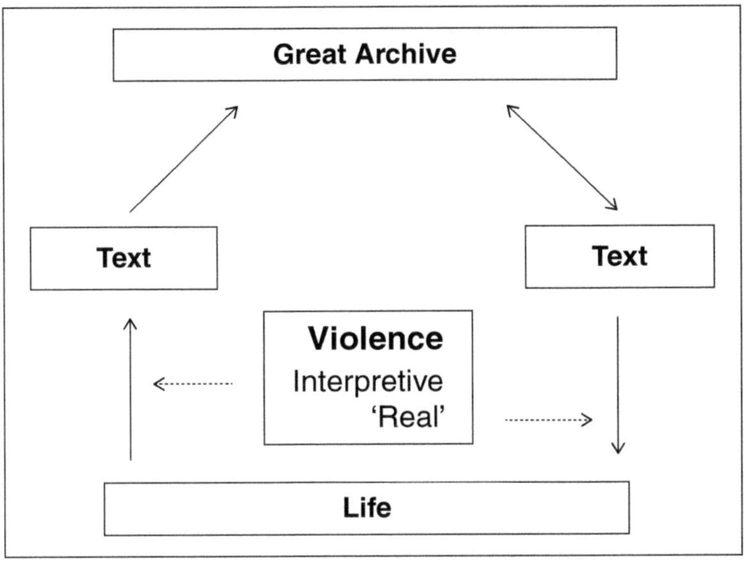

Figure 2.1 Schematic of modern legality.

However, digital legality as identified in *Caprica* challenges this schematic. Speed, autonomy and hybridity disturb these relationships and flows. Instead of paper, there is data. The archive has become dynamic and code can directly mediate the real. In *Caprica* what was manifest in the living avatars was a direct mediation of the archive with life without the human and textual inter-steps of modern law. Data and the virtual did not remain quarantined within the archive, but interfaced with the real directly. The immediate envisioning of this in *Caprica* were the military robots that Graystone Industry developed that became infected with the personality constructs made by the avatar program to become the deadly Cylons of *Battlestar Galactica*. In the robot the autonomy and hybridity of the digital was represented. The data crossed to the real and affected the real while retaining its virtuality. A less obvious representation was the absence of keyboards in the workplaces of *Caprica*. Graystone and his techs seemed to do their programming through graphic user interface (GUI) touchscreens; there were no representations of cutting code via alpha-numeric keystrokes. The icons of GUI suggest a much more active archive that limits data input according to the binary of yes and no. Instead of the analogue of text, GUI predetermines responses.[94]

94 "Past, Present and Future of User Interface Software Tools," Brad Myers et al. (1999), Carnegie Mellon University Research Showcase, accessed August 29, 2015, http://repository.cmu.edu/isr/732.

Each icon only allows a certain limited number of engagements; effectively a yes/no switch within a predetermined flow diagram.[95] What this means is that the schematics of digital legality is different to modern legality. The great archive interfaces directly with life; data is extracted by sensors and bots and data becomes real though robotic systems that directly control resources.[96] The human who read and decided at every stage in modern legality has been bypassed. This can be seen in Figure 2.2. In losing the human, in becoming ***inhuman***, those established and known concepts within modern legality of life, law, text and violence become atomised. Without human mediation the transitions between life, law, text and violence, digital legality seems rather alien.

The reality of this inhuman alien-ness of digital legality can be seen in the emerging system of traffic infringements arising from speed cameras as discussed by Richard Mohr and Francesco Contini.[97] Traffic infringement occupied a grey zone in modern legality, situated between the criminal justice system and the administrative machinery of the biopolitical state.[98] Nevertheless, in the heyday of modern legality for a sanction to be applied to a speeding motorist each of the stages in Figure 2.1 can be clearly discerned. First, a motorist was observed

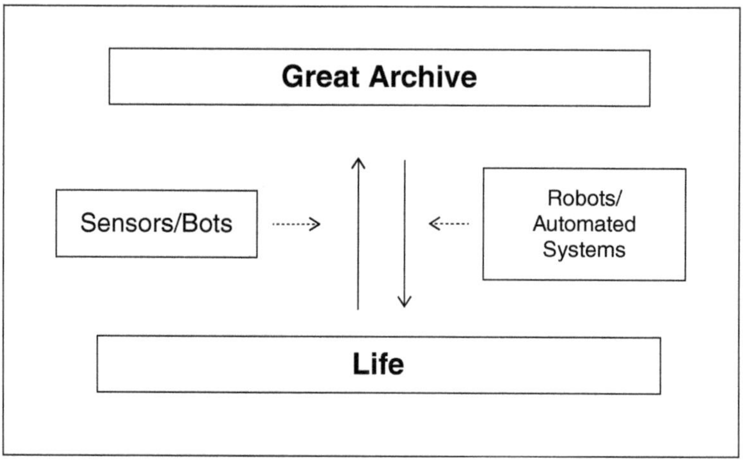

Figure 2.2 Schematic of digital legality.

95 Cornelia Vismann and Markus Krajewski, "Computer Juridisms" 29 *Grey Room* 90 (2008), 92.

96 David Murakami Wood and Stephen Graham, "Permeable Boundaries in the Software Sorted Society: Surveillance and Differentiations of Mobility" in *Mobile Technologies of the City*, ed. Mimi Sheller and John Urry (Routledge, 2006).

97 Richard Mohr and Francesco Contini, "Reassembling the Legal: 'The Wonders of Modern Science' in Court-Related Proceedings," 20 *Griffith Law Review* 994 (2011), 1006–1008.

98 Richard G. Fox, "On Punishing Infringements," 13 *Law in Context* 7 (1995).

speeding by a relevant officer and that officer wrote a report. A human extracted life to text. Second, various human agents took that text and engaged with many other texts within the great archive (road rules, driving licence and vehicle registrations, court procedures, summons/warrants, statements) to produce a file enclosing a textual avatar of that alleged speeding motorist that a decision maker (the superintendent of police or a local magistrate) would decide on. At various times and in various jurisdictions the shadow of the pre-modern oral legality could be seen in the provision or opportunity for an oral hearing at the decision stage. Third, the decision maker would then generate specific texts closing the file (transcripts or notes of decisions, orders/penalties on prescribed forms). These would move in two directions; be filed into the archive and feed into the enforcement mechanism. And fourth, if the motorists did not 'accept' the order, the order authorised the enforcement officers to violently enforce it.[99]

However, speed cameras change this process. The robotics of the camera (sensors in the road, the camera, the write-once-read-many disk, and the direct networking) sees and reports at first instance the violation. Data comprising the image of the vehicle, its velocity, the time and day is bundled together by the camera robot. The data is then transmitted to a central node. At that node image-reading software determines the registration of the vehicle from the picture of the vehicle's licence plate. The registration details of that vehicle are then searched through the database of vehicle registrations to find the contact details for the owner of the vehicle and an automatically generated infringement notice is issued to the owner.[100]

There are some striking contrasts with modern legality. Its speed is immediately obvious. Whereas in modern legality, time was needed to generate text and move files; the process from recording a transgression to issuing of a notice with speed cameras can be almost instantaneous. Paper has evaporated from the process, and humans have also vanished. Human involvement is limited to two possible sites. The first is where the clarity of the photograph means the image-reading software's algorithms cannot determine the details of the licence plate with sufficient probability and it is sent to a human for analogue interpretation.[101] The second is the workings of the enforcement mechanism where a driver does not respond to the infringement notice.[102] Further, these residual human involvements can be seen as transitory. Higher resolution cameras and next-generation image-reading software

99 These stages in modern legality's processing of a speeding infringement can be seen clearly in Emsley's account of motorists, police and law in the UK during the early twentieth century. Clive Emsley, "Mother, What *Did* Policemen Do When There Weren't Any Motors? The Law, the Police and the Regulation of Motor Traffic in England, 1900–1939," 36 *Historical Journal* 357 (1993).

100 These stages of the digital legality of speed cameras were documented by Mohr and Contini, "*Reassembling the Legal*," 1007.

101 Abru Elly, "Turning Back the Speedo," 83 *New South Wales Police News* 45 (2003).

102 Gaye Lansdell et al., "Infringement Systems in Australia: A Precarious Blurring of Civil and Criminal Sanctions?", 37 *Alternative Law Journal* 41 (2012).

could remove the need for human analogue interpretation of unclear photographs. The enforcement mechanism could also be further automated. Allowing the speed camera system to interface with the banking and finance system could facilitate automatic fine payments. Whereas *Caprica* presented digital legality in a dramatic fashion with living avatars operating between real and virtual worlds, speed camera systems present the mundane, everyday-ness of digital legality.

Speed cameras also show the inhumanity of digital legality – of how humans as the key mediators between life, law, text and violence – are becoming redundant. It does not mean that life, law, text and violence have necessarily become redundant; rather their core meaning in modernity of law as human life being written about and interpreted by humans in text facilitating violence by humans against humans, have dissipated. The touchstone of the human within each is changed. The 'violence' of an infringement regime is still violence in the sense of taking by force the assets of the person, regardless of whether the taking was modern law's human bailiffs seizing property or a piece of code directing a financial institution's system to debit an account. Human life is still the subject of 'violence,' but the agent of violence has changed. In digital legality its speed, automatism and hybridity has atomised modern legality's set relations between life, law, text and violence.

Programming of digital legality

The issue for legal theory is what to make of this change in the materiality, and with that, the essential features of law? There can be a utopian celebration of the digital. Positivism dreamed of the law machine. It told of a legal system where subjectivity, interpretation and discretion – all what had been seen as 'human' in modern legality – had been squeezed out; that the law should be a tool of social control that could reliably be deployed by political authority for whatever ends.[103] From this perspective, digital legality's speed, autonomy and hybridity potentially completes the positivist project. What is appreciated in this utopian assessment of digital legality is the reduction of legal transaction costs. Code means that the archive becomes dynamic, generating its own data and this data through autonomous robotic systems can effect change on life. The biopolitical machine can operate at greater efficiency. It will be quicker, there will be lower compliance costs as the number of subjective and expensive humans decrease, and it will be more uniform in its outcomes. In Lawrence Lessig's words 'the perfect technology of justice.'[104]

This techno-totality of autonomous data and code has a dystopian counterpoint. With the animation of the archive and its robotic doing-in-the-world, humans become an object of a system that they do not participate in. Human life is extracted from and then managed, but does not have any participation in the processes. It is highly tempting to see this in Agamben's terms as the

103 Carl Schmitt, *The Leviathan in State Theory of Thomas Hobbes: Meaning and Failure of a Political Symbol* (Greenwood Press, 1938).

104 Lawrence Lessig, "The Zones of Cyberspace," 48 *Stanford Law Review* 1403 (1996), 1411.

extinguishing of *bios* leaving only *zoe* subjected to the machine. The consequence for this removal of humans from legal decision making means that the exceptional circumstance, the compassionate, favourable interpretation, the possibilities of justice that Jacques Derrida identifies within modern legality's analogue textual existence is minimised.[105] *Caprica*'s basic genre was dystopian s/f. It showed a world and humanity in decline.[106] Code flows through a set of digital checkpoints of yeses and nos. The Cylon's 'by your command' was ironic. They gave the impression of compliance while bidding their time for revolution. As observed, one of the disappointments of *Caprica* was that humans were deprived of agency. Humanity was doomed the moment the divine angel/shadow/plot device of Zoe Graystone appeared to her childhood self and planted the seeds for the avatar program and the physical image of the military robot.[107]

It is here that the implications for legal theory of *Caprica* can be envisioned. Digital legality's inhumanity places humans outside of the emerging information gathering, processing and application networks. For much post-positivist legal theory the issue has been how to reconnect the human to the legal system as a participant. Under the operational question of how to ensure that the terrifying powers at modern legality's disposal to affect the future through changing life in the present were to be exercised appropriately – of how to prevent a legal system turning pathological – legal theory reinvigorated rights.[108] Rights gave the human object of the legal system *bios;* it gave it agency and involvement with the processes between life, text and archive and archive, text and life. Flimsy, contested and imperfect, rights functioned liked pause moments in the operation of modern legality. Rights, when they worked, made the machinery of modern legality slow down, consider more widely or closed off particular ways for life and text to interface.

In digital legality, what was aimed for in modern legality through rights can only be expressed as code. Code is something that legal theory has yet to adequately theorise. Yet the basic feature of code is it is programmability.[109] The issue has been what values and mechanisms should be expressed by that code. With digital legality's tendency to totality, to the exclusion of the humans that it processes, what many would require are pause moments in the code. Pause moments can be as simple as passwords or CAPTCHAs – the reverse Turing test that uses images to determine whether a data coming into a system originates with a human – or they could be as complex as allowing analogue inputs that are

105 Jacques Derrida, "Force of Law," 16–17; On this see, Kieran Tranter, "Come a Day There Won't be Room for Naughty Men Like Us to Slip About at All: the Multi-Medium Outlaws of Firefly/Serenity and the Possibilities of Post-Literate Justice," 16 *Law Text Culture* 277 (2012), 296.

106 Tom Moylan, *Scraps of the Untainted Sky: Science Fiction, Utopia, Dystopia* (Westview Press, 2000), 121.

107 Jutta Wimmler, "Masters of Cyber-Religion: The Female Body as God's 'Interface' in the TV Series *Caprica*," 3 *Journal of Religion, Media and Digital Culture* 120 (2014).

108 Costas Douzinas, *The End of Human Rights* (Hart Publishing, 2000), 109–117.

109 Lawrence Lessig, *Code and Other Laws of Cyberspace* (Basic Books, 1999).

then read or heard by human decision makers. What pause moments do is that they allow digital legality to be more responsive to the life-world. As has been identified in the extreme manifestation of digital legality the inputs are solely generated by sensors and bots. These take data from the life along predetermined paths. The sensor is triggered by a vehicle's velocity and a digital image is taken; or bots search the archive for information concerning an individual and knit that information together with other data to create a digital avatar.[110] The code is active and human life is passive.

Braidotti's reframing of Agamben's definitions of *zoe* and *bios* is illuminating. Under Agamben's scheme the emerging techno-totality of digital legality represents a stripping of *bios* leaving a bare, impoverished humanity. There is little hope in this vision – the techno-totality will paternalistically process human life without the textual and human-centred decision-making safeguards that ensured *bios* in a functional modern legal system. As noted when talking about the 'life-fulness' of the avatars in *Caprica*, Braidotti's *zoe* is the complex life-world in all its changing-ness. This vitalistic *zoe* surprises, always going beyond the known and expected. Having established *zoe* as generative, Braidotti's *bios* is the disciplined, refined, managed, known and regulated representation of life within techno-political, legal and cultural archives.[111] In the context of this chapter, the code of digital legality takes *zoe* and builds digital *bios*. What pause moments programmed into code can potentially allow is openness to the possibility of the surprisingness of *zoe*. The possibility of justice of modern legality ultimately was in the analogue potential that the human nodes of the legal system could appreciate unexpected difference and accordingly interpret and act differently. Rights were the mechanism for that difference to be communicated. The analogue through rights kept an openness to *zoe*; it allowed the possibility for life to present itself as something unexpected and exceptional where the normal workings should be suspended and changed. In digital legality, its tendency to totality means that this openness to *zoe* needs to be very clearly programmed into its code through pause moments. The task for legal theory is the embedded, technical task of envisioning how to program the program to pause. To return to *Caprica*, the digital Zoe needs to remain open to *zoe*.

Bibliography

Books and articles

Agamben, Giorgio. *Homo Sacer: Sovereign Power and Bare Life*. Stanford University Press, 1998.

Asimov, Isaac. "Introduction: The First Century of Science Fiction." In *Isaac Asimov Presents: The Best Science Fiction of the Nineteenth Century*, 9–12. Edited by Isaac Asimov. Knightsbridge, 1981.

110 Pearson and Tranter, "Code, Nintendo's *Super Mario* and Digital Legality."
111 Braidotti, *Transpositions*, 37.

Baron, Paula. "The Emperor's New Clothes: From Atticus Finch to Denny Crane." In *Alternative Perspectives on Lawyers and Legal Ethics: Reimagining the Profession*, 85–107. Edited by Reid Mortensen, Francesca Bartlett and Kieran Tranter. Routledge, 2011.

Baudrillard, Jean. *Simulacra and Simulation*. University of Michigan Press, 1994.

Beebe, Barton. "Law's Empire and the Final Frontier: Legalizing the Future in the Early Corpus Juris Spatialis." 108 *Yale Law Journal* 1737, 1999.

Biber, Katherine. "Evidence from the Archive: Implementing the *Court Information Act* in NSW." 33 *Sydney Law Review* 575, 2011.

Bignell, Jonathan. "Seeing and Knowing: Reflexivity and Quality." In *Quality TV: Contemporary American Television and Beyond*, 76–95. Edited by Janet McCabe and Kim Akass. I. B. Tauris, 2011.

Braidotti, Rosi. *Transpositions: On Nomadic Ethics*. Polity Press, 2006.

Broderick, Damien. *Reading by Starlight: Postmodern Science Fiction*. Popular Fictions Series, Routledge, 1995.

Brunsdon, Charlotte. *Screen Tastes: Soap Opera to Satellite Dishes*. Routledge, 1997.

Cadora, Karen. "Feminist Cyberpunk." 22 Science-*Fiction Studies* 357, 1995.

Cardwell, Sarah. "Is Quality Television Any Good? Generic Distinctions, Evaluations and the Troubling Matter of Critical Judgement." In *Quality TV: Contemporary American Television and Beyond*, 19–34. Edited by Janet McCabe and Kim Akass. I. B. Tauris, 2011.

Casey, Jim. "All This Has Happened Before: Repetition, Reimagination, and Eternal Return." In *Cylons in America: Critical Studies in Battlestar Galactica*, 237–250. Edited by Tiffany Potter and C. W. Marshall. Continuum, 2008.

Castronova, Edward. "The Right to Play." 49 *New York Law School Law Review* 185, 2004.

Csicsery-Ronay, Istvan. *The Seven Beauties of Science Fiction*. Wesleyan University Press, 2008.

Dauer, Edward A. and Arthur Allen Leff. "Law as Friend: Correspondence." 86 *Yale Law Journal* 573, 1976.

Derrida, Jacques. "Force of Law: The 'Mystical Foundations of Authority'." In *Deconstruction and the Possibility of Justice*, 3–67. Edited by Drucilla Cornell, Michel Rogerfield and David Grey Carlson. Routledge, 1992.

Douzinas, Costas. *The End of Human Rights*. Hart Publishing, 2000.

Dworkin, Ronald. *Taking Rights Seriously*. Harvard University Press, 1977.

——— "Law as Literature." In *The Politics of Interpretation*, 249–270. Edited by W J T Mitchell. University of Chicago Press, 1982.

Eberl, Jason T. *Battlestar Galactica and Philosophy: Knowledge Here Begins Out There*. Blackwell, 2008.

Elly, Abru. "Turning Back the Speedo." 83 *New South Wales Police News* 45, 2003.

Emsley, Clive. "Mother, What *Did* Policemen Do When There Weren't Any Motors? The Law, the Police and the Regulation of Motor Traffic in England, 1900–1939." 36 *Historical Journal* 357, 1993.

Fox, Richard G. "On Punishing Infringements." 13 *Law in Context* 7, 1995.

Freedman, Carl. *Critical Theory and Science Fiction*. Wesleyan University Press, 2000.

Fuller, Lon L. *The Morality of Law*, revised edition. Yale University Press, 1969.

Geraghty, Christine. "Aesthetics and Quality in Popular Television Drama." 6 *International Journal of Cultural Studies* 25, 2003.

Gillers, Stephen. "Taking *LA Law* More Seriously." 98 *Yale Law Journal* 1607, 1989.
Goodrich, Peter. *Languages of Law: From Logics of Memory to Nomadic Masks*. Weidenfeld and Nicolson, 1990.
Hart, H. L. A. *The Concept of Law*. Clarendon Press, 1961.
Hatch, Richard. *So Say We All: An Unauthorized Collection of Thoughts and Opinions on Battlestar Galactica*. BenBella Books, 2006.
Heidegger, Martin. "The Question Concerning Technology." In *The Question Concerning Technology and Other Essays*, 3–35. Harper and Row, 1977.
Henket, Maarten. "Digital Hercules?" 17 *International Journal for the Semiotics of Law* 277, 2004.
Hills, Matt. *Triumph of a Time Lord: Regenerating Doctor Who in the Twenty-First Century*. I. B. Tauris, 2010.
Hutchinson, Allan C. "A Postmodern Hart: Taking Rules Sceptically." 58 *Modern Law Review* 788, 1995.
Joseph, Paul R. "Science Fiction." In *Prime Time Law: Fictional Television as Legal Narrative*, 155–166. Edited by Robert M. Jarvis and Paul R. Joseph. Carolina Academic Press, 1998.
Jowett, Lorna. "Back to the Future: Retrofuturism, Cyberpunk, and Humanity in *Firefly* and *Serenity*." In *Investigating Firefly and Serenity: Science Fiction on the Frontier*, 101–113. Edited by Rhonda V. Wilcox and Tanya R. Cochran. I. B. Tauris, 2010.
Kapica, Steven. "'I Don't Feel Like a Copy': Poshuman Legal Personhood and *Caprica*." 23 *Griffith Law Review* 612, 2014.
Kaveney, Roz and Jennifer Stoy. *Battlestar Galactica: Investigating Flesh, Spirit and Steel*. I. B. Tauris, 2010.
Kincaid, Paul. "On the Origins of the Genre." 44 *Extrapolation* 409, 2003.
King, Laura and John Hutnyk. "The Eighteenth Brumaire of Gaius Baltar: Colonialism Reimagined in *Battlestar Galactica*." In *Breaching the Colonial Contract: Anti-Colonialism in the United States and Canada*, 237–250. Edited by Arlo Kempf. Springer, 2009.
Lansdell, Gaye et al. "Infringement Systems in Australia: A Precarious Blurring of Civil and Criminal Sanctions?" 37 *Alternative Law Journal* 41, 2012.
Lessig, Lawrence. "The Zones of Cyberspace." 48 *Stanford Law Review* 1403, 1996.
——— *Code and Other Laws of Cyberspace*, Basic Books, 1999.
Litowitz, Douglas E. "Has Technology Improved the Practice of Law." 21 *Journal of the Legal Profession* 51, 1997.
MacNeil, William P. "'You Slay Me!': Buffy as Jurisprude of Desire." 24 *Cardozo Law Review* 2421, 2003.
——— *Lex Populi: The Jurisprudence of Popular Culture*. Stanford University Press, 2007.
Malin, Brenton. *American Masculinity under Clinton: Popular Media and the Nineties "Crisis of Masculinity."* Peter Lang, 2005.
McCabe, Janet and Kim Akass. "Introduction: Debating Quality." In *Quality TV: Contemporary American Television and Beyond*, 1–11. Edited by Janet McCabe and Kim Akass. I. B. Tauris, 2011.
Mohr, Richard and Francesco Contini. "Reassembling the Legal: 'The Wonders of Modern Science' in Court-Related Proceedings." 20 *Griffith Law Review* 994, 2011.

Moylan, Tom. *Scraps of the Untainted Sky: Science Fiction, Utopia, Dystopia*. Westview Press, 2000.
Murakami, David Wood and Stephen Graham. "Permeable Boundaries in the Software Sorted Society: Surveillance and Differentiations of Mobility." In *Mobile Technologies of the City*, 177–191. Edited by Mimi Sheller and John Urry. Routledge, 2006.
Myers, Brad et al. *Past, Present and Future of User Interface Software Tools*. School of Computer Science, Carnegie Mellon University Research Showcase (1999). Available at <http://repository.cmu.edu/isr/732>.
Nelson, Robin. "Quality TV Drama: Estimations and Influences Through Time and Space." In *Quality TV: Contemporary American Television and Beyond*, 38–51. Edited by Janet McCabe and Kim Akass. I. B. Tauris, 2011.
Nicholls, Peter et al. *The Encyclopaedia of Science Fiction: An Illustrated A to Z*. Granada, 1979.
Oskamp, Anja and Arno R. Lodder. "Introduction: Law, Information Technology, and Artifical Intelligence." In *Information Technology and Lawyers*, 1–22. Edited by Arno R. Lodder and Anja Oskamp. Springer, 2005.
Pearson, Ashley and Kieran Tranter. "Code, Nintendo's *Super Mario* and Digital Legality." 28 *International Journal for the Semiotics of Law* 825.
Pohl, Fredrick and C. M. Kornbluth. *Gladiator-at-Law*, Pan Books, 1955/1964.
Potter, Tiffany and C. W. Marshall. *Cylons in America: Critical Studies in Battlestar Galactica*. Continuum, 2008.
Raz, Joseph. *The Concept of a Legal System*, Clarendon Press, 1980.
Rosen, Robert E. "Ethical Soap: *LA Law* and the Privileging of Character." 43 *University of Miami Law Review* 1227, 1989.
Ryan, Maureen. (2010) "'Caprica' Is Cancelled by Syfy." Available at <http://www.aoltv.com/2010/10/27/caprica-canceled>.
Schedle, Per. *Androids, Humanoids, and Other Science Fiction Monsters*. New York University Press, 1993.
Schmitt, Carl. *The Leviathan in State Theory of Thomas Hobbes: Meaning and Failure of a Political Symbol*. Greenwood Press, 1938.
Stark, Steven D. "Law on Television: Perry Mason Meets Sonny Crockett: The History of Lawyers and the Police as Television Heros." 42 *University of Miami Law Review* 229, 1986.
Steiff, Josef and Tristam D. Tamplin. *Battlestar Galactica and Philosophy: Mission Accomplished or Mission Frakked Up?* Open Court, 2008.
Stoy, Jennifer. "Of Great Zeitgeist and Bad Faith: An Introduction to *Battlestar Galactica*." In *Battlestar Galactica: Investigating Flesh, Spirit and Steel*, 1–37. Edited by Roz Kaveney and Jennifer Stoy. I. B. Tauris, 2010.
Strayer, Kirsten. "Reinventing the Inhumans: Avatars, Cylons, and *Homo Sapiens* in Contemporary Science-Fiction Television Series." 38 *Literature/Film Quarterly* 194, 2010.
Suvin, Darko. *Metamorphoses of Science Fiction; On the Poetics and History of a Literary Genre*. Yale University Press, 1979.
Swanson, Dorothy Collins. *The Stories of Viewers for Quality Television: From Grassroots to Prime Time*. Syracuse University Press, 2000.
Thompson, Robert J. *Television's Second Golden Age: From Hill Street Blues to ER*. Continuum, 1996.

Tranter, Kieran. "Terror in the Texts: Technology – Law – Future." 13 *Law and Critique* 75, 2002.

——— "'Frakking Toasters' and Jurisprudences of Technology: The Exception, the Subject and Techné in Battlestar Galactica." 19 *Law and Literature* 45, 2007.

——— "The Law and Technology Enterprise: Uncovering the Template to Legal Scholarship on Technology." 3 *Law, Innovation and Technology* 31, 2011.

——— "The Speculative Jurisdiction: The Science Fictionality of Law and Technology." 20 *Griffith Law Review* 817, 2011.

——— "'Come a Day There Won't be Room for Naughty Men Like Us to Slip About at All': The Multi-Medium Outlaws of Firefly/Serenity and the Possibilities of Post-Literate Justice." 16 *Law Text Culture* 277, 2012.

Travis, Mitchell. "Making Space: Law and Science Fiction." 23 *Law and Literature* 241, 2011.

Travis, Mitchell and Kieran Tranter. "Interrogating Absence: The Lawyer in Science Fiction." 21 *International Journal of the Legal Profession* 23, 2014.

Ury, Frederic S. "Atticus Finch and the Future of the Legal Profession." 18 *Southern-western Journal of International Law* 225, 2011.

Vismann, Cornelia. *Files: Law and Media Technology*. Stanford University Press, 2008.

Vismann, Cornelia and Markus Krajewski. "Computer Juridisms." 29 *Grey Room* 90, 2008.

Wan, Marco. "The Unwritten Law of Files." 22 *Law and Literature* 199, 2010.

Weber, Max, Guenther Roth and Claus Wittich. *Economy and Society: An Outline of Interpretive Sociology*. University of California Press, 1968.

Wimmler, Jutta. "Masters of Cyber-Religion: The Female Body as God's 'Interface' in the TV Series *Caprica*." 3 *Journal of Religion, Media and Digital Culture* 120, 2014.

Wolfe, Gary K. *Critical Terms for Science Fiction and Fantasy: A Glossary and Guide to Scholarship*. Greenwood Press, 1986.

Television series and episodes

Chase, David. *The Sopranos*. Chase Films, HBO, 1999–2007.

Frost, Mark and David Lynch. *Twin Peaks*. Lynch/Frost Productions, ABC, 1990–1991.

Gelbart, Larry. *M*A*S*H*. 20th Century Fox Television, CBS, 1972–1983.

Moore, Ronald D. and David Eick. *Battlestar Galactica*. David Eick Productions, Sci-Fi Channel, 2003–2010.

Moore, Ronald D., David Eick, Jane Espenson and Kevin Murphy. *Caprica*. Universal Cable Productions, Syfy, 2010.

——— "Caprica," *Caprica*, pilot. Directed by Jeffrey Reiner. Universal Cable Productions, Syfy, 2010.

——— "Rebirth," *Caprica*, season 1, episode 3. Directed by Jonas Pate. Universal Cable Productions, Syfy, 2010.

——— "Reins of a Waterfall," *Caprica*, season 1, episode 4. Directed by Ronald D. Moore. Universal Cable Productions, Syfy, 2010.

——— "Gravedancing," *Caprica*, season 1, episode 5. Directed by Michael Watkins. Universal Cable Productions, Syfy, 2010.

——— "Ghost in the Machine," *Caprica*, season 1, episode 9. Directed by Wayne Rose. Universal Cable Productions, Syfy, 2010.

——— "End of Line," *Caprica*, season 1, episode 10. Directed by Roxann Dawson. Universal Cable Productions, Syfy, 2010.

——— "Unvanquished," *Caprica*, season 1, episode 11. Directed by Eric Stoltz. Universal Cable Productions, Syfy, 2010.

——— "Retribution," *Caprica*, season 1, episode 12. Directed by Jonas Pate. Universal Cable Productions, Syfy, 2010.

——— "Things We Lock Away," *Caprica*, season 1, episode 13. Directed by Tim Hunter. Universal Cable Productions, Syfy, 2010.

——— "False Labor," *Caprica*, season 1, episode 14. Directed by John Dahl. Universal Cable Productions, Syfy, 2010.

——— "Here be Dragons," *Caprica*, season 1, episode 18. Directed by Michael Nankin. Universal Cable Productions, Syfy, 2010.

——— "Apotheosis," *Caprica*, season 1, episode 19. Directed by Jonas Pate. Universal Cable Productions, Syfy, 2010.

Whedon, Joss. *Buffy the Vampire Slayer*. Mutant Enemy, 20th Century Fox, 1998–2003.

——— *Firefly*. Mutant Enemy, 20th Century Fox, 2002.

Chapter 3

Don't blink: monstrous justice and the Weeping Angels of *Doctor Who*

Penny Crofts

Introduction

The *Doctor Who* episode "Blink" introduced the Weeping Angels,[1] aliens that when perceived look like statues of angels covering their eyes in sadness, but in the blink of an eye can touch their victims and send them to another time. The plot centres on Sally Sparrow (played by Carey Mulligan), a young woman who has never met the Doctor and only interacts with him for a few moments. She is a photographer, and when we first see her, she is breaking into an old, abandoned house. In the background is a beautiful statue of a crying angel. Sally's attention is drawn to a wall with words that are barely visible behind peeling wallpaper. She peels back the wallpaper in time to see that the words are a message addressed to her, telling her to duck. She does so, just in time to avoid being hit by a rock flying through the window – and just in time for us to notice that the beautiful statue has moved toward her.

A Weeping Angel – when seen – appears as a statue, carved into the shape of an angel, usually with its hands daintily covering its eyes as though it were weeping. When observed, it is serene and lovely. However, though still as stone when observed, a Weeping Angel is capable of extremely quick movements when not observed. If you blink, a Weeping Angel will have silently come up beside you. If the Weeping Angel touches you, then you are gone. Weeping Angels thrive by consuming all of the energy from the future lives of their victims. They deposit their victims in a past time, though not a time through which they have already lived. Their victims feel no pain and the rest of their lives are theirs to live as they are able in their new temporal and spatial locations. The Doctor states that they are 'the only psychopaths in the universe to kill you nicely.'[2]

The Weeping Angels render strange and threatening the familiar sight of statues of females in classic poses. Weeping Angels are portrayed not just as stone ornaments, but as mobile monsters that can take us away from ourselves. The Weeping Angels are visible only when quantum locked, but otherwise cannot

1 Stephen Moffat, "Blink," *Doctor Who*, series 3, episode 10, directed by Hetti MacDonald (BBC, 2007).

2 Moffat "Blink."

be seen by their victims or the television audience as they move on their prey. As their name would suggest, these figures normally take the appearance of a statue of an Angel. However, as the conclusion to the episode "Blink" implies, it is potentially *any* statue that can be a "Weeping Angel," with the Doctor providing the viewer a warning interposed with images of a variety of famous and publicly displayed statues. This chapter seeks to take up this warning by exploring the nature of the Weeping Angels in relation to the most ubiquitous statue for law and cultural legal studies – *Justicia* herself, adorning courthouses and courtrooms around the world. This chapter interrogates the intersections and dissonances of the Weeping Angels and *Justicia* to gain insight into the relationship between the visible emblem of *Justicia* and conceptions of justice, and its relationship between law and legal institutions. This alignment implies further, however, that like the Weeping Angels, *Justicia* may appear serene, beautiful and part of the ornamentation of buildings of law and justice, but in fact embodies a certain monstrousness that challenges our normal understanding of law. As such, by reading *Justicia* alongside the Weeping Angels, this chapter forms part of the project of cultural legal studies that identifies both how texts of popular culture (here, *Doctor Who*) and images of law (*Justicia*) intertwine in our envisioning of legality. Throughout this chapter, I use the word *Justicia* to refer specifically to statues of justice, and the word 'justice' to refer to all that *Justicia* represents and connotes. Historically, *Justicia* was one of four cardinal virtues, and in contemporary representations she is a blindfolded statue. Section 1 contextualises my analysis of the Doctor Who episode "Blink" within the cultural jurisprudence of science fiction and monstrosity. Section 2 considers the implications of the similarities between the Weeping Angels and *Justicia* – both are statues of females with their eyes covered, representing abstract concepts. Given these commonalities between the Weeping Angels and *Justicia*, section 3 considers the possibility of monstrousness that contests our conceptions of law's capacity to render justice.

Science fiction and monstrous justice

Law and science fiction both present and promise stories of utopian and dystopian alternatives – they both create worlds. They are both bound by self-constructed rules, which must be consistent with the narrative world created. Science fiction is often concerned with the relationship between state legitimacy, violence and justice, whether portraying the state's ambition for the perfection of its monopoly on violence,[3] or the breakdown of the state and the return to private violence.[4] In law, justice is a story, a 'narrative of jurisdiction that might constitute the texts

3 For example, *Hunger Games* and *Divergent* both present a tyrannical state seeking to sustain its monopoly of violence.

4 See, for example, Mezey's analysis of the western science fiction, *Deadwood*. Naomi Mezey, "Law's Visual Afterlife: Violence, Popular Culture, and Translation Theory," in *Imagining Legality: Where Law Meets Popular Culture*, ed. Austin Sarat (Tuscaloosa: University of Alabama Press, 2011).

that ground judicial commitments.'[5] Both science fiction and law are a literature and tradition of our wishes and fears of how we see ourselves, and who we would wish or fear to become. Just as with law, science fiction generates in its audience a desire for justice, whether or not this is delivered. In most science fiction, the narrative generally establishes a set of assumptions about what is just, which usually involves unmasking and punishing or resolving the villain/s and (sometimes) rewarding the good. Science fiction can also challenge its own portrayal of justice, particularly by shifting point of view and character development across a narrative arc, so that characters who initially appear evil may later be revealed as good. In *Doctor Who*, the series has at times challenged audience perceptions of a particular character as a villain;[6] however, the villains are almost always punished and the good are almost always rewarded. Science fiction enacts the possibility for justice to be delivered in imaginative ways, that can provide insight into the delivery of, and desires for, justice in the world.[7]

Doctor Who, which first premiered on the BBC in 1963, follows the adventures of the Doctor, a Timelord who travels across time and space in what appears to be a blue police box, called a TARDIS. He usually travels with a companion of some kind, and after some running from a threat by an alien or aliens, the Doctor saves the day with a clever resolution. The ending of each episode tends to provide a satisfying sense of justice and rarely requires overt force or violence by the Doctor, but may be imposed by some other character. The series has generated a sizeable body of fan and academic literature.

Within the series' considerable oeuvre, the episode "Blink" (2007) is a standout in terms of critical success and impact. It won the Hugo award for Best Dramatic Presentation, Short Form, and was nominated for the Nebula Award for Best Script. Its writer, Stephen Moffat, won the Best Academy of Film and Television Arts Craft and Cymru awards for best writer. The episode "Blink" is highly unusual in the *Doctor Who* series in that the Doctor is barely present: he is literally stuck in another time.[8] The primary protagonists are the intrepid Sally Sparrow and the terrifying Weeping Angels. "Blink" is regularly regarded as the most horrifying and best episode of entire *Doctor Who* series.[9] Throughout

5 Robert Cover, "The Folktales of Justice: Tales of Jurisdiction," *Capital University Law Review* 14 (1984–1985).

6 For example, in "Planet of the Ood," Tenth Doctor (David Tennant) with Donna Noble (Catherine Tate), the Ood appear to be evil but are reacting to centuries of enforced slavery. The episode concludes with the human villain Halpen becoming an Ood and the Ood liberated from slavery and able to sing again. Keith Temple "Planet of the Ood," *Doctor Who*, series 4, episode 8, directed by Graeme Harper (BBC, 2008).

7 See, for example, Stanley Cohen, *Visions of Social Control* (Cambridge: Polity Press, 1985). Cohen draws upon science fiction to analyse penal theories and the administration of justice.

8 The Tenth Doctor, David Tennant, makes only very brief appearances with his companion Martha.

9 Michelle Saint and Peter French, "The Horror of the Weeping Angels," in *Doctor Who and Philosophy: Bigger on the Inside*, ed. Courtland Lewis and Paula Smithka (Chicago: Open Court, 2010).

his career, the Doctor has faced a series of monsters, including the terrifying Daleks and the cyborg Cybermen. Whether technology-based or organic, these monsters are horrifying in and of themselves[10] and/or because of their evil plans (such as planetary destruction or universal domination). Despite the range of monsters the Doctor has faced, in a poll conducted by BBC, taking votes from 2,000 readers of the *Doctor Who Adventures* magazine, the Weeping Angels were voted the scariest monsters of 2007, with 55% of the vote; the Master and the Daleks took second and third place, with 15% and 4% of the vote.[11] In a 2012 poll of over 10,000 respondents conducted by the *Radio Times*, the Weeping Angels were again voted the best *Doctor Who* monster, with 49.4% of the vote. The Daleks came in second place, with 17%.[12] The Weeping Angels have since appeared in other episodes, but "Blink" remains the scariest and best, encapsulating the beauty and horror of the Weeping Angels.[13] It is this nature of the Weeping Angels – beautiful yet monstrous – that I would like to explore in relation to both the concept of the monstrous and that of justice.

But what do we mean by monstrous? The central characteristic of the monster is the transgression of borders of humanity. Monsters are conceptualised as beyond understanding, as incomprehensible to human beings. Derrida framed the idea of transgression in terms of undecidability;[14] Mary Douglas considered pollution and contamination fears of disorder from an anthropological perspective;[15] Kristeva explored the idea of abjection in *The Power of Horror*: '[i]t is thus not lack of cleanliness or health that causes abjection but what disturbs identity, system, order. What does not respect borders, positions, rules. The in-between, the ambiguous, the composite.'[16]

10 For example, the Daleks were inspired by the Nazis. Their catch cry 'Exterminate, exterminate' reflects their philosophy of genocide. Ed Webb and Mark Wardecker, "Should the Daleks Be Exterminated?," in *Doctor Who and Philosophy: Bigger on the Inside*, ed. Courtland Lewis and Paula Smithka (Chicago and La Salle: 2011).

11 Saint and French, "Horror."

12 Paul Jones, "Doctor Who: Weeping Angels Beat The Daleks to be Voted Fans' Favourite Ever Monsters," *Radio Times*, June 9, 2012, http://www.radiotimes.com/news/2012-06-09/doctor-who-weeping-angels-beat-the-daleks-to-be-voted-fans-favourite-ever-monsters (accessed December 20, 2016).

13 The Weeping Angels reappear in: Steven Moffat "The Time of Angels," *Doctor Who*, series 5, episode 4, directed by Adam Smith (BBC, 2010); Steven Moffat "Flesh and Stone," *Doctor Who,* series 5, episode 5, directed by Adam Smith (BBC, 2010); and Steven Moffat "The Angels Take Manhattan," *Doctor Who*, series 7, episode 5, directed by Nick Hurran (BBC, 2012).

14 The classic monsters of horror films, zombies, have been used to explain Derrida's ideas about undecidability. Zombies might be 'EITHER alive OR dead. But it cuts across these categories: it is BOTH alive AND dead. Equally, it is NEITHER alive NOR dead, since it cannot take on the "full" senses of these terms . . . in terms of life and death, *it cannot be decided*.' Jeff Collins and Bill Mayblin, *Derrida for Beginners* (Sydney: Allen and Unwin, 1996), 17–20.

15 Mary Douglas, *Purity and Danger: An Analysis of the Concepts of Pollution and Taboo* (London: Routledge and Kegan Paul, 1966/2002).

16 Julia Kristeva, *Powers of Horror: An Essay on Abjection* (New York: Columbia University Press, 1982), 4.

Foucault explicitly considers the production of monsters in *Abnormal*: '[e]ssentially, the monster is the casuistry that is necessarily introduced into law by the confusion of nature . . . it is a monster only because it is also a legal labyrinth, a violation of and an obstacle to the law, both transgression and undecidability at the level of the law.'[17] For Foucault, the production of monsters should be understood as a double breach of nature and law. According to Foucault each age had its 'privileged monster'[18] – bestial human in the Middle Ages, Siamese or conjoined twins in the Renaissance period, and the hermaphrodite in Classical Age.[19]

While there are significant differences between these theories, each of them stressed the idea that the disorderly, abject, or undecidable disturb, transgress or undermine identity, system, and order. The Weeping Angels, however, are unusual because although terrifying, they are not abject or disorderly, at least in their normal appearance. Monsters generate fear and fascination because they not only break rules and cross borders, but because they also challenge the border itself, by being both and neither one thing and another. Monsters resist and refuse easy categorisation. They are disturbing hybrids that refuse to participate in the classificatory 'order of things', problematising and challenging classifications built on hierarchy or binary oppositions.[20] Monster theory celebrates and fears monsters as agents of change – representing and enacting both threat and promise. Derrida wrote:

> The future is necessarily monstrous: the figure of the future, that is, that which can only be surprising, that for which we are not prepared . . . is heralded by species of monsters. A future that would not be monstrous would not be a future; it would already be a predictable, calculable, and programmable tomorrow.[21]

Monsters break apart the 'either/or' syllogistic logic with a kind of reasoning closer to 'and/or.' For example, vampires are the living dead – they are neither/both dead and alive. In "Blink", the Weeping Angels are trans-category – they are in/animate; alien yet familiar; im/mobile. They are impossible to conceptualise at all, except when they are quantum locked and thus cease to function. They disrupt our epistemological assumptions that 'to see is to know.'

17 Michel Foucault, *Abnormal: Lectures at the College de France 1974–1975* (New York: Picador, 2003), 64–65.

18 Foucault, *Abnormal*, 66.

19 Sharpe disputes Foucault's assertion of a linear development in monsters. He also notes that hermaphrodites were outside the monster category in English law. Andrew Sharpe, *Foucault's Monsters and the Challenge of Law* (London and New York: Routledge, 2010).

20 Jeffrey Cohen, "Monster Culture," in *Monster Theory: Reading Culture*, ed. Jeffrey Cohen (Minneapolis: University of Minnesota Press, 1996).

21 Jacques Derrida, "Passages – from Traumatism to Promise," in *Points . . . Interviews 1974–1994*, ed. E. Weber (Stanford: Stanford University Press, 1995).

In this sense, can justice be conceived as similarly concerned with transgressions or violations of borders and legal conceptual schemes, and therefore also as monstrous?[22] Does the figure of the monster provide a response to Goodrich's plea for different images of justice and for us 'to be playful, foolosophical with *Justicia*.' For us 'to be weened, made a little less dependent, a touch more irreverent, when it comes to justice and the politics of law.'[23] This chapter takes up this focus on both the monstrous and justice as transgressing law and nature, by exploring the intersections and dissonances of the portrayals of the Weeping Angels and *Justicia*, and what this means for the threat and promise of (monstrous) justice. The most striking parallel between the Weeping Angels and justice is that they are both abstract conceptions represented in stone as women, usually (but not always) with their eyes covered – whether by a blindfold or hands. As statues they are aesthetically pleasing, conveying an impression of serenity, loveliness, beauty and shyness, encouraging touch of their smooth stone exteriors. They are also ostensibly safe – despite *Justicia* being frequently armed with a sword – because inanimate. Given their allegorical representations and accoutrements, should our response to justice be the same as that excited in the viewer by the Weeping Angels? Can and should we regard justice as monstrous due to transgression and undecidability – breaching and obstructing law, capturing multiplicity and difference? On this account, does justice, like the Weeping Angels horrify? What are the implications of labelling justice monstrous? Justice is not just plural, contested and abstract. It can be frightening, immediate, real, irreducible and horrible. In what follows, I explore in turn the implications for conceptions of justice by its representation in stone, the significance of gender and blindness, and the links between aesthetic beauty and horror.

Visual representations of the 'creatures of the abstract'

The Weeping Angels are described by the Doctor as 'creatures of the abstract.' Nonetheless, they have concrete effects – they transport their victims to another time. When functioning as Weeping Angels, all we see are their effects, and those effects are the disappearance of a character. The figure of *Justicia*, also, is intended as a representation and claim of the abstract conception of justice. It has survived into modern times from a time when allegorical personifications were common.[24] We usually think of allegory as a representation of an abstract

22 Sharpe, *Foucault's Monsters*. See also Derrida's notion of justice as transgressive of law and legal categories: Jacques Derrida, "Force of Law: The 'Mystical Foundation of Authority' " *Cardozo Law Review* 11 (1990).

23 Peter Goodrich, "The Foolosophy of Justice and the Enigma of Law," *Yale Journal of Law and the Humanities* 24 (2012): 176.

24 Ruth Weisberg, "The Art of Memory and the Allegorical Personification of Justice," *Yale Journal of Law and the Humanities* 24 (2012).

idea, but allegories can also be a system of complex visual signs. *Justicia* is one of the Cardinal Virtues, along with Prudence, Fortitude and Temperance, that originated in Ancient Greece. Each virtue had a choice of attributes and props across the centuries to identify them and elucidate their meaning.[25] Originally, the accompanying attributes would have been easily read and understood[26] – but apart from *Justicia*, we have lost the ability to read the attributes of the Cardinal Virtues (who would now recognise Temperance holding a bridle?) and other groups of Virtues and Vices.[27] Of the Cardinal Virtues, only *Justicia* has remained legible – that is – her attributes are easily recognised and understood – scales, blindfold and sword.[28]

Justicia has been depicted since classical Roman times,[29] and was so ubiquitous in courthouses and law schools from the Renaissance that Capers has suggested that it had the weight of a 'given.'[30] Ruth Weisberg suggests that the reason why *Justicia* has remained legible, while the personification of the other Cardinal Virtues is largely forgotten, is because *Justicia* is attached to the law courts and the administration of justice.[31] Statues of *Justicia* are placed outside courtrooms to indicate or claim that here is a place where justice is or will be done.[32] Here, *Justicia* is a representation of a particular type of justice, an authoritative image of law, a state sanctioned expression of judicial values and governmental aspirations.[33]

25 Other symbols associated with *Justicia* include that she is carrying a sword and scale. In addition, historically she also carried a book, a bundle of lector rods, a globe, serpent, dog or skull. Dennis Curtis and Judith Resnik, "Images of Justice," *Yale Law Journal* 96 (1986).

26 Marina Warner, *Monuments and Maidens: The Allegory of the Female Form* (London: Weidenfeld and Nicolson, 1985), 158.

27 Most of the other sets are also female, except for the Vices, depicted as male. See Judith Resnik and Dennis Curtis, "Re-Presenting Justice: Visual Narratives of Judgment and the Invention of Democratic Courts," *Yale Journal of Law and the Humanities* 24 (2012).

28 Examples of the legibility of *Justicia* are demonstrated in forms of art where they are deployed in jest. For example, *Lady Justice Lucy* which stood in 2002 in front of William Mitchell College of Law in St Paul, Minnesota as part of that city's celebration of the cartoonist Charles Schultz, was a statue of a chunky child, draped, blindfolded and holding sword and scales, and yet was still legible and an obvious reference to law. Resnick and Curtis, "Re-presenting Justice," 29–30.

29 Linda Mulcahy, "Imagining Alternative Visions of Justice: An Exploration of the Controversy Surrounding Stirling Lee's Depictions of Justicia in Nineteenth-Century Liverpool," *Law, Culture and the Humanities* (2011).

30 Bennett Capers, "Blind Justice," *Yale Journal of Law and the Humanities* 24 (2012).

31 Ruth Weisberg, "The Art of Memory and the Allegorical Personification of Justice," *Yale Journal of Law and the Humanities* 24 (2012): 264.

32 For example, Resnik and Curtis note the use by the United States government of imagery of the court to gain legitimacy for 'Camp Justice' at Guantanamo Bay as a court, with the logo of the Office of Military Commissions echoing back to *Ma'at*, albeit substituting an eagle for a female with an ostrich feather in her cap. Resnik and Curtis, "Re-Presenting Justice," 87–90.

33 In the later episode, "The Time of Angels," the Weeping Angels are able to move through an image of a Weeping Angel. This reflects the assumption that placing *Justicia* outside a courtroom makes justice 'present.'

However, the image of *Justicia* is itself subject to subversive interpretations, other visions of justice. For example, theorists like Norman Spaulding have emphasised the tendency to place *Justicia* outside courtrooms, we must *pass* justice in order to enter courtrooms.[34] He argues that this reflects the ambivalence about whether law and justice occupy the same space. On this account, justice is both divided from, and related to, the authority of law.

The Weeping Angels and *Justicia* tend to be rendered in stone, suggesting stability, constancy and durability. For *Justicia,* the representation in stone is consistent with claims made of justice, such as that by Aristotle distinguishing between natural justice and conventional justice: '[t]hat which is by nature is unchangeable and has everywhere the same force . . . while they see change in things recognised as just.'[35] This statement is part of the natural law tradition that conceives of justice as timeless, permanent and universal. It asserts that the principles of natural law, including justice, guide how human law should be created and interpreted. On this account, natural justice is appropriately portrayed by the stone of *Justicia* – representing the claimed attributes of justice as timeless, permanent and universal. Her austere neutrality expresses durability and inspires deference and faith. But part of Aristotle's account is a recognition and assertion of another type of justice, conventional justice, which itself is contingent, variable and context-driven.

The Weeping Angels, however, raise questions about the celebration of a justice that is immobile, concrete and unchanging. When unperceived the Weeping Angels are swift assassins, but perceived, even by each other, they turn to stone. The Doctor states that 'their greatest asset is their greatest curse.' While a stone cannot be killed,[36] the Weeping Angels are unable to do anything while frozen. *Unlike* Justicia, the Angels *do* move – but it is only when we are not looking at them. It is the observation of them that quantum locks them and makes them immobile. This may suggest that there is something about the nature of looking at or for justice that locks it, renders it immobile and rigid, while in the process of turning away from a direct look at it, justice can be enacted. Accordingly, does justice require, at least in our modern times, a *failure* to observe it, a looking away from the rigidity of the law and allowing justice to occur in the space beyond it?

Representing and celebrating justice in the stone of *Justicia* outside of courtrooms may communicate and mirror a static and conservative form of justice. The

34 Norman Spaulding, "The Enclosure of Justice: Courthouse Architecture, Due Process and the Dead Metaphor of Trial," *Yale Journal of Law and the Humanities* 24 (2012): 312–313.

35 Aristotle, selections from *Nicomachean Ethics*, in *Lloyd's Introduction to Jurisprudence,* ed. M.D.A Freeman (London: Sweet & Maxwell, 2008), 137. See also Justinian: '[t]he laws of nature which are observed amongst all people alike, being established by a divine providence, remain ever fixed and immutable.' Justinian, selections from *Institutes*, in *Lloyd's Introduction to Jurisprudence*, ed. M.D.A. Freeman (London: Sweet & Maxwell, 2008), 138.

36 The Weeping Angels deteriorate like stone over many years. Moffat, "The Time of Angels."

conservatism and reductivism of the immobilisation of representations of justice is powerfully demonstrated in Mulcahy's analysis of Thomas Stirling Lee's bas reliefs of *Justicia* carved in Istrian marble on the side of St George's Hall (1841–7).[37] These images provide an example of alternative, more sensual visions of law than those usually portrayed by *Justicia*. The first panel depicts "The Childhood of Justice" and shows *Justicia* as a naked child being led by Conscience, instructed by Wisdom and followed by Joy. The second panel depicts "The Girlhood of Justice" showing a naked juvenile *Justicia* standing between Wealth and Fame. In these panels, *Justicia* is robbed of the usual props associated with authority and high status, and proffers a more complex account of justice than we are accustomed to. Here *Justicia* is not an authoritative Goddess but a vulnerable adolescent in need of tutoring not yet capable of authoritative judgment. She is a reflexive adjudicator rather than one unthinkingly bound by formal and rational rules.

Although there is no necessary relationship between *Justicia* and the concept that she represents, the image of *Justicia* has been used to reflect upon, critique, and express conceptions of justice at different times and places. That is, there is life and power invested in the image/allegory of *Justicia*.[38] *Justicia* was a symbolic figure of an ideal order from Roman times onwards until the 19th century, when the actual legal order excluded women from practising or being involved in justice.[39] It gave an illusion of bringing a feminine hand to justice when in fact female hands were absent.[40] As women and men of all colours gained recognition as rights holders, entitled to sue and be sued, to testify, and to judge, a female figure of Justice became less an abstraction and more a representation of a person. But who should decide how 'she' – *Justicia* – is to look? *Justicia* was called upon as an icon for feminists insisting on legal rights to equality,[41] and was represented as 'Mulatto' in South Carolina. The different appropriations and meaning of *Justicia* highlight not only her accessibility, but also her plasticity. Although portrayed in stone *Justicia* is 'sufficiently pliable' that she can serve multiple purposes.[42]

Blindfolds and the visibility of justice

Although depictions vary across time, place and artistic impulse, contemporary imagery tends to cover the eyes of *Justicia* with a blindfold. This covering of the eyes is another attribute in common with the Weeping Angels. In both sets of images, the covering of the eyes has multiple meanings. The name of the Weeping

37 Mulcahy, "Imagining Alternative Visions."

38 Mulcahy, "Imagining Alternative Visions."

39 Women were excluded under the doctrine of coverture, from practising law and from being jurors.

40 Capers, "Blind Justice."

41 Kristin Collins, "Representing Injustice: Justice as an Icon of Woman Suffrage," *Yale Journal of Law and the Humanities* 24 (2012).

42 Collins, "Representing Injustice," 192.

Angels comes from the assumption that they are covering their eyes in sadness, weeping at the follies of the world and the distance of humans from grace. However, the Weeping Angels are actually covering their eyes to avoid seeing each other – if they see each other, then they are permanently turned to stone.[43]

Historically, justice was not always depicted as blindfolded. This can be seen in Cesare Ripa's depictions of justice. Ripa was one of the most influential of popular European emblem books of the 16th and 17th centuries. He provided elaborate descriptions of the literary references and symbolic attributes associated with Virtues, Vices and Passions, as well as the arts and sciences. His work, *Iconologica*, featured memorable and dramatic woodcut figures with epigrammatic verses on moral themes. Ripa's worldly justice is shown with closed eyes, while divine justice had 'acute vision' and 'piercing eyes.'[44]

The blindfold, as well as blindness, was in Christian and Western traditions in earlier centuries wholly negative.[45] This was predicated on classical and biblical texts that repeatedly cast light as representing truth and darkness as misguided.[46] Blindness could preclude a person's entry into holy areas and to be struck blind was a form of punishment imposed by God. The blindfold was a sign of censure – when humans punished each other, they sometimes put blindfolds on their victims. When he discovered his wrongdoing, Oedipus put out his eyes; Ulysses puts his stake into the eye of the Cyclops and blinds him; Jesus was made sport of by being blindfolded, mocked and beaten.[47] Those who were blind or blindfolded had profound limitations.[48] In biblical terms, a blindfold denoted a wilful refusal to comprehend the light of redemption. Renaissance images placed a blindfold on Eros to mark the misguided nature of love, engendering foolishness and confusion. Fortuna was often blindfolded to denote irrationality and blindness. Blindfolds also adorned images of executed criminals, shown hanging and disgraced. Historically, the dominant motif was that blindness was linked with distress, to the extent that classicists have claimed that blindness was 'always associated with evil.'[49] The only exceptions to this general negativity associated with blindness were the sightless seers of Homer.

By covering their eyes, the Weeping Angels not only protect themselves from being quantum locked, but also camouflage themselves, highlighting the ubiquity

43 The Greek monster Medusa turned all who gazed on her directly into stone. She was beheaded by Perseus who looked at her reflection in his mirrored shield.

44 Cesare Ripa, *Iconologia* (New York: Garland Publishing Company, 1611/1976), 201.

45 E.g. Thomas St Aquinas, *Summa Theologica* (Westminster MD: Christian Classics, 1225–1274/1981).

46 *Job* 11:20: 'Blindness will fall on the wicked.'

47 *Mark* 14:65: 'Some began to spit on him, blindfolded him, and struck him with their fists.'

48 E.g. *Exodus:* 23:8: 'bribery makes the discerning man blind and the just man give a crooked answer.' *Job* 9:24: 'the land is given over to the power of the wicked and the eyes of its judges are blindfolded.'

49 Erwin Panofsky, "Blind Cupid," in *Studies in Iconology: Humanistic Themes in the Art of the Renaissance* (New York: Harper and Row, 1962), 109.

of statues with covered eyes. Why then, did a blindfolded *Justicia* gain currency and what did this mean? Positive explanations of the deliberate occlusion of sight have been proffered, particularly that the blindfold purported impartiality. The blindfold may serve as a buffer so that judges are not tempted away from using reason. For example, Ripa posited that only one of his seven Justices was to sport a blindfold. This was the type of Justice that is exercised in the Tribunal of judges and secular executors:

> She is wearing white because judges should be without the stain of personal interest or of any other passion that might pervert Justice, and this is also why her eyes are bandaged – and thus she cannot see anything that might cause her to judge in a manner that is against reason.[50]

Here, blindfolding was a symbol of law's commitment to rationality and even-handedness, consistent with Lutheran theology – truth was to come from inner light (as with Homer's seers). The blindfold represented inner wisdom, lack of distraction, incorruptibility, and encouraged abstention from corrupt, self-interested dealing.[51] The once-hostile gesture of affixing a blindfold has been attributed to scepticism about law and judges in the context of both the Reformation and the Inquisition.[52] In the 19th century, the blindfold was used to denote a new idea about the position of the judge – independence. Judges were untethered from the governments that employed them and were no longer servile to God and to rulers.

The image of the blindfold continues to provoke commentary about what it denotes about the relationships between sight, knowledge, wisdom, judgment and justice, and the role of law. In modern accounts, the blindfold has been utilised to represent positive aspects of justice. For example, Rawls' highly influential account of justice relied upon a 'veil of ignorance' to put one into an 'original position' that precluded knowledge about one's own class, social status, intelligence, abilities etc. Veiled, one could develop principles without knowing whether one was 'advantaged or disadvantaged . . . by the outcome of natural choice or the contingency of social circumstances.'[53] But the blindfold has also been appropriated by the law's critics. Given the emphasis upon sight in law expressed through various optical metaphors in legal doctrine and popular discourse about justice,[54] theorists have relied upon the image of the blindfold

50 Ripa, *Iconologica*, 203.

51 Thus a traditional pictorial representation of injustice shows a devil breaking the scales of justice and tearing the blindfold from her eyes. Judith Shklar, "Giving Injustice Its Due," *Yale Law Journal* 98 (1991).

52 Resnik and Curtis, "Re-presenting Justice," 58–59.

53 John Rawls, *A Theory of Justice* (Cambridge, MA: The Belknap Press, 1971), 12.

54 Thus one 'appears before the law', 'justice must be seen to be done.' Acts of Parliament and the King's Bench reaffirmed the right of confirmation, that 'accusing witnesses be brought

to interrogate the implications of occluded vision. In Bruegel's *Justicia*, printed in 1559, Justice personified stands on a pedestal blindfolded, sword in one hand, scales in the other. All around her 'justice' is being done – one man is beheaded, while another is strapped to a bench while boiling liquid is poured down his throat, others are hanging from the gallows.[55] Here the blindfold can be regarded as signalling *Justicia's* indifference and/or weakness. *Justicia* is represented as a bystander – there is a divorce between the symbol of justice and the action surrounding *Justicia*. But given that the action was presumably made in *Justicia's* name, *Justicia* could be regarded as either complicit for allowing it to happen, or ineffective in preventing it.[56] The political and legal theorist Judith Shklar extended this analysis to passive injustice – looking away from injustice,[57] averting eyes from wielders of violence.[58] Here *Justicia* is representative of law as an apparatus of complicity, a failure to act, collaborating with injustice.

The efficacy of the horror of "Blink" is in part due to its presentation and use of the idea of different sightlines or viewing positions. The perspective of the protagonist Sally Sparrow is predominant, but the audience sees more than Sally. Her vision is limited in time and place, while the audience is more able to perceive the threat of Weeping Angels and also see what happens to characters after they have been touched by an Angel. The audience can see the Weeping Angels closing in on Sally, while she is unaware of the threat. We never see from the perspective of the Weeping Angels – they remain unknown and unknowable. "Blink" thus emphasises how different viewers have different knowledge and perspectives. The image of *Justicia's* blindfold has been used to denote the perspectives of different viewers. Cartoonists regularly rely on a blindfolded *Justicia* to denote injustice.[59] The image of the blindfold has been utilised to critique colour-blind justice. Capers argues that *Justicia's* blindness blinds the spectator, it 'lulls and

'face to face' with the defendant.' Richard D Friedman and Bridget McCormack, "Dial-in Testimony," *University of Pasadena Law Review* (2002). The law also places great emphasis upon seeing evidence, for example, s 10A *Oaths Act NSW* requires that a driver's license is seen. Signatures on legal documents must be witnessed.

55 *Justice*, etching, attributed to Phillip Galle, circa 1559, after the 1539 drawing by Pieter Bruegel the Elder.

56 Desmond Manderson, "Blindness Visible: Law, Time, and Bruegel's Justice." Lecture at ANU School of Literature, Languages and Linguistics, 31 March 2014.

57 Shklar quotes Cicero: 'Who does not oppose wrong when he can, is just as guilty of wrong as if he deserted his country.' Cicero, *The Offices*, bk II at ch. 8; bk I at ch. 10 and ch. 7 (W. Miller trans 1951). Shklar, 1148.

58 Cover, "Folktales," 200.

59 For example, in 1988, the *Los Angeles Times* ran the Paul Conrad cartoon in which Justice holds a coat hanger instead of scales to suggest the cruder methods used to induce abortions prior to the Supreme Court's recognition that abortion rights were constitutionally protected. Justice, if banning abortions, is rendered blind to the harm of the coat hanger abortions that would ensue. *Alternative to Roe vs Wade, LA Times*, November 21, 1988, 115. Resnik and Curtis, "Re-presenting Justice," 62.

tricks us into not seeing our own blindness.'[60] Procedural rules limit the sorts of information available to jurors, imposing a kind of blindness in decision-making – which depending on perspective can be positive or negative.[61] Peter Goodrich has argued that 'the eyes are the gates of justice and that if they are closed, if Justice can neither see nor be seen, then access is denied.'[62] If the eyes are windows to the soul, why then is *Justicia* blindfolded – so she cannot see our souls and we cannot see hers? Both the images of the Weeping Angels and *Justicia* denote multiple meanings of the covered eyes.

Aesthetic beauty and horror

Only some individuals or groups are at any given historical moment demonised by the term monster. Heroes like Superman and the Doctor are also unnatural and inexplicable, so there is more to a monster than the transgression of laws and classificatory systems. Monster status is always an effect of interpretation, and 'central to the interpretative task . . . is an assessment of any threat posed to, and the possibility and degree of their incorporation within, the legal order.'[63] In his seminal analysis of horror, Noel Carroll argues that monsters are produced not only because they are transgressive but because they elicit an affect of horror, a mixture of fear and disgust.[64] I will explore why the Weeping Angels excite such horror even though they seem almost benign and beautiful when compared with other baddies, and apply these insights to the question of whether we should fear justice.

Fear of the monstrous

A central aspect of horror is fear. Horrific monsters are threatening – whether physically, psychologically, morally or socially. They are destroyers – frightening in their capacity to harm. Alex Sharpe also emphasises this notion of threat in her legal history of monsters noting the legal distinction between monstrosity and 'mere' deformity. Why, compared with other monsters represented in *Doctor Who*, such as the Daleks (exterminate) or the Cybermen (take over a victim's soul and body), is this modus operandi of the Weeping Angels of moving their victim to another time so frightening? The Weeping Angels are particularly terrifying because of the unknown – one moment a person is there, and in another they have disappeared without any explanation or noise. The Weeping Angels are a nightmare-like private threat, rather than the politically organised Daleks and Cybermen.

60 Bennett Capers, "Blind Justice," 184.

61 Katherine Biber, "How Silent is the Right to Silence," *Cultural Studies Review* 18(1) (2012).

62 Goodrich, "Foolosophy," 155.

63 Sharpe, *Foucault's Monsters*, 15.

64 Noel Carroll, *The Philosophy of Horror or Paradoxes of the Heart* (New York: Routledge, 1990).

By removing victims to another time, Weeping Angels threaten to destroy personhood. Dislocation in time is a common trope in science fiction, and often portrayed in positive terms.[65] But the Weeping Angels are scary because they act without negotiation or consent, and there is no way back to the life that the Weeping Angels have taken you away from. This shows the significance of time in the construction of personal identity. Alasdair MacIntyre maintains that persons construct their identities via coherent narratives. People integrate the various facts and roles of their lives together into meaningful, continuous timelines by filtering relevant from irrelevant features followed by foregrounding the most relevant elements and allowing the rest to fade into the background. This means that a person is a 'storytelling animal', whose ability to understand herself depends on her ability to understand what narratives are available through her life.[66] In effect, we create our personal identities by the stories we tell about ourselves and others about what we care about, in a particular time and context.[67] By ripping Kathy out of her location in time and space and placing her in another point of time, the Weeping Angels are tearing Kathy away from everything she cares about. She finds herself instantly in a land as foreign to her as another country, without any access to those things she cared about, that were important to her. By removing Kathy from all those things that mattered to her, the Weeping Angels have 'demolished a large part of Kathy's identity;'[68] they have removed Kathy from herself.

The Weeping Angels inflict an inexplicable type of violence upon characters, not only upon the person transported back in time, but also the people that they leave behind. The tragedy of the loss of what might have been is demonstrated by the transportation of Billy, whom Sally meets only a few minutes before he becomes a victim of the angels. At the time that they meet, it is implied that this is Sally's future husband. Billy is sent to 1969 London, where he lives a normal lifespan, and later dies on the same day he first met Sally. The tragedy is thus for what might have been, even though both Sally and Billy have created (second) lives for themselves. The Weeping Angels highlight the extent to which we are time and place bound. A person's identity is not just bound up with their physical body or even a particular mind, but with who and what a person cares about. Thus the Weeping Angels are feared because of the potential harm they can inflict. They threaten the dissolution of personal identity – they can rob a person of who they are, hence the Doctor regarding this fate as a form of 'death.'

The harm inflicted by the Weeping Angels raises questions about the modus operandi of justice and the extent to which justice generates fear through

65 In the *Doctor Who* series, time travelling is predominantly presented as desirable, exciting and empowering.

66 Alasdair MacIntyre, *After Virtue: A Study in Moral Theory*, Second ed. (Notre Dame, IN: University of Notre Dame Press, 1984), 201.

67 Saint and French, "Horror," 304. Martha Nussbaum, *Upheavals of Thought: The Intelligence of Emotions* (Cambridge: Cambridge University Press, 2001).

68 Saint and French, "Horror."

threats to personhood. The idea of *Justicia* as exciting fear is not necessarily problematic – the wicked should fear justice. For example, in his description of seven Justices Ripa emphasises fear. Thus Rigorous Justice was described as:

> A skeletal figure like that used to depict death, in a white robe . . . we can see her face, feet and hands with a bared sword and scales . . . This figure teaches us that rigorous justice does not pardon any crime, no matter the excuse given . . . just like death, who is not touched by excuses and who has no regard for the station or quality of that person . . . The fearsome aspect of this figure demonstrates that this sort of Justice is frightening to the people and that there is no occasion for the law to be interpreted lightly.[69]

The tendency to provide *Justicia* with a sword also denotes a threat of the force of law, of law's violence.[70]

The Weeping Angels suggest that *Justicia's* threat extends beyond the wicked and could affect anyone. If justice is done through the law, then we should examine the ways in which a subject experiences legal subjectivity. The legal subject does not pre-exist law, but is constituted and constructed by and through language. The law provides a means by which messy human emotions and/or actions are redrawn/reconstructed/translated into legal categories. It provides a basic model of our understanding of other people and for our understanding of ourselves. By emphasising particular attributes, and ignoring or excluding other attributes as irrelevant the law may undermine, transform or remove what a person cares most about. Our personal identities depend, at least in part, on there being a comprehensive thread of narrative in our lives, about past, present and future. Much has been written about the restriction, selection and exclusion of the narratives of participants in the courtroom.[71] The legal system, in the process and claims of doing justice, removes participants from their everyday lives and forces them to fit within a particular legal narrative or not be heard. This results in a disruption to an integral aspect of what it means to be human. Our narratives of what matters to us, often at moments of great stress and importance, are forced to fit within general formulae not of our making.

The effect of the Weeping Angel's touch – removing a person from a particular time and all that they care about – reflects also the touch of justice, which 'kill(s) you nicely.' One reading of the historical shift in punishment away from capital and corporal methods towards imprisonment is as a progress towards treating the criminal more 'nicely.' At the same time, however, imprisonment can be understood as contributing to a destruction of personhood. It removes a person from

69 Ripa, *Iconologica*, 204.
70 Robert Cover, "Violence and the Word," *Yale Law Journal* 95 (1986).
71 See, for example, Alison Young re: the restricted narratives of rape victims. Alison Young, "The Waste Land of the Law, the Wordless Song of the Rape Victim," *Melbourne University Law Review* 22 (1998).

time and space – it disrupts their normal life trajectory without the benefit of amnesia: '[i]n jail, I lost everything that made me *me*: my family, dog, business, house, studies, friends, freedom, clothes, make-up, choices. All I had was myself, my mind and my heart.'[72] Although imprisonment is regarded as more benign than physical punishment the Weeping Angels encourage us to question whether this is necessarily so. Imprisonment removes a person from their life, they might be permitted limited contact with family and friends, but this is in an restricted, artificial environment. A prisoner is removed from many of the cares of his or her life prior to imprisonment. Even though a sentence may be finite, the long-term stigma of imprisonment may be such that hopes and stories are disrupted.

Likewise, the Weeping Angels keep their victims physically and mentally unchanged while shattering their identity as the persons they were – shattering their sense of self temporally. Virtually no one's identity-defining cares are ahistorical. We invest ourselves contextually, and the Weeping Angels pluck us from our contexts and deposit us elsewhere. Arguably, the same is done in the name of justice – whether through restrictions on narratives of integral significance to our personhood telling us what is important, (ir)relevant, or through imprisonment removing us from the cares by which we defined ourselves. Both the Weeping Angels and the judiciary avoid shedding blood literally, but the removal of a person from themselves could be regarded as a fate worse than death, and theorists such as Cover have used the imagery of 'blood on their hands' to capture effects of judicial decision-making.[73] Accordingly, the experience of being touched by justice is potentially the same as being touched by a Weeping Angel.

Disgust for the monstrous

Carroll has argued that we feel horror of monsters not only due to fear, but also disgust. He argues that monsters are something that humans do not want to have contact with – we recoil from them and feel nauseated by them, even when the threat of harm has been removed. They 'make one's skin creep.'[74] However, the Weeping Angels question this assumption of disgust as a necessary component of horror. The Weeping Angels are attractive, aesthetically pleasing, inviting us to look and touch them: they are 'monsters of beauty.'[75] Both Weeping Angels and *Justicia* have classic female forms – neither excite disgust. Their beauty can be contrasted with another type of statue – gargoyles. Although gargoyles have had multiple meanings, their ugliness was intended to represent evil, a comforting

72 Danielle Stewart, a former prison inmate, quoted by Susan Chenery, "Out of the Void," *Good Weekend, Sydney Morning Herald*, May 4, 2013, 10–15, 15.

73 Robert Cover, "*Nomos* and Narrative," *Harvard Law Review* 97 (1983).

74 Carroll, *Philosophy of Horror*, 32.

75 Clive Cazeaux, "Beauty is Not in the Eye-Stalk of the Beholder," in *Doctor Who and Philosophy: Bigger on the Inside*, ed. Courtland Lewis and Paula Smithka (Chicago: Open Court, 2010), 317.

notion that evil was easily recognised through external stigma. They have been explained as scaring people into coming into churches by reminding them of evil in the world, or to assure that evil was not inside the church. When the Weeping Angels are on the attack, they become increasingly horrifying, caught in threatening poses with arms raised and vampiric teeth exposed. But by the time their victims and the audience see beneath their beauty it is too late.

Given their ostensible beauty, why then are the Weeping Angels so horrific? This is because they work their evil by using a natural process, blinking, in order to attack humans. The Weeping Angels impose a burden on potential victims to save themselves – that is, one must not blink in order to save one's identity. "Blink" reminds viewers of the anxiety most humans feel about controlling their bodily functions and extends it unnaturally over something we know that we can never wholly control.[76] The Weeping Angels play on archetypal fears of what might happen when we are not looking. They are ostensibly inspired by the childhood game 'statues', where while one child is turned away, the other children move towards him or her. The Weeping Angels are particularly unsettling for the viewer, as through editing and our natural compulsion to blink, we feel as though the Weeping Angels have moved while we have blinked. We feel empathy for the plight of the fictional victims. Monsters that turn the vulnerabilities and inadequacies of their victims against themselves, making their survival depend on their accomplishing an impossible task, directly linking the sense of impotency to the monster's ability to harm, are truly horrific.[77]

Can and should we consider justice in the same terms? We do not tend to see law or justice at work. The law affects, constructs and drives our actions, yet the law tends to operate without being seen. We are governed and yet we do not know about it. The law is relatively invisible in its operation, and like the Weeping Angels, it moves without being seen. This is particularly exacerbated by the modern shift of formal administration dissolving into techniques of summary execution.[78] In addition, if to err is human, should we fear justice because it requires us to exercise control over something that we cannot? On Derrida's account, justice demands the impossible of judges. We fear monsters because they expose our powerlessness.

The Weeping Angels also horrify because of their inexorability and limited modus operandi – they consistently and solely send their victims to another time, and each angel can only send victims to one time.[79] This raises questions about the limited modus operandi of what is permitted, expected and available to contemporary justice. This restriction upon the modus operandi of justice can be

76 Saint and French, "Horror," 307.

77 Saint and French "Horror," 307.

78 Russell Hogg, "Law's Other Spaces," *Law/Text/Culture* 6 (2002).

79 There is some ambiguity beyond this core capacity. For example, the Weeping Angels appear to have power of electricity (they can switch off lights so that they cannot be seen), and in a later episode they can possess and speak through their victims.

seen in our limited depiction of *Justicia*. As noted above, historically justice and *Justicia* were depicted in many different ways and regarded as one virtue among many.[80] Now, standing alone outside courtrooms, the singular legible survival of representations of the Virtues, justice is regarded as transcendent and intrinsic, foundational and all-encompassing. Her ethical primacy and descriptive adequacy are unchallenged.[81] Does the increasingly narrow, singular depiction of *Justicia* reflect and reinforce the restricted repertoire and thus inexorability of justice?

In "Blink," a neat form of justice is ostensibly delivered – the Doctor uses the Weeping Angels' powers and weaknesses against them. He gets Sally Sparrow to unwittingly send the TARDIS back in time so that the Weeping Angels surrounding her and the TARDIS are entrapped staring at each other. The *Doctor Who* series delivers a kind of faith-driven 'trust me' philosophy of justice.[82] In every episode, the Doctor comes up with a plan that delivers some satisfying form of closure. This theory of justice is demonstrated in "Blink." The Doctor does not tell Sally Sparrow his plan to send the TARDIS back in time, leaving her behind. When she realises what is happening she feels betrayed, but ultimately realises, along with the audience, that it is a clever solution. Sally Sparrow is saved and the Weeping Angels are quantum locked. The Doctor provides no explanation, and his reasoning becomes apparent only after the TARDIS has gone. The *Doctor Who* series is based on the premise that the Doctor knows best. However, in recent episodes the Doctor's hero status is questioned, as his victims challenge his extreme actions. The Weeping Angels are like our own private monsters haunting our nightmares, and the Doctor delivers a form of justice that satisfies a nightmare logic that does not require reason or negotiation. Moreover, we realise at the end of the episode that the Doctor did not know what he was doing either – he received only a partial explanation from Sally later in time. Which then raises the question of where and how Sally obtained her information and knowledge that she later gives to the Doctor. By playing with the concept of time, the Doctor's knowledge and authority is based on a kind of circular logic requiring infinite regression.[83]

The ending of "Blink" demonstrates that justice *may not be* timeless and eternal – it is situational and perspectival. What is justice for one group may not be justice for another. From the perspective of the viewer of *Doctor Who*, the horror that is felt in response to the Angels, the concern for Sally and her companion,

80 Ripa, *Iconologica*, 202.

81 Wai Chee Dimock, *Residues of Justice: Literature, Law and Philosophy* (Berkeley, Los Angeles, London: University of California Press, 1996).

82 Desmond Manderson, "Trust Us Justice: *24*, Popular Culture, and the Law," in *Imagining Legality: Where Law Meets Popular Culture*, ed. Austin Sarat (2011).

83 Jean-Francois Lyotard, *The Differend: Phrases in Dispute*, trans. Georges van den Abbeele (Minneapolis: University of Minnesota Press, 1988), s 203, p 142. Attempts at legitimating authority lead to vicious circles (I have authority over you because you authorise me to have it), to question begging (the authorisation authorises authority), to infinite regressions (x is authorised by y, who is authorised by z), and to the paradox of idiolects (God, Life, etc, designate me to exert authority, and I am the only witness of this revelation).

the desire for the Doctor to 'save them,' means that the episode satisfies our expectations. The Weeping Angels are quantum locked until the end of time. The Doctor provides a singular form of justice that satisfies Sally and the audience, but we still know next to nothing about the Weeping Angels, and whether this was a just solution or not.

Monster theory emphasises that regarding a threat as monstrous justifies and requires extreme measures. It raises the question of whether in the process of stopping monsters we have become monstrous ourselves.[84] From the perspective of the Angels, what is the nature of justice? Are they able to do other than what they do? Such a response is a rationalist approach – one that the Doctor often adopts. Instead of allowing the monster to remain in the space of the abject and that which makes us afraid, it is brought into the light and rendered visible and logical. Yet, at the same time, the monsters that the Doctor faces – and the Angels in particular – are some of the most horrifying fare on television. In our modern, rational age, we watch that which horrifies as entertainment – but what does it mean that our imaginary is still filled with monsters? How does this feed our legal imaginary and our vision of justice – is justice thus *not* the figure of the austere and serene *Justicia*, but rather the Angel's face distorted, mouth open in a frozen scream of rage, arms outstretched towards us? Maybe the monster, therefore, reflects justice more than *Justicia* does.

This brings us back to the title of the episode, "Blink," and the Doctor's instruction 'Don't Blink' – if we *don't blink*, if we continue to see, we are able to elude and escape that which haunts us. By bringing into the light the operations of the monster – and of justice – we are able to escape that which makes such things horrific or monstrous. The exhortation from the Doctor *not* to blink is therefore an exhortation to keep everything in sight, drawn to the rational gaze and observation. Yet, of course, the exhortation *not* to blink is an impossibility. The vision of a completely rational justice is one that is beyond the human – a vision that is monstrous in itself.

Conclusion

The commonalities of the Weeping Angels and *Justicia* suggest that if the Weeping Angels are monsters, then justice, too, can and should be regarded as such. Justice transgresses cherished categories and challenges systems of law, and it generates horror because of the potential to inflict harm and its inexorability. The Weeping Angels can be regarded as another, more terrifying face of justice, reminiscent of the mythological Furies, motivated by vengeance, hunting blood.[85]

84 See, in particular, Cole's analysis of anti-terrorist legislation. Phillip Cole, *The Myth of Evil* (Edinburgh: Edinburgh University Press Ltd, 2006).

85 Margaret Visser, "Vengeance and Pollution in Classical Athens," *Journal of the History of Ideas* 45(2) (1984).

Theorists emphasise not only the threat but also the promise of monsters.[86] Monsters capture difference and multiplicity rather than sameness, they are impure and hybrid creatures. Justice as monster is a challenge to legal taxonomies, understandings and categories, particularly those premised on binary thinking. On this account, justice is a rebuke to boundary and enclosure, imperilling traditional methods of organising knowledge and human experience. The category of monster offers a site from which to launch a counter or 'reverse-discourse'[87] concerning the term of key legal distinctions. Sharpe argues that in response to monsters we might adopt a strategy of demonsterisation – one that seeks to resist legal attempts to place particular bodies outside of law and nature. Alternatively, Sharpe suggests that we might aim to lay claim to and embrace the very ground that the monster occupies: '[h]owever, they amount to the same thing. For challenge to legal constructions of nature, and to legal taxonomies, premised as they are on binary thinking, necessarily paves the way and creates a space for hybridity, and therefore the monster.'[88] This regards *Justicia* as monstrous – as disruptive, threatening and promising the possibility of change. It is scary because of the potential suspension and change to cherished categories and borders. The closing scenes of "Blink" emphasise and threaten that the Weeping Angels could embody any statue, taking over the imaginary that informs our operations of law and justice. That is, the figure of *Justicia* outside our courtrooms may, in fact, be a Weeping Angel, a figure of monstrous justice herself.

Bibliography

Aquinas, Thomas St. *Summa Theologica*. Westminster MD: Christian Classics, 1225–1274/1981.

Aristotle. Selections from *Nicomachean Ethics*. In *Lloyd's Introduction to Jurisprudence*, edited by M.D.A Freeman. London: Sweet & Maxwell, 2008.

Biber, Katherine. "How Silent is the Right to Silence." *Cultural Studies Review* 18(1) (2012): 1–14.

Capers, Bennett. "Blind Justice." *Yale Journal of Law and the Humanities* 24 (2012): 179–89.

Carroll, Noel. *The Philosophy of Horror or Paradoxes of the Heart*. New York: Routledge, 1990.

Cazeaux, Clive. "Beauty is Not in the Eye-Stalk of the Beholder." In *Doctor Who and Philosophy: Bigger on the Inside*, edited by Courtland Lewis and Paula Smithka, 313–324. Chicago: Open Court, 2010.

Cohen, Jeffrey. "Monster Culture." In *Monster Theory: Reading Culture*, edited by Jeffrey Cohen, 3–25. Minneapolis: University of Minnesota Press, 1996.

Cohen, Stanley. *Visions of Social Control*. Cambridge: Polity Press, 1985.

86 See, for example, Cohen, *Visions*; Judith Halberstam, *Skin Shows: Gothic Horror and the Technology of Monsters* (Durham, NC: Duke University Press, 1995); Sharpe, *Foucault's Monsters*.

87 Michel Foucault, *The History of Sexuality Volume 1* (New York: Pantheon, 1978), 101.

88 Sharpe, *Foucault's Monsters*, 12.

Cole, Phillip. *The Myth of Evil.* Edinburgh: Edinburgh University Press Ltd, 2006.
Collins, Jeff, and Bill Mayblin. *Derrida for Beginners.* Sydney: Allen and Unwin, 1996.
Collins, Kristin. "Representing Injustice: Justice as an Icon of Woman Suffrage." *Yale Journal of Law and the Humanities* 24 (2012): 191.
Cover, Robert. "The Folktales of Justice: Tales of Jurisdiction." *Capital University Law Review* 14 (1984–1985): 179–203.
——— "*Nomos* and Narrative." *Harvard Law Review* 97 (1983): 4.
——— "Violence and the Word." *Yale Law Journal* 95 (1986): 1601.
Curtis, Dennis, and Judith Resnik. "Images of Justice." *Yale Law Journal* 96 (1986): 1727.
Derrida, Jacques. "Force of Law: The 'Mystical Foundation of Authority'." *Cardozo Law Review* 11 (1990): 919.
——— "Passages – from Traumatism to Promise." In *Points . . . Interviews 1974–1994*, edited by E. Weber, 372–395. Stanford, CA: Stanford University Press, 1995.
Dimock, Wai Chee. *Residues of Justice: Literature, Law and Philosophy.* Berkeley, Los Angeles and London: University of California Press, 1996.
Douglas, Mary. *Purity and Danger: An Analysis of the Concepts of Pollution and Taboo.* London: Routledge and Kegan Paul, 1966/2002. 1966.
Foucault, Michel. *Abnormal: Lectures at the College de France 1974–1975.* New York: Picador, 2003.
——— *The History of Sexuality, Volume 1.* New York: Pantheon, 1978.
Friedman, Richard D., and Bridget McCormack. "Dial-in Testimony." *University of Pasadena Law Review* (2002): 1171.
Goodrich, Peter. "The Foolosophy of Justice and the Enigma of Law." *Yale Journal of Law and the Humanities* 24 (2012): 141–178.
Halberstam, Judith. *Skin Shows: Gothic Horror and the Technology of Monsters.* Durham, NC: Duke University Press, 1995.
Hogg, Russell. "Law's Other Spaces." *Law/Text/Culture* 6 (2002): 29–38.
Justinian. Selections from *Institutes.* In *Lloyd's Introduction to Jurisprudence*, edited by M.D.A. Freeman. London: Sweet & Maxwell, 2008.
Kristeva, Julia. *Powers of Horror: An Essay on Abjection.* New York: Columbia University Press, 1982.
Lyotard, Jean-François. *The Differend: Phrases in Dispute.* Translated by Georges van den Abbeele. Minneapolis: University of Minnesota Press, 1988.
MacIntyre, Alasdair. *After Virtue: A Study in Moral Theory*, 2nd edn. Notre Dame, IN: University of Notre Dame Press, 1984.
Manderson, Desmond. "Trust Us Justice: *24*, Popular Culture, and the Law." In *Imagining Legality: Where Law Meets Popular Culture*, edited by Austin Sarat, 22–47. Tuscaloosa: University of Alabama Press, 2011.
Mezey, Naomi. "Law's Visual Afterlife: Violence, Popular Culture, and Translation Theory." In *Imagining Legality: Where Law Meets Popular Culture*, edited by Austin Sarat, 65–100. Tuscaloosa: University of Alabama Press, 2011.
Mulcahy, Linda. "Imagining Alternative Visions of Justice: An Exploration of the Controversy Surrounding Stirling Lee's Depictions of Justicia in Nineteenth-Century Liverpool." *Law, Culture and the Humanities* (2011): 1–19.
Nussbaum, Martha. *Upheavals of Thought: The Intelligence of Emotions.* Cambridge: Cambridge University Press, 2001.

Panofsky, Erwin. "Blind Cupid." In *Studies in Iconology: Humanistic Themes in the Art of the Renaissance.* New York: Harper and Row, 1962.

Rawls, John. *A Theory of Justice.* Cambridge, MA: The Belknap Press, 1971.

Resnik, Judith, and Dennis Curtis. "Re-Presenting Justice: Visual Narratives of Judgment and the Invention of Democratic Courts." *Yale Journal of Law and the Humanities* 24 (2012): 19–93.

Ripa, Cesare. *Iconologia.* New York: Garland Publishing Company, 1611/1976.

Saint, Michelle, and Peter French. "The Horror of the Weeping Angels." In *Doctor Who and Philosophy: Bigger on the Inside*, edited by Courtland Lewis and Paula Smithka, 297–312. Chicago: Open Court, 2010.

Sharpe, Andrew. *Foucault's Monsters and the Challenge of Law.* London and New York: Routledge, 2010.

Shklar, Judith. "Giving Injustice Its Due." *Yale Law Journal* 98 (1991): 1135–1151.

Spaulding, Norman. "The Enclosure of Justice: Courthouse Architecture, Due Process and the Dead Metaphor of Trial." *Yale Journal of Law and the Humanities* 24 (2012): 311–343.

Visser, Margaret. "Vengeance and Pollution in Classical Athens." *Journal of the History of Ideas* 45(2) (1984): 193–206.

Warner, Marina. *Monuments and Maidens: The Allegory of the Female Form.* London: Weidenfeld and Nicolson, 1985.

Webb, Ed, and Mark Wardecker. "Should the Daleks be Exterminated?" In *Doctor Who and Philosophy: Bigger on the Inside*, edited by Courtland Lewis and Paula Smithka, 177–89. Chicago and La Salle: Open Court, 2011.

Weisberg, Ruth. "The Art of Memory and the Allegorical Personification of Justice." *Yale Journal of Law and the Humanities* 24 (2012): 259–266.

Young, Alison. "The Waste Land of the Law, the Wordless Song of the Rape Victim." *Melbourne University Law Review* 22 (1998): 442.

Chapter 4

'Seeing' justice done: envisioning legality in Christopher Nolan's *The Dark Knight Trilogy*

Timothy D. Peters

> A long line of cases shows that it is not merely of some importance but is of fundamental importance that justice should not only be done, but should manifestly and undoubtedly be seen to be done . . . Nothing is to be done which creates even a suspicion that there has been an improper interference with the course of justice.[1]
>
> Lord Hewart CJ, R v Sussex Justices; Ex parte Macarthy

> Greater love has no one than this, that someone lay down his life for his friends.[2]
>
> John 15:13

Introduction

What vision of legality is driving, undergirding and being propounded by the dominance of the superhero genre on screen and beyond today? While there are a variety of explanations for the remarkable resurgence and prominence of the superhero on film in recent years—with a particular focus being the post-9/11 'war on terror' and politics of the exception—this chapter seeks to examine the underlying visions of law, legality and justice in the superhero genre through a 'reading' of one of the most significant series of texts within this resurgence: Christopher Nolan's *The Dark Knight Trilogy* (made up of *Batman Begins* (2005), *The Dark Knight* (2008) and *The Dark Knight Rises* (2012)).[3] In doing so, it explores the way in which Nolan both draws on the superhero genre and Batman mythos, but also transcends and transforms that genre and its traditional tropes—including the genre's inherent critique of the law. Nolan's transformation

1 *R v Sussex Justices; Ex parte Macarthy* [1924] 1KB 256 at 259 per Lord Hewart CJ.

2 John 15:13 (English Standard Version).

3 *Batman Begins,* directed by Christopher Nolan (Warner Brothers Pictures, 2005); *The Dark Knight,* directed by Christopher Nolan (Warner Brothers Pictures, 2008); *The Dark Knight Rises,* directed by Christopher Nolan (Warner Brothers Pictures, 2012). For analysis of *Batman Begins,* see Timothy D. Peters, "Unbalancing Justice: Overcoming the Limits of the Law in *Batman Begins,*" *Griffith Law Review* 16(1) (2007): 247. For a more detailed exploration of *The Dark Knight,* see Timothy D. Peters, "Beyond the Limits of the Law: A Christological Reading of Christopher Nolan's *The Dark Knight,*" *Griffith Law Review* 24(3) (2015): 418.

of the superhero genre can be understood in relation to two key thematic 'readings' of the genre itself: the 'legal' reading, which sees the superhero as the figure beyond the law who is able to achieve justice where a fallible and inept legal system fails (often depicted with a sense of vigilantism as embodied by characters such as Daredevil and Batman); and the 'theological' reading of the superhero genre which sees the superhero as a Christological or messianic saviour-figure who, with great strength, virtue and valour, is able to 'show the way' to humanity and save the city, country or world from peril (clearly embodied in Superman's filmic representations). Christopher Nolan's *The Dark Knight Trilogy*, however, challenges and 'makes strange' these 'standard' readings of the superhero genre—and of Batman specifically—and, instead of presenting a simple superhero critique of the law, presents a more foundational critique of our vision of law itself.[4]

This chapter progresses its reading of Nolan's films via an analysis of these competing visions of legality and the way in which they oscillate around a particular image—that of the 'heroic lawyer,' Harvey Dent. While Batman is traditionally positioned as the vigilante-superhero, embodying the genre's critique of law, this function is displaced in Nolan's rendering and is taken up by Dent as the lawyer-cum-villain who, in the end, seeks to enforce a retributive justice—a punishing of the criminal—where the law fails to achieve this. On the other hand, the Christological or messianic reading of the superhero is transformed from a god-like Superman type, to the human and non-heroic positioning of Nolan's Batman who, at the end of *The Dark Knight*, takes the blame for the murders committed by Harvey Dent in order to save his reputation and good works in Gotham City. In this sense, Batman undertakes a work of atonement at the end of *The Dark Knight* so as to 'save' the reputation and 'image' of Harvey Dent. Batman is then condemned in *The Dark Knight Rises* as a 'murderer and a thug,' whose actions provided the political justification for the *Dent Act*, a 'tough on crime' legal instrument that allows the police to 'clean up the streets.' However, the *Dent Act* here reflects not so much the public image of Dent that is remembered, but rather aspects of what Dent became as the villain 'Two-Face.' That is, there is a fundamental connection between the vision of legality promulgated by the different figurings of Harvey Dent: as the 'heroic lawyer'; as the vigilante; and enshrined in the authoritarian legislation that bears his name. In contrast, despite traditionally being seen as a vigilante, Batman's actions at the end of *The Dark Knight* represent a different vision of legality—not a form of exceptional superhero who goes beyond the law in order to fulfil a justice that it cannot achieve itself, but rather a legality based on forgiveness, trust and compassion as the basis for founding community. It is in this sense that Batman's actions are taken so that the city can 'have its faith rewarded' and that a theological vision of legality—one which founds a community based on trust and hope, rather than the ever-present

4 For an articulation of Cultural Legal Studies as a method of 'making strange,' see Timothy D. Peters, "Reading the Law Made Strange: Cultural Legal Studies, Theology and Speculative Fiction," in *Cultural Legal Studies: Law's Popular Cultures and the Metamorphosis of Law*, ed. Cassandra Sharp and Marett Leiboff (New York: Routledge, 2016), 252.

threat of evil—in, through and beyond the law is presented. Such a reading is in stark contrast to the critical and fan-based reactions to the films (which saw them as either validating or criticising the tactics of the 'war on terror,' Occupy Wall Street and conservative politics) but opens up the way in which Nolan's trilogy provides an alternate vision of legality to the superhero genre which dominates our screens and informs our legal imaginary.

The chapter begins in section two, which outlines the traditional cultural legal studies approach to the superhero genre in terms of its critique of the fallibility of the law, and the way that these themes are taken up in *The Dark Knight Trilogy*. Section three then proceeds to unpack the transformation of this 'traditional' superhero vision of legality in relation to the transmogrification of Harvey Dent into the villain Two-Face. Here we see embodied quite specifically a critique of the procedural justice of the law, which focuses on justice being *seen* to be done, as opposed to the vigilante superhero who focuses on justice *being* done. Section four then contrasts this presentation of justice to the figure of Batman operating *not* as a superhero in either the vigilante or saviour modes, but as one who founds a sense of community and legality based on trust and faith in each other rather than the force of law—either in its ordinary or exceptional operation. The final section then turns to the question of the image and fiction in relation to the nature of Nolan's filmmaking, and the vision of theological legality that I am arguing for. Nolan's films point to a different understanding of justice and legality that responds to the prevalence of legal and biopolitical exceptionalism, both on screen in terms of the dominance of the superhero genre, and in the practice and operation of law—revealing the intertwined nature of representation and reality in our envisioning of legality.

'You either die a hero or you live long enough to see yourself become the villain': Dark Knights and heroic lawyers

The Dark Knight introduced into Nolan's re-telling of the Batman mythos the classic Batman villain, the Joker (played with a sadistic brilliance by the late Heath Ledger). In Nolan's Batman origin story, *Batman Begins*, we see Bruce Wayne's (Christian Bale) experience of the murder of his parents, and his initial desire for vengeance. This desire for vengeance is transformed, with the encouragement of childhood friend Rachel Dawes (Katie Holmes) and training from Ra's Al Ghul (Liam Neeson) and the League of Shadows (who he then fights after discovering their plan to destroy Gotham City to rid the world of its corruption), into a desire to fight injustice, which he channels into becoming Batman. Despite the final battle with Ra's and the League of Shadows, Bruce Wayne's reason for becoming Batman presented in *Batman Begins* was to deal with the domination of the mob and the corruption of Gotham—corruption that had, in part, been the cause of his parents' murder. Following directly from this goal, the first third of *The Dark Knight* tracks Batman's attempts (with the aid of Harvey Dent (Aaron Eckhart) and Commissioner Gordon (Gary Oldham)) to take down the mob. As his mission continues, Bruce Wayne begins to question his role as Batman—particularly in contrast to the 'legitimate' figure of Harvey Dent, the new District Attorney.[5] When Dent manages to put the entire mob in jail in one day—and does so without wearing a mask—Bruce believes that the day when Batman is no longer needed is coming and that he can pass his mantle on to Harvey. However, at that point in time, the Joker (who was engaged by the mob to take down Batman, though he eventually turns on the mob as well), wreaks chaos on Gotham City with a range of 'social experiments' designed to get Gotham's citizens to turn on one another. He also challenges Batman by declaring that for each day Batman does not remove his mask, he will go on killing people. The Joker kidnaps both Rachel (Maggie Gyllenhaal) and Dent, threatening to blow them up. While Batman is able to save Harvey (though half his face is physically deformed from burns), Rachel dies. Batman eventually captures the Joker, ending his reign of terror, but the conclusion of the film lies not with the showdown between Batman and the Joker, but the face-off between Batman and Dent, who has now gone to seek justice for all those involved in Rachel's murder. The film concludes with Dent falling to his death after Batman saved the life of Commissioner Gordon's son (whom Dent was threatening as a way of punishing Gordon for working with crooked cops). Instead of allowing Gotham to lose hope in its 'white knight,' the film concludes with Batman taking the blame for Harvey's killings and being hunted as an outlaw.

In the final installation of Nolan's trilogy, *The Dark Knight Rises*, the image of Harvey Dent haunts the film. Despite his disfiguration at the end of his life, and the 'murders' that he had committed avenging the death of his fiancé Rachel, he has been upheld as a shining beacon of law and justice and whose death (now attributed to Batman, who has not been seen in eight years) is the political foundation for the *Dent Act*, which gave law enforcement 'teeth' (tougher sentencing, no parole) to 'clean up the streets' of Gotham and eliminate organised crime. The revelation of this 'lie' to the public, forms part of Bane's (the new leader of the League of Shadows, played by Tom Hardy) 'revolution' and encouragement of the people of Gotham to 'take back' their city from the 'corrupt'—aided by the threat of a nuclear explosion if anyone tries to stop the revolution. Batman comes out of retirement, but is initially defeated by Bane. With his back broken, he is sent to a prison in the Middle East from where he will watch as Gotham is destroyed. Bruce, after regaining his strength, escapes, returns to Gotham and manages to defeat Bane and Talia Al Ghul,[6] saving Gotham. In doing so, Batman

5 This, of course, follows from the actions that Bruce took in *Batman Begins* in order to become Batman, and his close friend Rachel Dawes identifying that this meant that it was the face behind Batman's mask that was truly feared by the criminal underworld. She points to the possibility of a time when Gotham would no longer need Batman.

6 Talia is Ra's Al Ghul's daughter who had been masquerading as Miranda Tait (Marion Cotillard), one of the board members of Wayne Enterprises.

appears to have been killed when the bomb he is carting out to sea explodes (the audience discovers, however, that he is not dead).

One of the interesting things about Nolan's trilogy is that both the first and third films focus specifically on lesser-known (at least to the non-comic book fan audience) villains—Ra's Al Ghul, the League of Shadows and Bane. While he is alluded to at the end of *Batman Begins* and he is the dominating figure in *The Dark Knight*, the Joker disappears and is not even remembered or referred to in *The Dark Knight Rises*.[7] Rather, the figure of Harvey Dent and his image and reputation becomes the central link between *The Dark Knight* and *The Dark Knight Rises*.[8] In addition, *The Dark Knight* depicts a structural doubling not just between Batman and the Joker, but also between Dent and Batman—with Dent even turning himself in as the Batman to appease the people of Gotham. What are we to make of the significance of this doubling of Batman and Harvey Dent who is depicted, more than anything else, as the 'heroic lawyer'?

This focus on Dent goes to the critical interrogation of the superhero genre by Nolan and, in particular, of one of its dominant themes: the failure of the law and legal system. As Cassandra Sharp notes, it is this failure of the legal system that gives rise to the need for the superhero. Justice appears to *not* be done by the law and the superhero is the means by which this failure is remedied—by taking justice into his (or her) own hands, removing it from the 'public' and open means implemented by the legal system, the superhero achieves a form of vigilante-justice beyond the law.[9] A range of cultural legal scholars have analysed this genre and, as Jason Bainbridge notes, the way in which 'superheroes . . . personify the tension between a modern adherence to the rule of law' and pre- or post-modern explorations of justice.[10] As both Bainbridge and Sharp point out, modern legality has a focus on the rule of law, of a *system* of justice and of due process. But the superhero presents

7 Noting that extra-textually, part of the reason for not returning to the figure of the Joker in *The Dark Knight Rises* was because of the death of Heath Ledger.

8 Christopher Nolan and David Goyer also acknowledge the centrality of the role of Dent to their initial work on *Batman Begins*. The role of the 'heroic lawyer' is specifically alluded to there with the character Rachel Dawes (Katie Holmes) who, as Assistant District Attorney and childhood friend, challenges the young Bruce Wayne about the need for 'good people' to help save Gotham. See Christopher Nolan and David S. Goyer, "Introduction: A Conversation with Christopher Nolan and David S. Goyer," in Jeph Loeb and Tim Sale, *Batman: The Long Halloween* (New York: DC Comics, 2011).

9 See Cassandra Sharp, " 'Riddle Me This . . .?' Would the World Need Superheroes if the Law Could Actually Deliver 'Justice'?" *Law Text Culture* 16 (2012): 353.

10 Jason Bainbridge, " 'This is the Authority. This Planet is Under Our Protection'—An Exegesis of Superheroes' Interrogations of Law," *Law, Culture and the Humanities* 3(3) (2007): 457. There is also a growing criminological literature that explores the representations of justice and the legitimacy of the criminal justice system in superhero comics. See, for example, Scott Vollum and Cardy D. Adkinson, "The Portrayal of Crime and Justice in the Comic Book Superhero Mythos," *Journal of Criminal Justice and Popular Culture* 10(2) (2003); Bradford W. Reyns and Billy Henson, "Superhero Justice: The Depiction of Crime and Justice in Modern-Age Comic Books and Graphic Novels," *Sociology of Crime, Law and Deviance* 14 (2010).

a fundamental critique of the ability of the modern system of law to achieve 'true justice.' As Sharp notes, '[t]he very existence of the superhero . . . presupposes that justice has not and cannot be achieved by the legal system.'[11] The role of the superhero then seems to be fundamentally in tension with the law and even where a superhero is potentially working with police or state authorities—that is, working alongside the law and not beyond it—their very nature takes them beyond the law. As Desmond Manderson notes, the superhero 'is heroic precisely *because* his actions transcend laws, whether those of physics or of society.'[12]

The rise and rise of the superhero film (along with the genre's developing success on television) has seen an increasing demonstration of this need for justice in the face of law's impotence.[13] Furthermore, given the post-9/11 context of the renaissance of the superhero genre, a number of scholars have drawn on the terminology of jurist Carl Schmitt and his modern reader Giorgio Agamben to describe the superhero. That is, in the state of exception or emergency the superhero, out of necessity, goes beyond the law and operates as if it is suspended in order to deal with the crisis and restore the social order.[14] The superhero is a figure beyond the law who can operate as an 'exception' to it and this is why superhero films are so easily incorporated into conservative post-9/11 ideologies around the need for exceptional measures in the 'war on terror.'[15] When there

11 Sharp, "'Riddle Me This . . .?'," 359. Desmond Manderson also notes '[t]he superhero's preparedness to act against and despite due process and law is surely an implicit—indeed, increasingly explicit—critique of the established order's ability to achieve justice at all.' Desmond Manderson, "Trust Us Justice: *24*, Popular Culture, and the Law," in *Imagining Legality: Where Law Meets Popular Culture,* ed. Austin Sarat (Tuscaloosa: University of Alabama Press, 2011): 33.

12 Manderson, "Trust Us Justice," 33. See also Todd McGowan, "The Exceptional Darkness of The Dark Knight," *Jump Cut* 51 (2009); Jason Bainbridge, "Spider-Man, The Question and the Meta-Zone: Exception, Objectivism and the Comics of Steve Ditko," *Law Text Culture* 16 (2012): 217–242.

13 On the rise of the Superhero film, see Shaun Trent, "How America Learned to Stop Worrying and Cynically ENJOY! The Post-9/11 Superhero Zeitgeist," *Communication and Critical/Cultural Studies* 6(1) (2009): 103. See also Richard J. Gray and Betty Kaklamanidou, eds, *The 21st Century Superhero: Essays on Gender, Genre and Globalization in Film* (Jefferson, NC: McFarland & Company, 2011).

14 Carl Schmitt, *Political Theology: Four Chapters on the Concept of Sovereignty,* trans. George Schwab (Chicago: University of Chicago Press, 2005); Giorgio Agamben, *The State of Exception,* trans. Kevin Attell (Chicago: University of Chicago Press, 2005). For discussions of Agamben's work in relation to superheroes, see Mervi Miettinen, "Representing the State of Exception: Power, Utopia, Visuality and Narrative in Superhero Comics," in *Images in Use: Towards the Critical Analysis of Visual Communication,* ed. M. Tocchetti and K. Kukkonen (Amsterdam: John Benjamins Publishing Company, 2011); Bainbridge, "This is the Authority"; Bainbridge, "Spider-Man"; Jason Bainbridge, "'The Call to Do Justice': Superheroes, Sovereigns and the State During Wartime," *International Journal for the Semiotics of Law,* 28(4) (December 2015); Peters, "Beyond the Limits of the Law."

15 See, for example, Spencer Ackerman, "Batman's 'Dark Knight' Reflects Cheney Policy," *The Washington Independent,* 21 July 2008; Andrew Klavan, "What Bush and Batman Have in

is a state of emergency in which the law can no longer fulfil its role of ensuring order, a state of exception is called which suspends the operations of the law in order to deal with the crisis. The 21st-century superhero (to borrow Gray and Kakliamando's term) appears to specifically embody this exceptional dealing of justice and restoring of order in the face of crisis.[16]

This turn to Schmitt's jurisprudence of 'the exception' also responds to the question of the *legitimacy* of the role of the superhero, which is fundamental to the genre. For the superhero that goes beyond the law is, in many respects, an illegitimate figure engaging in *criminal* activity.[17] Batman's actions, for example, are on the whole unauthorised and illegal—they go *against* the law in exacting justice.[18] However, the crisis circumstance or failure of the law that the superhero responds to provides the basis for their claim to legitimacy—whether it is in terms of 'popular sovereignty,' or whether it goes to the nature of the sovereign decision on the exception itself.[19] In Schmitt's jurisprudence the figure of the sovereign is what ties the exception to law.[20]

Nolan's Batman films, and *The Dark Knight* in particular, provide one of the most explicit interrogations of these themes in the post-9/11 superhero genre. In terms of the traditional aspects of the genre, the supervillains that Batman fights (Ra's Al Ghul, the Joker, Bane) all create chaos and exceptional emergencies that require the actions of Batman beyond the law, because of the failure of the police to be able to deal with these villains. At the same time, however, in

---

Common," *Wall Street Journal,* 25 July 2008; Joe Allen, "Batman's War on Terror," *Counterpunch,* 2 August 2008; Andrew Bolt, "Batman Bush True Dark Knight," *Herald Sun,* 30 July 2008. For a discussion of these claims—and their inaccuracies—see John Ip, "The Dark Knight's War on Terrorism," *Ohio State Journal of Criminal Law* 9(1) (2011): 227.

16 Gray and Kakliamando, *21st Century Superhero,* 1–2. Michael Nichols reads this particular narrative framework as a modernised version of the 'combat myth' with the hero (Batman) defeating the chaos monster (the Joker) and restoring order: Michael Nichols "'I think you and I are destined to do this forever': A reading of the Batman/Joker comic and film tradition through the combat myth," *Journal of Religion and Popular Culture* 23(2) (2011).

17 For example, see Miettinen's discussion of Frank Miller's *The Dark Knight Returns,* where Superman pontificates about Batman's acceptance of the superheroes as criminals. Miettinen, "Representing the State of Exception," 135; Frank Miller, Klaus Janson and Lynn Varley, *The Dark Knight Returns* (New York: DC Comics, 1986).

18 Though Joshua Lisk argues that Batman can be seen as a 'state actor' in American jurisprudence: Joshua Lisk "Is Batman a State Actor? The Dark Knight's Relationship with the Gotham City Police Department and the Fourth Amendment Implications," *Case Western Reserve Law Review* 64(3) (2014): 1419–1440.

19 On the superhero acting on the basis of 'popular sovereignty,' see Sharp, "'Riddle Me This . . .?'," 360 and, in relation to Agamben's work on the 'state of exception', 365. In terms of the superhero's appropriation of the sovereign decision, see Bainbridge, "'The Call to Do Justice,"' 754–757 and Peters, "Beyond the Limits of the Law," 420–425. See also Neil Curtis, "Superheroes and the Contradiction of Sovereignty," *Journal of Graphic Novels and Comics* 4(2) (2013).

20 This is captured in Schmitt's famous quote: '[s]overeign is he who decides on the exception.' Schmitt, *Political Theology,* 5.

The Dark Knight Bruce Wayne openly questions the role of Batman in Gotham City, believing that he has found a more legitimate supplement to the law in the District Attorney Harvey Dent. In contrast, Dent articulates a case for the *legitimacy* of the superhero. Early in the film, at a dinner with Dent, Rachel Dawes and the Russian ballet dancer, Natascha, Bruce Wayne poses the question 'Who appointed the Batman?' Harvey *immediately* responds with a well-thought-out defence:

> We did. All of us who stood by and let scum take control of our city . . . When their enemies were at the gates, the Romans would suspend democracy and appoint one man to protect the city. And it wasn't considered an honour it was considered a public service.

Instead of subscribing to the idea that Batman is a criminal vigilante on a personal vendetta for justice (which is how Natascha describes Batman in the conversation—and also how the Gotham City Police Department 'officially' refer to the Batman), Dent legitimises the role that Batman has taken by providing a specifically *legal* argument for that role—an argument that has a significant history. For, as Ip rightly points out, Dent's references to Rome links Batman to the tradition of legal 'dictatorship' (though emerging from popular consensus).[21] Agamben, however, in his genealogy of the state of exception, distinguishes between the legal idea of 'dictatorship,' which involves a specific appointment and empowering of a particular magistrate to act on behalf of Rome, and that of the *iustitium*, which involves a suspension of law—and at which point the magistrates are treated as ordinary citizens, and 'ordinary citizens' themselves then have the 'imperium' to take whatever action needed to defend the city/state.[22] So, when Dent argues that Batman is an 'ordinary citizen standing up for what is right,' he is articulating Batman not so much as a dictator who has been appropriately appointed, but rather as someone operating in the 'state of exception' in Gotham City.

Dent further develops his legal arguments in relation to Batman later in the film. When the Joker has wreaked chaos on Gotham and threatens to continue killing people unless Batman takes off his mask, Dent addresses a press conference. There he is challenged about protecting an 'outlaw vigilante' rather than the lives of citizens. While Dent acknowledges that Batman *is* an outlaw, he notes that the city has been willing for him to clean up the streets—that Batman has been accepted by the people of Gotham and that it is to the people of Gotham (not a terrorist) that he will have to account for the laws he's broken. Dent's articulation of Batman here as an 'outlaw' and *not* as a criminal, however, also points to the fact that the transgression of the law by Batman falls into a different

21 Ip, "The Dark Knight's War on Terrorism," 227.
22 Agamben, *State of Exception*, 47–49.

category to the transgression of the law by criminals. Identifying Batman as an outlaw reinforces the nature of Batman's activities as being connected to the sovereign exception, for, as Agamben explains, the outlaw falls into the same structural place in relation to the law as the sovereign does—included via their exclusion.[23]

Dent's articulation of the legal justifications and role of the superhero, falls neatly within the general arguments around the need for exceptional measures in exceptional circumstances—the need to suspend the normal operation of the law in the case of emergency. That is, it is the character of Harvey Dent that provides the legal grounding of *The Dark Knight* within the post-9/11 arguments about the nature of the exception. These arguments do not, however, come from Batman, who still sees Dent as the *legitimate* figure of the law, who should be the hero the city 'needs,' not the *illegitimate* figure of the superhero.[24] Dent, on the other hand, is the figure that explains the role of the superhero in relation to law. As we shall now see, when Dent becomes 'Two-Face' he also fundamentally takes up the superhero's *critique* of the law.

The superhero critique of the law: Harvey 'Two-Face' as vigilante superhero?

The superhero genre in general, and the discussion of Batman in Nolan's *The Dark Knight Trilogy*, pits a 'modern' form of justice embodied in the system of law and governance, with a 'pre-modern' form of justice embodied in the costumed crime fighter (focused on crime control).[25] The superhero *as such* is understood as a challenge to modern legality. By donning cape and mask, he asks us to 'trust' that he is doing the right thing, rather than having any recourse to a system of checks and balances, of due process, appeals and of the rule of law.[26] Of course, in the depictions of the superhero on screen, we almost always get visual confirmation that the superhero *is* right—that is, that the criminals that they capture and punish *have done* illegal and often horrendous things and they have not been captured or brought to justice by the law. Yet, this focus on 'trust'

23 Giorgio Agamben, *Homo Sacer: Soveriegn Power and Bare Life*, trans. Daniel Heller-Roazen (Stanford, CA: Stanford University Press, 1998), 104–111.

24 These two positions—seeing the superhero as a legitimate or illegitimate figure in relation to the law—correspond to the different trajectories in Agamben's genealogy of the 'state of exception,' between arguments that the exception should be specifically provided for within law and arguments that see it as something that cannot be provided for because it is fundamentally beyond or outside the law. Agamben *also* notes the way in which both Carl Schmitt and Walter Benjamin also articulate, in a more sophisticated fashion this difference—Schmitt consistently trying to tie the sovereign exception to law, Benjamin founding the position by pushing the exception beyond or outside the law. See Agamben, *State of Exception*, 9–31 and 52–64.

25 Bainbridge, "This is the Authority," 460–466.

26 Manderson, "Trust Us Justice," 40–44.

itself as opposed to a system of justice is one of the issues that the superhero and their 'pre-modern' form of justice raises. This is why Batman, in *The Dark Knight*, sees the superhero as an *illegitimate* figure and Dent as the legitimate figure of justice. He makes this claim explicit by telling Dent that his 'stand against organized crime is the first legitimate ray of light in Gotham in decades.' Harvey is the one who could implement justice *through* the law via his skills as an advocate, his knowledge of nuances of legal cases and legislation and his use of both legal and political strategy. Dent is presented as Gotham's 'white knight,' the legitimate role of the 'heroic lawyer' who can replace the illegitimate role of the superhero.[27] This also depicts, for Batman, an apparent return to normalcy, an end to the exceptional situation, which needs the superhero, and a return to the normal operation of the law where Batman is no longer needed.[28] However, a shift to the legitimate role of the lawyer does not elide the need for a supplement to the law in order for it to achieve justice. The very need for a 'heroic lawyer' points to the fact that the 'impartial system' of the law cannot operate by itself without assistance. It is still a system reliant on the individuals who carry it out, and will only achieve justice if there are those willing to go 'above and beyond' in order to see justice done.[29] This means that rather than being at odds with one another, there is a continuum between the role of the 'heroic lawyer' and the 'superhero' beyond the law. That is, the 'impartial' system of law is still determined by the fallible hands of always potentially corrupt police, lawyers and judges, and is therefore reliant on the 'heroic lawyer' to manipulate the system to get a 'just' outcome.[30]

These two aspects of the role of Dent, first that he is the one to articulate a legitimate role for Batman, and second that even as the 'legitimate' figure of justice he needs a degree of heroism, points to a fundamental continuity, rather than tension, between the role of the superhero and the operation of the law. Whereas, as Manderson points out, at one level the superhero's approach to justice hearkens back to an earlier theological model based not on a system of justice but on individual judgment,[31] at the same time modern legality *also* embodies a

27 For a more detailed version of this analysis of Dent, specifically in the context of *The Dark Knight*, rather than the trilogy as a whole, see Peters, "Beyond the Limits of the Law," 431–435.

28 It is worth noting, that this theme is uncommon within the superhero narrative, where there is generally a reason for the superhero to continue, even after the emergency has ended.

29 The Hollywood 'heroic lawyer' trope regularly depicts Perry Mason-style lawyers willing to do whatever it takes to achieve justice for their client. In this sense, the superhero version (whether it is Daredevil or She-Hulk or Harvey Dent) only emphasises this trope, rather than reinventing it.

30 For a related critique of the guarantees of the law, which are always reliant on the fallibility of the agents of the law, see John Milbank, "Paul Against Biopolitics," in *Paul's New Moment: Continental Philosophy and the Future of Christian Theology*, ed. John Milbank, Slavoj Žižek and Creston Davis (Grand Rapids: Brazos Press, 2010), 53.

31 Manderson, "Trust Us Justice," 35–36.

particular aspect of individual judgment through the operation of the exception. While in the normal course justice is systematised through the law, there is always the possibility of the law being suspended in an emergency or state of exception. It would appear that the superhero as figure of exception is in contrast to the modern system of justice, but it in effect embodies the exception as central to modern law. For, as Agamben points out, the modern roots of the state of exception arise from that very 'modern' of events—the French Revolution.[32] The state of exception is not a return to a pre-modern position but rather an embodiment of this specifically modern notion, stripped of its theological context.[33] Nolan's representation of the transformation of Harvey Dent, from a figure of modern law into a figure of vigilante justice, reflects this fundamental continuity between law and the exception.

When Dent, having been disfigured by an explosion and lost his fiancé Rachel, takes up the role of 'Two-Face' (the nickname used by the cops that had been investigated by Harvey when he was working for Internal Affairs), he shifts along the continuum from the role of the 'heroic lawyer' to the figure of vigilante justice. We can thus read Harvey in relation to the superhero-lawyer characters such as Daredevil or She-Hulk who, while using the law to achieve justice during the day, will deal retribution where the law fails at night.[34] Yet, when Harvey goes out killing those that were involved in Rachel's kidnapping, he is not simply out seeking vengeance. Rather, his commitment to justice and legality take over. Instead of looking at the fallible justice of a legal system reliant on multiple individuals who are all possibly corrupt, Harvey uses the 'toss of the coin'—an action based on a 50–50 chance—as the means to justice. At the same time Harvey's rendering of legality encompasses a critique of legal justice in terms of its formality—its focus on due process and fairness *before* the law, which is a systematic reliance on a particular individual to fulfil the rule of law itself. Harvey embodies the traditional critique of law found in the superhero genre—that modern legality is at times deficient, only ever reactive and cannot sufficiently protect us against the threat of violence either in the normal course or during times of emergency. The superhero genre, then, according to this trajectory, provides us a way of thinking through a pre-emptive notion of justice—one which, in line with the post-9/11 environment, which *The Dark Knight* was so clearly connected to, might actually provide justice.[35] For, despite all of its procedural requirements, the law is reliant on the actions of individuals that can be corrupted and the decisions of

32 Agamben, *State of Exception,* 4–5; Milbank, "Paul Against Biopolitics," 25.

33 Though, of course, Schmitt's articulation of the notion of exception is in the context of his political theology. What this points to, however, is not that there is a return to theological concepts of the past but rather than modern secular law embodies those theological concepts in a new form. See Schmitt, *Political Theology,* 36–52.

34 For discussions of Daredevil and She-Hulk, see Bainbridge, "This is the Authority"; Sharp, "'Riddle Me This . . .?'"; Dale Mitchell, "Paradoxes and Patriarchy: A Legal Reading of She-Hulk," *Griffith Law Review* 24(3) (2015), 446.

35 See Bainbridge, "This is the Authority," 468–471.

individuals that could be arbitrary. The premise of the law, at one level, is a divine justice, and yet the human implementation of the law can never be measured against this justice. As such, the law is measured against procedural aspects—has due process been followed—rather than substantive ones which are always left to the indeterminacy of the legal decision. It is this potential for arbitrariness and corruption—the law's fallibility itself—that Harvey reveals in *The Dark Knight* and attempts to bypass by implementing a vision of legality that, despite seeming to oscillate between due process and vigilantism, actually encompasses an expression of modern legality taken to its limits—in terms of a *system* of law bound by objectivity, certainty and a form of rationality and without the potential fallibility of its actors by rendering justice in the objective act of the toss of a coin.

This vision of legality is taken even further in *The Dark Knight Rises*. Whereas Dent as 'Two-Face' embodies the belief that justice can only be done via a completely purified and objectified system of law that removes the discretion of the judicial decision by replacing it with the toss of a coin, Gotham in *The Dark Knight Rises* has enshrined this objectifying and discretionless form of legality in legislation. The viewer is given very little knowledge of the substantive provisions of the *Dent Act*, other than it 'gave law enforcement teeth' and that there are 1,000 criminals locked up in Blackgate prison as a direct result of the Act's implementation. What is implied, however, is that the Act reduced normal protections, involved mandatory sentencing and no parole—that is, it reduced the very aspects of due process and of judicial discretion that are part of the legal system's 'normal' protections and operations. By imposing mandatory sentencing, the discretion of Gotham's judges to take into account the circumstances is removed thus rendering the law *more* objective, more machine-like, more systematic.[36] In this sense, the legislation that bear's Dent's name takes up not so much the position that Dent describes as the one he embodies as Two-Face. At the same time, after Bane's 'revolution,' this aspect of legality is parodied with the 'insane' Crane (one of the minor villains from *Batman Begins*, played by Cillian Murphy) overseeing not trials but 'sentencing hearings' where the guilt of those brought before him is pre-determined.[37] The outcome of these 'hearings' is also constrained, with the 'guilty' being given the illusion of two options: death or exile (both sentences involve the forcing of people to walk out on the frozen river separating Gotham from the mainland—everyone falls through the fragile ice to their death).

Furthermore, if the *Dent Act* takes up Two-Face's vigilante retributive justice through an 'objective system' of law, Bane's revolution, which explicitly invokes Dickens' retelling of the French Revolution in *A Tale of Two Cities*, takes the

36 As will be discussed below, this shift to an objective, machine-like operation of law is *also* one of the outcomes of the move to secular authority. See Manderson, "Trust Us Justice," 35–36.

37 I owe the point about Crane's trials as parodying the *Dent Act* to discussions with my students in the 2016 class of *6039LAW Cultural Legal Studies: Critical Engagements between Law and Popular Culture*.

superhero critique of the law to its other extreme.[38] Bane's revolution charges 'the people' with taking back power from the oppressed and dealing 'true justice.' Is this not a literal encompass of the vigilante ethos, of 'taking the law into one's own hand' *en masse*? Revolution encompasses an extreme version of the superhero/vigilante ethos—where *everyone* is called upon to overthrow the law, which fails to achieve justice, and to seek justice beyond the law. While, of course, this depiction of revolution is stylised (as was Dickens')—and the revolution is illusory in nature because the nuclear bomb that Bane uses to threaten the city is set to go off no matter what—it points to one of the challenges of rational modern law. For the French Revolution is a symbol *not* of the *ancien regime* and traditional natural law, but one of the founding moments of modernity and *modern* legality.[39]

As such, the supposedly 'legitimate' role of Dent as 'heroic lawyer' shares a structural homology with his objectification of the law as Two-Face, its systematisation in terms of the *Dent Act* and finally its literalisation in the overthrowing of law by Bane's revolution in *The Dark Knight Rises*. Where does this leave the role of Batman in the films? My argument is that Batman's challenge to the law is not of an exceptional justice beyond the law, but instead a more fundamental challenge to the nature and basis of modern legality. It is in the way Nolan's version of Batman takes up, but also transfigures or 'makes strange,' the traditional theological aspects of the superhero genre that this critique of modern law can be understood and an alternative vision of legality is revealed. This will be unpacked in relation to a particular claim: that Batman operates as a Christological Type.

A theology of the non-heroic: Batman as Christological type

At first glance, to argue that Batman is a type of Christ is, despite the claims of some critics about a Christological 'ultimate sacrifice' in *The Dark Knight Rises*,[40]

38 The numerous allusions to Dickens' novel are made explicit by the reading from the concluding pages over the empty grave of Bruce Wayne by Commissioner Gordon: 'I see a beautiful city and a brilliant people rising from the abyss . . . I see the lives for which I lay down my life, peaceful, useful, prosperous and happy . . . I see that I hold a sanctuary in their hearts, and in the hearts of their descendants, generations hence . . . It is a far, far better thing that I do, than I have ever done; it is a far, far better rest that I go to, than I have ever known.' See Charles Dickens, *The Complete Works of Charles Dickens: A Tale of Two Cities* (New York: Cosimo Books, 2009), 358.

39 As Agamben specifically notes, the 'modern state of exception is a creation of the democratic-revolutionary tradition and not the absolutist one.' Agamben, *State of Exception*, 5. Walter Benjamin also flags the terror of the French Revolution as the ideological foundation for the modern natural law thought which sees violence as a 'product of nature . . . the use of which is in no way problematical, unless force is misused for unjust ends.' Walter Benjamin, "Critique of Violence" in *Reflections: Essays, Aphorisms, Autobiographical Writings*, ed. Peter Demetz, trans. Edmund Jephcott (New York: Schocken Books, 1986), 277–278.

40 See, for example, Tyler O'Neil, "Dark Knight and Occupy Wall Street: The Humble Rise," *Hillsdale Natural Law Review*, 21 July 2012, https://hillsdalenaturallawreviewdotcom.

would appear to be an odd claim to make. If any superhero was going to be compared to Christ, surely it would be Superman and not Batman. Superman, coming from the heavens (another planet, Krypton), with the mission given to him by his heavenly father (Jor-El) to show us the way and his supernatural, god-like powers captured within 'human' form (along with his desire to *save* humanity), demonstrates a range of theological and messianic references—particularly emphasised in Superman's filmic representations (such as Bryan Singer's *Superman Returns* (2006) and Zack Snyder's *Man of Steel* (2013)).[41] These representations bring a heightened visual reference to comic-book writer Grant Morrison's description of Superman as an 'American Christ' and Bryan Singer's description of him as 'the Jesus Christ of Superheroes.'[42]

C. K. Robertson understands the character of Batman as directly opposed to Superman's 'Christological' connections and is, rather, the real *humanist* myth—the appropriate heir to Nietzsche's self-made *Übermensch* to which we should aspire. Batman as a 'self-made' superhero, relying on his training and technology instead of any inherent divine powers, points to a more humanist myth. This Nietzschean reading of Batman has significant merit, particularly if we read the superhero genre in relation to the tales of the Roman and Greek heroes and gods, which embodied a heroic virtue that responds to and overcomes evil. Surely, if anything, the focus of the super-*hero* is to demonstrate their virtuous nature by dealing with the evil that arises. From the Christian perspective, however, the problem with this type of virtue is that it secretly celebrates as its occasion a *prior* evil.[43] The virtuous in the Greek and Roman traditions was focused on a heroic overcoming of violence and evil, which means that there

> can only *be* virtue where there is something to be defeated, and virtue therefore consists for them, not only in the attainment and pursuit of a goal desirable in itself, but also in a 'conquest' of less desirable forces, which is always an exercise of strength *supplementary to*, although supporting, a 'right desire.'[44]

---

wordpress.com/2012/07/21/dark-knight-and-occupy-wall-street-the-humble-rise (accessed 31 October 2016). See also, the discussion in Slavoj Žižek, "The People's Republic of Gotham," *New Statesman*, 24–30 August, 2012.

41 *Superman Returns,* directed by Bryan Singer (Warner Brothers, 2006); *Man of* Steel, directed by Zack Snyder (Warner Brothers, 2013). For a discussion of the Christological aspects of the Superman mythos and in particular its filmic incarnations, see Ken Schenk, "Superman: A Popular Culture Messiah," in *The Gospel According to Superheroes: Religion and Popular Culture*, ed. B. J. Oropeza (New York: Peter Lang, 2005); Adam Barkman, "Superman: From Anti-Christ to Christ-Type," in *Superman and Philosophy: What Would the Man of Steel Do?*, ed. Mark D. White (West Sussex: John Wiley & Sons, 2013).

42 See Grant Morrison, *Wizard: The Comics Magazine*, 143, 1 August 2003, 180; Adam Barkman, "Superman," 117, quoting Singer.

43 John Milbank, *The Word Made Strange* (Oxford: Blackwell Publishers, 1997), 219–221.

44 John Milbank, *Theology and Social Theory: Beyond Secular Reason*, 2nd edn (Malden: Blackwell Publishing, 2006), 393.

While there are clear Nietzschean elements to the Batman mythos, Nolan's cinematic interpretation displaces them onto the villains. The Joker's first line in *The Dark Knight*—'I believe, whatever doesn't kill you, only makes you *stranger*'—is a reworking of Nietzsche's famous 'whatever doesn't kill you, only makes you stronger.'[45] But the Nietzschean villain is much more clearly depicted in the form of Ra's Al Ghul in *Batman Begins* (and the references back to him in *The Dark Knight Rises*), who is attempting to destroy Gotham and its people because of its corruption. When Bruce Wayne challenges Ra's noting that he will be destroying millions of lives, Ra's responds by saying 'Only a cynical man would call what these people have lives, Wayne. Crime, despair, this is not how man was supposed to live.' Ra's is envisioning a form of humanity or life beyond that of the human, which is regularly corrupt and despairing—he desires a new order of humanity that will supersede the corruption that Gotham exhibits. Bruce's response specifically recalls the debate between God and Abraham in the Old Testament, when God threatens to destroy Sodom. Bruce says, 'Gotham isn't beyond saving. Give me more time. There are good people here.' Ra's responds by saying that Bruce is defending a city so corrupt that they have infiltrated every level of its infrastructure.[46] He tells Bruce that, as his greatest student, he should be the one 'standing by my side saving the world.' Bruce's response is that he will be standing where he belongs—between Ra's and the people of Gotham. This mediatory role of Batman—standing between the agent of justice and the sinful city of Gotham—also has a Christological aspect to it, where the only thing that stands between sinful humanity and the wrath of divine judgment is Christ as defender and advocate.

The Christological aspect to Nolan's trilogy, however, is more strongly emphasised in *The Dark Knight* with the opposition between Batman and the Joker. The Joker is traditionally conceived as a trickster figure and presented as an agent of chaos—a figurative version of Satan whose 'main purpose is to sow chaos, confusion, and destruction among human beings.'[47] This becomes particularly apparent in the way that the Joker takes up a similar position as Satan or 'the Accuser' in the Biblical Book of Job. There, Satan is presented as an accuser who challenges God's valorisation of Job. Whereas God boasts to Satan that there is none like Job on earth, that he is a 'blameless and upright man, who fears God

45 Nietzsche's original is '*From the Military School of Life*—Whatever does not kill me makes me stronger.' See Friedrich Nietzsche, *Twilight of the Idols: or How to Philosophize with a Hammer*, trans. Duncan Large (Oxford: Oxford University Press, 1998). See also McGowan "The Exceptional Darkness."

46 Genesis 18:22–33, ESV.

47 Charles K. Bellinger, "The Joker is Satan and So are We: Girard and The Dark Knight," *Journal of Religion and Film* 13(1) (2009): para [5]. Bellinger notes that in the same way that Satan is the most interesting character in Milton's *Paradise Lost*, 'the Joker is clearly the most interesting character in *The Dark Knight*, and he is obviously a figurative version of Satan.' Nichols, who reads *The Dark Knight* in relation to the traditional 'combat myth', also identifies the Joker as a figure of Satan (the chaos monster in the Christian tradition). Michael Nichols, "'I Think You and I Are Destined to Do This Forever'," 238.

and turns away from evil,' Satan challenges the reason for Job's goodness.[48] He argues that it is only because God has blessed Job (that he is rich, well thought of and prosperous), that he is good and that if he lost it all he would turn and curse God.[49] God therefore allows Satan to test Job, initially destroying his children and possessions and then finally inflicting his health.[50] Job, of course, passes the test, refuting Satan's challenge that goodness and integrity are purely dependent on good circumstances. It is this accusatory nature of Satan that is referenced by the Joker's operation and behaviours in Gotham. In the most detailed face-to-face interaction between the Joker and Batman (in the 'interrogation' scene at the Gotham Police Station), the Joker describes the morals and code of society as just a bad joke 'dropped at the first sign of trouble.' His critique is that people are 'only as good as the world allows them to be . . . when the chips are down, these . . . these "civilised people," they'll eat each other.' That is, he argues that the 'good' aspects of humanity are simply dependent on circumstances.[51]

The Joker's 'social experiments' reflect the 'tests' that Satan puts to Job. In the same way that Satan believes that Job simply has not yet experienced enough suffering to prove him right, when there is an initial lack of response to the Joker's provocations to the people of Gotham, he ups the ante. But, even his biggest social experiment—the 'prisoner's dilemma' with the ferries, where a ferry full of prisoners and a ferry full of 'innocent civilians' are tasked with blowing each other up or being blown up themselves—fails to generate the outcome that the Joker desires.[52] While the Joker is somewhat dumbfounded by the failure of anyone to blow up the boats, Batman challenges him: 'What were you trying to prove? That deep down, everyone's as ugly as you? . . . This city just showed you that it's full of people that are ready to believe in good.' So, like Satan in regards to Job, the Joker's 'social experiments' fail to demonstrate that people *will* always act in a self-interested fashion. However, the Joker's final accusation comes in a form of a challenge to their hope, which he believes they will lose when:

> their spirit breaks completely. [When] they get a look at the real Harvey Dent and all the heroic things he's done. You didn't think I'd risk losing the

48 Job 1:8, ESV.

49 Job 1:8–11, ESV.

50 After the initial destruction of Job's possessions and children, the text notes that 'In all this Job did not sin or charge God with wrong.' When God then presents this to Satan, he again identifies Job as a blameless and upright man who held fast to his integrity despite the destruction wreaked against him for no reason. Satan again challenges Job's goodness, arguing that if God takes Job's health from him then 'he will curse you to your face.' Job 1:22 and 2:3–5, ESV.

51 For a more detailed analysis of the Joker, see Peters, "Beyond the Limits of the Law," 425–431. See also Bellinger, "The Joker is Satan."

52 Though, as Todd McGowan points out, this is not in the straightforward sense of 'the people' deciding to not go through with the action—the 'innocent civilians' decide *to* blow up the criminals (though cannot go through with it), while it is one of the criminals who throws their trigger out the window. See McGowan, "The Exceptional Darkness."

> battle for Gotham's soul in a fistfight with you? No, you need an ace in the hole. Mine's Harvey . . . I took Gotham's white knight and I brought him down to our level. It wasn't hard. See madness, as you know, is like gravity. All it takes is a little push.

Here, while Nolan is drawing on Alan Moore's classic exposé of the Joker, *The Killing Joke*, his position of this discussion of madness and Harvey Dent continues the Satan-like accusation.[53] As Job loses initially his wealth and children, and then subsequently his health, here the Joker's actions against Harvey mean that he has lost his family (with his fiancé Rachel having died) and his health (in terms of the disfiguration and the agony it leaves him in). In this sense, then, the transformation of Harvey Dent into 'Two-Face' is a direct result of the Joker's Satan-like accusations and the suffering that he has inflicted on Dent.

Another aspect of the story of Job becomes relevant here: the fact that Job does not know why he is suffering, but the readers do. That is, there are two settings for the story: heaven, where God and Satan discuss Job's character, and earth, where Job actually experiences the suffering inflicted by Satan (with God's acquiescence) and is then 'comforted' by his theological friends. It is in the midst of this dichotomy between the reader having received an explanation for Job's suffering that Job never receives, and Job's faithful endurance in his position that he did not deserve the suffering inflicted upon him, that the Book's critical engagement of justice in relation to suffering becomes most relevant. For Job, as Slavoj Žižek points out, continuously resists the attempts to attribute meaning to his suffering.[54] The role of the theological friends in the narrative is an attempt to provide ideological meaning to what Job is experiencing. They articulate what Benjamin L. Berger describes as the 'conventional account of justice': 'that if you do good, you will be rewarded, and if you do evil, you will be punished.'[55] Job's friends determine that, given Job is suffering, he must have committed some specific sin. However, the reader is aware that this is not the case—for God has declared him a 'blameless and upright man.' As such, to Job, his suffering seems completely unjust—and the reason for his suffering is never explained to him. The Book of Job thus 'explores the idea that there is a durable gap between the undeniable presence of injustice in the world and the profound desire to make sense out of experience.'[56]

Yet, the desire to makes sense of suffering and injustice is part of what is demanded of the law: the criminal law's punishing of the perpetrator and acknowledgment of the suffering of the victim is an attempt to provide a degree of societal

53 Alan Moore and Brian Bolland, *Batman: The Killing Joke* (New York: DC Comics, 2011).

54 Slavoj Žižek, *Violence* (London: Profile Books, 2009), 152–157. See also Slavoj Žižek, "The Fear of Four Words: A Modest Plea for the Hegelian Reading of Christianity," in *The Monstrosity of Christ: Paradox of Dialectic?*, ed. Creston Davis (Cambridge, MA: The MIT Press, 2009), 50–57.

55 Benjamin L. Berger, "On the Book of Job, Justice and The Precariousness of the Criminal Law," *Law, Culture and the Humanities,* 4 (2008): 105.

56 Berger, "On the Book of Job," 105.

meaning in response to the senseless suffering of the victim.[57] Furthermore, the superhero genre critique of the law is one that responds to the sense of the law's failure to be able to provide this degree of meaning (which, of course, the precarious nature of modern law, always concerned about its own fallibility and inability to adequately determine the guilt of a perpetrator, is only ever able to achieve in a limited fashion).[58] It is in the face of this type of senseless suffering and, moreover, the failure of the law to adequately address and provide meaning to such suffering that Harvey Dent becomes Two-Face. Unlike Job, who persists in denying the meaning to his suffering, the denial of the logical response of his friends, Dent desires to reinstitute a degree of order. Dent's recourse (at the Joker's provocation) to the fairness of chance and the toss of the coin is a means of objectifying the operation of justice. Dent's fall and failure, then, is not that he goes beyond the law and discards it, but rather that he maintains too great a commitment to it—he demands too much meaning from it and when the ordinary operation of the legal system fails to provide such meaning, he extends it and transforms it into his own objectified system which responds to the nature of the chaos of the world. As he shouts, in the final scenes, to Batman and Gordon that 'The world is cruel and the only morality in a cruel world is chance: unprejudiced, unbiased, fair.'

The greater question, however, that Dent is asking is the one that all victims ask: 'Why me?' And while the law may provide a degree of justice and a degree of meaning by punishing the perpetrator of the criminal act inflicted on the victim, such punishment will never answer that question of 'Why me?'[59] In the context of *The Dark Knight*, it becomes clear that the reason that Dent suffered was the *same* reason that Job did—not because he had done anything wrong, but specifically *because* the Joker/Satan wanted to prove that the goodness of an individual was dependent on pathological motives (i.e. the desire to be rewarded) and not any innate ethical position.[60] All the Joker's apparent radical anarchism and recourse to chaos are there to try and demonstrate a conservative view of law and justice: that if you do good, you will be rewarded, and if you do evil, you will be punished, *and therefore the reason someone does good is to be rewarded and not punished*. As Batman points out, Dent was chosen 'Because you were the best of us. He wanted to show that even someone as good as you could fall.' Here is the crucial difference between Dent and Job—in relation to Dent, 'He was right.'

It is in direct response to this point that we can understand Batman's actions at the end of *The Dark Knight*. For in taking the blame for Dent's killings, he does so as a means of *saving* Dent, so that, like Job at the end of his narrative, Dent is remembered not as a vigilante who lost faith in the law, but as an 'upright and blameless' man—Gotham's 'white knight.' In the same way that Christ's death

57 Ibid., 106–109.
58 Ibid., 109–112.
59 Ibid., 108.
60 See the analysis of the Joker's 'social experiments' in relation to Kantian ethics in McGowan, "The Exceptional Darkness."

on the cross is understood as an atoning action, by which he takes the sins of humanity upon himself so that they can be rendered forgiven and viewed as innocent, Batman's actions (which respond specifically to the Joker's accusation of Dent and demonstration of his failures) have an atoning dimension to them. Batman puts forward the image of Dent not as someone who has lost faith and who believes that justice is arbitrary or a result of chance, but as someone who maintained a belief in law and justice, as a good and upright man. One of the problems of this Christological reading, however, is that it therefore privileges or condones the act of deception undertaken by Batman and Gordon—the promotion of a lie rather than the truth. It is because of this deception that the conclusion to *The Dark Knight* is distinctly uncomfortable and there were a number of critics who criticised this apparently compromising action.[61] Furthermore, the narrative of *The Dark Knight Rises* seems to reveal Nolan's own sense of discomfort because the promulgation of this 'lie' and the resulting revelation of the 'truth' by Bane forms one of the key themes of the concluding film, and is the basis for the revolution that Bane leads. In order to read Batman's actions as something *more* than simply the promulgation of an ideological 'lie' in order to deceive the people of Gotham and allow an authoritarian and oppressive response to crime, we have to see Batman as providing a different vision of legality and community—one that is not based simply on 'the truth' of the actions committed by Dent, nor purely on the just punishment of sin and retribution. This different vision of legality is caught up specifically with the notion of the 'lie,' as it is intertwined with the nature of the medium we are analysing: cinematic fiction.

Envisioning legality: legal truth in the fictional image

Todd McGowan's insightful analysis of Nolan's films focuses specifically on the nature of the 'lie' in Nolan's filmmaking. Each of Nolan's films (not just the Batman ones) are based on a particular deception that is presented to the audience at the beginning of the film, only to be revealed as a lie later in the film and replaced with a higher truth. Nolan does this not by 'showing events that aren't really happening'[62] but by showing 'events that actually transpire in the filmic universe, [where] the formal structure leads the spectator to misinterpret these events.'[63] It is the *form* that operates as a deceit, rather than the content: '[t]he structure of the films deceive the spectator about the meaning of the events seen.'[64] Nolan's use of

61 See, for example, the discussion by Dennis A. Rendleman, "Two Faces of Criminal Prosecution: Harvey Dent, Mike Nifong, Craig Watkins," *The Journal of the Institute of Justice & International Studies*, 9 (2009), 180.

62 Todd McGowan, *The Fictional Christopher Nolan* (Austin: University of Texas Press, 2012), 1.

63 McGowan, *Fictional Christopher Nolan*, 1.

64 Ibid., 1. McGowan goes on to note that, '[t]he lie, as Nolan depicts it, is what misleads both characters and spectators. Lies encourage us to draw incorrect conclusions and to misunderstand

the lie is not in the form of traditional moral cinema, which focuses on illustrating the 'priority of deceit in order to denounce lying and insist on the importance of truthfulness.'[65] Rather, it is ethical cinema because of the way in which it 'redefines the relationship between ethics and truthfulness.'[66] 'Nolan inverts the traditional priority of truth and deception: the quest for truth originates with a lie, just as the cinematic fiction itself creates a terrain for the discovery of truths.'[67]

What is important to note here, of course, is that cinema itself is structurally based on lies and deception—it is fictional (even 'non-fiction' or documentary cinema deploys this fictional mode of presentation). While at one level we go to the cinema to escape or divert ourselves from the everyday, the power of filmic fictions to deceive manifests 'the truth of the extra-cinematic social reality.'[68] Taking into account this nature of cinema in general, and Nolan's cinematography in particular, what are we to make of the 'lie' that operates both at the end of *The Dark Knight* and as the thematic basis of *The Dark Knight Rises*—Batman's taking the blame for Dent's murders. At one level the saving of the image of Harvey Dent picks up an aspect of the superhero genre's hearkening back to an earlier form of Christian justice, rooted in the Western legal tradition. Whereas modern law's project was to 'replace a vision of justice deriving from God with a vision of justice as deriving from Man' medieval and early modern Europe's depiction of law was infused with a 'Christ-centred model of justice' where judges were responsible to Christ for their actions.[69] This saw a much more personal notion of justice than we expect of modern law and modern law's institutions. 'Just as Christ appears as the model of one whose character was the guarantee of justice, so too the principal criterion for the judge lay in *his* goodness and character, and therefore his capacity to assess this divine insight.'[70] Secular modernity thus moved away from a focus on the character of the judge to the effectiveness of an institutional system of justice.[71] The superhero, by donning cape and mask, asks

actions and events . . . But the lie also points to the truth that it hides. We understand the lie as a lie through its relationship to a truth that we finally distinguish from the lie.' Ibid., 3.

65 Ibid., 3.

66 Ibid., 3.

67 Ibid., 10.

68 Ibid., 7. McGowan notes that, by 'highlighting the power of film to decide and by remaining faithful to film's fictional structure, Christopher Nolan unveils the ethical potential of the cinema.'

69 Manderson, "Trust Us Justice," 35.

70 Manderson, "Trust Us Justice," 36. Manderson draws here on the work of French art historican Robert Jacob: Robert Jacob, *Images de la Justice* (Paris: Le Leopard d'Or, 1994). See also Martin Jay, "Must Justice Be Blind? The Challenges of Images to the Law," in *Law and the Image: The Authority of Art and the Aesthetics of Law*, ed. Costas Douzinas and Lynda Nead (Chicago: University of Chicago Press, 1999).

71 Manderson, "Trust Us Justice," 35–36. As Manderson notes: 'The crucial move to secular authority led to the modern obsession with the construction of hierarchical institutions and interpretive norms in which the role of the judge would be specific, circumscribed, and subservient. Thus the promise of justice was replaced by the guarantee of law, and divinely

us to *trust* that he is doing the right thing. Harvey Dent makes explicit reference to this type of trust when he affirms to reporters that, despite not knowing Batman's plans, he 'trusted him to do the right thing' (which, he flippantly adds, was 'saving my ass'). This sense of *trust* in the superhero, though, falls outside our modern sense of legality which looks not to trust but to institutional structures to attain justice—a sense of justice that is embedded in process as much as, or even more than, substance. Modern law thus finds itself caught in a dichotomy between the *doing* of justice and the *appearance* of justice being done.[72]

Furthermore, *The Dark Knight* unpacks this question about the issue of the appearance of justice specifically in relation to Harvey Dent and his prosecution of the mob. After having charged 549 mobsters, the Mayor points out to Dent:

> they're all gonna come after you now. And not just the mob. Politicians, journalists, cops—anyone whose wallet's about to get lighter. Are you up to it? You better be, because if they find anything on you then those criminals are back on the streets, followed swiftly by you and me.

This concern highlights the need for the appearance of propriety on behalf of Dent. This connects *both* to modern legality's concern with due process and open justice but *also* to the historical concern with the character of the judge as the one delivering justice.[73] If Harvey Dent is shown not to be completely beyond reproach, then the case that he has argued may be thrown out on procedural grounds. The concern is specifically with Harvey Dent's *character* and his *appearance.* Batman further emphasises this after the attempted killing of the Mayor, when Dent captures one of the Joker's pawns and interrogates him at gunpoint using his 'lucky' two-sided coin. Batman accuses Dent of leaving a man's life to chance, outlining, as noted above, the importance of Dent using legitimate means (as opposed to Batman's illegitimate ones) and that if anyone sees Dent's actions 'everything would be undone. All the criminals you pulled off the streets would be released and Jim Gordon [who at that stage is believed to be dead] will have died for nothing.'[74] It is this concern with the *appearance* of impartiality

inspired insight into the former transformed into rote obedience to the latter. The spirit of justice was replaced by the letter of the law. Judges and government became technicians in a structure that, as much as possible, was to run automatically, like a machine.'

72 This dichotomy is captured in the much quoted maxim from Lord Hewart CJ in *R v Sussex,* that justice should not only be done, but should be seen to be done: *R v Sussex Justices; Ex parte Macarthy* [1924] 1KB 256 at 259 per Lord Hewart CJ. Note, however, J. J. Spigelman's questioning of the true source of this maxim: J. J. Spigelman AC, "The Principle of Open Justice: A Comparative Perspective," *UNSW Law Journal* 29(2) (2006): 147–150.

73 For a comparison of Dent to 'real life' issues of the character of district attorneys, see Rendleman, "Two Faces of Criminal Prosecution."

74 After Dent has died, Gordon also refers to this concern about appearance—particularly now given the killings by Dent: 'The Joker won. Harvey's prosecution, everything you fought for, undone. Whatever chances you had of fixing our city, dies with Harvey's reputation. We bet it all on him. The Joker took the best of us and tore him down. People will lose hope.'

that gets taken up at the end of the film in relation to the *image* of Harvey Dent and the killings he committed. For, while Dent's face is partially scarred, leaving one side deformed and the other side normal, it is Dent's image that is being protected—the perfect, good-looking District Attorney which is symbolic of his 'good' character and actions (as opposed to the disfigured 'Two-Face' and his illegitimate, vengeful killings). This focus on the image goes to the ocular nature of the vision of law being presented: that it is not simply the *ends* for achieving justice, whether justice itself is done, but about the justness of the *means* to such ends—that justice must be *seen* to be done.

My use of the word 'image' here has a double meaning—it refers both to the speculative or imagined image of Dent, his character and actions in the mind of the people of Gotham City, but also to the very specific photographic image of Dent that is constantly presented (at his funeral both in the concluding scenes of *The Dark Knight* and their reproduction at the beginning of *The Dark Knight Rises*, the memorial day service in *The Dark Knight Rises*, and then finally, the image that is torn in half by Bane). When Gordon, in the concluding scenes of *The Dark Knight* presents a eulogy of Dent, in the background are multiple pictures of the smiling Dent, undamaged and undeformed—but these are not a range of *different* pictures of Dent, but rather multiple copies of the *same* picture. The use of this image then accompanies the words of Gordon's eulogy: 'A hero, not the hero we deserved, but the hero we needed. Nothing less than a knight, shining.' The actions of Batman which enable the presentation of Dent as a hero is aimed specifically at counteracting the Joker's accusations, and his final ironic words about 'all the heroic things' Dent has done. Batman describes his reasoning for promoting this 'lie' as follows: 'sometimes the truth isn't good enough. Sometimes people deserve more. Sometimes people deserve to have their faith rewarded.' What this points to, then, is that what is being promulgated is not so much a *lie about* Harvey Dent, but a *belief in* Harvey Dent—in who he was and what he achieved. This idea of a 'belief' in Harvey Dent is prefigured by Bruce's earlier reference to Gordon's campaign slogan: 'I believe in Harvey Dent.'

While the cinematography that begins *The Dark Knight Rises* parallels the conclusion of *The Dark Knight*, a shift in the role of the image occurs. At the end of *The Dark Knight*, Batman stands over the body of the dead Dent and turns his face so that the focus shifts from the disfigured side to the non-disfigured side—suggesting that the truth of who Dent was is not limited to his actions at the end of his life. In *The Dark Knight Rises*, however, at the Dent Day memorial celebration, there are once again multiple images of the good and non-deformed Dent, but when Gordon gets up to tell the 'truth' about Harvey Dent, the viewer gets a flashback to the disfigured Dent holding a gun to Gordon's son. The implication for the viewer, then, is that the 'truth' about Harvey Dent really lies in these actions at the end of his life and thus that Gordon had been promulgating a lie. Gordon, however, decides *not* to reveal this 'truth,' but reiterates the deception by referring to the number of people locked in Blackgate Prison and that Dent's death was therefore not in vain.

Gordon's speech about the 'truth' of Harvey Dent is later found and then read out on television by Bane as he exhorts the people of Gotham to throw off the chains of their oppressors and release those imprisoned in Blackgate under Dent's name. In doing so, the same image of the good and perfect Dent is held up by Bane and then torn in two—the implication then being that the lies have now been uncovered and the 'truth' revealed. Yet, of course, the viewer discovers later that Bane has his own deception about the use of the nuclear bomb he threatens the city with. It would appear at this point that the issue that Nolan is attempting to deal with is the problems of lying—a point which Alfred (Michael Caine) then tries to make to Bruce by saying that 'maybe it's time we all stop trying to outsmart the truth and let it have its day.' In the context of Nolan's filmmaking, however, such a straightforward approach to the issues of lying and the need for truth is rendered problematic. This can be understood first in relation to Nolan's use of the flashback in the film. Normally flashbacks are used to present an aspect of the fictional reality to the audience not otherwise available. The obvious reason for including the flashback to Dent's threatening of Gordon's son is to ensure that those who have not seen or cannot remember the previous film are 'up to speed.' The problem with this straightforward narrative-based reading is that the operation of the other flashbacks within the film are all deceptive—the appearances of Ra's Al Ghul to Bruce when he is in prison, the depictions of the story of Ra's' child and flashbacks to the earlier films make the viewer (and Bruce) believe that Bane is the child of Ra's. It is then revealed in the end that Talia, not Bane, is Ra's' child. If, therefore, Nolan's use of the flashback is *not* about revealing a fictional truth, then the flashback to Dent at the beginning of the film *also* fails to reveal the truth of Dent, but is part of a specific deception.

Of course, Dent *did* actually threaten Gordon's son and he *did* actually kill a number of people. So, how is this flashback image of the 'truth' of Harvey Dent actually a deception? It goes to the nature and purpose of the image. For, when Bane proclaims the 'truth' of Harvey Dent, what he is saying is factually true *but* because of the way and context in which he says it, it is actually a lie—a lie, as Slavoj Žižek would say, 'in the guise of the truth.'[75] This is most clear in the way Bane argues that none will interfere with the 'true justice' that will be implemented by 'the people,' and yet, in truth the nuclear bomb that Bane is threatening the city with is set to go off no matter what happens. The revolution is thus *not* a means of instituting a new legality and a new form of justice, it simply has the same aim of the League of Shadows—to destroy the decadent and corrupt people of Gotham in their entirety. What this means is that, even though we are seeing specifically the same image of Dent in the conclusion to *The Dark Knight* and in *The Dark Knight Rises*, the function of these images is not the same. At the conclusion of *The Dark Knight*, while what is being presented is not, at one level, factually accurate, it *is* the truth—that is, in contrast to Bane's presentation

75 Žižek, *Violence,* 85.

of a lie in the guise of the truth, Batman presents the truth in the form of a lie: the truth being that Dent *did not* become the monster that it would appear on the facts he did because Batman stopped him. Whereas the killing of mobsters and corrupt cops, while extra-legal, did actually encompass a sense of doing justice, the killing of Gordon's son in order to punish Gordon is not in the same category. When Batman stops Dent from killing Gordon's son, it is not only a means of saving the boy, but it is *also* a saving of Dent—stopping him doing something he would later regret and which would have transformed him into a monster. Whereas Gordon only remembers the fact that Dent *threatened* his son, what he has forgotten is that he *did not kill* his son. The truth of the circumstances, then, are more powerful than the actions that were averted.

The point of Batman's actions were to foreground a trust and faith—not in the Batman (which is part of the theme of *The Dark Knight Rises*), but as the basis of community itself. This provides a contrasting reading to that of the two traditional lines of the superhero. For the superhero genre seems to point either to an infallible justice beyond the law *or* to a recognition of the limits of modern law that we should live with. The orientation and conclusion of *The Dark Knight*, however, which foregrounds neither Batman as the hero, nor the need for the community to 'trust' Batman, presents another alternative: the identification of faith and trust in each other as the basis of community itself. It is this notion of faith and trust that counts the fallibility of the law, its always 'too human' limitations, as well as the mechanisms of suspicion that it institutes. What we should take away from Nolan's critical interrogation of the superhero genre is not so much that we should believe in the 'heroic lawyer' or the superhero as the figure of justice, but rather that we should look to believe and have faith in each other—despite the fact that we will constantly fail each other. Such a mechanism of faith and trust is the only foundation of community that will counter the biopolitical tendencies of modern law and its exception.[76]

Conclusion: trust, law and second chances

The dominance of the superhero genre on screen seems to call for more from modern legality than it is able to provide. It provides a sense of affective satisfaction in the viewer's literal ability to see justice being done. And yet, that role of seeing is one which modern law is not privy to. For the viewing of the actions on screen—the ability to see the crimes committed by the criminal and their guilt, along with the punishment rendered upon them by the superhero—is the very thing that the law cannot see, its vision restricted by the immanence of its secular orientation. Modern law works only with limited knowledge and never has the divine certainty that the screen almost inevitably seems to provide. Nolan's filmic working through of the superhero genre, however, is distinctly aware of this

76 See Milbank, "Paul Against Biopolitics"

problem of the limited vision of modern law. Nolan's Batman does not promote simply an overthrowing of the law or its fulfilment via the exception. It offers an alternative approach, which looks towards a grounding of community in faith and trust in each other, rather than in the nature of the law. It is in this sense that Batman does not fight for 'justice' in terms of demanding higher punishment of criminals or greater measures of law enforcement (such articulations of justice are captured better by the villains that Batman fights against). Batman's actions reference a vision of community that encompasses an ability to forgive, to express a trust in each other, which provides a stronger foundation for solidarity and togetherness than the protections of the law which are demanded.[77] Rather than seeing the theological resonances of the superhero genre as a pre-modern critique of the law, Nolan's rendering offers a more substantial vision of the superhero: not as a messianic-saviour figure of judgment, but as a figure that is willing to trust in others to do good and not evil, even when such trust may be broken.

We find this sense of trust in the interactions between Bruce/Batman and Selina Kyle (the 'cat burglar') in *The Dark Knight Rises*. There, despite her continually 'letting him down' and proving to be self-serving and self-interested, Bruce provides multiple opportunities for a 'second chance.' He trusts in Selina Kyle to do the right thing despite constant evidence to the contrary. This trust is one that steps out in knowledge that the other can be more than they have been in the past—it is a trust that encourages the other to also trust and to act in the right way. It is certainly not a trust that will never be broken—Selina Kyle misleads Batman, turns him in to Bane and appears to abandon him at a number of points in the film—but it is a trust that expects more of the other than they would think that they have in themselves. In a time when trust seems to be scarce, where our political leaders seem to be constantly mired in scandal, suspicion and self-interest, perhaps it is a time when trust is most important. If we rely on a vision of legality based on mistrust, then we will believe nothing and yet, as Nolan shows us, be thoroughly deceived.[78] It is in the very process of trusting others that we gain a knowledge of them and of community that cannot be gained by a mistrust that always requires law to shore up protection against the other, because in believing nothing it is always ready to believe the worst of the other. We need to focus instead on a trust that, as Kierkegaard might say, 'believes everything' and yet 'is never to be deceived.'[79] It is with such a trust in each other and not the law that we may have our 'faith rewarded.'

77 Ibid., 53.

78 As I have noted elsewhere, drawing on Søren Kierkegaard, 'the cynic who mistrusts is the one who misses the efficiency of the appearance itself (however fleeting, fragile and elusive it is). The true believer (the one who loves) sees the goodness of the other and the dimension through the appearance.' Peters, "Unbalancing Justice," 263. See also Søren Kierkegaard, *Works of Love*, trans. David F. Swenson and Lillian Marvin Swenson (Port Washington, NY: Kennikat Press, 1972), 182–183; Slavoj Žižek, *The Fragile Absolute—Or Why is the Christian Legacy Worth Fighting For?* (London: Verso, 2000), 127; 1 Cor. 13:7, ESV.

79 Kierkegaard, *Works of Love*, 182–183.

Bibliography

Cases

R v Sussex Justices; Ex parte Macarthy [1924] 1KB 256.

Books and articles

Agamben, Giorgio. *Homo Sacer: Soveriegn Power and Bare Life*. Translated by Daniel Heller-Roazen. Stanford, CA: Stanford University Press, 1998.

Agamben, Giorgio. *The State of Exception*. Translated by Kevin Attell. Chicago: University of Chicago Press, 2005.

Bainbridge, Jason. " 'The Call to Do Justice': Superheroes, Sovereigns and the State During Wartime." *International Journal for the Semiotics of Law*, 28(4) (December 2015): 745–763.

Bainbridge, Jason. "Spider-Man, The Question and the Meta-Zone: Exception, Objectivism and the Comics of Steve Ditko." *Law Text Culture* 16 (2012): 217–242.

Bainbridge, Jason. " 'This is the Authority. This Planet is Under Our Protection'—An Exegesis of Superheroes' Interrogations of Law." *Law, Culture and the Humanities* 3(3) (2007): 455–476.

Barkman, Adam. "Superman: From Anti-Christ to Christ-Type." In *Superman and Philosophy: What Would the Man of Steel Do?*, edited by Mark D. White, 111–120. West Sussex: John Wiley & Sons, 2013.

Bellinger, Charles K. "The Joker is Satan and So are We: Girard and The Dark Knight." *Journal of Religion and Film* 13(1) (2009).

Benjamin, Walter. "Critique of Violence." In *Reflections: Essays, Aphorisms, Autobiographical Writings*, edited by Peter Demetz, 277–300. Translated by Edmund Jephcott. New York: Schocken Books, 1986.

Berger, Benjamin L. "On the Book of Job, Justice and the Precariousness of the Criminal Law." *Law, Culture and the Humanities* 4 (2008): 98–118.

Curtis, Neil. "Superheroes and the Contradiction of Sovereignty." *Journal of Graphic Novels and Comics* 4(2) (2013): 209–222.

Dickens, Charles. *The Complete Works of Charles Dickens: A Tale of Two Cities*. New York: Cosimo Books, 2009.

Gray, Richard J. and Betty Kaklamanidou, eds. *The 21st Century Superhero: Essays on Gender, Genre and Globalization in Film*. Jefferson, NC: McFarland & Company, 2011.

Ip, John. "The Dark Knight's War on Terrorism." *Ohio State Journal of Criminal Law* 9(1) (2011): 209–229.

Jacob, Robert. *Images de la Justice*. Paris: Le Leopard d'Or, 1994.

Jay, Martin. "Must Justice Be Blind? The Challenges of Images to the Law." In *Law and the Image: The Authority of Art and the Aesthetics of Law*, edited by Costas Douzinas and Lynda Nead, 19–35. Chicago: University of Chicago Press, 1999.

Kierkegaard, Søren. *Works of Love*. Translated by David F. Swenson and Lillian Marvin Swenson. Port Washington, NY: Kennikat Press, 1972.

Lisk, Joshua. "Is Batman a State Actor? The Dark Knight's Relationship with the Gotham City Police Department and the Fourth Amendment Implications." *Case Western Reserve Law Review* 64(3) (2014): 1419–1440.

Manderson, Desmond "Trust Us Justice: *24,* Popular Culture, and the Law." In *Imagining Legality: Where Law Meets Popular Culture,* edited by Austin Sarat, 22–52. Tuscaloosa: University of Alabama Press, 2011.

McGowan, Todd. "The Exceptional Darkness of The Dark Knight." *Jump Cut* 51 (2009).

McGowan, Todd. *The Fictional Christopher Nolan.* Austin: University of Texas Press, 2012.

Miettinen, Mervi. "Representing the State of Exception: Power, Utopia, Visuality and Narrative in Superhero Comics." In *Images in Use: Towards the Critical Analysis of Visual Communication,* edited by M. Tocchetti and K. Kukkonen, 269–290. Amsterdam: John Benjamins Publishing Company, 2011.

Milbank, John. "Paul Against Biopolitics." In *Paul's New Moment: Continental Philosophy and the Future of Christian Theology,* edited by John Milbank, Slavoj Žižek and Creston Davis, 21–73. Grand Rapids: Brazos Press, 2010.

Milbank, John. *Theology and Social Theory: Beyond Secular Reason*, 2nd edn. Malden: Blackwell Publishing, 2006.

Milbank, John. *The Word Made Strange.* Oxford: Blackwell Publishers, 1997.

Mitchell, Dale. "Paradoxes and Patriarchy: A Legal Reading of She-Hulk." *Griffith Law Review* 24(3) (2015): 446–481.

Nichols, Michael. " 'I Think You and I Are Destined to Do This Forever': A Reading of the Batman/Joker Comic and Film Tradition Through the Combat Myth." *Journal of Religion and Popular Culture* 23(2) (2011).

Nietzsche, Friedrich. *Twilight of the Idols: or How to Philosophize with a Hammer.* Translated by Duncan Large. Oxford: Oxford University Press, 1998.

Peters, Timothy D. "Beyond the Limits of the Law: A Christological Reading of Christopher Nolan's *The Dark Knight.*" *Griffith Law Review* 24(3) (2015): 418–445.

Peters, Timothy D. "Reading the Law Made Strange: Cultural Legal Studies, Theology and Speculative Fiction." In *Cultural Legal Studies: Law's Popular Cultures and the Metamorphosis of Law,* edited by Cassandra Sharp and Marett Leiboff, 252–273. New York: Routledge, 2016.

Peters, Timothy D. "Unbalancing Justice: Overcoming the Limits of the Law in *Batman Begins.*" *Griffith Law Review* 16(1) (2007): 247–270.

Rendleman, Dennis A. "Two Faces of Criminal Prosecution: Harvey Dent, Mike Nifong, Craig Watkins." *The Journal of the Institute of Justice & International Studies* 9 (2009): 171–181.

Reyns, Bradford W. and Billy Henson. "Superhero Justice: The Depiction of Crime and Justice in Modern-Age Comic Books and Graphic Novels." *Sociology of Crime, Law and Deviance* 14 (2010): 45–66.

Schenk, Ken. "Superman: A Popular Culture Messiah." In *The Gospel According to Superheroes: Religion and Popular Culture*, edited by B. J. Oropeza, 33–48. New York: Peter Lang, 2005.

Schmitt, Carl. *Political Theology: Four Chapters on the Concept of Sovereignty.* Translated by George Schwab. Chicago: University of Chicago Press, 2005.

Sharp, Cassandra. " 'Riddle Me This . . .?': Would the World Need Superheroes If the Law Could Actually Deliver 'Justice '?" *Law Text Culture* 16 (2012): 353–378.

Spigelman AC, J. J. "The Principle of Open Justice: A Comparative Perspective." *UNSW Law Journal* 29(2) (2006): 147–166.

Trent, Shaun. "How America Learned to Stop Worrying and Cynically ENJOY! The Post-9/11 Superhero Zeitgeist." *Communication and Critical/Cultural Studies* 6(1) (2009): 103–109.

Vollum, Scott and Cardy D. Adkinson. "The Portrayal of Crime and Justice in the Comic Book Superhero Mythos." *Journal of Criminal Justice and Popular Culture* 10(2) (2003): 96–108.

Žižek, Slavoj. "The Fear of Four Words: A Modest Plea for the Hegelian Reading of Christianity." In *The Monstrosity of Christ: Paradox of Dialectic?*, edited by Creston Davis, 24–109. Cambridge, MA: The MIT Press, 2009.

Žižek, Slavoj. *The Fragile Absolute—Or Why is the Christian Legacy Worth Fighting For?* London: Verso, 2000.

Žižek, Slavoj. *Violence*. London: Profile Books, 2009.

Films

Batman Begins. Directed by Christopher Nolan. Warner Brothers Pictures, 2005.

The Dark Knight. Directed by Christopher Nolan. Warner Brothers Pictures, 2008.

The Dark Knight Rises. Directed by Christopher Nolan. Warner Brothers Pictures, 2012.

Man of Steel. Directed by Zack Snyder. Warner Brothers, 2013.

Superman Returns. Directed by Bryan Singer. Warner Brothers, 2006.

Comic books and graphic novels

Miller, Frank, Klaus Janson and Lynn Varley. *The Dark Knight Returns*. New York: DC Comics, 1986.

Moore, Alan and Brian Bolland. *Batman: The Killing Joke*. New York: DC Comics, 2011.

Nolan, Christopher and David S. Goyer. "Introduction: A Conversation with Christopher Nolan and David S. Goyer." In *Batman: The Long Halloween*, by Jeph Loeb and Tim Sale. New York: DC Comics, 2011.

Newspaper articles, magazine articles, blogs

Ackerman, Spencer. "Batman's 'Dark Knight' Reflects Cheney Policy." *The Washington Independent*, 21 July 2008.

Allen, Joe. "Batman's War on Terror." *Counterpunch*, 2 August 2008.

Bolt, Andrew. "Batman Bush True Dark Knight." *Herald Sun*, 30 July 2008.

Klavan, Andrew. "What Bush and Batman Have in Common." *Wall Street Journal*, 25 July 2008.

Morrison, Grant. *Wizard: The Comics Magazine*, 143, 1 August 2003, 180.

O'Neil, Tyler. "Dark Knight and Occupy Wall Street: The Humble Rise." *Hillsdale Natural Law Review*, 21 July 2012, https://hillsdalenaturallawreviewdotcom.wordpress.com/2012/07/21/dark-knight-and-occupy-wall-street-the-humble-rise (accessed 31 October 2016).

Žižek, Slavoj. "The People's Republic of Gotham." *New Statesman*, 24–30 August, 2012.

Chapter 5

Machiavellian fantasy and the game of laws: rex, sex and lex in George R. R. Martin's *A Song of Ice and Fire*

William P. MacNeil

Fantastic jurisprudence: popular culture's law of genres and genre of laws in *Game of Thrones*

How are cultural legal scholars to understand the instant cult status accorded to HBO's recently screened and baroquely rich televisual adaptation of George R. R. Martin's *Game of Thrones*,[1] the first in his celebrated cycle, *A Song of Ice and Fire*?[2] This chapter locates its runaway success in terms of three prime-time programming *absences*, the previous *presences* of which seeded a variety of audiences that have been interpellated by *Game of Thrones*. First, there are those Tolkienistas and Potter-maniacs who long for a good fantasy flight which, if not quite reproductions of the Shire or Hogwarts, will take them somewhere *else* equally enchanted by its 'sword 'n' sorcery.' Second, there are those history buffs keen for the kind of costumed sexual shenanigans—*The Tudors*, *Rome*, *The Borgias*—which turn out to be nothing more than a highly pornified version of yesteryear. Finally, there are the gothic 'scream queens' (myself included) who can't quite get *over Buffy the Vampire Slayer*, but can't quite get *with* the *Twilight* programme, all longing for a horror with less of Edward's sparkle and more of Spike's fang. *Game of Thrones* 'hails,' in the purest Althusserian sense, all of these subject-spectators,

1 David Benioff and D. B. Weiss, prods, *Game of Thrones: The Complete First Season* (USA: Home Box Office, 2011) [DVD, TV programme]. See also: David Benioff and D. B. Weiss, prods, *Game of Thrones: The Complete Second Season* (USA: Home Box Office, 2012) [DVD, TV programme]; David Benioff and D. B. Weiss, prods, *Game of Thrones: The Complete Third Season* (USA: Home Box Office, 2013) [DVD, TV programme]. While the novel is entitled *A Game of Thrones*, the television series (and subsequent tie-in textual reprint) dropped the indefinite article 'A,' rendering the title simply *Game of Thrones*. As the focus of this chapter is the television series, this chapter adopts the latter title. However, references which are quoted or cited from the former text retain that title.

2 George R. R. Martin, *A Game of Thrones* (New York: Bantam Books, 1996). The sequels are: *A Clash of Kings* (New York: Bantam Books, 1999); *A Storm of Swords* (New York: Bantam Books, 2000); *A Feast for Crows* (New York: Bantam Books, 2005); *A Dance with Dragons* (New York: Bantam Books, 2011); *The Winds of Winter* (forthcoming); *A Dream of Spring* (forthcoming).

fusing them into a collective that is even more devoted in its following than Daenerys' army of Unsullied *castrati*. With a narrative bristling with dark lords, evil sorceresses, powerful wizards, hobbit-like 'children of the Earth' and magically empowered youngsters, the series more than delivers the high fantasy its Tolkien/Rowling fanbase demands. Not to mention a rollicking historical yarn that strays from throne room to bedroom and, with it, the full-frontal nudity and (barely) simulated copulation captured in 'money shots' that out-rival the racy romps of *The Tudors, et.al.* To say nothing of a horror that can be neither slain nor penetrated, not domesticated or gentrified in the zombie-like, living dead White Walkers—the Others of Westerosi myth and legend, now once again abroad in the land—who seem to reach out, *Ring*-like, from the screen, transfixing, indeed staking recovering Slayerettes and their coven's fellow travellers: True Blooders, Vampire Diarists, Twihards and other Goth wannabes.

So fantasy, history and horror: all three genres, I claim, account for the tremendous appeal of *Game of Thrones*. To which I will add what Northrop Frye would call yet another 'mode of emplotment,'[3] namely, the rhetorical register of the law. 'The law,' my reader may mutter to herself, 'in a text as seemingly *lawless* as *Game of Thrones*?' Replete with breaches and betrayals of conventions which are sexual and social, how can this criminal narrative of murder and mayhem be *anything* but lawful? Of course, as any lawyer well knows, criminality always implies a codified law, the provisions of which are chronically infringed by egregious wrong-doings; and the next two sections of this chapter will map, in some detail, the deeply dialectical relationship between Westerosi legality (Section Two) and its flagrant contraventions (Section Three) throughout *Game of Thrones*. Ultimately, though, the end-game for which the series' principal characters play is nothing less than raw, brute *power*, an unrelenting story arc that, seemingly, takes all of them far beyond the law and puts what might be the real TV *auctoritas* for *Game of Thrones*—*The West Wing*—to shame. This drives home the key point of this chapter as propounded in Section Four: that for all its high fantasy flourishes, all its mediaevalising historical trills, all its zombie horror subtext, *Game of Thrones* is a work driven by a power *politics* of a particularly amoral, even immoral, kind. 'Machiavelli meets magic'[4] is how many critics and journalists greeted the series when first broadcast earlier this year, referencing, of course, the (god)father of modern *Realpolitik*, Renaissance humanist scholar, man of letters and politician, Niccolò Machiavelli (1469–1527). Two of Machiavelli's germinal meditations on the nature of power—*The Prince* (1515) and the

3 Northrop Frye, "Historical Criticism: Theory of Modes," in *Anatomy of Criticism: Four Essays*, Northrop Frye (Princeton, NJ: Princeton University Press, 1957), 49.

4 See, for example: "George R. R. Martin: Barbarians at the Gate," *Guardian*, Thursday 14 April 2011, http://www.guardian.co.uk/books/2011/apr/13/george-rr-martin-game-thrones; or "George R. R. Martin's *Game of Thrones* is Machiavelli's *The Prince*," *The Examiner*, Thursday 11 August 2011, http://www.examiner.com/review/george-r-r-martin-s-game-of-thrones-is-machiavelli-s-the-prince-1.

Discourses on Livy (1517)—will be relevant to this chapter's argument, as further developed in Section Four; for each text adumbrates a politics,[5] whether the state be princely or republican, a dominion or a *civis*, where strategic aims and overriding objectives are realised, as Malcolm X would put it, 'by any means necessary.'

That those means, often thought unscrupulous and scheming to the highest degree—in short, axiomatically Machiavellian—turn out to be, as *Game of Thrones* vividly dramatises, *lawful*, will be this chapter's core conclusion, laid out in its final two sections. There, Section Five argues that Martin's series repositions Machiavelli as much a theorist of the *lex natura* (the *lex* of my title) as that of the pragmatic *politique* of 'the prince' (*rex*) or the city-state's Pocockian 'virtue, trade and commerce' (sex).[6] That is, as a law of *nature*, the *lex* of which—however much it may constrain *rex*, even regulate sex—is, nonetheless, *critical* in its Machiavellian as Martinian reconception in that it must go *through* politics with all of its contingencies and indeterminacies, *aporias* and ambiguities, before arriving at its astonishing teleological destination: a radically reconceived *Recht*. So the law in both Martin and Machiavelli is, first and foremost, a politics of the law, combusting as it constructs notions of sovereignty and 'the social,' pointing its readers and spectators towards a law of *post*-politics. That post-political law potentially sketches, so Section Six concludes, a new relationship between *natura naturans* and humanity, one which is made all the more urgent and necessary as the Anthropocene winds to a close in both Westeros and Earth: the latter, figuratively iced over in the unending winter to come; the former literally melting away, like today's polar ice caps, with global warming. Averting this environmental disaster, both real and imagined, is nothing less than an ecological *Begriffsjurisprudenz*, which, for all its 'dungeons 'n' dragons' fancy dress, *Game of Thrones* vividly dramatises as the aleatory outcome of a game of laws in and around a reconstituted nature-as-Gaia.

Westerosi crime and punishment: 'lealty,' feudal hierarchy and the stark justice of Lord Eddard Stark

However, before turning to the series' overarching juridical metaphorisation—of a 'higher law' immanent in, rather than transcending nature—this section will examine, as a threshold issue, the way in which juridical processes, as well as institutions and concepts, are enacted in *Game of Thrones* in the strictest of socio-legal senses. Indeed, the *diegesis* proper opens with a strongly staged scene of law—or more, precisely, a site of law's execution; specifically, in the punishment of the

5 Niccolò Machiavelli, *The Prince and The Discourses*, trans. Luigi Ricci (Toronto: Random House Inc., 1950).

6 John (J. G. A.) Pocock, *Virtue, Commerce and History* (New York: Cambridge University Press, 1985), 43–50.

hapless Will, the Night's Watch recruit found wandering far from The Wall, and perforce guilty of desertion.[7] Of course, the viewer knows from the narrative's prologue that Will's desertion is, in fact, a panic reaction, a desperate flight from a sanguinary sortie with the deadly White Walkers, upon whom he stumbles while on patrol with two other rangers—Gared and Ser Waymar—and of which he is the only (and highly traumatised) survivor.[8] That explanation-as-excuse, however, in no way amounts to a defence; and Will's sentence—death—is carried out here, with unflinching resolve, by Sean Bean's Lord Eddard Stark, at once judge, jury and executioner. Such a conflation of nomological roles puts paid to the Coverian notion that the law occurs against a background of 'pain and suffering';[9] for, here, such miserable and immiserating *affect* is front row and centre as the scene's audience is forced to watch, in all its gory details, Will's beheading with the same sense of visceral discomfort that Bran Stark feels, as a witness to this scene of 'crime and punishment.'[10]

Despite the punitive severity on graphic, indeed grisly, display here, this bloody sentence is absolutely necessary because '(t)he law' is 'the law,' as Ser Rodrik Cassel, the master at arms, unhesitatingly says to Catelyn, Lady Stark.[11] This pithy positivist distillation calls up and turns on a formalism in which the law is to be followed *to the letter*; that is, a narrow and unyielding legalism which admits no exceptions to its sanctions, even if it produces a kind of rough justice of Will's beheading. But make no mistake about it; no matter how *rough* this justice may be—and the series abounds in characters who have had not only heads, but tongues, hand, feet, breasts and cocks cut off—there is what Carol Gilligan might call a *logic* of justice operative in this scene and the 'imagined community' for which it stands, synecdochically.[12] Nowhere more so than in the character of Lord Eddard Stark, whose probity, integrity and honour renders him this world's exemplary figure. For Stark is a man of such sterling principle that, for the Westerosi, he seems to incarnate 'the Law' itself: a personification which, for all its rigidity, is balanced, mitigated and mollified—as most legal systems are—by an innate sense of equity. This equitable or, more technically, *fiduciary* duty is amply evidenced in the way Ned honours, *uberimma fides*, all those dependent upon him: not only his loving wife and cherished children, not only his ever loyal household staff and faithful attendants; but also his insolent ward-hostage,

7 David Benioff and D. B. Weiss, prods, "Winter is Coming," *Game of Thrones*, season 1, episode 1, directed by A. Taylor, D. Minahan, D. Nutter, B. Kirk, T. Van Patten, A. Sakharov, D. Petrarca, A. Graves, M. Maclaren (USA: Home Box Office, 2011). See also Martin, *A Game of Thrones*, pp.13–17.

8 Benioff and Weiss, "Winter is Coming." See also Martin, *A Game of Thrones*, 1–11.

9 Robert Cover, "Violence and the Word," *The Yale Law Journal* 95(8) (1986): 1601.

10 Benioff and Weiss, "Winter is Coming." See also Martin, *A Game of Thrones*, 13–17.

11 Benioff and Weiss, "Winter is Coming.".

12 Carol Gilligan, *In a Different Voice: Psychological Theory and Women's Development* (Cambridge, MA: Harvard University Press, 1982), 134.

Theon Greyjoy, even his moody bastard, Jon Snow. Indeed, Lord Stark's Winterfell seems, itself, to be a space of law at its most *natural*, watched over by the old gods of the Weirwood who ensure a place for everyone—aristocrats, servants, tenants—and everyone in their place.[13]

Surely, here is a vision of society at its most nostalgically feudal; specifically, a backward-looking *utopos* of caste where all and sundry 'love the Starks' *as* their overlords, each singing the ruling clan's praises in a way that is the fantasy equivalent to Merrie Olde England's 'bless the squire and his relations/ . . . And always know our proper stations.'[14] Dickens' rhyming paean to the deference society—of which Winterfell is both an analogue and a microcosm—is quoted here because it could be applied to the Seven Kingdoms as a whole. For Martin's cycle renders in *faerie* terms what a certain strain of Anglo-Saxon historicist legal theory, inspired by Sir Henry Maine, would call the 'society of status.'[15] Or what a more Francophile school of thought—that of Émile Durkheim's—would nominate as 'the mechanical,'[16] presumably because, there, everyone is soldered into place, like the spokes of a wheel or the pistons of an engine. No wonder, then, that each televised episode of *Game of Thrones* opens with a sweeping Middle-earth map which springs to life in a most un-Tolkien, even steampunk way: specifically, with all sorts of dials turning, tops spinning, and cylinders ascending, thereby literalising the mechanical that constitutes this domain, and impliedly its omnipresent juridicism. For is there a more lawful, indeed law-*full* (meaning 'full of law') sphere than this mechanical, deferential, feudal jurisdiction where every institution, every event, every relationship or person is ordered by some norm, governed by some precept, the amalgam of which amounts to, with all due respect to Jeremy Bentham,[17] a kind of unwritten but no less 'pannomial' code of conduct ensuring a strict *hierarchy* of the most top-down kind—of king, lord, bannerman, hedge knight, sellsword, small folk and so on.

At that hierarchy's apex sits the fount of law himself, the King of Seven Kingdoms, secure on his Iron Throne, and surrounded by his trusty advisors: for example, the prime ministerial Hand who, as a scatological aside, would have it, 'wipes' while the king 'shits';[18] the Grand Maester who functions as a kind of lord chancellor, or counsellor and confessor; and even more sinister figures, such

13 Martin, *A Game of Thrones*, 22–23.

14 Charles Dickens, *A Christmas Carol and Other Stories* (Westminster, MD: Modern Library, 2000) 149.

15 Henry S. Maine, *Ancient Law: Its Connection with the Early History of Society and Its Relation to Modern Ideas* (London: Hasell, Watson & Viney Ltd, 1906), 174.

16 Émile Durkheim, *The Division of Labour in Society* (New York: Macmillan, 1933), 70–110.

17 Jeremy Bentham, "Anarchical Fallacies," in *Nonsense upon Stilts: Bentham, Burke and Marx on the Rights of Man*, ed. Jeremy Waldron (New York: Methuen, 1987).

18 David Benioff and D. B. Weiss, prods, "Lord Snow," *Game of Thrones*, season 1, episode 3, directed by A. Taylor, D. Minahan, D. Nutter, B. Kirk, T. Van Patten, A. Sakharov, D. Petrarca, A. Graves, M. Maclaren (USA: Home Box Office, 2011).

as the chief of the secret police, the scheming eunuch Lord Varys, who seems to have stepped out of a version of *Arabian Nights* as retold by Robert Ludlum. Clustering around the king and his council—and functioning, collectively, as a royal court when assembled in the capital, King's Landing—are the lordly representatives of the Great Houses. Proudly bearing their armigerous sigils (a dire wolf for the Starks, a lion for the Lannisters, and so on), encomiastically touting their family mottos (such as the Starks' 'Winter is coming' or the Lannisters' 'Hear Me Roar!') and ruling, now as imperial satraps, ancestral lands over which once they were supreme (e.g., for the Starks, the North; for the Lannisters, Casterly Rock), all of these grandees are hunkered down in their vast castellated fastnesses, staffed with a retinue of relations and retainers, including kinfolk, masters, septons, guards, servants and so forth. Below them are the bannermen, lesser noble houses attached as vassals to their Great House lieges, and which include some of the key players in the series: for example, Jon Snow's Billy Bunter-ish sidekick, Sam Tarly,[19] whose house is pledged to the Tyrells of Highgarden; or, to take another example, the far more sinister Freys of the Crossing, turncloak lieges of the Tullys, whose over-ripe fecundity is legend, its members ever-replicating versions (both 'Little' and 'Big') of their insatiably ram-like paterfamilias, Walder. To say nothing of the Boltons of the (aptly named) Dreadfort: those psychopaths of the Seven Kingdoms, whose obscene *enjoyment* in and of torture—flaying their victims alive, like the hapless Theon—inject a very *Dexter*-ish, 'serial killer' horror story into the narrative.[20]

Underneath these not-so-gentle gentry are the hedge knights, landless crusaders who could easily shade into, and often become sellsword *condottieri*—like Tyrion's defender, Bronn;[21] but nonetheless, by reason of their fighting prowess, armour and mount remain socially superior to the vast majority of Westerosi: namely, the 'small folk.' Of whom we meet many in the Arya narrative, once she becomes separated from both her family and the Night's Watch protectors, thereby bringing her, in her loneliness, in contact with smithies and sailors, innkeeps and barrow-boys (like Hot Pie[22]—my personal characterological favourite)

19 Martin, *A Game of Thrones*, 262. David Benioff and D. B. Weiss, prods, "Cripples, Bastards, and Broken Things," *Game of Thrones*, season 1, episode 4, directed by A. Taylor, D. Minahan, D. Nutter, B. Kirk, T. Van Patten, A. Sakharov, D. Petrarca, A. Graves, M. Maclaren (USA: Home Box Office, 2011).

20 Martin, *A Dance with Dragons*, 167; David Benioff and D. B. Weiss, prods, "Dark Wings, Dark Words," *Game of Thrones*, season 3, episode 2, directed by A. Taylor, D. Minahan, D. Nutter, B. Kirk, T. Van Patten, A. Sakharov, D. Petrarca, A. Graves, M. Maclaren (USA: Home Box Office, 2013).

21 Martin, *A Game of Thrones*, 423; Benioff and Weiss, "Cripples, Bastards, and Broken Things."

22 Martin, *A Clash of Kings*, 32; David Benioff and D. B. Weiss, prods, "Fire and Blood," *Game of Thrones*, season 1, episode 10, directed by A. Taylor, D. Minahan, D. Nutter, B. Kirk, T. Van Patten, A. Sakharov, D. Petrarca, A. Graves, M. Maclaren (USA: Home Box Office, 2011).

in her strange, Huck Finn-ish journey around Westeros—if, that is, Huck Finn ever trained as an assassin's apprentice.[23] Finally, at the very bottom of this society are those adrift and displaced: the aforementioned sellswords, the exiles, the outlaws, the dwarves, and especially the bastards. But note how, even here, in the dregs of society, conventions and customs hold sway, signifying and situating the *absence* of legitimacy in the highly whimsical—and region-specific—names each Great House bestows on bastardy: Flowers, for the blooming botanical gardens of the South; Rivers for the riparian valley of the Trident; and Snow for the frozen wastes of the North. All of which suggests a lawful place for even those whose respective accidents of birth have branded as *hors-loi*.

Holding together this finely calibrated and artfully layered hierarchy of *legal* status is an overarching value; specifically, a *grundnorm*,[24] the ethico-juridical baseline of which is loyalty or fidelity to one's liege, one's house, and one's word. Not for nothing is one of the common adjectives in the text 'leal,' an old Scottish word meaning faithful; because it is this attitude of lealty which is most prized by the community here, functioning as the moral adhesive which binds its tiered structure of functional and familial estates—and the correlative *doctrinal* rights and responsibilities attaching to each, from the most frivolously playful to the most solemnly serious, ceremonialising all Westerosi persons, places and processes. Consider, for example, all the *rites* enacted in the series, taking the most seriously sacramental first. For what is one of the first scenes of *Game of Thrones* if not a religious ritual, the elaborate state funeral of John Arryn, Lord of the Vale, carried out by the Silent Sisters, an order of the Seven.[25] This is, shortly thereafter, followed by Jon Snow's avowal of allegiance to the Night's Watch before the arboreal gods of the pagan North, literally present, as *genius loci*, in the groves of the sacred.[26] Finally, there are those hideous human sacrifices to the new 'God' from the East, the intensely monotheistic Rh'llor, the Lord of Light, whose fires consume his victims, like the *auto-da-fés* of Counter-Reformation Spain—only here the point is not, as it was with the Inquisition, to dispatch heresy, but to conjure up and send forth new, ever more terrifying supernatural forces (such as an uncanny *golem*-like double of Stannis Baratheon) in a Seven Kingdoms' war *of* (rather than *against*) terror.[27] That is to say, *rites* are everywhere in this world, as a set of practices which bleed into—literally, more often than not—*rights*. Such

23 Martin, *A Feast for Crows*, 138–139.

24 Hans Kelsen, *The Pure Theory of Law*, trans. Max Knight (Berkley: University of California Press, 1967), 221–276.

25 Benioff and Weiss, "Winter is Coming."

26 Martin, *A Game of Thrones*, 522; David Benioff and D. B. Weiss, prods, "You Win or You Die," *Game of Thrones*, season 1, episode 7, directed by A. Taylor, D. Minahan, D. Nutter, B. Kirk, T. Van Patten, A. Sakharov, D. Petrarca, A. Graves, M. Maclaren (USA: Home Box Office, 2011).

27 Martin, *A Clash of Kings*, 149–150, 623; Martin, *A Game of Thrones*, 522; David Benioff and D. B. Weiss, prods, "The Ghost of Harrenhal," *Game of Thrones*, season 2, episode

as the right to participate in this world's preferred extreme sport of choice and leisure activity: the *Ivanhoe*-like tournament, itself sited within a context of law as much as valour, being minutely regulated as to what to wear, how to joust, what constitutes fair play, the nature of a good win, and so forth.[28]

As faithless as a Frey: oaths, kingslaying and the politics of transgression

In its rule-bound violence, however, the tournament gives us a clue to how the law operates here in Westeros and makes sense of all its beheadings, eviscerations, mutilations, and so on. For what the tourney's elaborate codification drives home is how, in the series, violence functions according to, and as a *rule*; so much so that one can say that this is a society that expects and is bounded by a rule of violence as much as its violence of the rule. To that end, look no further for the binding nature of this counter-, even anti-, *nomos*—the daemonic parody of Dicey's Rule of Law[29]—than the scenes set in the vertiginous Eyrie of the Arryns; and, especially, the 'trial by ordeal' of Tyrion Lannister, whose sellsword substitute, Bronn, dispatches Lysa Arryn's knightly master of arms, Sir Vardis, through the Moon-Door making him, in the words of the cruelly infantile Lord Robert, 'fly.' What is astonishing about this extended sequence is its end-game; that is, here, in the Vale's neurasthenic, *angst*-ridden court, presided over by the clearly cracked Lysa and her febrile, halfwit heir and offspring (still suckling at his mother's teat at the age of seven), the Imp and his mercenary sidekick get off scot-free, blithely decamping—what a scattercash toss of coin—from the Eyrie, via the *front* door rather than the Moon-Door because the code of chivalry and its basic norm of fidelity still thoroughly subtends this Occidental 'floating world.'[30] So here is a domain in which the rules of the game—the game of thrones—are sacrosanct, even inviolate, rendering Westoros a 'warlocks 'n' wizards' version of the *Rechstaat*.

If, that is, the rules of the game were not being violated all the time, ruptured so much that Lysa's release of Tyrion looks like the exception that *proves* the following

5, directed by A. Taylor, D. Minahan, D. Nutter, B. Kirk, T. Van Patten, A. Sakharov, D. Petrarca, A. Graves, M. Maclaren (USA: Home Box Office, 2012).

28 Martin, *A Game of Thrones*, 295–297, 522; David Benioff and D. B. Weiss, prods, "The Wolf and the Lion," *Game of Thrones*, season 1, episode 5, directed by A. Taylor, D. Minahan, D. Nutter, B. Kirk, T. Van Patten, A. Sakharov, D. Petrarca, A. Graves, M. Maclaren (USA: Home Box Office, 2011).

29 A. V. Dicey, *An Introduction to the Study of the Law of the Constitution* (London: Macmillan, 1959).

30 Martin, *A Game of Thrones*, 422–428, 522; David Benioff and D. B. Weiss, prods, "A Golden Crown," *Game of Thrones*, season 1, episode 6, directed by A. Taylor, D. Minahan, D. Nutter, B. Kirk, T. Van Patten, A. Sakharov, D. Petrarca, A. Graves, M. Maclaren (USA: Home Box Office, 2011).

rule: there are no rules here—or, if there are rules, then those rules are *made* to be *broken*.[31] Even the most cursory review of *Game of Thrones* yields a litany of breach with transgression abounding in almost every sphere of codified conduct. Take, for instance, the private realm of hearth and hospitality that, by Westerosi convention, is subject to the binding principle that once you have broken bread in someone's home, no harm can befall you. This hard-and-fast rule is spectacularly contravened by the faithless Freys, who lure the King of the North, Robb Stark, to the Two Towers under the pretext of a military alliance; but who, upon their guest's arrival, slaughter both him and his followers as payback for Stark's clandestine marriage to a slip of girl from the minor *noblesse*—Lady Jeyne Westerling—rather than, as previously agreed, one of the far more adiposally substantial Waldas on offer from their own house.[32] Or take another example: that of desire, and its 'laws,' principally those of love, sexuality and procreation, all of which have their fixed place and appointed time in the Westerosi schema of directives, stabilising human relations. Significant here is the high heteronormativity of the Ned-Catelyn marriage.[33] In its combination of affection and duty—a love match arising out of, and issuing from an alliance, arranged for the perpetuation of power, as much as progeny—the Stark connubial relationship provides an outlet for free-floating phallic *eros* (typified elsewhere in the series in the louche and lewd Tyrion, who, in his whoring, seems to have wandered in from one of Chaucer's more ribald tales),[34] as much as channels richly sentimental romance (embodied, at least early in the series by the dreamy Sansa, with her courtly love tales of Symeon Star Eyes).[35]

So a representation emerges here of Winterfell as a bower of marital bliss regulated and ruled over by a law of desire. But for, of course, the signal *exception* of Jon Snow, whose very existence as Ned's by-blow is a living rebuke to his wedding vows and a constant irritant to Cat,[36] his exceptionality always threatening to upset her very ordered world. Elsewhere, the disorder takes firm hold and deepens, this very exceptionality—Jon's bastardy—becoming the rule, with illegitimacy cropping up everywhere (think of Ramsay Bolton,[37] Edric Storm[38] and Gendry,[39] to name but a few), and illicit coupling the norm (including homosexual partners,

31 Martin, *A Game of Thrones*, 422–428; Benioff and Weiss, "A Golden Crown."

32 Martin, *A Storm of Swords*,193–201; David Benioff and D. B. Weiss, prods, "The Rains of Castamere," *Game of Thrones*, season 3, episode 9, directed by A. Taylor, D. Minahan, D. Nutter, B. Kirk, T. Van Patten, A. Sakharov, D. Petrarca, A. Graves, M. Maclaren (USA: Home Box Office, 2013).

33 Martin, *A Game of Thrones*, 22; Benioff and Weiss, "Winter is Coming."

34 Martin, *A Game of Thrones*, 679–681; David Benioff and D. B. Weiss, prods, "The Kingsroad," *Game of Thrones*, season 1, episode 2, directed by A. Taylor, D. Minahan, D. Nutter, B. Kirk, T. Van Patten, A. Sakharov, D. Petrarca, A. Graves, M. Maclaren (USA: Home Box Office, 2011.

35 Martin, *A Game of Thrones*, 139; Benioff and Weiss, "The Wolf and the Lion."

36 Martin, *A Game of Thrones*, 65; Benioff and Weiss, "The Kingsroad."

37 Martin, *A Storm of Swords*, 484; Benioff and Weiss, "Dark Wings, Dark Words."

38 Martin, *A Clash of Kings*, 565.

39 Martin, *A Game of Thrones*, 280; Benioff and Weiss, "Cripples, Bastards, and Broken Things."

such as gay lovers, Renly Baratheon and Ser Loras Tyrell).[40] Nowhere more so than with the *faux*-Baratheon dynasty, all of whom turn out to be pure Lannister—the lovely Myrcella, the *naïf* Tommen and that baddest of 'bad seeds,' the sadistic Joffrey—because each and every one of its tow-headed tots is, as their golden locks amply attest (first to Jon Arryn, then Ned Stark), the product of incest; specifically, between their uncle, Ser Jaime Lannister, the dashing Lord Commander of the Kingsguard, and his twin sister, their mother, the coldly beautiful Queen Cersei Baratheon (*née* Lannister).[41] It is their vigorous love-making which little Bran Stark has the ill luck to stumble upon, then tumble to his (near) death,[42] defenestrated by the startled guilty subjects of his transfixed gaze.

Not that this is the only instance in this world of what Gilles Deleuze and Felix Guattari would call anti-*Oedipe*;[43] for the deposed royal line, the Stuart-style 'kings across the water'—the Targaryen pretenders—routinely married, pharaonically, their own sisters. Only an all-too-necessary bride price (of a Dothraki army, required for Westeros's *Reconquista*) spared the ethereal Daenerys from a similar conjugal fate and the lifetime of matrimonial hell that would clearly have followed nuptials to her manifestly deranged brother, the 'beggar-king,' Viserys.[44] Of course, the Targaryens are a very special instance here, set off from the general Westerosi run: what with their old Valyrian origins, their dragon-riding prowess, and their silvery tresses' unearthly glow, they seem less a fantasy equivalent of *mitteleuropa*'s intermarrying Habsburgs (for that, see Frank Herbert's *Dune*, and its *Almanache de Gotha* of planetary Great Houses)[45] and more akin to the High Elves of Tolkien's Lothlorien. All of which is to say, that by virtue of their supernatural in/humanity, the Targaryens, may very well be *exempt*, as a species apart, from the incest taboo that has obtained, historically, in Westeros, the writ of which continues to run, and indeed is renewing itself with added vigour, under the Rh'llor' cult's Mosaic-like iteration of incest as 'abomination.'[46] It remains unclear, however, whether this nay-saying form of religious fundamentalism—with its implacably prohibitive 'No! In thunder'—would excuse the Targaryens.

Most certainly *not* eligible for relief, though, would be those sibling *sweet*-hearts, (the anything but sweet) Jaime and Cersie, whose ukase-defying coital lust is all too *human*, thereby rendering any sort of Targaryen-like, species-ist special pleading unavailable.[47] Mention of Jaime, popularly known as 'the Kingslayer,' brings this section to the last (but certainly not least) Westerosi example of lealty's limits and legality's failures. This is because, despite all the professions of fidelity

40 Martin, *A Clash of Kings*, 348; Benioff and Weiss, "The Wolf and the Lion."
41 Martin, *A Game of Thrones*, 486; Benioff and Weiss, "Winter is Coming."
42 Martin, *A Game of Thrones*, 85; Benioff and Weiss, "Winter is Coming."
43 Gilles Deleuze and Felix Guattari, *Anti-Oedipus: Capitalism and schizophrenia*, trans. R. Hurley, M. Seem, and H. Lane (New York: Viking Press, 1977).
44 Martin, *A Game of Thrones*, 32.
45 Frank Herbert, *Dune* (New York: Ace Books, 1990).
46 Martin, *A Clash of Kings*, 158.
47 Martin, *A Game of Thrones*, 85; Benioff and Weiss, "Winter is Coming."

made here, all the submissions to law on display, the principal denizens of Westeros are, to a man, oathbreakers—be they cruel Bolton or courageous Baratheon, false Frey or honest Tully, money-loving Lannister or noble Stark. For, indeed, all the Great Houses—Tyrell, Martell, Hightower, Arryn, Manderly—are kingslayers, guilty, by association, of conspiring with the actual regicide, Jaime Lannister who, in stark violation of his Kingsguard oath, murdered His Grace King Aerys II, the last (and worst) of the reigning Targaryen dynasty.[48] Of course, Aerys was mad—with all that inbreeding, who would not be?—enjoying nothing more than boiling his rivals alive (as he did to Ned's father and brother).[49] So a 'just' end to an unjust reign, Aerys being lawfully executed for his crimes rather than unlawfully usurped, then assassinated? Such is the historical consensus here, at least as retroactively told by the victors, the supporters of the Baratheon succession.

This tale turns darker—and far less palatable—as the narrative proceeds, revealing *en passant*, further details about the deposition of the former ruling family. For 'mad Aerys' was not the only Targaryen the rebels disposed of here, their murder squad's spree extending to his son, Prince Rhaegar, Rhaegar's Dornish born wife, Princess Elia, and—here's the real clincher—the royal couple's two young children, Prince Aegon and Princess Rhaenys.[50] So, in this instance, we have not just oathbreakers, not even 'kingslayers,' but—like the Bolsheviks at Ekaterinburg[51] or Vader at the Jedi Temple[52]—heinous kiddie-killers, all in the name of expediency. Which suggests that the Seven Kingdoms is not the state of law, immutable and unchanging, that the series' opening and subsequent scenes seem to suggest; it is rather, a realm of and in juridical flux, subject to a peculiar kind of *politics* in which no one is safe and nothing sacred, where all is up for grabs, with everyone and everything subject to yet another contingent spin of Dame Fortuna's wheel.

The postmodern condition as premodern conflict: *Il Principe*, Shakespeare's histories and the theatre of Realpolitik

This means that the sort of politics as practised in *A Game of Thrones* as either *pre*-modern or *post*-modern—yet anything but 'high modern.' For modernity, as represented some time ago by Jean-François Lyotard,[53] defined politics in terms

48 Martin, *A Game of Thrones*, 116; Benioff and Weiss, "The Kingsroad."

49 Martin, *A Clash of Kings*, 796–799.

50 Martin, *A Game of Thrones*, 112–117; Benioff and Weiss, "The Kingsroad."

51 On the murder of the Russian Imperial family, see: Chris Cook and John Stevenson, *The Longman Handbook of Modern European History 1763–1991* (New York: Longman Group, 1992), 148, 311.

52 *Star Wars: Episode III—Revenge of the Sith*, directed by George Lucas (USA: Twentieth Century Fox Film Corporation, 2005).

53 Jean-François Lyotard, *The Postmodern Condition: A Report on Knowledge*, trans. Geoff Bennington and Brian Massumi (Minneapolis: University of Minnesota Press, 1989).

of two overarching, ideological scripts: one turning on the economic question of 'who owns?' (the Marxist script), the other on the identic question of 'who has rights?' (the liberal script)—both now exhausted, their sell-by dates long expired. The narrative desuetude of which *Game of Thrones* affirms in a portrayal of politics which is post-ideological in the extreme, deploying even the fanatical faith of the 'Church militant'—Rh'llor as code for Islam, the Seven as Roman Catholicism, and so on—on purely strategic grounds (rather than as an end in itself), all the while dispensing with modernity's binarised scripts' respective characterological fixities, split between permanent friends (for Marxism, the proletariat; for liberalism, the autonomous subject) or enemies (for Marxism, the *bourgeoisie* of global finance capital; for liberalism, the nanny state, either leftist or authoritarian) and substituting, instead, a notion of the Schmittian-like 'frenemy,'[54] useful only to the extent that one's kaleidoscopically shifting interests and ever-changing agendas are advanced. Central here is the personage of Lord Peter Baelish, the *arriviste* 'Littlefinger' being a classic instance of the *novo hominem*, ever on the make, rising onwards and upwards, but always an aporetic figure of radical indeterminacy, of ambiguity: can he be trusted? Is he ally or foe? On which side is he? The Starks'? The Lannisters'? Both? Neither? The answers to which turn out to be as otiose as the questions posed because, in the game of thrones, there are no sides—only that of one's *survival*.[55] The success of which turns on a strategisation which might be best distilled, in a trite contemporary apothegem, as 'looking out for "number one"'; that is, being ready, willing and able to advance one's cause by any necessary means: in Littlefinger's case, taking the life of his not-so-fair lady wife, the eminently disposable, Lysa Arryn, all the while further plotting to exterminate his pathetic little step-son, Lord Robert, the heir to The Eyrie and the guardianship of the West.[56] This murder of children suggests a literary analogue that situates the series politically as much as aesthetically. Who, after all, is the most famous murderer of children in world literature, if not Shakespeare's Richard III; as Duke of Gloucester, he ordered the execution of his two nephews, the 'princes in the tower,' one of the most despicable criminal acts in English history and certainly the most reprehensible in Shakespeare's history plays about the War of the Roses, of which *Richard III* is the last, and the best.[57] Shakespeare is referenced here, and the Elizabethan period against which his plays—comedies, tragedies, but especially *histories*—were written, because it precisely *historicises* the kind of politics that Martin invokes in the series.

54 Carl Schmitt, *Political Theology: Four Chapters on the Concept of Sovereignty*, trans George Schwab (Cambridge, MA: MIT Press, 1985).
55 Martin, *A Game of Thrones*, 529; David Benioff and D. B. Weiss, prods, "The Pointy End," *Game of Thrones*, season 1, episode 8, directed by A. Taylor, D. Minahan, D. Nutter, B. Kirk, T. Van Patten, A. Sakharov, D. Petrarca, A. Graves, M. Maclaren (USA: Home Box Office, 2011).
56 Martin, *A Storm of Swords*, 1115.
57 William Shakespeare, *King Richard III*, ed. Antony Hammond (London: Methuen, 1981).

In terms of historical context, this series is more 'renaissance' than 'mediaeval,' because for all its self-conscious referencing of 'the waning of the Middle Ages'—with knights errant and damsels in distress—the politics trumpeted here turns, not so much on a divinely anointed king, as it does on an ambitious *prince*, driven by glory and ever ready, as it were, to *carpe diadem*; that is, seize the crown of the Seven Kingdoms by any and all modalities, ascending the Iron Throne regardless of legitimacy, religion, right or reason. So the figure who bestrides *Game of Thrones*, and indeed the cycle as a whole, is that of 'the Prince,' who seems to have stepped out of Niccolò Machiavelli's *Il Principe*.[58] Not that this connection is unique to me, many fans (and critics) of the series have hailed, as noted before in the introduction, *A Song of Ice and Fire* as something like a 'Machiavellian fantasy,' a glib throw-away depiction which this chapter proposes to take *seriously* because, as with Shakespeare's *oeuvre*, Martin's series is giving its readers yet another literary formulation of Machiavellianism. Though, in this case, one which speaks to and expresses our postmodern times of the twenty-first century as much as Shakespeare's Machiavellian *dramatis personae*—not only Richard III, but Iago, Malvolio, and so on—reflected his premodern world of the sixteenth century.

The difference being, of course, that while Shakespeare's Richard III is repulsively *faux*-Machiavellian in his Tyrion-esque misshapen bile, Martin's Robert Baratheon is not *nearly* Machiavellian enough in the true sense of the word. Of course, he looks like one of the Sforzas, even the Medicis, those Machiavellian *beau ideals*-as-dynasts—at least at the start of his reign, if Ned, Cersei and others' flashbacks are to be relied upon: that is, Robert as the charismatic leader and military genius.[59] Yet as king, Robert has no *capacity* for rule, and lacks the key trait demanded, according to Machiavelli, for sustaining a princely regime: namely, *prudence*,[60] itself based on sound advice-taking[61] and yielding a *juris*prudence of sensible policy- and rule-making. If anything, Robert goes out of his way to be *imprudent*, by squandering the treasury on fripperies, like the King's Landing tourney; by ruining his figure and health by endless gourmandising and profligacy; finally, by surrounding himself with a nest of vipers—his scheming in-laws, as powers not so much *behind*, as encircling the throne, like a noose around a soon-to-be-hanged neck.[62] Not only does Robert enable his own untimely end by providing the Lannisters-as-executioners all too easy access to himself, he practically *guarantees* it by antagonising each and every one of them through neglect or insult—Cersie, Jaime, Lancel, Tywin: all people who never, ever *forget*, let alone forgive.[63] Even when he displays remnants

58 Machiavelli, *The Prince and The Discourses*.
59 Martin, *A Game of Thrones*, 112–117.
60 Machiavelli, *The Prince and The Discourses*, 11, 61.
61 Machiavelli, *The Prince and The Discourses*, 88–89.
62 Martin, *A Game of Thrones*, 40, 193–195, 485–488.
63 Martin, *A Game of Thrones*, 427–430.

of his old 'derring do' character—for example, in his undying love for Lyanna Stark, long gathered to her ancestors—such passionate commitment only serves to alienate further his embittered and vengeful Queen. And, in the process, feed his own ever-growing appetite for avenging Lyanna's untimely death against the Targaryens-in-exile: that man-child who would be king, Viserys, and, of course, Daenerys.[64] Though both are innocent of any crime here, a sanguinary Robert would have smothered each of the royal siblings in their cradles *but* for the counsel of mentor Lord Jon Arryn and friend Lord Eddard Stark, in turn, benighted Hands of the King.

Robert's shortfall of prudence is devastating because it produces the kind of parody of Machiavelli that so terrified the Renaissance, and still resonates darkly for us today, as it conjures up a world of retribution, conspiracy, denunciation, the stab in the back; in short, the secret state of Lord Varys, whose minions—his 'little sparrows'—are everywhere, their whispers even more menacing than the 'dark wings, dark words'[65] of the ravens used for distance communication. No wonder Lord Eddard loses his head; it would be very surprising indeed if he kept it, so inimical in his *virtu* to the game of thrones, and its fractious 'time of troubles.' For this is an epoch in which not only, as Hamlet said, the '*time* is out of joint,'[66] but *narrative* is as well. This is precisely why, according to this chapter, the *form* of *A Song of Ice and Fire* is one of multiple, highly individualised narrators. Unlike Tolkien's *Lord of the Rings*, where an omniscient narrator is very much in charge of determining the plot, with the occasional look-see into select characters' consciousness, here in the novelistic *A Game of Thrones* and elsewhere in the written (as opposed to televised) cycle the story is *said*, if that solecism can be permitted, from a series of very limited, even at times unreliable points of view, each with their own vocal inflection *upon* and reflection *of* the event they record: the ironic distance of Tyrion,[67] the trickster wiliness of Arya,[68] the girlish gush of Sansa,[69] the controlled *ressentiment* of Jon,[70] and so forth. What this narrative form conveys is important in terms of context; that is, how the tale is told—fractured, multiple, individual, as well as lacking any clear linearity of cause and effect—gestures towards, indeed enacts aesthetically the kind of landscape against which its plotted action takes place. Which, for all its 'dungeons 'n dragons' touches, is *ours*: a postmodern world in which relativism reigns in the wake of any metanarrative's collapse—be it Marxist, liberal or, even, theological with a 'return of the religious repressed' sermonising on either an axis of evil or the clash of civilisations.

64 Martin, *A Game of Thrones*, 298–301, 351–358.
65 Martin, *A Game of Thrones*, 480.
66 William Shakespeare, *Hamlet* (Chandni Chowk, Delhi: Global Media, 2007), 43.
67 Martin, *A Game of Thrones*, 87.
68 Martin, *A Game of Thrones*, 215.
69 Martin, *A Game of Thrones*, 139.
70 Martin, *A Game of Thrones*, 49.

Essos' Arab spring and the return of the queen: Daenerys Stormborn as Mater Draconisa

This is a world in which, as Jean Baudrillard would put it, there are no laws, only rules;[71] and, as noted before, these rules are made not only to be *broken* but, even more, smashed to smithereens—like Old Valyria of myth and legend, blown to bits during its ominous 'Doom.'[72] That this historic, Atlantis-like catastrophe is referenced repeatedly throughout the cycle suggests an inescapable conclusion: specifically, if 'collapse'[73]—as Jared Diamond would term it—has come before to this world, *it will come again*. And, indeed, it looms all too palpably, as Westeros—*and* Essos—slide into civil strife, each continent torn apart by its feuding houses and marauding *khalasars*, whose respective bloodletting leaves nothing in their wakes but a wasteland of pillage, rapine and scorched earth.[74] What—or, more to the point, *who*—will arrest this senseless spin of the historical cycle, intervening in the game of thrones before it destroys all of its players? The answer, surely, lies in the 'return of the King'—or, rather, Queen, the exiled Daenerys, the 'Stormborm,' Khaleesi of the Dothraki, the *fin de ligne* of the blood of the dragon. It is her triumphant march across the East, liberating the slave cities of Astapor, Mexereen, Yunkai and Volantis,[75] that seems to have taken a leaf out of Machiavelli's 'art of war'[76] because, instead of the mercenaries preferred by her opponents, she gathers round her an army of emancipation: the now free Unsullied, joining the remnants of her old *khalasar* as well as voluntary camp-followers. This gathering strikes a note that resonates in a register hitherto alien to the game of thrones; for it chimes in with the startling suggestion that 'the Queen across the water,'[77] Daenerys—as *the* figure of *ancien regime* legitimacy, and consequently nomological tradition—may usher in a *new* law of *Recht*, and with it a new order, one horizontal rather than vertical, egalitarian rather than hierarchical: as Antonio Negri and Michael Hardt (as well as Machiavelli) would say, a society of the democratic 'multitude' rather than monarchical 'Empire.'[78]

The only—but alas *fatal*—problem here is that these noble experiments in Skinnerian 'civic republicanism' are so short-lived.[79] Liberty transmogrifies all

71 Jean Baudrillard, *The Transparency of Evil: Essays on Extreme Phenomena*, trans James Benedict (New York: Verso, 1993), 36, 160.

72 Martin, *A Game of Thrones*, 24.

73 Jared Diamond, *Collapse: How Societies Choose to Fail or Succeed* (New York: Viking, 2005).

74 Martin, *A Game of Thrones*, 665–674.

75 Martin, *A Storm of Swords*, 571–589; Martin, *A Dance with Dragons*, 84.

76 Niccolò Machiavelli, *The Art of War*, trans. and ed. Christopher Lynch (Chicago: University of Chicago Press, 2003).

77 Martin, *A Clash of Kings*, 986.

78 Michael Hardt and Antonio Negri, *Empire* (Cambridge, MA: Harvard University Press, 2000), 61–63. See also Michael Hardt and Antonio Negri, *Multitude: War and Democracy in the Age of Empire* (New York: The Penguin Press, 2004).

79 Gisela Bock, Quentin Skinner and Maurizio Viroli (eds), *Machiavelli and Republicanism*, (Cambridge: Cambridge University Press, 1990).

too easily into tyranny the moment—for example, in Astapor—Queen Daenerys and her 'coaliation of the willing' move on to other (though hardly greener) pastures.[80] That Cleon, the Ghiscari butcher-turned-demagogue, subverts so quickly Astapori responsible government bespeaks not only its fragility but the core problem,[81] identified by Machiavelli, inherent with the multitude itself: they are too deracinated, free-floating and unanchored by any kind interest, propertied or otherwise.[82] In short, the multitude has no *ownership*, literal and figurative, in or of the *socius* of which they are a part. This is why their enfranchising efforts always revert, as Machiavelli implies in the *Discourses*,[83] to dictatorship. And not only here in the Essos' mysterious and highly orientalised East, for a similar sort of theme is being sounded at the opposite end of the series' world with that emblem of exclusion—the Wall—and the way in which the very human Wildings are fleeing south, bringing their radically libertarian values with them, very much at odds with those hieratic ones of the Night's Watch, sworn to military chains of command.[84] That it is the outsider *par excellence*, Eddard Stark's bastard Jon Snow, who becomes Lord Commander of the Night's Watch at the very moment of its unlikely alliance with the Wildlings is one of the many ironies in a text full of ironies,[85] suggestive of a legality of right, here at the other end of Empire, which is as inclusive as that of Daenerys: one that forges a new collective of Wildling and Westerosi who are led, not ruled over, by an elected head, himself outlaw.[86] If only, that is, the Wildlings were, in fact, the 'noble savages' the cycle makes them out to be, living in a 'state of nature,'[87] autonomically. Far from it; they look, instead, like something out of Sigmund Freud's *Totem and Taboo*,[88] with, for example, Craster, who, as both father *and* husband of his children, functions as a figure of obscene *jouissance*, endlessly enjoying his symptom in the free-for-all of licence (rather than liberty) that exists beyond the Wall.

Not that a demonic *demos* or a cruel despotism are the *only* political choices here. In fact, there is a 'third way,' which, incidentally, is far worse than either, being thoroughly corrupting in its valorisation of *exchange* rather than use, prioritising money as not only its means but *ends*, reifying all—agents, allies, armies—as the wage slaves of a *bourgeois* oligarchy. Here is the true meaning of the sobriquet 'rich as a Lannister,' because it points to the fact that, despite their ancient

80 Martin, *A Storm of Swords*, 774–792.
81 Martin, *A Storm of Swords*, 982–984.
82 Machiavelli, *The Prince and The Discourses*.
83 Machiavelli, *The Prince and The Discourses*.
84 Martin, *A Clash of Kings*, 995.
85 Martin, *A Storm of Swords*, 1093–1097.
86 Martin, *A Storm of Swords*, 95–104.
87 John Locke, "Selections from Two Treatises of Government (Civil Government)," in *Lloyds Introduction to Jurisprudence*, ed. Michael (M. D. A.) Freeman (London: Sweet and Maxwell, 1994).
88 Sigmund Freud, *Totem and Taboo: Resemblances between the Psychic Lives of Savages and Neurotics*, trans. A. A. Brill (London: Routledge and Sons, 1919).

descent as one of the great houses, the Lion's values are profoundly plutocratic rather than aristocratic, contract (rather than combat) being their overarching *modus operandi*, as suggested in the highly telling mercantile phrase 'A Lannister always pays his debts.'[89] That this looming commonwealth of contract, which the Lannisters, as the Rothschilds of Westeros, so clearly represent and portend—gold sprouting from their heads as much, so the apocrypha goes, their bottoms—is precisely the kind of society Machiavelli feared the most, at least according to historian of ideas J. G. A. Pocock's reading: a place where everything was up for sale, and where all could be bought and sold.[90] Counterposed against this sort of fundamentally venal *ethos*—which knows the price of everything but the value of nothing—is another sort of polity, a different kind of *socius*: connected yet independent, individual yet collective, peaceful yet ready to fight for its freedom: in short, Machiavellian democracy, as sketched in the *Discourses*,[91] and which is '*a venir*,' or 'to come' in the cycle. Not that this 'Machiavellian moment'[92] which the text longs for looks ever to arrive, an 'Event'[93] of Badiouvian proportions, not only postponing it indefinitely but forever interrupting the game of thrones,[94] and its ever-revolving options for democracy, tyranny and oligarchy. That event is captured in the Starks often-repeated mantra, 'Winter is coming,'[95] itself a presage of *our* contemporary climate change: only here, unlike global warming, it could leave this continent, and others frozen by a New Ice Age, and overrun by the return of the White Walkers—the living dead.[96]

Who, or rather *what* (to reverse my earlier question) will defeat this zombie army, arrest the wintering of the world and save the day? *Game of Thrones* affords its spectators (and readers) a tantalising solution in the first season's (and novel's) mesmerising final scene, one which suggests that only *nature* can tame nature, its fundamental law—the *lex natura*[97]—overshadowing any and all of humanity's power-playing games. This re-emergence of nature and its law is vividly realised in the concluding scene of Season 1 of *Game of Thrones*. There, the portrayal of a naked and charcoal-smeared Daenerys, slowly rising amid the smoking embers of Khal Drogo's funeral pyre and nursing her newly hatched dragons, is pregnant with meaning, both literally and figuratively.[98] Figurative in the sense that here

89 Martin, *A Game of Thrones*, 456.

90 J. G. A. Pocock, *The Machiavellian Moment: Florentine Political Thought and the Atlantic Republican Tradition* (Princeton, NJ: Princeton University Press, 1975).

91 Machiavelli, *The Prince and The Discourses*.

92 Pocock, *The Machiavellian Moment*.

93 For an introduction to this concept of the 'event,' see Alain Badiou, *Being and Event* (New York: Continuum, 2005).

94 Martin, *A Storm of Swords*, 841.

95 Martin, *A Game of Thrones*, 24; Benioff and Weiss, "Winter is Coming."

96 Martin, *A Game of Thrones*, 240.

97 Thomas Aquinas, "Selections from Summa Theologica," in *Lloyds Introduction to Jurisprudence*, ed. Michael (M. D. A.) Freeman (London: Sweet and Maxwell, 1994).

98 Martin, *A Game of Thrones*, 804–807; Benioff and Weiss, "Fire and Blood."

Daenerys has been elevated by the scene to a kind of madonna-like status: the *mater draconisa*, whose reptilian loved ones—the un/holy trinity of Viserion, Rhaegal and Drogon—will inaugurate, in their fulfilment of the Targaryen law of 'waking the dragon,' a 'new dispensation,' promising salvation for us all.[99] No wonder the scene concludes with Daenerys worshipped as something like a *theotokos* or God-bearer; only, here, she is *dracotokos*, or 'mother of dragons' and, with it, an instantiation of the miraculous love between mariological parent and divine child.

'Can spring be far behind?': the wintering of Westeros as climate change and the game of laws' principle of hope

As tempting as it is, this chapter resists such a typological reading, opting instead for a more literal one that takes this scene of 'natural supernaturalism' at its most physical, its most material. Theology accedes to biology in the *love* dramatised between Daenerys and her dragons; and this accession—the corporeal displacing the otherworldly—is, according to Haig Patapan's brilliant book, *Machiavelli in Love,* profoundly Machiavellian.[100] As 'Machiavellians in love,' Daenerys and her dragons complement and complete each other in their somatic mutual need, each having a vital 'lack' which the other fills and, indeed, *must* have to survive: the 'Unburnt'—as Daenerys is now called, having become herself a force of nature—*must* have the dragons to ride, if ever she is to return to Westeros; and the dragons *must* have Daenerys, if ever they are to live on to be ridden, as in fact they are most clearly intended (and want) to be. Thus, this relationship is predicated on an organic bond that distinguished philosopher of science, Isabelle Stengers, would call 'the symbiotic.'[101] The obligatory mutuality of the symbiotic is in bold contrast to 'the parasitism' of the White Walkers,[102] who inhabit and, in so doing, obliterate their victims. This obliteration is, if ever there was one, a grim metaphor of our own relationship with nature; particularly, the way it comes back to bite modernity as a direct consequence of its own devastating game of thrones. Which, in turn, presses home all the more the necessity for a new relationship between wo/man and nature that, as staged in the scene between Daenerys and her dragons, turns on reciprocal advantage rather than unilateral exploitation. In so doing, this scene blurs the boundaries between, even levels the positionality of subject and object, user and used so that what was a parasite—for example, man's dominion, so-called, over nature—becomes a symbiote, the negotiations, indeed

99 Martin, *A Clash of Kings*, 188–192.

100 Haig Patapan, *Machiavelli in Love: The Modern Politics of Love and Fear* (Lanham, MD: Lexington Books, 2006).

101 Isabelle Stengers, *Cosmopolitics I (Posthumanities),* trans. Robert Bononno (Minneapolis: University of Minnesota Press, 2010), 35–36.

102 Martin, *A Game of Thrones*, 8–11.

adjudication of its up-for-grabs 'game of laws,' trumping, then superseding the miasmal mess of the Earth made by the game of thrones.

That last point, however, is more this chapter's bottom line than Martin's, as *A Song of Ice and Fire* is far from over, two books remaining in its heptalogy. Given this open-endedness, it is still unclear from the story whether the symbiotic[103] is capable of turning the tide against the parasitic, or the latter's game of thrones being overturned by the former's game of laws. But one can only hope. Moreover, Martin, himself, may fuel that hope, holding out, in the prospect of the Law of Nature-as-'*natural* supernaturalism,'[104] an(O)ther 'game' that would constrain, and override, sovereignty's ultimately self-destructive *divertissement* of politics. Which is why, ultimately, Martin is a necessary supplement to, and corrective of Machiavelli, the latter having been in/famously silent on the entire sphere of natural law. Why? Presumably, because, as a realm of moral absolutes, natural law's 'transcendental truths' would threaten, even trump the notion of game-like contingency so integral to Machiavelli's political machinations. Martin, though, out-'machiavellies' Machiavelli by demonstrating how contingency is writ large, as much in the *lex natura's* 'great chain of being' as the *lex humana's civis*, the former being just as contested, just as conflicted (parasitic White Walkers vs symbiotic dragon riders) as the latter (venally timocratic Lannisters vs the virtuously *noblesse oblige* Starks). In short, Martin 'machiavellianises' the law of nature by turning its timeless truisms, its static sublimity into an ever-changing, always dynamic and utterly riven competition ('survival of the magically fittest'?) where, much like the game of thrones, the risks are great, the stakes high and the outcome anything but certain.

And a good thing that is too, providing, as it does, for not just the aleatory vagaries of chance but the responsibilities of free will's *choice*: the choice to win or to lose, to live or to die. Now whether that choice in the game of laws Martin sketches is for the living win of the symbiotic or the deathly loss of the parasitic remains obscure; but the die may already be cast in this *spiel*, plumping for the former rather than the latter. This is because, for all the abundant pessimism on offer here in the social, political and economic ills this cycle allegorises—the global financial crisis (as Lannisterian kleptocracy), the Arab awakening (as Essos' slave revolts) and, especially, climate change (as either global cooling or warming), Martin strikes an optimistic note, especially in his valorisation, over White Walker parasitism,[105] of humanity and nature's symbiosis: as cooperative, as interactive, and as interdependent, imaged in the relationship of Daenerys with her dragons. In so doing, I think Martin may not only offer hope, but hope that—as distinguished law-and-*litterateuse* Mme Justice Jeanne Gaakeer

103 Stengers, *Cosmopolitics I (Posthumanities)*, 35–36.

104 M. H. Abrams, *Natural Supernaturalism: Tradition and Revolution in Romantic Literature* (New York: Norton, 1973).

105 Martin, *A Game of Thrones*, 8–11.

might advise—'*springs* eternal,' literally.[106] Here, Martin does so by echoing, and alluding to that most *hopeful* of Romantic poems, Shelley's tribute to nature, 'Ode to the West Wind,' especially, in its closing three lines which, as if premonitory of *Game of Thrones*' ecology, expectantly suggest a thaw to follow the freeze-to-come: 'Be through my lips to unawakened Earth/ . . . The trumpet of a prophecy! O wind/ . . . If Winter comes, can Spring be far behind?'[107]

Bibliography

Books, book chapters, journals

Abrams, M. H. *Natural Supernaturalism: Tradition and Revolution in Romantic Literature*. New York: Norton, 1973.

Aquinas, Thomas. "Selections from Summa Theologica." In *Lloyds Introduction to Jurisprudence*. Edited by M. D. A. Freeman. London: Sweet and Maxwell, 1994.

Badiou, Alain. *Being and Event*. New York: Continuum, 2005.

Baudrillard, Jean. *The Transparency of Evil: Essays on Extreme Phenomena*. Translated by James Benedict. New York: Verso, 1993.

Bentham, Jeremy. "Anarchical Fallacies." In *Nonsense upon Stilts: Bentham, Burke and Marx on the Rights of Man*. Edited by Jeremy Waldron. New York: Methuen, 1987.

Bock, Gisela, Skinner, Quentin and Viroli, Maurizio (eds). *Machiavelli and Republicanism*. Cambridge: Cambridge University Press, 1990.

Cook, Chris and Stevenson, John. *The Longman Handbook of Modern European History 1763–1991*. New York: Longman Group, 1992.

Cover, Robert. "Violence and the Word." *The Yale Law Journal* 95(8) (1986): 1601–1629.

Deleuze, Gilles and Guattari, Felix. Anti-*Oedipus: Capitalism and Schizophrenia*. Translated by R. Hurley, M. Seem, and H. Lane (New York: Viking Press, 1977).

Diamond, Jared. *Collapse: How Societies Choose to Fail or Succeed*. New York: Viking, 2005.

Dicey, A. V. *An Introduction to the Study of the Law of the Constitution*. London: Macmillan, 1959).

Dickens, Charles. *A Christmas Carol and Other Stories*. Westminster, MD: Modern Library, 2000.

Durkheim, Émile. *The Division of Labour in Society*. New York: Macmillan, 1933.

Freud, Sigmund. *Totem and Taboo: Resemblances between the Psychic Lives of Savages and Neurotics*. Translated by A. A. Brill. London: Routledge and Sons, 1919.

Frye, Northrop. "Historical Criticism: Theory of Modes." In *Anatomy of Criticism: Four Essays*, by Northrop Frye. Princeton, NJ: Princeton University Press, 1957.

Gaakeer, Jeanne. *Hope Springs Eternal: An Introduction to the Works of James Boyd White*. Amsterdam: Amsterdam University Press, 1998.

106 Jeanne Gaakeer, *Hope Springs Eternal: An Introduction to the Works of James Boyd White* (Amsterdam: Amsterdam University Press, 1998).

107 P. B. Shelley, "Ode to the West Wind," in *Shelley: Poetical Works*, ed. Thomas Hutchinson (London: Oxford University Press, 1970).

Gilligan, Carol. *In a Different Voice: Psychological Theory and Women's Development.* Cambridge, MA: Harvard University Press, 1982.
Hardt, Michael and Negri, Antonio. *Empire.* Cambridge, MA: Harvard University Press, 2000.
———. *Multitude: War and Democracy in the Age of Empire.* New York: The Penguin Press, 2004.
Herbert, Frank. *Dune.* New York: Ace Books, 1990.
Kelsen, Hans. *The Pure Theory of Law.* Translated by Max Knight. Berkeley: University of California Press, 1967.
Locke, John. "Selections from Two Treatises of Government (Civil Government)." In *Lloyds Introduction to Jurisprudence.* Edited by Michael (M. D. A.) Freeman. London: Sweet and Maxwell, 1994.
Lyotard, Jean-François. *The Postmodern Condition: A Report on Knowledge.* Translated by Geoff Bennington and Brian Massumi. Minneapolis: University of Minnesota Press, 1989.
Machiavelli, Niccolò. *The Prince and The Discourses.* Translated by Luigi Ricci. Toronto: Random House Inc., 1950.
———. *The Art of War.* Translated and edited by Christopher Lynch. Chicago: University of Chicago Press, 2003.
Maine, Henry S. *Ancient Law: Its Connection with the Early History of Society and Its Relation to Modern Ideas.* London: Hasell, Watson & Viney Ltd, 1906.
Martin, George R. R. *A Game of Thrones.* New York: Bantam Books, 1996.
———. *A Clash of Kings.* New York: Bantam Books, 1999.
———. *A Storm of Swords.* New York: Bantam Books, 2000.
———. *A Feast for Crows.* New York: Bantam Books, 2005.
———. *A Dance with Dragons.* New York: Bantam Books, 2011.
———. *The Winds of Winter.* Forthcoming.
———. *A Dream of Spring.* Forthcoming.
Patapan, Haig. *Machiavelli in Love: The Modern Politics of Love and Fear.* Lanham, MD: Lexington Books, 2006.
Pocock, John (J. G. A.). *The Machiavellian Moment: Florentine Political Thought and the Atlantic Republican Tradition.* Princeton, NJ: Princeton University Press, 1975.
———. *Virtue, Commerce and History.* New York: Cambridge University Press, 1985.
Schmitt, Carl. *Political Theology: Four Chapters on the Concept of Sovereignty.* Translated by George Schwab. Cambridge, MA: MIT Press, 1985.
Shakespeare, William. Edited by Antony Hammond. *King Richard III.* London: Methuen, 1981.
———. *Hamlet.* Chandni Chowk, Delhi: Global Media, 2007.
Shelley, P. B. "Ode to the West Wind." In *Shelley: Poetical Works.* Edited by Thomas Hutchinson. London: Oxford University Press, 1970.
Stengers, Isabelle. *Cosmopolitics I (Posthumanities).* Translated by Robert Bononno. Minneapolis: University of Minnesota Press, 2010.

Films

Star Wars: Episode III—Revenge of the Sith. Directed by George Lucas. USA: Twentieth Century Fox Film Corporation, 2005.

Television

Series

Benioff, David and Weiss, D. B., prods, *Game of Thrones: The Complete First Season.* USA: Home Box Office, 2012.
———, *Game of Thrones: The Complete Second Season.* USA: Home Box Office, 2012.
———, *Game of Thrones: The Complete Third Season.* USA: Home Box Office, 2013.

Episodes

Benioff, David and Weiss, D. B., prods, "Winter is Coming," *Game of Thrones*, season 1, episode 1. Directed by A. Taylor, D. Minahan, D. Nutter, B. Kirk, T. Van Patten, A. Sakharov, D. Petrarca, A. Graves, M. Maclaren. USA: Home Box Office, 2011.
Benioff, David and Weiss, D. B., prods, "The Kingsroad," *Game of Thrones*, season 1, episode 2. Directed by A. Taylor, D. Minahan, D. Nutter, B. Kirk, T. Van Patten, A. Sakharov, D. Petrarca, A. Graves, M. Maclaren. USA: Home Box Office, 2011.
Benioff, David and Weiss, D. B., prods, "Lord Snow," *Game of Thrones*, season 1, episode 3. Directed by A. Taylor, D. Minahan, D. Nutter, B. Kirk, T. Van Patten, A. Sakharov, D. Petrarca, A. Graves, M. Maclaren. USA: Home Box Office, 2011.
Benioff, David and Weiss, D. B., prods, "Cripples, Bastards, and Broken Things," *Game of Thrones*, season 1, episode 4. Directed by A. Taylor, D. Minahan, D. Nutter, B. Kirk, T. Van Patten, A. Sakharov, D. Petrarca, A. Graves, M. Maclaren. USA: Home Box Office, 2011.
Benioff, David and Weiss, D. B., prods, "The Wolf and the Lion," *Game of Thrones*, season 1, episode 5. Directed by A. Taylor, D. Minahan, D. Nutter, B. Kirk, T. Van Patten, A. Sakharov, D. Petrarca, A. Graves, M. Maclaren. USA: Home Box Office, 2011.
Benioff, David and Weiss, D. B., prods, "A Golden Crown," *Game of Thrones*, season 1, episode 6. Directed by A. Taylor, D. Minahan, D. Nutter, B. Kirk, T. Van Patten, A. Sakharov, D. Petrarca, A. Graves, M. Maclaren. USA: Home Box Office, 2011.
Benioff, David and Weiss, D. B., prods, "You Win or You Die," *Game of Thrones*, season 1, episode 7. Directed by A. Taylor, D. Minahan, D. Nutter, B. Kirk, T. Van Patten, A. Sakharov, D. Petrarca, A. Graves, M. Maclaren. USA: Home Box Office, 2011.
Benioff, David and Weiss, D. B., prods, "The Pointy End," *Game of Thrones*, season 1, episode 8. Directed by A. Taylor, D. Minahan, D. Nutter, B. Kirk, T. Van Patten, A. Sakharov, D. Petrarca, A. Graves, M. Maclaren. USA: Home Box Office, 2011.
Benioff, David and Weiss, D. B., prods, "Fire and Blood," *Game of Thrones*, season 1, episode 10. Directed by A. Taylor, D. Minahan, D. Nutter, B. Kirk, T. Van Patten, A. Sakharov, D. Petrarca, A. Graves, M. Maclaren. USA: Home Box Office, 2011.
Benioff, David and Weiss, D. B., prods, "The Ghost of Harrenhal," *Game of Thrones*, season 2, episode 5. Directed by A. Taylor, D. Minahan, D. Nutter, B. Kirk, T. Van Patten, A. Sakharov, D. Petrarca, A. Graves, M. Maclaren. USA: Home Box Office, 2012.
Benioff, David and Weiss, D. B., prods, "Dark Wings, Dark Words," *Game of Thrones*, season 3, episode 2. Directed by A. Taylor, D. Minahan, D. Nutter, B. Kirk, T. Van

Patten, A. Sakharov, D. Petrarca, A. Graves, M. Maclaren. USA: Home Box Office, 2013.

Benioff, David and Weiss, D. B., prods, "The Rains of Castamere," *Game of Thrones*, season 3, episode 9. Directed by A. Taylor, D. Minahan, D. Nutter, B. Kirk, T. Van Patten, A. Sakharov, D. Petrarca, A. Graves, M. Maclaren. USA: Home Box Office, 2013.

Other

"George R. R. Martin: Barbarians at the Gate." *Guardian*, Thursday 14 April 2011, http://www.guardian.co.uk/books/2011/apr/13/george-rr-martin-game-thrones.

"George R. R. Martin's *Game of Thrones* is Machiavelli's *The Prince*." *The Examiner*, Thursday 11 August 2011, http://www.examiner.com/review/george-r-r-martin-s-game-of-thrones-is-machiavelli-s-the-prince-1.

Part II

Juridical spectators

Chapter 6

Ambivalence and the spectatorship of violence: viewing *Inglourious Basterds*

Alison Young

One of the central tenets of recent critical research in cultural legal studies has been that the subject of law is discursively constructed. Although there is empirical solidity to the experiences involved in the commission of any act categorised as criminal under the law, it is through discourse that we generate a vocabulary for the various subject positions involved ('victim,' 'criminal,' 'witness,' 'judge,' and so on). One strand of this overarching interest in subject formation through culture has involved engagement with the cinematic image. In studying how the image is envisioned as an image of law and legality, it is crucial to examine it as a point of attachment and identification – as a subject position through which we speak and think. In respect of the criminal law, while the idea of actual victimisation is something that most individuals fear, crime fascinates: the consumption of images of crime is a staple of leisure activities, featuring in literature (where it has its own genre), computer games, television drama and cinema. In cinematic images of crime, the various crimes that make up the category we call violence are far more frequently represented on screen than any other. And although the violent encounter is regarded as something to be avoided in everyday life, it is a source of excitement and entertainment when it appears on the cinema screen. Such a complicated and contradictory relation to violence (fearing its actuality, yet desiring its representation) encourages investigation of the vicissitudes of our affective relation to the cinematic image of violence.

There is no singular format to the violent image; rather, films make use of a range of genres in which violence is an integral part: sometimes violence is envisioned as legitimate because it is carried out by the hero; in other genres, violence is linked to retributive justice or to vigilantism.[1] This chapter examines violence within a well-known cinematic genre; that of the war movie, as revised in *Inglourious Basterds*, directed by Quentin Tarantino (Universal Pictures, 2009). My focus is the specific subject position of *ambivalence* about violence in the

1 See, variously, Alison Young, "The Screen of the Crime: Judging the Affect of Cinematic Violence," *Social & Legal Studies* 18(1) (2009); *The Scene of Violence: Cinema, Crime, Affect* (London: Routledge 2010); and Alexandra Heller-Nicholas, *Rape-Revenge Films: A Critical Study* (New York: Mcfarland, 2011).

context of World War II, both as an affective relation between spectator and image, and also as an effect sought by the film. Such a focus allows consideration of some of the ways in which the constitutive role of images of crime and law is not straightforward. Indeed, our relation to the 'crime-image' is a deeply paradoxical one.[2] As Richard Sparks has pointed out, in the context of television crime drama, images of crime can soothe anxieties in the face of uncertainty.[3] It is not hard to see the pleasures that can be gained through discrete and compelling narratives of crime and punishment, as, 'terrified of darkness and death, of the horizon and the limit of the visible, we turn to the image as the bearer of light, we seek to destroy the horizon, we ask the image for consolation.'[4] However, the image is an uncertain source of comfort, and there is no guarantee that comfort will be forthcoming. Spectators watch the screen knowing that what they see is an image, a representation that holds out the possibility of contiguity with everyday life but which remains separate from it. Such a gap is both reassuring and terrifying: the image is 'only an image,' and therefore not real, yet the image can only be understood through its deployment of tropes of realism that offer synonymity with 'real life.'[5] To look real and yet not be real: such a gap prompts an irredeemable ambiguity.

Inglourious Basterds confronts the spectator with the ambiguities that may permeate the image, rendering its consolations limited and uncertain. Indeed, the spectator to *Inglourious Basterds* is compelled to adopt a viewing position that allows no possibility of a comfortable and soothing certainty about violence and law, but rather only ambivalence – and an ambivalence in which legality itself is proposed to be undecidable. To investigate the construction and implications of such a subject position within the film, it is necessary to read it as an 'encountered sign,' asking not so much 'What does it mean?' or 'How is violence depicted in the film?' but rather, borrowing from Jill Bennett, 'How does the image of violence work in *Inglourious Basterds*?' and 'How do we watch it?'[6]

Such an approach constructs what we see on screen as a 'crime-image' in order to open up the affective and ethical dimensions binding the spectator to the screen.[7] As such, my reading, which follows Gilles Deleuze's perspectives on film, examines the spectator's desire for attachment to the image (that is, through instances in which to experience affective intensity) rather than modes

2 Young, *The Scene of Violence: Cinema, Crime, Affect.*

3 Richard Sparks, "Dramatic Power: Television, Images of Crime and Law Enforcement," in *Censure, Politics and Criminal Justice*, ed. C. Sumner (Milton Keynes: Open University Press, 1990), 123.

4 Alison Young, *Imagining Crime: Textual Outlaws and Criminal Conversations* (London: Sage, 1996), 20.

5 Slavoj Žižek, *Everything You Always Wanted to Know About Lacan (but Were Afraid to Ask Hitchcock)* (London: Verso, 1992).

6 Jill Bennett, *Empathic Vision: Affect, Trauma and Contemporary Art* (Palo Alto, CA: Stanford University Press, 2005), 45.

7 See further, Young, *The Scene of Violence: Cinema, Crime, Affect.*

of identification arising through the operation of the gaze (as is conventional in structuralist or psychoanalytic approaches to film).[8] The chapter will investigate both the contours and cinematic devices of the film itself, and its critical reception, by analysing reviews of the meaning and implications of the film. The aim is to examine the spectator's predicament when ambivalence is the sole affective subject position offered in relation to violence and to law.

Watching *Inglourious Basterds*

The film tells a story of revenge and retribution, as is common to many crime films, but, as I will show, its tale of vengeance refuses to conform to spectators' expectations about how violent retribution should be carried out. It has two main narrative strands: the first revolves around Shosanna Dreyfus (Mélanie Laurent), seen early in the film escaping from Colonel Hans Landa (Christoph Waltz) after he orders the massacre of her family, who have been hiding out on a farm in rural occupied France. Shosanna changes her name to Emmanuelle Mimieux, and moves to Paris, where she manages a cinema. She meets Frederick Zoller (Daniel Brühl), German war hero and star of Joseph Goebbels's latest propaganda film, *Nation's Pride*; Zoller persuades Goebbels to hold the film's premiere in Shosanna's cinema, prompting her to plot the assassination of all those who will attend the film's screening.

The second strand centres upon a squad of American soldiers in France, the eponymous 'basterds,' whose mission is to kill Nazis and 'strike fear into the German's subconscious.' These are Jewish American soldiers, led by a southerner, Lieutenant Aldo Raine (Brad Pitt), part hillbilly, part Native American from Tennessee. The basterds spend their time ambushing German patrols and slaughtering soldiers. The squad is ordered to participate in a mission called 'Operation Kino,' for which they, together with a British officer disguised as a German, must rendezvous with a German film star turned British agent, in order to infiltrate the screening of *Nation's Pride*. Although the rendezvous goes desperately wrong, Operation Kino proceeds, and the two narrative strands converge in the final section of the film, in which both Shosanna and the surviving basterds wreak revenge upon the assembled Germans at the film screening.

Inglourious Basterds is thus a war movie, but it is set during a very specific war: the one that is considered to constitute a break with all previous forms of armed conflict, that introduced notions of the possible criminality of war itself, and that is regarded, thanks to the enfolding of the Holocaust within it, as an event that must not recur: 'never again' is a touchstone of its discursive representation. Films about World War II therefore offer spectators the opportunity to consider violence perpetrated in the name of national identity and under the mantle of military engagement, framed within a conflict that is already understood to represent

8 Gilles Deleuze, *Cinema 1: The Movement-Image* (London: The Athlone Press, 1986); *Cinema 2: The Time-Image* (London: The Athlone Press, 1989).

the worst excesses of violence against humanity itself. As a war movie, *Inglourious Basterds* is thus located within a pre-existing discursive frame, in which spectators expect to see Nazis and Allied soldiers as opposing armed forces, while the atrocity of the Holocaust takes place across Europe. The film certainly offers those themes, but presents them through a series of inversions and in a mode where their meanings are rendered indeterminate.

That *Inglourious Basterds* confronts spectators with a series of challenges and difficulties, many of which relate to its refusal to provide a subject position on violence that does not involve ambivalence, can be seen from the critical response to its release, which fell into three distinct categories. In the first, extravagant praise was showered upon the film: in the *Chicago Sun-Times*, Roger Ebert called it 'a considerable film'; for Peter Travers in *Rolling Stone*, it had a 'power punch' that 'comes from cinema itself'; in the *Village Voice*, J. Hoberman called it 'energetic, inventive, swaggering fun' and 'a consummate Hollywood entertainment' with 'enthusiastic performances and terrific dialogue'; and, writing in *The Independent*, Anthony Quinn found it 'an enjoyable reminder of why we sat up and noticed him in the first place.'[9] In this category of critical commentary, the film's narrative of oppression, war and vengeance was framed as something that could be experienced pleasurably thanks to formal aspects of the film's making (cinematography, editing, screenplay, and so on). In the second category can be found detraction of any merit that the film might have: in the *New York Times*, Manohla Dargis called it 'repellent,' and 'vulgar in the extreme'; and Sukhdev Sandhu in *The Telegraph* thought it was 'a film that's only interested in film; a gorgeously-constructed self-pastiche.'[10] Peter Bradshaw, film critic for the *Guardian*, described it as a film containing 'great heavy lumps of nothing':

> exasperatingly awful and transcendentally disappointing . . . a colossal, complacent, long-winded dud, a gigantic two-and-a-half hour anti-climax', in which 'over-stretched scene follows over-stretched scene in plonkingly conventional narrative order and each is stuffed with dull dialogue which made it feel like Mogadon was somehow being pumped into the cinema's airconditioning.[11]

The American film critic Jonathan Rosenbaum declared on his personal blog that the film was 'deeply offensive,' and complained that it transmitted 'the sort

9 Roger Ebert, "*Inglourious Basterds*," *Chicago Sun-Times*, 19 August 2009; J. Hoberman, "Quentin Tarantino's Inglourious Basterds Makes Holocaust Revisionism Fun," *Village Voice*, 18 August 2009; A. Quinn, "Dog Soldiers," *The Independent*, 21 August 2009; P. Travers, "*Inglourious Basterds*," *Rolling Stone Magazine*, 20 August 2009. All quoted reviews are unpaginated unless otherwise stated.

10 M. Dargis, "*Inglourious Basterds*: Tarantino Avengers in Nazi Movieland," *New York Times*, 21 August 2009; S. Sandhu, "*Inglourious Basterds*," *The Telegraph*, 20 August 2009.

11 P. Bradshaw, "Inglourious Basterds," *Guardian*, 19 August 2009.

of malaise that made [him] wonder periodically what it was (and is) about the film that seems morally akin to Holocaust denial, even though it proudly claims to be the opposite of that.'[12] In this second category, diametrically distinct in its conclusions from the previous one, the same formal aspects of filmmaking were interpreted as providing an interpretive frame entirely inadequate to the subject matter of World War II and the Holocaust. However, both categories, the film's proffered ambivalence is repressed through extremes of praise or condemnation.

A third category of critical response to the film is characterised by a compulsion to temper any negative criticism with praise, and to undercut praise with reservations. David Denby wrote in the *New Yorker* that the film occupies 'an uneasy nowhereseville between counterfactual pop fantasia and trashy exploitation,' and Sandhu stated: 'Thinking of it as a historical fantasy unbound by usual dramatic conventions would be true, although also too kind.'[13] In *Salon*, Stephanie Zecharek commented:

> Tarantino has taken a huge leap and made a movie that doesn't fully work, which presents those of us who love his work, hate his work, or love-hate his work – which should cover just about everybody – with a confounding question: Do we praise the leap, or shake our fists at the result?[14]

Although oscillation between praise and condemnation can sometimes be a consequence of the genre of the film review (in which the reviewer lists the aspects of the film she enjoyed and juxtaposes them with a declaration of the film's flaws), reactions to *Inglourious Basterds* go beyond the oscillations of conventional liberal even-handedness. These commentators tapped into the anxiety flowing from the inability to fix a single and definite meaning to the intentions of the director, to the meaning of the film, or to the emotional investments of the spectator herself. The critic James Wood wrote in the *London Review of Books*: 'What's impossible to know is how Tarantino himself views this story. Irony is not his thing, but stupidity isn't either,' as though certainty as to the director's intention would provide a means of calming the agitations of the text.[15] The unsettling nature of the film results in a need to fix its meaning in the face of what Zygmunt Bauman calls 'the horror of ambiguity': to *assimilate* its uncertainties into comfortable categories of discourse.[16] As Bauman states, 'Literally, assimilation

12 J. Rosenbaum, "Recommended Reading: Daniel Mendelsohn on the New Tarantino," 2009.

13 D. Denby, "Inglourious Basterds," *The New Yorker*, 31 August 2009; Sandhu, "Inglourious Basterds."

14 S. Zecharek, "*Inglourious Basterds*," *Salon*, 23 August 2009.

15 Wood quoted in B. Walters, "Debating *Inglourious Basterds*,." *Film Quarterly* 63(2) (2009): 19.

16 Zygmunt Bauman, "Modernity and Ambivalence," in *Global Culture: Nationalism, Globalization and Modernity*, ed. M. Featherstone (London: Sage, 1990), 151.

means making alike,' and much of the critical discourse on the film seeks ways to allocate it to a comprehensible category so that it can be explained and judged.[17] However, *Inglourious Basterds* does not make this easy, and the predicament of the spectator lies in the impossibility of locating a settled meaning in the ambiguities of the text. In place of certainty, the film offers indeterminate meanings, shifting affects, and ethical quandaries: an interim space on the borderlines of cinematic representation. In what follows, I will investigate the contours of the film's 'uneasy nowheresville' and the subject positions on violence and vengeance created within it.

The crime-image of *Inglourious Basterds*

> Order is . . . a fight of determination against ambiguity, of semantic precision against ambivalence.[18]

The interpretation of a movie takes place within the framework of the meanings that it encourages the viewer to attribute to it. The *preferred reading* ensures that audiences tend to laugh, cry, and gasp when appropriate (although such responses are never guaranteed, and most spectators will have witnessed various unexpected reactions from other audience members – laughing instead of crying, for example – or will perhaps have experienced moments when their own reactions did not conform to that which was expected of them). But a film's preferred reading generally aligns the viewer in predictable and patterned ways with the structural and stylistic features of a particular cinematic text. It is an effect of many distinct elements: genre, tone, cinematographic style, narrative, characterisation, and so on. The affective ambivalence generated in *Inglourious Basterds* derives from the combined effect of all these constitutive features, although it is not clear whether critics at times thought that ambiguity was a result of a flaw in the filmmaking (resulting from inadequacies in plotting, lapses in continuity of narrative, unevenness of tone, and so on) or was in fact the preferred reading that the film was offering (in that the film might be suggesting that its subject matter was one that had shifting meanings). Irrespective of the diagnosis being offered, critics variously judged as problematic or lacking the film's genre, cinematography, narrative, characterisation and, in particular, its depictions of vengeance and violence in the context of the Holocaust. It is worth examining how each of these tropes and devices contributes to the production of a subject position of ambivalence with concomitant uncertainty of ethical engagement for the spectator.

In terms of cinematic genre, *Inglourious Basterds* is ostensibly a 'Second World War movie,' belonging to a genre that came to prominence during that conflict

17 Bauman, "Modernity and Ambivalence," 155.
18 Bauman, "Modernity and Ambivalence," 164.

and has retained popularity over the intervening decades.[19] However, calling *Inglourious Basterds* a Second World War movie falls short of the task of categorisation. As with most of Tarantino's films, *Inglourious Basterds* merges genres and moves seamlessly between them; and sometimes it may appear to belong to one genre while subverting its characteristics. Quinn comments: 'No modern filmmaker has paid such an obsessive tribute to genre while subverting it at the same time.'[20] Since *Reservoir Dogs* in 1992, Tarantino's corpus has depended upon a simultaneous invocation and subversion of genre expectations, in which the characteristics of one genre can be used to tell a story that would normally belong in another genre entirely. Genre mixing has become one of the identifying characteristics of his work: one reviewer calls him 'a pick'n'mix, smash-and-grab postmodernist.'[21] Such constitutive dependence upon the merging and submerging of genre forms means that the remark of one individual during the shooting of *Inglourious Basterds*, to the effect that Tarantino was making his first Western, therefore seems inevitable and predictable.[22]

Tarantino is not content merely to marry the war movie to the Western: he also gives one of the strands of *Inglourious Basterds* the specific shape of the 'band of soldiers' story (also found in films such as *The Dirty Dozen*, *Saving Private Ryan* and *Platoon*) and the dénouement of *Inglourious Basterds* invokes the narrative trajectory of *The Dirty Dozen* with its vengeful slaughter of Germans in a confined space. Since vengeance drives both the basterds' activities in occupied France and Shosanna's decision to burn down the cinema, *Inglourious Basterds* is, in common with previous Tarantino films such as *Kill Bill vols. 1 and 2* and the later *Django Unchained*, very much a revenge movie and its depiction of vengeance will be discussed in more detail later. In the face of the co-mingling of so many different genres into the confines of one film, the viewer is left uncertain as to how to position the film generically, with all the spectatorial expectations attendant upon genre categorisation being forced into suspension.

The spectator's viewing position is unsettled in further ways. Cinematographic style is choppily variable throughout the film. Some scenes feature sudden flashbacks; there is intermittent and unexplained use of voice-over; one action scene contains a fleeting slow motion sequence in the style of Hong Kong action films. Flashbacks are used to establish detail about one character (a member of the

19 On the relationship between war and cinema, see P. Virilio, *War and Cinema: The Logistics of Perception* (London: Verso, 1989), 9–10. Movies specifically about World War II were also popular during the 1950s, but declined in number and in acclaim throughout the next two decades. As a broader genre, however, the war movie more generally has had a long lasting magnetism, and more contemporary films such as *Platoon*, *Full Metal Jacket*, *Three Kings*, *The Thin Red Line*, *Jarhead*, *Letters from Iwo Jima* and *Saving Private Ryan* continue to put the experience of armed conflict in the foreground, in a variety of locations and historical periods.

20 Quinn, "Dog Soldiers."

21 Sandhu, "Inglourious Basterds."

22 R. Gilbey, "Days of Gloury," *Sight and Sound*, 19(9) 2009.

basterds), but not for any others; whereas a parenthetical scene (a sudden insertion of images of him having dominating sex with a collaborating Frenchwoman) is used to flesh out the character of Goebbels. Lighting varies from one chapter to another. The moving image is occasionally annotated by yellow pencil and an arrow, naming characters in the crowded cinema. The sudden, but irregular and only occasional, appearance of these devices is uncomfortable for the viewer: *Inglourious Basterds* is not a film into which the viewer is pleasurably immersed: rather, it is a film of sudden shifts in pace, visual jolts, and erratic stylistic transformations.

Its segmented narrative structure and inconsistent modes of characterisation further contribute to the viewer's destabilisation. Tarantino divides the story into five distinct sections, marked by intertitles (a favourite device of Tarantino's). Common in the era of silent film, they are used rarely by contemporary filmmakers. They are anti-naturalistic devices, inevitably interrupting narrative progression and pointing out a film's constructedness. Their inclusion in *Inglourious Basterds* contributes to the disjointedness complained of by many critics: Philip French in *The Observer*, for example, called the film's narrative structure 'uneven and fractured.'[23] Thus, in the first chapter, 'Once Upon a Time in Occupied France,' we are introduced to Colonel Hans Landa and, briefly, to Shosanna. By means of a lengthy interrogation masquerading as a civilised conversation over a glass of milk, we witness Landa's embodiment of charm, cultivation and ruthlessness, establishing him as the film's villain; Shosanna flees from the massacre of her family at Landa's behest, establishing her simultaneously as victim, survivor and hero.

However, these two figures immediately drop out of cinematic sight; the second chapter, 'Inglourious Basterds,' shifts period and location to introduce Aldo Raine and his squad of basterds more than two years later, prior to their mission in occupied France, and then carrying out their work of executing Nazis. In the third chapter, 'German Night in Paris,' Shosanna re-enters the film. As a result of the German soldier Frederick Zoller's infatuation with her, she is introduced to Goebbels and then, once again, to Landa. It is after this encounter with Landa that Shosanna decides to assassinate the German high command at the screening of Goebbels's film at her cinema.

After this chapter, the narrative shifts again for 'Operation Kino,' in which we encounter Archie Hicox (Michael Fassbender), a former film critic, on a secret mission to France. His attempt to rendezvous with a German film star who is spying for the Allies goes badly wrong and results in the deaths of Hicox and a number of the basterds. The final chapter, 'The Revenge of the Giant Face,' brings together both the remaining central characters (Shosanna, Zoller, Landa, the German film star, and Raine) and the two separate strands of the narrative, as both Shosanna's and Operation Kino's objectives are put in motion (at the film's end, only Raine and Landa are still alive).

23 P. French, "*Inglourious Basterds*," *The Observer*, 23 August 2009.

The story oscillates between one strand and another, each section building up momentum and then releasing it as the film abandons one set of characters for another. Such narrative choppiness has implications for the intensity of affect experienced by the spectator in relation to these characters, modulating identification by creating lapses and surges of attachment throughout the film. Furthermore, within the chapters, the narrative relies on a small number of extended, static, emblematic scenes (almost all of which culminate in intense violence), rather than on conventional storytelling through a variety of scenes moving events and characters around. Thus, in addition to frustration when attachment to a character is interrupted by their disappearance for extended periods, when those characters are on screen, it is often during scenes that either verge on boredom or feature discomfiting violence. Added to the difficulties of investing spectatorial attachment in the main characters is the fact that several minor ones enter and leave the film abruptly. Some characters initially seem to occupy heroic roles but are summarily dropped, such as the farmer who has been hiding the Dreyfus family but then confesses their presence to Landa, and who is not seen again after the opening chapter; while Hicox, the film critic turned secret agent, appears only in the fourth chapter.

With those characters who do endure throughout the film (Landa, Shosanna and Raine), affective attachment to them is challenged in a number of ways. Landa is the film's most richly drawn of the film's various villains (who include Hitler and Goebbels): cold, brutal, charming, charismatic and ruthless, and revealed towards the film's end to be a pragmatic traitor, happy to participate in the assassination of his leaders if he can engineer a fortuitous exit strategy for himself. Throughout the film, the spectator is supposed to view Landa with a mixture of marvel and horror, his charm always offset by his sadism, meaning that the spectator's desire for attachment cannot readily be sustained. Heroism could be embodied in the figure of Aldo Raine, leader of the basterds, but it is a dubious heroism. He is a figure as outlandish as Landa, equally marvellous and equally cruel. His cruelty is directed at German soldiers: he orders his men to each bring him one hundred Nazi 'scalps' – an order meant quite literally. Raine shows unremitting violence towards the German soldiers he encounters and flouts the 'rules' of war without hesitation. A figure of folksy humour and swaggering determination, the gruesomeness and excess of Raine's violence mean that for many viewers, he too is ambiguous, represented without clarity as to whether his retributive mission is admirable or odious.

Shosanna, combining victim, survivor and avenger, is the most obvious candidate for spectatorial investment: persecuted as a Jew, pluckily surviving Landa's massacre of her family, enduring the obligation to screen Riefenstahl movies in her cinema in occupied Paris, and then finally conceiving and executing a plan to assassinate the Nazi cinema-goers. The film allows her to occupy a more heroic role, but when in the final chapter, she is shot dead by Frederick Zoller and must wreak her revenge in spectral form through the projection of a pre-recorded speech spliced into *Nation's Pride*, the spectator's attachment to her is abruptly and forcibly transformed. We see her achieve her desired revenge, but in such a way that she exists only as a fleeting image on a cinema screen. As Zecharek commented, the resulting image of Shosanna's 'face projected on a wall of smoke' is 'so illusory and so beautiful that it makes you want to reach towards the screen to touch it,' but this investment in an after-image delivers, instead of narrative satisfaction, only the discomfort felt by those who live on when confronted with images of those who do not survive.[24] Shosanna, then, is shown at the end of the film to be not so much a survivor as a victim, albeit one who wreaks revenge as she dies.

What unites the depictions of Raine and Shosanna is that they are shown engaging in *vengeance* rather than resistance. The war movie conventionally depicts resistance as noble and praiseworthy; it rarely deals in retribution for its own sake. The insistence on vengeance in *Inglourious Basterds* alters the affective expectations located in the genre of the war movie: the spectator is left uncertain as to how to view vengeance. Shosanna's vengeance is the more easily palatable of the two: it follows the murder of her family and is sparked by the encroachment of the Nazis into her cinema. Even so, it is presented to the viewer as brutal: in burning down the cinema she chooses to kill not only members of the German army but also their civilian partners and family members.

Retribution is not incompatible with the war movie, since films such as *The Dirty Dozen* incorporate vengeance into their sensibility, but *Inglourious Basterds* foregrounds the violence necessitated by retribution and dwells at length on the corporeal effects of the mission undertaken by Raine and his men. In addition to the scalpings, which are depicted in detail, the basterds evince an aggression which seems to be without limit or restriction: one of the basterds, known as the 'Bear Jew,' beats a prisoner to death with a baseball bat, complete with his own sports commentary on the killing; Raine tortures a woman by sticking his finger in a bullet hole in her leg, shoots a German prisoner who has surrendered, and carves swastikas into the foreheads of captured Germans. The film's ambiguous 'nowheresville' therefore features an inversion of the war film's conventional brutality and refuses to specify a framework through which to interpret these scenes. The spectator is left wondering whether the scalping of Nazis is simply included to allow the filmmaker to blend a trope from the western into the activities of a World War II movie or whether the basterds' vengeful violence is depicted to show what 'fighting back' might look like.

For some commentators, the ambiguity of these scenes necessitated their condemnation, and those involving Sergeant Donny Donowitz (the so-called 'Bear Jew'), wielding his baseball bat with such devastating effect and emptying his machine gun into the panic-stricken Germans fleeing the inferno in the cinema, were the most reviled. Donowitz has been described as 'ferocious,' 'turning murder into a parodic game,' and 'enjoy[ing] clubbing people to death.'[25]

24 Zecharek, "Inglourious Basterds."

25 Bradshaw, "*Inglourious Basterds*"; D. Mendelsohn, "*Inglourious Basterds*: When Jews Attack," *Newsweek*, 14 August 2009; Sandhu, "*Inglourious Basterds.*"

Meanwhile, the performance of the actor playing Donowitz has also been criticised, with Dargis for example calling it 'dreadful.'[26] To say that Donowitz was played by an 'actor' is inaccurate; the role was taken by Eli Roth, director of the *Hostel* series, films notorious for their refinement (if that is the right word) of the cinematic genre variously called 'exploitation,' 'torture horror' or 'torture porn.' Roth's casting provided an intertextual underscoring of Donowitz's brutality, but Roth himself added to the debate about vengeance, by commenting that *Inglourious Basterds* is 'kosher porn.'[27] Roth expanded on this as follows:

> It's almost a deep sexual satisfaction of wanting to beat Nazis to death, an orgasmic feeling . . . My character gets to beat Nazis to death. That's something I could watch all day. My parents are very strong about Holocaust education.[28]

The notion that the film might be offering itself as 'kosher porn' prompted additional ambivalence, with some naming such violence in *Inglourious Basterds* impermissible because it was carried out by Jews acting *as if they were Nazis*. Locking individuals in the confined space of the cinema and burning them to death or machine-gunning them as they tried to escape; carving symbols onto the bodies of prisoners; killing surrendered prisoners and civilians – all these acts were perpetrated by the Nazis and are inverted by *Inglourious Basterds* so that Jews do them to Nazis instead of the other way round.[29] In this, as Hoberman notes, '*Inglourious Basterds* . . . push[es] wish fulfilment to a near-psychotic break with reality.'[30]

Several scenes in *Inglourious Basterds* explicitly challenge dichotomies familiar from conventional representations of World War II, ensuring that the interim space occupied by the film lacks those traditional semantic markers. Two scenes are exemplary. One features the basterds at work, after their ambush of a German patrol. Most are occupied in the work of scalping their victims; Raine, however, is interrogating three prisoners, seeking information as to the whereabouts of another patrol. Their exchange plays with spectatorial assumptions as to how Allied soldiers and German captives should behave. Dialogue between the two characters repeatedly undercuts any attempt on the part of the viewer to identify with Raine (as a conventional war film would expect) or even (far less comfortably) with the captured German. Raine's attempt to gain information seems understandable; however, threatening death in order to gain the information is torture, something that 'heroic Allied soldiers' do not usually perform on screen.

26 Dargis, "*Inglourious Basterds*: Tarantino Avengers in Nazi Movieland."
27 Quoted in Hoberman, "Quentin Tarantino's Inglourious Basterds Makes Holocaust Revisionism Fun."
28 J. Goldberg, "Hollywood's Jewish Avenger," *Atlantic Monthly*, September 2009.
29 See, on this point, Mendelsohn, "*Inglourious Basterds*: When Jews Attack."
30 Hoberman, "Quentin Tarantino's Inglourious Basterds Makes Holocaust Revisionism Fun."

The German soldier will not give him information, saying that he refuses to do so, 'respectfully'; for the viewer, this seems admirable (since a soldier's betrayal of his nation is rarely sanctioned cinematically), but such momentary attachment is undercut by the German's use of the epithet 'Jew dogs' for the basterds. When Raine invites Donowitz to beat the prisoner to death with a baseball bat, the moment is horrific and brutal; but when Donowitz pauses to ask the soldier if he won his medals 'killing Jews,' the film seems to suggest to the viewer that a German soldier *perhaps* deserves even this brutality. To intensify the spectator's discomfort as they confront this issue, Raine comments that 'watching Donny beat Nazis to death is as close as we get to going to the movies.' The very role of spectator is thus implicated in the extremities of the violence depicted.

Many of Tarantino's previous films have sought to provoke discomfort in the spectator. In *Reservoir Dogs* (Miramax Films, 1992), the claustrophobic use of a confined location (inside a warehouse) for almost the entire duration heightened the violence being intermittently depicted on screen. In *Kill Bill* (particularly *vol.1*) (Miramax Films, 2003) there are numerous ways in which Tarantino invites viewer to revel in the violent revenge carried out by his central character, whether she is murdering a redneck rapist who has sexually assaulted her while she was in a coma or the members of the entire Crazy 88 gang headed by her former colleague O-Ren Ishii.

But with *Inglourious Basterds*, Tarantino takes a step closer to the outright critique of spectatorship generated by a number of earlier films depicting violence. In *Henry: Portrait of a Serial Killer*, directed by John McNaughton (Maljack Productions, 1986), the film seems to be showing us a scene in which Henry and his accomplice, Otis, murder a family whose home they have invaded; however, the film suddenly stops, and we hear a voice say, 'Let's watch it again.' In that moment, the film points out the identical position of the viewer and Henry and Otis, watching scenes of homicide. Another film involving a home invasion performs an even more explicit indictment of the spectator for her choice in watching the film's violence. In *Funny Games*, directed by Michael Haneke (Filmfonds Wien, 1997), two young men take a family captive within their home, initially playing a range of disturbing pranks that soon become more threatening.

Suddenly, one of the young men breaks the 'fourth wall,' directly addressing the film's audience, warning them that they have thirty seconds to leave the cinema before the violence begins. He poses questions to the spectator: 'Who do you think will survive?' and 'What shall we do with them now?.' As with *Henry*, the film being watched by the spectator is doubled with a film being watched in the movie: the audience sees an apparent opportunity for the family to escape, but this is rewound by the young men and a new version screens in which all family members are killed. In its seemingly offhand comment about how watching one of the basterds kill Nazis is akin to being at the movies for the rest of the troop, the viewer is invited to think about the pleasures of watching acts of killing onscreen. *Inglourious Basterds*, along with *Henry* and *Funny Games*, therefore belongs to what can be called the cinema of co-implication, in which the viewer's gaze at the screen generates complicity with the violent acts depicted.

Another destabilisation occurs in the final moments of the film, which show Raine shooting one surrendered German soldier and visiting vengeance upon Landa by marking him with a swastika carved agonisingly into his forehead. As with the prior scene of brutality, the spectator's position can only be one of ambivalence. Should the viewer take pleasure in the sight of Landa receiving what could be considered his just deserts? Should the viewer deem the violence excessive? Landa himself is appalled when Raine shoots the German soldier; thus offering two polarised viewing positions, one aligned with the morally repugnant German who asserts that Raine has breached the rules of surrender (which is correct); the other aligned with Raine, who has acted in a way normally condemned both by war movies and the law. The answer is undecidable: of the two positions, neither one nor the other is being advocated, while at the same time, either one or the other is available. Is Raine a war hero or a war criminal? Is vengeance admirable or despicable? The resolution of binary oppositions brings order and certainty in the face of doubt: *Inglourious Basterds*, however, will not choose on the viewer's behalf. As Bauman comments: '[undecidables] brutally expose the fragility of a most secure of separations. They bring the outside into the inside, and poison the comfort of order with the suspicion of chaos.'[31] Unable to resolve the film's ambiguities into 'secure separations,' the viewer is forced into the precariousness of the interim space: condemned to ambivalence in the face of vengeance.

More than the effects of any individual scenes, destabilisation of the spectator's viewing position is brought about by the film's telling of a story of violent *Jewish* vengeance within the context of the Holocaust. Among all the film's tropes, this provoked the most intense anxiety. In *Newsweek*, Daniel Mendelsohn wrote:

> Tarantino, the master of the obsessively paced revenge flick, invites his audiences . . . to take . . . a deep emotional satisfaction in turning the tables on the bad guys. ('The Germans will be sickened by us', Raine tells his corps of Jewish savages early on.) But these bad guys were real, this history was real, and the feelings we have about them and what they did are real and have real-world consequences and implications. Do you really want audiences cheering for a revenge that turns Jews into carbon copies of Nazis, that makes Jews into 'sickening' perpetrators?[32]

Despite the obvious flaws in this argument – as Charles Taylor points out, for the claim that Tarantino turns Jews into Nazis to be true, his Jews would have had to have acted in a way that denied all humanity to an entire people – for some, this question required a resounding rejection of the film's indeterminacies in its

31 Bauman, "Modernity and Ambivalence," 146.
32 Mendelsohn, "*Inglourious Basterds*: When Jews Attack."

representation of violent Jewish vengeance.[33] The film critic of the *Guardian* newspaper, Peter Bradshaw, described himself as 'traumatized' by the film; at the *New York Times*, Dargis found the film's inversion of conventions 'repellent'; while for Rosenbaum, it was 'a gleeful celebration of savagery' and 'akin to Holocaust denial.'[34] For these viewers, the film failed to meet norms for the depiction of World War II and the Holocaust, either falling short of acceptable cinematic versions (such as *Saving Private Ryan* or *Schindler's List*) or joining a group of films whose effect is claimed to be a dilution of knowledge about the reality of the war. Rosenbaum, in expanding upon why he considered the film to be 'akin to Holocaust denial,' stated: '*Inglourious Basterds* makes the Holocaust harder, not easier, to grasp *as a historical reality*. Insofar as it becomes a movie convention – by which I mean a reality derived only from other movies – it loses its historical reality.'[35] For Mendelsohn, *Inglourious Basterds* was

> the latest, if the most extreme, example of a trend that shows just how fragile memory can be – a series of popular World War II films that disproportionately emphasised armed Jewish heroism (*Defiance*) and German resistance (*Valkyrie*, *White Rose*) or elicited sympathy for German moral confusion (*The Reader*).

Such a trend, for Mendelsohn, distorts the true past in which 'passive victims, alas, vastly outnumbered those who were able to fight back.'[36] Although there are certainly criticisms that can be levelled at these films, it merits consideration why 'World War II films' should be uniform in their approach to representation. In asserting that *Inglourious Basterds* reveals the fragility of memory and is capable of distorting the past, history itself is constructed as under threat, with culture the means by which the realities of the past might be rendered mere options in a flux of narrative possibilities. Ambiguity, then, is feared for its potential to render the past precarious and to untether history from facticity.

The interim space of ambivalence

Ambivalence is difficult. It involves the holding of simultaneously conflicting feelings, and it positions the subject in tension between polar oppositions, or between shifting alliances. It is a position of uncertainty, hesitation and reservation. It requires the withholding of judgment, since it prevents the endorsement

33 Charles Taylor, "Violence as the Best Revenge: Fantasies of Dead Nazis," *Dissent* 57(1) (2010): 106.

34 Bradshaw, "*Inglourious Basterds*"; Dargis, "*Inglourious Basterds*: Tarantino Avengers in Nazi Movieland"; Rosenbaum, "Recommended Reading: Daniel Mendelsohn on the New Tarantino."

35 Rosenbaum, "Some Afterthoughts About Tarantino," 2009.

36 Mendelsohn, "*Inglourious Basterds*: When Jews Attack."

of one side over another. It demands a continual openness to the views of two contrary positions. It cannot be readily resolved. When a film refuses a singular position and opts instead to trace the borderlines between opposing positions, the viewer's resulting anxiety demands that the indeterminacies of the text be resolved into more familiar and less confronting categories. *Inglourious Basterds* slides away from categorisation, refuses all demands to state its definitive meaning, and undercuts any possibility of a settled viewing position. As noted earlier, indeterminacy prompts a desire to categorise, to resolve ambiguities with certainty: film reviewer Manohla Dargis resolved the indeterminacies of *Inglourious Basterds* by comparing it to an award-winning film which has become a cultural benchmark for the depiction of Nazis and the Holocaust: 'unlike those in "Schindler's List", Mr. Tarantino's Nazis exist in an insistently fictionalized cinematic space where heroes and villains converge amid a welter of movie allusions.'[37] 'Fictionalized' here has the same rhetorical function as when Jay condemns the way in which 'wholesale postmodernist fictionalizing of the past' makes it hard for some images to 'resist the outrages of Holocaust denial.'[38] And just as *Inglourious Basterds* is juxtaposed with *Schindler's List,* so Tarantino himself is juxtaposed with Steven Spielberg: Hoberman describes Tarantino's comment about 'the excitement he experienced in asserting his will over history' as 'tasteless' in comparison with the sensitivity of Spielberg.[39]

After making *Schindler's List*, Spielberg established the Shoah Visual History Foundation, which he dedicated to the collection of testimony from Holocaust survivors. As if in an implicit endorsement of the ethical engagement offered by Spielberg's film and Spielberg's Foundation, Mendelsohn proposed that instead of enacting 'sickening' violent revenge upon the Nazis, the Jews in *Inglourious Basterds* should have undertaken 'an alternative and morally superior form of "revenge"': that is, the 'preserv[ation] and perpetuat[ion of] the memory of the destruction that was visited upon them, precisely in order to help prevent the recurrence of such mass horrors.'[40] Both Spielberg's film and his work in creating a memory archive implicitly function as a measure against which Tarantino and his film can be judged. Failing to reach the standards set by *Schindler's List* and Spielberg's Foundation, *Inglourious Basterds* and its director can thus be declared ethically inadequate.

Where *Schindler's List* is regarded as ethically sound and documentary-like in its commitment to realism, the most common trope deployed in the deprecation of *Inglourious Basterds* has been the assertion of its *fantastic* nature. The

37 Dargis, "*Inglourious Basterds*: Tarantino Avengers in Nazi Movieland." See, on *Schindler's List* as a cultural benchmark, S. Felman, "A Ghost in the House of Justice: Death and the Language of the Law," in *Cultural Analysis, Cultural Studies and the Law*, ed. A. Sarat and J. Simon (Durham, NC: Duke University Press, 2003).

38 M. Jay, *Refractions of Violence* (London: Routledge, 2003), 57.

39 Hoberman, "Quentin Tarantino's Inglourious Basterds Makes Holocaust Revisionism Fun."

40 Mendelsohn, "*Inglourious Basterds*: When Jews Attack."

terms 'fantasy' or 'fantastical' appear in several accounts of the film and are used to draw a distinction between the tale actually told by *Inglourious Basterds* and the narrative that *should* have been provided.[41] 'Fantasy' denotes caprice, whim, invention without solid foundation, something unreal, a hallucination; a fantastic text is segregated from history and from the real. It can be distinguished from testimony, where the subject recounts an experience or responds to questioning, which has become the dominant trope in descriptions of how the Holocaust and World War II should be represented.[42]

The relationship of testimony to the real and to history is one unmediated by invention or by caprice; it is a solemn, worthy relationship, channelling experiences into the archive of memory. *Schindler's List* would never be described as a fantasy, even though it is based on a novelistic rewriting of events: rather, it is regarded by many as a cinematic version of testimony. But *Inglourious Basterds* is not just a fantasy failing its testamentary obligations: some writers called *Inglourious Basterds* a 'fantasia.'[43] 'Fantasia' is a musical term for a composition in whimsical or irregular form or style; it is also used to describe compositions in which well-known melodies are blended together amid interludes and with embellishments. Although in some ways this does indeed seem to fit the cinematic approach of Tarantino, who embellishes his films with adornments snatched from elsewhere, the epithet is further significant in that it connotes a minor musical form that lacks seriousness or import. Thus, if *Inglourious Basterds* is merely a 'fantasia,' the film's ambivalence need not be taken seriously.

Conclusions

In pointing out the implications of the categorisation of *Inglourious Basterds* as a fantasy or fantasia, I do not wish to claim that it is, in fact, truthful, or that any of the events depicted happened, or that war really is 'like that.' Nor is my aim to argue that *Schindler's List* is or, is not, 'historically accurate' or 'objective.' Some have made these counter-claims: pointing out that violent Jewish resistance did take place during World War II, or arguing that *Schindler's List* is in fact a story of 'Christian redemption' rather than an account of the Holocaust.[44] Rather, my aim is to point out the ways in which oppositions such as playful/serious, fact/fantasy, and whim/testimony function as ways of resolving the anxiety resulting when

41 Bradshaw, "*Inglourious Basterds*"; Goldberg, "Hollywood's Jewish Avenger"; Hoberman, "Quentin Tarantino's Inglourious Basterds Makes Holocaust Revisionism Fun"; Mendelsohn, "*Inglourious Basterds*: When Jews Attack"; Rosenbaum, "Recommended Reading: Daniel Mendelsohn on the New Tarantino"; Walters, "Debating *Inglourious Basterds*."

42 See, especially, S. Felman and D. Laub, *Testimony: Crises of Witnessing in Literature, Psychoanalysis and History* (London: Taylor & Francis, 1992).

43 Denby, "*Inglourious Basterds*"; T. McCarthy, "*Inglourious Basterds*," *Variety*, 20 May 2009; Quinn, "Dog Soldiers."

44 Goldberg, "Hollywood's Jewish Avenger"; Taylor, "Violence as the Best Revenge: Fantasies of Dead Nazis."

ambivalence is the only subject position on offer regarding an event that encompasses not simply a crime but years of violent atrocity. In the domain of images of World War II and the Holocaust, these oppositional tropes dominate the terrain of cinematic representation to the extent that the demand for facticity, seriousness and testimony can justify the automatic censure of texts dealing in other registers.

At present, a number of frameworks and genres (such as memoir, survivor account, testimony, historical documentation) exist for representations of World War II, and these have become culturally legislated and deeply sedimented. The war has achieved what Slavoj Žižek has called, in relation to discourses on the Holocaust, 'untouchable status,' whereby narrative structures (irrespective of cultural form) reappear with regularity, acquiring the iconic status of truth through repetition and familiarity.[45] Such frameworks perform worthwhile functions, including the maintenance of cultural awareness about the gravity of the atrocities committed during the war, a role that arguably becomes more pressing as the years pass and subsequent generations are exposed less to survivor accounts and depend more upon secondary cultural production. However, must these frameworks exclude all others? Is there *any* place for ambivalence in cultural representations of World War II?

Given the status of the war as moral, ethical and cognitive rupture, it is no surprise that aesthetic order is sought in cultural representations. As Bauman writes: 'The "other" of order is the miasma of the indeterminate and unpredictable: uncertainty, the source and archetype of all fear.'[46] Ambiguous texts are thus

> the true hybrids, the monsters: not just unclassified, but unclassifiable. They therefore do not question this one opposition here and now: they question oppositions as such, the very principle of the opposition, the plausibility of dichotomy it suggests. They unmask the brittle artificiality of distinction – they destroy the world . . . They must be tabooed, disarmed, suppressed, exiled physically or mentally – or the world may perish.[47]

The discomfort in the subject positions offered by *Inglourious Basterds* arises from the fact that the spectator is asked to view World War II through a different lens than that used to create the iconic images conventional its representation. The critical condemnation of *Inglourious Basterds* as fantasy reveals the contemporary cultural legislation as to the cinematic depiction of the war and the Holocaust, in which the imaginary is outlawed in favour of documentary, and in which both the spectator's viewing position and the image on the screen require the certainty of the real in favour of the ambivalence of possibility.

The importance of *Inglourious Basterds* is that it invites investigation of our spectatorial desires: how we want, or expect, or hope to depict and view Jews

45 Slavoj Žižek, *Violence* (London: Profile Books, 2008), 92.
46 Bauman, "Modernity and Ambivalence," 165.
47 Bauman, "Modernity and Ambivalence," 148–9.

in World War II, and how we want, or expect, or hope to depict and view the Holocaust. Whatever is uncomfortable, inspiring, horrifying or repugnant in *Inglourious Basterds* demands careful examination rather than relegation to the categories of fantasy or fictionalisation. Ambivalence in *Inglourious Basterds* recognises our affective investment in dominant genres, narratives and structures of characterisation, interrogates the implications of this investment for the criminological understanding of *verstehen*, and allows us to question why certain events require their stories to be told in particular ways. The resultant investigation of uncertainty and ambiguity can, in turn, assist cultural legal research into the meanings and implications of the images through which we tell history and in which we make sense of everyday life. Viewing a profoundly ambiguous film such as *Inglourious Basterds* reminds us that cultural texts must be read with openness to uncertainty, contestation and dispute. Meaning is not singular; interpretations may be multiple; and the task of cultural legal analysis is to put legality and vision into an oscillating relation mediated through the cinematic form.

Bibliography

Bauman, Zygmunt. "Modernity and Ambivalence." In *Global Culture: Nationalism, Globalization and Modernity*, edited by M. Featherstone, 143–69. London: Sage, 1990.

Bennett, Jill. *Empathic Vision: Affect, Trauma and Contemporary Art*. Palo Alto, CA: Stanford University Press, 2005.

Bradshaw, P. "*Inglourious Basterds*." *Guardian*, 19 August 2009.

Dargis, M. "*Inglourious Basterds*: Tarantino Avengers in Nazi Movieland." *New York Times*, 21 August 2009.

Deleuze, Gilles. *Cinema 1: The Movement-Image*. London: The Athlone Press, 1986.

——— *Cinema 2: The Time-Image*. London: The Athlone Press, 1989.

Denby, D. "*Inglourious Basterds*." *The New Yorker*, 31 August 2009.

Ebert, Roger. "*Inglourious Basterds*." *Chicago Sun-Times*, 19 August 2009.

Felman, S. "A Ghost in the House of Justice: Death and the Language of the Law." In *Cultural Analysis, Cultural Studies and the Law*, edited by A. Sarat and J. Simon, 259–303. Durham, NC: Duke University Press, 2003.

Felman, S., and D. Laub. *Testimony: Crises of Witnessing in Literature, Psychoanalysis and History*. London: Taylor & Francis, 1992.

French, P. "*Inglourious Basterds*." *The Observer*, 23 August 2009.

Gilbey, R. "Days of Gloury." *Sight and Sound*, 19(9) 2009.

Goldberg, J. "Hollywood's Jewish Avenger." *Atlantic Monthly*, September 2009.

Heller-Nicholas, Alexandra. *Rape-Revenge Films: A Critical Study*. New York: Mcfarland, 2011.

Hoberman, J. "Quentin Tarantino's Inglourious Basterds Makes Holocaust Revisionism Fun." *Village Voice*, 18 August 2009.

Jay, M. *Refractions of Violence*. London: Routledge, 2003.

McCarthy, T. "*Inglourious Basterds*." *Variety*, 20 May 2009.

Mendelsohn, D. "*Inglourious Basterds*: When Jews Attack." *Newsweek*, 14 August 2009.

Quinn, A. "Dog Soldiers." *The Independent*, 21 August 2009.
Rosenbaum, J. "Recommended Reading: Daniel Mendelsohn on the New Tarantino," 17 August 2009, http://www.jonathanrosenbaum.net/2009/08/recommended-reading-daniel-mendelsohn-on-the-new-tarantino.
——— "Some Afterthoughts About Tarantino," 27 August 2009, http://www.jonathanrosenbaum.net/2009/08/16606.
Sandhu, S. "*Inglourious Basterds.*" *The Telegraph*, 20 August 2009.
Sparks, Richard. "Dramatic Power: Television, Images of Crime and Law Enforcement." In *Censure, Politics and Criminal Justice*, edited by C. Sumner. Milton Keynes: Open University Press, 1990.
Taylor, Charles. "Violence as the Best Revenge: Fantasies of Dead Nazis." *Dissent* 57(1) (2010): 19306.
Travers, P. "*Inglourious Basterds.*" *Rolling Stone Magazine*, 20 August 2009.
Virilio, P. *War and Cinema: The Logistics of Perception*. London: Verso, 1989.
Walters, B. "Debating *Inglourious Basterds.*" *Film Quarterly* 63(2) (2009): 19–20.
Young, Alison. *Imagining Crime: Textual Outlaws and Criminal Conversations.* London: Sage, 1996.
——— *The Scene of Violence: Cinema, Crime, Affect*. London: Routledge 2010.
——— "The Screen of the Crime: Judging the Affect of Cinematic Violence." *Social & Legal Studies* 18(1) (2009): 5–22.
Zecharek, S. "*Inglourious Basterds.*" *Salon*, 23 August 2009.
Žižek, Slavoj. *Everything You Always Wanted to Know About Lacan (but Were Afraid to Ask Hitchcock)*. London: Verso, 1992.
——— *Violence*. London: Profile Books, 2008.

Chapter 7

Trench, trail, screen: scenes from the scopic regime of sovereignty

*Desmond Manderson**

Introduction

Christian Metz coined the phrase 'scopic regime'[1] to express the idea that not just what we see but *how* we see it and make sense of it is structured differently in different times and places. Nowhere is this clearer than in the depiction of acts of sovereign power. Since the US Civil War, visual images have played a key role in the representation of State-sanctioned violence. More generally, they frame the relationship between legal authority and its subjects. How violence and death is justified in war is not unrelated to how it is justified in peace. As Tom Conley writes in his foreword to Louis Marin's *Portrait of the King*, 'in the arts of representation are found the real origins and organs of social control.'[2] Marin insists that 'the representation of power' and 'powers of representation' are much the same.[3] Since power is best exercised when least expended, discourses of representation allow it to be to 'modalized' (i.e. put into action) and 'valorized' (i.e. legitimated) almost infinitely. The painting of a monarch or a state waging war is almost the paradigm of a claim to its sovereign authority.

Photography seems to bear a direct relationship to reality; even Roland Barthes said that there was something 'necessarily real' about a photograph.[4] Yet Barthes had already shown how photography works by grafting ideology onto selected fragments of material reality.[5] The camera's image gives an ideological cast to the

* The ARC's support for the essay in this collection is gratefully acknowledged

1 Christian Metz, *The Imaginary Signifier: Psychoanalysis and the Cinema* (Bloomington: Indiana University Press, 1982), Part I; Hal Foster, ed., *Vision and Visuality* (New York: New Press, 1988); Martin Jay, "Cultural Relativism and the Visual Turn," *Journal of Visual Culture* 1 (2002): 267–278, 268.

2 Tom Conley, "Foreword," in Louis Marin, *Portrait of the King*, trans. Martha House (Minneapolis: University of Minnesota Press, 1988), vi.

3 Ibid., 6–7.

4 Roland Barthes, *Camera Lucida* (New York: Farrar, Straus & Giroux, 1981); see also Susan Sontag, *On Photography: Regarding the Pain of Others* (Harmondsworth: Penguin, 1979).

5 Roland Barthes, "Myth Today," in *Mythologies*, trans. Annette Lavers (New York: Farrar, Straus & Giroux, 1972), 109; "Le Message Photographique," *Communications* 1 (1961): 127–138.

real and provides a basis in reality for ideology.[6] The 'capturing' of a moment, whether or not it is 'natural' or 'staged,' uses a contingent event to confirm or justify a reading with which it is already ideologically or culturally pregnant. Ironically then, the image appears real because it consolidates a certain idea or belief. But in a powerful feedback loop, its relationship to reality reaffirms those ideological constructions. As John Tagg explains it, the photograph reveals not the truth of an event but the underlying belief system that governs it.

> What lies 'behind' the paper or 'behind' the image is not reality—the referent—but reference: a subtle web of discourse through which realism is enmeshed . . . a whole hidden corpus of knowledge, a social knowledge that is called upon through the mechanism of connotation.[7]

The word *cliché* is doubly appropriate: in French, the word for a photographic negative and in English, a negative word for a commonplace. Read in both these senses, the cliché is the hidden template which bears the imprint of the 'common sense' of a generation.[8]

Such a perspective helps to shift our attention from 'the analysis of the signifieds' to an analysis of signifiers or, as Christian Metz put it, from the *enoncé* (the content uttered) to the *enunciation* (the act of utterance).[9] Too often we examine cultural representations in terms of the objects depicted by them rather than in terms of the frame or style that organizes them, and the focalizing position which orients our position as 'juridical spectators.' The Cambodian Genocide Program Photographic Database held at Yale University, for example,[10] comprises several thousand passport photos of Cambodian men and women taken shortly before they were killed by the genocidal Pol Pot regime. The photos reveal a fetish for record-keeping as the exercise of state power. The photos say, 'your body and your image belongs to us now.' Yet now these same photos testify to something very different: to the existence of those the regime sought to erase; to the inhumanity of those who took and catalogued the photographs. For the Khmer Rouge, the photos shamed the criminals whose lives were taken. For the Cambodian Genocide Program, the photos shamed the criminals who took them. The very same photos bear an opposite interpretation. What has changed is not the signified but the signifier. Images of the relationship between violence and

6 Caroline Brothers, *War and Photography: A Cultural History* (Abingdon, Oxon: Routledge, 1997), 16–27; Stuart Hall, "The Determination of News Photographs," in Stanley Cohen and Jock Young, eds, *The Manufacture of News: Social Problems, Deviance and the Mass Media* (London: Constable, 1981), 236–243.

7 John Tagg, *The Burden of Representation* (Amherst: University of Massachusetts Press, 1988), 100.

8 Brothers, *War and Photography,* 3; see also 18–25.

9 Christian Metz, "The Imaginary Signifier," *Screen* 16(2) (1975): 14–76, 14.

10 See http://www.yale.edu/cgp/img.html.

the State always incite us to respond; but they do so in different names and in different ways, and from distinct subject-positions.[11]

To further this approach, I focus on three sets of images. These images are not in any way secondary to more orthodox 'legal' materials about sovereignty and the use of violence. The foundations of law are embedded in a cultural imaginary. Only by turning to and properly examining the images and texts that shape it can we understand the nature of authority, order, power and justice. The exercise of sovereignty by governments today, and how we as citizens relate to it and are constituted by it, is intimately connected to the modes and discourses through which we experience it on a daily basis.

The first two sections address iconic work by two Australians who are among the greatest photo-journalists of the twentieth century—Frank Hurley in World War I and Damien Parer in World War II. The third section considers contemporary and global images of sovereign violence in the context of video game technology. A comparison, not just in terms of what is represented but *how,* will help us articulate three different scopic regimes of war, power and subjectivity, in which these and many other images are significant constitutive forces. In the first, sovereign power is transcendent. The violence of war is related to the power of god, as an event outside our control and already determined. The sovereign speaks in the past tense and mandates our awe. In the second, the sovereign State is immanent. The violence of war and invasion is related to the power of the nation, as a crisis which demands our action and remains undetermined. The sovereign speaks in the present tense and mandates our engaged voice. In the third, sovereign violence is presented as omnipotent. The violence of war is related to the power of technology, as a procedure which warrants our admiration and continues indefinitely. This time, the sovereign speaks in the future tense and mandates our silent acquiescence.

These images help us see how sovereign power's claims, and the social relations that sustained it, are advanced through different visual discourses of spectatorship. My purpose is not to be overly schematic or dogmatic about the relationship between these scopic regimes and different historical moments. I only want to show the diverse ways in which images of war constitute different vocabularies for the expression and the legitimation of sovereign authority, that we may be better attuned to how these vocabularies are deployed in the contemporary world. Photographs, films and videos, 'representations of power' in Marin's words, actively participate in the socio-legal trends that they pretend merely to document. By pursuing differences in the scopic regime I do not mean to inaugurate a new formalism or to surpass a political economy of sovereignty, but rather to extend it, the better to recognize the power of aesthetic elements within it. In the twenty-first century, in a world saturated with images, overwhelmed by aesthetics, and engulfed in violence, this aspiration has surely lost none of its critical edge.

11 Walter Benjamin, "The Work of Art in the Age of Mechanical Reproduction," in *Illuminations*, Hannah Arendt, ed. (London: Schocken Press, 1968), 214–218.

Sovereignty as the transcendence of God

Some of the most compelling images of World War I were taken by the first official photographer to the Australian Imperial Forces, Frank Hurley.[12] His work demonstrates the constructed nature of photography; many were 'composites' from multiple negatives, carefully superimposed and adjusted to heighten their effect. Hurley's boss, the official war historian C. E. W. Bean, initially refused him permission to exhibit his photographs, condemning them as 'fakes.'[13] Yet as I argued above, the truths of these photos understood not as the record of historical events but their social meaning, is not compromised by the ways in which they were constructed.

Hurley's work shows considerable engagement in the daily rounds and routines of military life. Individual soldiers are often its focus. This creates a structure of identification which assumed a particular importance in the context of the myth of the ANZACS—the Australian and New Zealand Army Corps, whose formation and endeavours during World War I, so soon after the two countries achieved their independence early in the new century, created a central rallying-point for the idea of the nation and the character of its citizens. Yet what is most distinctive about Hurley is his aesthetic imagination, his composition, lighting and tone. Hurley's layering of tones and textures, facilitated by his composite techniques, give a remarkable three-dimensionality to the pictures. The effect is to draw the viewer deeply into the image. One is reminded of the 'panorama,' a mix of painting and model-making developed during and after the Napoleonic Wars.[14] By providing a series of detailed models and images around the sides of a vast room, the panorama gave nineteenth-century spectators a sense of detail and scale which constituted them as awe-struck and humbled witnesses. In Hurley's photographs—originally exhibited as huge images several feet high—one likewise becomes drawn into the emotional and sensory experience of the picture, rather than held at a distance. But Hurley's use of light, sky and clouds, and his careful deployment of destroyed buildings, overwhelm us with their grandeur and loss. If we are drawn into the image, we are also made small by their majesty. His work conveys transcendence.

In a work like *Battle-Scarred Sentinels* (Figure 7.1), the title ambiguously refers to both soldiers and pillars, and highlights the work of time and decay.

> The word 'history'stands written on the countenance of nature in the characters of transience. [. . .] In the ruin history has physically merged into the setting. And in this guise history does not assume the form of the process of an eternal life so much as that of irresistible decay.[15]

12 See Alisdair Macgregor, *Frank Hurley: A Photographer's Life* (New York: Viking, 2004). For a representative gallery of images, see http://www.greatwar.nl/hurley/forward.html.

13 Paul Gough, "'Exactitude is Truth': Representing the British Military through Commissioned Artworks," *Journal of War and Culture Studies* 1 (2008): 341–356.

14 Mary Favret, *War at a Distance* (Princeton, NJ: Princeton University Press, 2010).

15 Walter Benjamin, *The Origin of German Tragic Drama*, trans. John Osbourne (London: NLB, 1977), 177–178.

Figure 7.1 Frank Hurley, *Battle-Scarred Sentinels* (1917). Reproduced by kind permission of the Estate of the late Frances Antoinette Mooy. Image courtesy of the State Library of NSW.

The ruin survives only as the trace of time past. It reeks of death.[16] Its temporal *pastness* connotes our impotence in the face of the work of time. Both in Hurley's

16 Hannah Arendt, "Introduction," in Benjamin, *Illuminations*, 13; Bradley Stephens, "Reading Walter Benjamin's Concept of the Ruin in Victor Hugo's *Notre Dame de Paris*," *French Studies* 61 (2007): 155–166.

symbols of decay and transience, and in the great skies and visions of eternity that he sets against them, we do not experience our political agency but its lack. Again, like the panorama, Hurley awakens feelings of awe and subservience to an overwhelming power, sovereign, divine or natural.

> War happened, it happened all around you and your fellow citizens, you were up close to it but had no role other than spectator . . . Through the elimination of distance and the offer of unbearable detail, it . . . harnesses the event to an overwhelming, incontrovertible force.[17]

This is the romantic sublime. Like a painting by Caspar David Friedrich,[18] Hurley's image does not elicit a feeling of pastoral peace, progress or reconciliation, but rather the sublime surrender to an irresistible force that carries us violently away.

Hurley's sublime aesthetic reaches its apotheosis in *Dawn* (or *Morning) at Passchendaele* (Figure 7.2). That it should be called dawn or morning when it is in fact *after* the battle of Passchendaele demonstrates how much war was imagined as *amor fati*, a destiny rather than a choice. But it also suggests the possibility of new worlds after the destruction of the present one. It is true that Paul Fussell, in his classic work on the writers of World War I, argues that the trope of dawn is inflected with a powerful irony.[19] But the light that bathes *Dawn at Passchendaele* does not seem to me predominantly ironic. For one thing, Fussell's texts typically concern the shadow of retrospectivity in which what happens (tinted with hope) is haunted by what we know will happen (tainted by disillusionment). This ironic juxtaposition is not Hurley's. So too, irony works through the discordant surprise of otherness. But there is nothing fortuitous in Hurley's composites. To read the figure of dawn ironically would not account for the care Hurley has lavished on the image and the soldiers on one another. Dawn literally enlightens and blesses the soldiers' work (notably tending the wounded and burying the dead). Both nature and culture combine in an experience of *agape*.

The transcendental yearning of *Passchendaele* should come as no surprise. For many artists—Erich Remarque, T. S. Eliot, Siegfried Sassoon, Wilfred Owen, Otto Dix—the war demanded a new reckoning with the unheroic reality of modern combat. But this was by no means the whole story.[20] World War I also saw the resurgence of romanticism in politics and legal philosophy, precisely *in response to* this widespread sense of crisis and ruin. The war shook Europe out of its cultural and intellectual complacency. No institutions, values or cultural forms remained

17 Favret, *War at a Distance*, 218–219.

18 Caspar David Friedrich, *Monk by the Sea,* oil on canvas, 110 x 172 cm (Berlin: Nationalgalerie, 1809); *Winter – Cloister Ruins and Church*, oil on canvas (Hamburg: Hamburger Kunsthalle, 1826).

19 Paul Fussell, *The Great War and Modern Memory* (New York: Oxford University Press, 1975).

20 Desmond Manderson, *Kangaroo Courts and the Rule of Law: The Legacy of Modernism* (London: Routledge, 2012), 25–51.

Figure 7.2 Frank Hurley, *Dawn (or Morning) at Passchendaele* (1917). Reproduced by kind permission of the Estate of the late Frances Antoinette Mooy. Image courtesy of National Film and Sound Archives, Australia.

untouched. Movements in literary and artistic modernism repudiated the positivist orthodoxies of nineteenth-century realism. For D. H. Lawrence, for example, the best symbol for the modern predicament was the phoenix, a mythical bird from the ashes of whose self-immolation new life emerges. Like the phoenix, it is only through annihilation that we can truly start afresh. War was a moment of dreadful ruin, of decay and nothingness, but at the same time it opened the possibility of an unimaginable future which could only be achieved by surrender to forces much greater than ourselves. Hurley's works explicitly confront the destruction of war. But that does not make him indifferent to war's purifying fire. The title no less than the image plays on the relationship between morning and mourning.[21]

Romantic idealism was not confined to artists. It formed an important element of the legal and political visions of the inter-war years. 'Reactionary modernism,'[22] as it has been called, sought an escape from the hegemonic structure of technological and instrumental positivism whose moral and political bankruptcy had been exposed by the catastrophe of the war.[23] A cognate spirit—although with very different political implications—infects Walter Benjamin's evocation of 'divine violence,' the philosophy of Martin Heidegger, or Max Weber's dying declarations against modernity. In the wake of the Great War, Weber warned that we were entering an 'iron cage' of technological and bureaucratic rationality, a 'polar night of icy darkness.'[24] In the realm of legal theory, Carl Schmitt likewise urged us to discard the facade of 'due process' and embrace the uncontainable and exceptional power of the sovereign.[25] Sovereignty and violence[26] are thought *together* here, not as opposites but as partners. Only by liberating sovereign violence from the false constraints of instrumental rationality could justice be recovered from the ashes of the old order. The desire for some kind of *deus ex machina*—a leader, a dictator (as Schmitt put it), a prophet (Weber), an orator, a general strike (Benjamin), or even a *Führer*—runs through the legal debates on sovereignty and emergency in the 1920s and 1930s. It underscores the collapse of the Weimar Republic and the rise of fascism, but also colours the rhetoric of F. D. R. and the New Deal.[27]

There is a tension in Hurley's image as to whether dawn is a blessing or a reproach. In a writer like Carl Schmitt, the sublime is appropriated for political purposes in a way that undoes or represses that tension, exactly as Benjamin

21 See William Styron, *Sophie's Choice* (New York: Vintage Books, 1979); Gillian Rose, *Mourning Becomes the Law* (Cambridge: Cambridge University Press, 1996).

22 Jeffrey Herf, *Reactionary Modernism* (Cambridge: Cambridge University Press, 1986).

23 See Manderson, Kangaroo Courts and the Rule of Law, 25–51.

24 See Peter Baehr, "The 'Iron Cage' and the 'Shell as Hard as Steel': Parsons, Weber, and the *Stahlhartes Gehäuse* metaphor in the Protestant Ethic and the Spirit of Capitalism," *History and Theory* 40(2) (2001): 153–169; Asher Horowitz and Terry Maley, eds, *The Barbarism of Reason: Max Weber and the Twilight of Enlightenment* (Toronto: University of Toronto Press, 1994).

25 See David Dyzenhaus, ed., *Law as Politics: Carl Schmitt's Critique of Liberalism* (Durham, NC: Duke University Press, 1998); Carl Schmitt, "Der Führer schützt das Recht," *Deutsche Juristen-Zeitung* 39 (1934): 945–950; Carl Schmitt, *Political Theology,* trans. Gary Schwab (Cambridge, MA: MIT Press, 1985).

26 Carl Schmitt, *Concept of the Political,* trans. Gary Schwab (Chicago: University of Chicago Press, 2007).

27 Ira Katznelson, Fear Itself: The New Deal and the Origins of Our Time (New York: Liveright, 2012).

predicts.[28] Yet the seeds of such a move can be found in the way Hurley's images frame the horrors of war through the lens of the sublime. A certain relationship to the sovereign actions that lead to war is thereby constituted—a surrender to transcendental violence beyond our ken or control, a sense of the modern world in ruins, and of the actions and forces that have destroyed it as destined and completed. This temporal distance and aesthetic height interpellates the viewer or subject as the awestruck witness to a distant force. In 1917, after a zeppelin raid on London, D. H. Lawrence wrote with millenarian rapture, 'So it seems our cosmos is burst, burst at last, the stars and moon blown away . . . So it is the end—our world is gone, and we are like dust in the air.'[29] This language seems to express perfectly this sense of a temporal closure and our own cosmic insignificance. Ruins and ashes, light and dawn. Hurley, Schmitt, Lawrence—even Benjamin—seem willing to embrace the wasteland of established human structures in the name of a new world and a new justice summoned by the angel of violence. Sovereignty is expressed in the past tense and legitimated in terms of a god-like and humbling transcendence.

Sovereignty as the immanence of the nation

A version of this aesthetic ideology formed the basis of Nazi propaganda in World War II, most notably in the 'reactionary modernism' of Leni Riefenstahl.[30] It was otherwise for the Allies. There, the photographic archive, particularly the cinema newsreel, was almost always constructed to build a social commitment to the war. The question of sovereign power is connected therefore not to its sublime distance, both temporally and politically, but to demotic appeals to immediacy and participation. In these newsreels we find ourselves much closer to the action—closer, specifically, to our own troops—at the very moment when their own fate lay in the balance, and in which our solidarity would help determine the outcome.

Damien Parer's celebrated Australian documentary, *Kokoda Front Line!* (Figure 7.3) exemplifies this, portraying the experience of Australian soldiers—close-ups of the soldiers' feet in the rain and the mud of New Guinea—against an unmistakably Christian iconography of suffering, mercy and sacrifice. The images themselves convey both an intimate presence and urgency. But the sound and narration were only added in post-production. Both the romanticism of the musical score and the orotund voice-over, control the meaning of these pictures, literally orchestrating our affective responses. We see the world up close; we

28 See Benjamin, *Origins of Baroque Drama;* Walter Benjamin, "Critique of Violence," in *Reflections*, trans. Edmund Jephcott (New York: Schocken, 1986), 277–300; Schmitt, *Concept of the Political*; Schmitt, *Political Theology.*

29 D. H. Lawrence, *Letters,* quoted in Peter Fjågesund, *The Apocalyptic World of D. H. Lawrence* (Oslo: Norwegian University Press, 1991), 29–31.

30 Steven Bach, *Leni—The Life and Work of Leni Riefenstahl* (New York: Knopf, 2007).

Figure 7.3 Still from Damien Parer, *Kokoda Front Line!* (Cinesound Review, No. 0568, 1942). Reproduced by permission of Rightsmith.

judge it from afar. This disjunction between images filmed on location and studio sound is one of the hallmarks of the newsreel. Just like a wildlife documentary, the highly artificial superimposition of music and text couples the myth of our authentic presence with a way of seeing carefully manipulated by the unseen narrator, and a way of feeling transmitted by the musical score.

The narrator is in charge. His voice dispenses emotional, spiritual and political instruction, from high above and far away. Parer's use of jungle scenery, distant shots and slow dissolves, while it positions the viewer close to the soldiers in some ways, yet separates us from them through a jungle mist or a blurry lens. We see the soldiers' lips move, but we never hear them speak. The only voice is that of the narrator, and he uses it to directly interpellate the Australian citizen. 'This is happening not three hundred miles from the Australian coastline,' says the narrator. 'Are they getting all the support they need, from the mines, from the factories, from the ordinary civilian? Can every man and woman in this country truthfully say—I've done all I can, given all I can?' Sovereignty—legally justified violence—is framed in the grammar of the third person plural: it is not 'they' who suffer it, but 'we' who sustain and consent to it. The temporality of

Frank Hurley's images is the past perfect. War is pre determined, over. In Damien Parer, on the other hand, we find ourselves in the continuous present. 'There is a dramatic reality about this which cannot be escaped,' intones the narrator. 'All this is happening,' insists the narrator, 'men are sweating, suffering, dying in that jungle.' Events are presented in the film as still unfolding, and we are actively called upon to participate in their outcome. Sovereignty is expressed in the present tense and legitimated in terms of the demotic immanence and active participation of the nation.

The *personal* nature of the obligation between community and soldier is consolidated by Damien Parer's personal appearance at the very end of the film. By speaking at the end of the film rather than at the beginning, Parer does not so much introduce a subjective perspective as confirm the narrator's didactic veracity. 'I've seen the war and I know what your husbands, sweethearts and brothers are going through,' says Parer to the camera. His words provide a necessary link in the chain of evidence that connects the jungles of New Guinea to the political argument of *Kokoda*. He speaks not as a film-maker but as a *witness*. Metz argued that in cinematic fiction the signifier 'disappears,'[31] allowing us to accept unquestioningly the narrative on the screen. But this was never the case with documentary. The question of signifier or subjective position raised issues of authenticity and truth that became and continue to be difficult to answer. At the end of the war, the camera's relationship to truth reached perhaps its most urgent moment when the first photo-journalists entered the Belsen and Buchenwald concentration camps. Some further link in the chain of evidence was needed to confirm the veracity of those obscene images. The camera served as a witness to the witnesses, whose truth-value lay ultimately in their own presence. When Lee Miller sent the first pictures of Dachau back to her editor in New York, she wired the editor, 'I implore you to believe this is true.'[32] Miller would appear to have intuited the problem that Holocaust deniers have exploited ever since, and that only the integrity of the eye-witness can actually dispel.

Sovereignty as the omnipotence of technology

The sovereignty of the West shows an impressive capacity to adapt to a changed scopic regime. While it is undoubtedly true that recent photographic and

31 Metz, *The Imaginary Signifier*, 119–129; Frank Burke, "'How'd You Like to Disappear?:' The Subject in Film," *CTHEORY* 13.1–2 (1989): 25–43. Compare Mikhail Bakhtin, who would seem to argue the opposite in the case of the history and development of the novel: see *The Dialogic Imagination: Four Essays by M. M. Bakhtin*, trans. Caryl Emerson and Michael Holquist, trans. (Austin: University of Texas Press, 1981); Mikhail Bakhtin, *Problems of Dostoevsky's Poetics,* trans. Caryl Emerson (Minneapolis: Minnesota University Press, 1984).

32 Mary Warner Marien, *Photography: A Cultural History*, 2nd edn (London: Laurence King, 2002), 301.

televised images of war encompass a great diversity of perspectives, the normalization of new visual forms of signification suggest important changes in our legal subjectivity.

Since the Vietnam War, the US military in particular (but by no means they alone), have paid much greater attention to the visual representation of combat. In both the first Gulf War (1990–91) and even more so during the Iraq War and in Afghanistan, photographers and journalists have been subject to strict controls on what and how images can be collected and reported. 'Embedded' journalists and cameramen have been given unprecedented access to military personnel. The perspective from which a great deal of the reporting of these wars took place, therefore, is over the shoulders of the troops themselves. Both independent reporting and daily military briefings have meanwhile tended to focus on images of technology. Modern warfare invokes metaphors of medicine (as in surgical strikes and lasers), patriotism (as in missiles), and intelligence (the bombs are smart, the drones less so).[33] What we are shown on the screen is increasingly nothing but a mirror of our *own* technology.

The virtual *invisibility* of military opposition during 'Operation Desert Storm' (1990–91) led Jean Baudrillard, somewhat infamously, to claim that 'the gulf war did not take place.'[34] He did not mean that no one died. Quite the contrary.[35] He meant that, from the Gulf War onwards, the obsession with warfare as technology by other means renders unrepresentable the actual deaths that are suffered on the ground. This is not simply about visibility but about tactics. Faced with this technological inequality, the enemy avoids direct confrontation, hides, and fights battles of insurgency. As Baudrillard noted, the result of 'Desert Storm' was the refusal of the Iraqi army to fight, the *status quo ante* in Kuwait and the continuance in power of Saddam Hussein. One might say something similar about the war against the Taliban. They too chose not to fight so much as to disrupt and wait it out. The Gulf War was played out in the circulation of displays and spectacles. This, of course, was not entirely without consequences. The Pentagon got to parade its hardware and justify its budget. In the minds of the West, the conflict instilled a message of technological supremacy, and provided a sort of 'masturbatory' satisfaction.[36] Like masturbation, we could satisfy a fantasy of omnipotence,[37] without experiencing any messy reality (or more enduring relationship) to complicate it.

One thing certainly seems to have changed in the annals of war and sacrifice. Wilfred Owen's famous poem about World War I recalled Horace's line,

33 See Mary Louise Pratt, "Harm's Way: Language and the Contemporary Arts of War," *PMLA* 124(5) (2009): 1515–1531; Fredric Jameson, "War and Representation," *PMLA* 124(5) (2009): 1532–1547.

34 Jean Baudrillard, *The Gulf War Did Not Take Place,* trans. Paul Patton (Sydney: Power, 2000).

35 See Patton, "Introduction," in Baudrillard, *The Gulf War,* 6–19.

36 Baudrillard, *The Gulf War,* 32–41.

37 Ibid., 75.

Dulce et decorum est pro patria mori.[38] But no one thinks that any more. There is nothing sweet or honourable in dying for your country: only in killing for it. The new photography of war consistently glorifies those who kill not those who die. Indeed the US military now prevents reporters filming the return of dead soldiers. War has become engulfed in publicity; death has become shrouded in secrecy. Increasingly, the journalist reports on these events not from the front line but from behind a screen located many hundreds or thousands of miles away. Images are remediated through multiple editorial manipulations. War is no longer more real to us than a video game or a movie. These second-, third-, or fourth-hand images provide us with a sense of technological power accompanied by a psychological *mis en abyme*, a 'postmodern sublime.'[39]

Increasingly, images of war adopt a *bomb's eye view*. Walter Benjamin had long foreshadowed this development, arguing that the camera was the ideal agent of modern warfare, spatializing, organizing and distancing its objects. We are framed as beings for whom technical mastery constitutes our identity and our meaning. Under its spell, we seek not to understand nature but to *capture* it, as the camera does an image or a weapon a target.[40] Heidegger's position complements that of the Frankfurt School.

> Rationality is being transformed from a critical force into one of adjustment and compliance. Autonomy of reason loses its meaning in the same measure as the thoughts, feelings and actions of men are shaped by the technical requirements . . . and the subordination of thought to pre-given external standards.[41]

This process is further exacerbated by the very speed of war's representation, which increases sensation and decreases the time for a measured assessment.[42] Both Marcuse and Heidegger thought that the illusion of technical mastery creates a myth of control at the very moment that we become increasingly enslaved to it. Our *identification* with technology is the route to less and less intellectual or social autonomy with respect to it.

38 Wilfred Owens, *The War Poems,* ed. John Stallworthy (London: Chatto & Windus, 1994), 29.

39 Ibid., 23; Richard Sherwin, *Visualizing Law in the Age of Digital Baroque* (London: Routledge, 2011).

40 Martin Heidegger, "The Question of Technology," in *The Question of Technology and Other Essays,* trans. W. Lovett (New York: Harper & Row, 1977); Paul Nadal, "Heidegger's Critique of Modern Technology: On 'The Question Concerning Technology'," *Be Late, a Blog by Paul Nadal* (2010).

41 Herbert Marcuse, "Some Social Implications of Modern Technology," in *Technology War and Fascism: Collected Papers of Herbert Marcuse*, ed. Douglas Kellner (London and New York: Routledge, 1998), 49.

42 Favret, *War at a Distance,* 196–197; Paul Verilio, *Desert Screen: War at the Speed of Light,* trans. Michael Degener (London: Athlone Press, 2001).

It is no coincidence that the weapon as signifier is echoed in other genres of representation. 'First Person Shooter' video games (FPS) adopt exactly the perspective of the 'embedded' player who experiences the world through the scope of a gun. Early FPS games such as *Doom* came out shortly after the Gulf War. Later variants including *Quake* and the *Call of Duty* franchise radically expanded the highly immersive video environment they create.[43] New heights of realism and therefore of ideological integration were reached in games such as *Six Days in Fallujah* (2005). While properly classed as a third person shooter game, because we do not see the world out of the eyes of a soldier but over his shoulder—embedded in the action like a journalist—*Six Days'* close tracking of a Marine action undertaken during 'Operation Iraqi Freedom' created a sense of both experiential and technical reality. The game was released while the war was still underway. The aesthetic environment in which the player is enveloped is intensely claustrophobic. Lines of sight are limited. Sounds of breathing are amplified as if we are inside a hazmat or space suit. There is no sense of the player/soldier acting in consort with others. He is utterly isolated *by* the technology that protects him. Within that solitary bubble, the soldier is sense-poor but data-rich. Without a broader perspective and subject to these data flows, his capacity to respond is almost entirely limited to the immediate threats around him: kill or be killed. He is removed from the kind of social or cultural context that would, were he to abandon his technological muffler, leave him far more exposed but with a much more diverse set of possible options. The game conveys then the isolation, anxiety and technological determinism that seems to have defined the sovereign world-view of much of the West over the past decade or so.

Video games like *Six Days* present the rules and goals of the game as given, and reward those who can best adapt their behaviour and skills to them. The more immersive and comprehensive the video game environment the more the user becomes a creature of its framework and an instrument of its instrumentalization. There is no space for critique. When was the last time a video game adopted the point of view of a bystander, or a civilian, or an out-gunned resistance? How often has technology been correlated with injustice? Of course the argument does not all go one way. The Arab spring is often taken to provide evidence for modern technology's ability to provide the tools of political empowerment; although three years on and the argument is starting to look a little naive. And a writer like Katherine Hales defends the 'posthuman' imbrication of bodies and technologies as opening the door to new potentials and new relationships.[44] No doubt there is some truth in this. But I am too old-fashioned not to see real dangers in the overbearing relationship between technology and instrumentalization, including

43 *Doom*, id Software, 1993; *Quake*, id Software, 1996; *Call of Duty*, Infinity Ward/Activision, 2004–2011.

44 Katherine Hales, *How We Think: Digital Media and Contemporary Technogenesis* (Chicago: University of Chicago Press, 2012); *How We Became Post-human: Virtual Bodies in Cybernetics, Literature and Informatics* (Chicago: University of Chicago Press, 1999).

its effects on our bodies and our desires, on unconscious optics and unconscious impulses.

Furthermore, the structures of signification of the images of war over the past twenty years are beginning to reframe our understanding of the limits and justifications of sovereign violence, even in legal terms. As Judith Butler points out, this logic is now extended to law. It too is increasingly imagined not as an ethical control or limit but as a technology of mastery. 'The law is not that to which the State is subject nor that which distinguishes between lawful state action and unlawful, but is now expressly understood as an instrument of power that can be applied and suspended at will.'[45] Law then becomes a technology to be mobilized but by no means an obligatory framework or an ethical limit.

The fundamental question confronting Western power, says Butler, is 'the differential allocation of precariousness' across the globe.[46] Terrorist acts arise precisely out of an effort to redistribute that precarity. And the displacement of Western sovereign power externally is aimed at reinstating it, rendering ever more visible our own technological force and ever less visible those who are damaged by it. The technological determinacy of the West places it in the position of being able to impose the risks of its own existence onto other places and peoples, whose very backwardness is thought to impose an unacceptable risk to Western security and in the name of whose backwardness further backwardness is then dropped on them.

In this era of securitization, sovereignty is increasingly articulated not as a response to action but as an effort to pre-empt anxiety, which is then displaced externally, onto other cultures and other places.[47] Since the fear of risk constantly generates new anxiety as it rubs up against the limits of our ability to control our destiny, the protection against the precariousness of life becomes ever more invasive. The anxiety and therefore the sovereign violence needed to protect against it are no longer containable territorially. Legal sovereignty presents itself as entitled to *export* violence in order to defend against its own risks. Indeed increasingly, law, rights and sovereign violence go together. The global technological violence that has expanded over the past ten or more years is treated not as an abuse of human rights—which surely it is, whether or not it has been justifiable for other reasons—but as the phoenix-like immolation that will, in the end, permit their expansion.

> It follows from such a viewpoint that the destruction of such populations, their infrastructure, their housing, and their religious and community institutions, constitutes the destruction of what threatens the human, but not the human itself. It is also precisely this particular conceit of a progressive history that positions 'the West' as articulating the paradigmatic principles of the human.[48]

45 Judith Butler, *Precarious Life: The Powers of Mourning and Violence* (New York: Verso, 2006), 83.

46 Ibid.; Judith Butler, *Frames of War* (New York: Verso, 2010).

47 Butler, *Precarious Life*, 14–25.

48 Butler, *Frames of War* (London: Verso, 2009), 125.

From the point of view of governmentality, an endless discursive cycle of anxiety, displacement and security creates a climate in which states of exception, particularly through scopic regimes of surveillance, are increasingly normalized.[49] Increasingly, suspensions of the rule of law do not reveal a Foucauldian disjunction between sovereignty and governmentality but rather their collaboration. Each of them are ways of undermining the rule of law, the first by promoting a spatial exceptionalism and the second by promoting a temporal exceptionalism[50] 'that lead us, in the name of sovereignty, to defend a border in one instance and to violate it in another with impunity.'[51] The exception is displaced externally and intensified internally. Yet the rhetoric of external threat acts to conceal those very processes of intensification.

Above all, the images of war of this latest period inaugurate a radically new temporality.[52] These recent images propel us towards the *future* not the past. Through the cross-hairs of a weapon, in the laser sights as they lock on to a target, or in the trajectory of a bomb, we are implicated in a decision that is *about* to happen—a button which is about to be pressed, a missile which is launched and traces an arc in the sky. The sovereign violence of the West is thus represented neither as a fatality that has already happened, nor as a crisis for which we are actively responsible, but rather as an ever-present *potential.* The sovereign actions represented by these images are neither extensive nor discontinuous. Rather they are intensive, punctuated, endlessly repeatable and directed towards a future which will continue indefinitely. Like a Constitution, this visual discourse gains its power on the one hand from its ability to turn problematic and perhaps even illegal acts now into a destiny on which we will one day look back and legitimate, and on the other hand from its constant recitation, which makes each moment the new affirmation of this mythic *Bildungsroman* of endless discipline exerted over other peoples and over ourselves.

The image of an omnipotent technology justifies sovereignty in terms of a future that will never arrive, and an instrumentalism that leaves us little choice. Again like the aesthetic elements of a Constitution, for example—carved into monuments, repeated as oaths, sung as anthems, celebrated on special days—images of war are not merely evidential, but performative. They *do* something. They implicate us in alienated and instrumental relationships that generate a complicated dance of spectacle and surveillance.[53] As we have already seen with Hurley and Parer, our engagement with the legitimation of sovereignty is not just intellectual but emotional. Images forge pathways of desire, indispensable to the juridical and political manifestations of sovereign power.

49 Damian Cox, Michael Levine and Saul Newman, eds, *Politics Most Unusual: Violence, Sovereignty and Democracy in the 'War on Terror'* (Basingstoke: Palgrave Macmillan, 2009.

50 See, for example, Butler, *Precarious Life*, 53–56.

51 Butler, *Frames of War*, 48.

52 See Virilio, *Desert Screen*.

53 Guy Debord, *The Society of the Spectacle,* trans. Donald Nicholson-Smith (New York: Zone Books, 1994).

Of course the modern world is saturated in images of sovereignty of all kinds, some of which specifically address the suffering of war, technological inequality, and so on. But the consequences of this surfeit are not so clear.[54] Hannah Arendt suggests that pity does not necessarily disrupt a bureaucratic, instrumental, technological determinism but instead *privatizes* and *compartmentalizes* suffering, separating it from the discourse of politics. There is a real danger that humanitarian war is invested in the persistence of the suffering to which it claims to respond.[55] The monks had a word for all this, *acedia,* the sin of feeling good about feeling bad; 'the specific form of sin that a penitent commits if his sadness substitutes itself for work.'[56] As we watch the latest YouTube uploads on a small laptop by ourselves, in the middle of the night, the bombardment of images seems to be accompanied by a greater experience of alienation. In fact by privatizing images of suffering, we might well create a sense of shame and impotence about our public lives. The aesthetics of shame and the aesthetics of satisfaction—the politics of suffering and the politics of violence, the law of rights and the law of security—swing us from one emotional extreme to the other but rigorously compartmentalize them in a way that repeats the cycle. Many addictions work this way. They are nourished by contradiction; self-loathing only fuels the destructive cycle of behaviour.

Conclusion: time, affect, and the image

The scopic regime underscores not the meaning of images but their governance. What is signified in these images is not as important as *how* it is signified, through whose eyes actions are framed and understood, and by whom we are interpellated. This frame organizes not only how we see the world around us, but the relationship between sovereignty and responsibility in relation to it. Each of the images or sets of images we have looked at is characterized by a distinct temporality. The ruined past of Hurley's images contains a determinacy on which we gaze like a spectacle. The presence and urgency of Parer's documentary demands a commitment. Images of the relationship between war and sovereignty, from Iraq or Afghanistan, implicates our bodies in a repetitive future which will continue *ad nauseum*, imposing violence on other communities as it none-too-subtly disciplines our own.

Different modes of signification have different affective registers. Hurley's historic grandeur incites awe and transcendence in which we are invited not to *participate* but to surrender to the power of the sovereign. In the work of Parer, the

54 Nicholas Mirzoeff, *Watching Babylon: The War in Iraq and Global Visual Culture* (London: Routledge, 2005).

55 See Mark Antaki, "Genre, Critique, and Human Rights," *University of Toronto Quarterly* 82(4) (2013): 974–996.

56 Robert Meister, *After Evil: A Politics of Human Rights* (New York: Columbia University Press, 2012).

sense of history as resting on *our* shoulders incites feelings of demotic solidarity. In a video game or an image of a smart bomb or a surgical strike, sovereignty is seen as the realization of an omnipotent technology which is framed in terms of efficiency and fear.

Perhaps this is one way to think about the notorious images of US soldiers mugging for the cameras with their captives at Abu Ghraib.[57] Even more than they enact a power differential they record a presence—not of the objects in the photograph but of the subject who is shown, grinning, as if against the backdrop of a tourist attraction. We take a selfie to establish *our* identity; the scenery hardly matters. So again the image shows itself to be Janus-faced, the position of the witness double-edged. Although it confirms one existence when it was taken, it reveals a blindness to another when it begins to circulate. This ambiguity is the camera's secret weapon. It has the remarkable capacity to point in two directions simultaneously, towards its subject as well as its object, towards a signifier as well as a signified. It reveals not one set of relations but two: the relation between the figures in the image, and the frame that organizes and controls those relations. By honing our skills of double reading, the camera might become again, as Barthes and Benjamin imagined it: an instrument through which to interrogate our complicity with sovereign violence, and to glimpse our mortality.[58] The term 'scopic regime' originated in a book entitled *The Imaginary Signifier*. The task for the twenty-first century is to make sure that the signifier remains neither imaginary nor invisible.

Bibliography

Books and articles

Antaki, Mark. "Genre, Critique, and Human Rights." *University of Toronto Quarterly* 82(4) (2013): 974–996.

Arendt, Hannah. "Introduction." In Walter Benjamin, *Illuminations*, edited by Hannah Arendt. London: Schocken Press, 1968.

Bach, Steven. *Leni—The Life and Work of Leni Riefenstahl*. New York: Knopf, 2007.

Baehr, Peter. "The 'Iron Cage' and the 'Shell as Hard as Steel': Parsons, Weber, and the *Stahlhartes Gehäuse* Metaphor in the Protestant Ethic and the Spirit of Capitalism." *History and Theory* 40(2) (2001): 153–169.

Bakhtin, Mikhail. *The Dialogic Imagination: Four Essays by M. M. Bakhtin*. Translated by Caryl Emerson and Michael Holquist. Austin: University of Texas Press, 1981.

57 See, in particular, the photos of specialists Charles Graner and Sabrina Harman, ABC News, 19 May 2006: http://www.antiwar.com/news/?articleid=8560. For further discussion, Phillip Gourevitch and Errol Morris, *The Ballad of Abu Ghraib* (New York: Penguin, 2009); Brian Johnsrud, "Putting the Pieces Together Again: Digital Photography and the Compulsion to Order Violence at Abu Ghraib," *Visual Studies* 26(2) (2011): 154–168.

58 Barthes, *Camera Lucida;* Walter Benjamin, "A Short History of Photography," trans. Paul Patton, *Artforum* 15 (1977): 46–61.

Bakhtin, Mikhail. *Problems of Dostoevsky's Poetics.* Translated by Caryl Emerson. Minneapolis: Minnesota University Press, 1984.
Barthes, Roland. *Camera Lucida.* New York: Farrar, Straus & Giroux, 1981.
Barthes, Barthes."Le Message Photographique." *Communications* 1 (1961): 127–138.
Barthes, Roland. "Myth Today." In *Mythologies.* Translated by Annette Lavers. New York: Farrar, Straus & Giroux, 1972.
Baudrillard, Jean. *The Gulf War Did Not Take Place.* Translated by Paul Patton. Sydney: Power, 2000.
Benjamin, Walter. "Critique of Violence." In *Reflections.* Translated by Edmund Jephcott. New York: Schocken, 1986.
Benjamin, Walter. *The Origin of German Tragic Drama.* Translated by John Osborne. London: NLB, 1977.
Benjamin, Walter. "A Short History of Photography." Translated by Paul Patton. *Artforum* 15 (1977): 46–61.
Benjamin, Walter. "The Work of Art in the Age of Mechanical Reproduction." In *Illuminations*, edited by Hannah Arendt. London: Schocken Press, 1968.
Brothers, Caroline. *War and Photography: A Cultural History.* Abingdon, Oxon: Routledge, 1997.
Burke, Frank. "'How'd You Like to Disappear?': The Subject in Film." *CTHEORY* 13.1–2 (1989): 25–43.
Butler, Judith. *Frames of War.* New York: Verso, 2010.
Butler, Judith. *Precarious Life: The Powers of Mourning and Violence.* New York: Verso, 2006.
Conley, Tom. "Foreword." In Louis Marin, *Portrait of the King.* Translated by Martha House. Minneapolis: University of Minnesota Press, 1988.
Cox, Damian, Michael Levine and Saul Newman, eds. *Politics Most Unusual: Violence, Sovereignty and Democracy in the 'War on Terror.'* Basingstoke: Palgrave Macmillan, 2009.
Debord, Guy. *The Society of the Spectacle.* Translated by Donald Nicholson-Smith. New York: Zone Books, 1994.
Dyzenhaus, David, ed. *Law as Politics: Carl Schmitt's Critique of Liberalism.* Durham, NC: Duke University Press, 1998.
Favret, Mary. *War at a Distance.* Princeton, NJ: Princeton University Press, 2010.
Fjågesund, Peter. *The Apocalyptic World of D. H. Lawrence.* Oslo: Norwegian University Press, 1991.
Foster, Hal, ed. *Vision and Visuality.* New York: New Press, 1988.
Fussell, Paul. *The Great War and Modern Memory.* New York: Oxford University Press, 1975.
Gough, Paul. "'Exactitude is Truth': Representing the British Military through Commissioned Artworks." *Journal of War and Culture Studies* 1 (2008): 341–356.
Gourevitch, Phillip and Errol Morris. *The Ballad of Abu Ghraib.* New York: Penguin, 2009.
Hales, Katherine. *How We Became Post-human: Virtual Bodies in Cybernetics, Literature and Informatics.* Chicago: University of Chicago Press, 1999.
Hales, Katherine. *How We Think: Digital Media and Contemporary Technogenesis.* Chicago: University of Chicago Press, 2012.
Hall, Stuart. "The Determination of News Photographs." In *The Manufacture of News: Social Problems, Deviance and the Mass Media*, edited by Stanley Cohen and Jock Young, 236–243. London: Constable, 1981.

Heidegger, Martin. "The Question of Technology." In *The Question of Technology and Other Essays*, translated by W. Lovett. New York: Harper & Row, 1977.
Herf, Jeffrey. *Reactionary Modernism*. Cambridge: Cambridge University Press, 1986.
Horowitz, Asher and Terry Maley, eds. *The Barbarism of Reason: Max Weber and the Twilight of Enlightenment*. Toronto: University of Toronto Press, 1994.
Jameson, Fredric. "War and Representation." PMLA 124(5) (2009): 1532–1547.
Jay, Martin. "Cultural Relativism and the Visual Turn." *Journal of Visual Culture* 1 (2002): 267–278.
Johnsrud, Brian. "Putting the Pieces Together Again: Digital Photography and the Compulsion to Order Violence at Abu Ghraib." *Visual Studies* 26(2) (2011): 154–168.
Katznelson, Ira. *Fear Itself: The New Deal and the Origins of Our Time*. New York: Liveright, 2012.
Macgregor, Alisdair. *Frank Hurley: A Photographer's Life*. New York: Viking, 2004.
Manderson, Desmond. *Kangaroo Courts and the Rule of Law: The Legacy of Modernism*. Routledge: London, 2012.
Marcuse, Herbert. "Some Social Implications of Modern Technology." In *Technology, War and Fascism: Collected Papers of Herbert Marcuse*, ed. Douglas Kellner. London and New York: Routledge, 1998, 49.
Marien, Mary Warner. *Photography: A Cultural History*, 2nd edn. London: Laurence King, 2002.
Meister, Robert. *After Evil: A Politics of Human Rights*. New York: Columbia University Press, 2012.
Metz, Christian. "The Imaginary Signifier." *Screen* 16(2) (1975): 14–76, 14.
Metz, Christian. *The Imaginary Signifier: Psychoanalysis and the Cinema*. Bloomington: Indiana University Press, 1982.
Mirzoeff, Nicholas. *Watching Bablyon: The War in Iraq and Global Visual Culture*. London: Routledge, 2005.
Owen, Wilfred. *The War Poems*. Edited by John Stallworthy. London: Chatto & Windus, 1994.
Pratt, Mary Louise. "Harm's Way: Language and the Contemporary Arts of War." PMLA 124(5) (2009): 1515–1531.
Rose, Gillian. *Mourning Becomes the Law*. Cambridge: Cambridge University Press, 1996.
Schmitt, Carl. *Concept of the Political*. Translated by Gary Schwab. Chicago: University of Chicago Press, 2007.
Schmitt, Carl. "Der Führer schützt das Recht." *Deutsche Juristen-Zeitung* 39 (1934): 945–950.
Schmitt, Carl. *Political Theology*. Translated by Gary Schwab. Cambridge, MA: MIT Press, 1985.
Sherwin, Richard. *Visualizing Law in the Age of Digital Baroque*. London: Routledge, 2011.
Sontag, Susan. *On Photography: Regarding the Pain of Others*. Harmondsworth: Penguin, 1979.
Stephens, Bradley. "Reading Walter Benjamin's Concept of the Ruin in Victor Hugo's *Notre Dame de Paris*." *French Studies* 61 (2007): 155–166.
Styron, William. *Sophie's Choice*. New York: Vintage Books, 1979.
Tagg, John. *The Burden of Representation*. Amherst: University of Massachusetts Press.
Virilio, Paul. *Desert Screen: War at the Speed of Light*. Translated by Michael Degener. London: Athlone Press, 2001.

Works of art

Friedrich, Caspar David. *Monk by the Sea,* oil on canvas, 110 x 172 cm. Berlin: Nationalgalerie, 1809.

Friedrich, Caspar David. *Winter – Cloister Ruins and Church*, oil on canvas. Hamburg: Hamburger Kunsthalle, 1826.

Websites

Nadal, Paul. "Heidegger's Critique of Modern Technology: On 'The Question Concerning Technology'." *Be Late, a Blog by Paul Nadal*, 12 July 2010, https://belate.wordpress.com/2010/07/12/heidegger-modern-technology.

Video games

Call of Duty, Infinity Ward/Activision, 2004–2011.

Doom, id Software, 1993.

Quake, id Software, 1996.

Chapter 8

The confessor: Oprah Winfrey, James Frey and the logic of confession

Karen Crawley and Desmond Manderson

> That this man is standing in front of me and everyone else in this room is lying to us is heresy. The truth is all that matters. This is fucking heresy.
>
> James Frey, *A Million Little Pieces*[1]

Confession's DNA

Saint Augustine may be said to have founded the genre of the confession in the year 397 AD. He declared: 'I wish to act in truth, making my confession both in my heart before you and in this book before the many who will read it.'[2] The mode of truth-telling, which beats at the contrite heart of the confession, has two faces. The external confession of sins 'in this book' and 'before the many' serves as a model of transformation. It operates to enable the conversion of others. But equally importantly, the internal confession of sins 'in my heart' and 'before God' serves as a model of humility. It operates as a submission before a transcendent and final figure of judgment. The external face is public and objective – it operates in the realm of meaning, which is to say, what we know. Its internal correlative is private and subjective – it operates in the realm of affect, which is to say, how we know. The relationship to truth of both the external and the internal dimensions of confession are equally pivotal. In the first case, were St Augustine to fail to speak the truth – the whole truth, nothing but the truth – he would divert others from following his footsteps. In the second case, failing to speak the truth would be an even worse crime. He would be guilty in that case of heresy – not only a refusal to accept the might of God, but an assumption that He could be conned. A more scandalous blasphemy could scarce be imagined.

Foucault seized on this dual register in his diagnosis of the diffuse functions of confession in the modern world. In *The History of Sexuality* he argued that confession is the means through which networks of power and knowledge converge and

1 James Frey, *A Million Little Pieces* (New York: Random House, 2003), 178.

2 Saint Augustine of Hippo, *Confessions* (Harmondsworth: Penguin Books, 1961), Book X, Chapter 1.

circulate. It spread beyond Christianity to become 'employed in a whole series of relationships: children and parents, students and educators, patients and psychiatrists, delinquents and experts,'[3] and assumed new forms: 'interrogations, consultations, autobiographical narratives, letters.'[4] 'Western man,' he concluded, 'has become a confessing animal.'[5] But confession still contains within its DNA this double helix relationship to truth. On the one hand, the external dimension pertaining to the content of what is confessed reaffirms the prevailing social ideology; on the other, the internal dimension pertaining to the affect of what is confessed disciplines the bodies and souls of individual men and women within discourses – church, police, army, educational institutions, media – that maintain a transcendent authority over the confessing self. The intimate therapeutics of the confessional implicates the modern subject ever deeper within these lattice-works of power.

Hence the double helix that binds truth and confession: a narrative that confirms ideology by presenting evidence of its reality; a disposition that confirms subservience by the naked vulnerability of what is exposed. Indeed, the external and internal dimensions ramify one another, making complicit not just the author but the vast audience that witnesses its spectacle of humility and obedience. From early in the Romantic era onward, Western literature has made the confessional mode a crucial kind of self-expression that is supposed to manifest sincerity and authenticity and to bear witness to the truth of the individual personality. The contemporary manifestations of popular autobiographical discourse, such as tell-all memoirs and self-help books focused on overcoming personal tragedy, resonate strongly with this centuries-old genre. In this era of representational legality, when the theatre of sound and the moving image has taken over the public sphere, confession has become spectacularised, embodying the extremes of intimacy and publicity that reach their zenith in that paragon of modern television, the therapeutic talk show.[6] As Walter Benjamin perceived in 'The Work of Art,' the mechanical reproduction of the mode of confession does not diffuse and weaken its intensity, but rather enhances it through a logic of collective, shared and witnessed intimacy.[7]

3 Michel Foucault, *The History of Sexuality Volume 1: An Introduction,* trans. Robert Hurley (New York: Vintage, 1990; New York: Pantheon, 1978), 63; see also 68.

4 *Ibid.*

5 *Ibid.*, 59.

6 See further, Eva Illouz, *Saving the Modern Soul: Therapy, Emotions and the Culture of Self-Help* (Berkeley, CA: University of California Press, 2008), Jane M. Shattuc, *The Talking Cure: TV Talk Shows and Women* (New York: Routledge, 1997), Patricia Joyner Priest, *Public Intimacies: Talk Show Participants and Tell-All TV* (Cresskill, NJ: Hampton Press, 1997), Mimi White, *Tele-Advising: Therapeutic Discourse in American Television* (Chapel Hill: University of North Carolina Press, 1992).

7 Walter Benjamin, "The Work of Art in the Age of Its Mechanical Reproducibility," *Zeitschrift für Sozialforschung* (May 1936), in Walter Benjamin, *Selected Writings, Vol. 3–1935–38*, ed. Howard Eiland and Michael Jennings (Cambridge, MA: Belknap Press, 2006), 101–33; revised version in Walter Benjamin, *Selected Writings, Vol. 4–1938–40*, ed. Howard Eiland and Michael Jennings (Cambridge, MA: Belknap Press, 2006), 251–283.

A confession requires a confessor – one who is authorised to hear a confession. As Foucault reminds us, confession is 'a ritual which unfolds in a relation of power, since one does not confess without the presence, at least the virtual presence, of a partner who is not simply an interlocutor but the agency that requires the confession, imposes it, weighs it, and intervenes to judge, punish, pardon, console, reconcile.'[8] The High Priest of the secular theology of confession is, of course, Oprah Winfrey.[9] Routinely described as the most powerful woman in media, in America, and even in the world, Oprah is a 'cultural icon, spiritual guru, and media mogul.'[10] In her thirty-year stint as host of *The Oprah Show,* and now continuing with her cable network, print publication network and online presence, she has built a career out of eliciting and performing confessions. When former Tour de France champion Lance Armstrong was stripped of his medals and banned from professional cycling in light of evidence that he had used performance-enhancing drugs throughout his career, he turned to Oprah as confessor. Yet in his special televised interview[11] Armstrong refused to adopt the requisite redemptive attitude of true atonement, describing what he did as 'leveling the playing field' – a performance widely seen as lacking meaningful remorse.[12] The ritual of confession must be performed properly in order to appease the audience and to realise its transformative potential of producing 'intrinsic modifications in the person who articulates it: it exonerates, redeems, and purifies him; it unburdens him of his wrongs, liberates him, and promises salvation.'[13]

This chapter turns to an earlier episode in Oprah's confessional oeuvre to unravel this dual relationship between confession and truth: the controversy concerning James Frey's *A Million Little Pieces.* After Oprah chose Frey's supposed 'memoir' for her Book Club in September 2005, *A Million Little Pieces,*

8 Foucault, *The History of Sexuality*, 61.

9 In this chapter we follow Allan G. Borst's practice of referring to Oprah Winfrey as 'Oprah' in order to underscore the imbrication of her brand and her status as an individual, i.e. to simultaneously name the person and the enterprise: Allan G. Borst, "Managing the Crisis: James Frey's *A Miliion Little Pieces* and the Addict-Subject Confession," *Cultural Critique* 75 (2010): 148–176.

10 Janice Peck, "The Secrets of Her Success: Oprah Winfrey and the Seductions of Self-Transformation," *Journal of Communication Inquiry* 34(1) (2010): 9; see further Sherryl Wilson, *Oprah, Celebrity and Formations of Self* (New York: Palgrave Macmillan, 2003), Jeffrey Louis Decker, *Made in America: Self-Styled Success from Horatio Alger to Oprah Winfrey* (Minneapolis: University of Minnesota Press, 1997), Eva Illouz, *Oprah Winfrey and the Glamour of Misery: An Essay on Popular Culture* (New York: Columbia University Press, 2003); Trystan T. Cotton and Kimberly Springer, *Stories of Oprah: The Oprahfication of American Culture* (Jackson: University Press of Mississippi, 2010), Kathryn Lofton, *Oprah: The Gospel of an Icon* (Berkeley: University of California Press, 2011).

11 It aired January 17–18, 2013 on the OWN channel.

12 Steven R. Thomsen and Harper Anderson, "Using the Rhetoric of Atonement to Analyse Lance Armstrong's Failed Attempt at Redeeming His Public Image," *Journal of Sports Media* 10(1) (2015): 93.

13 Foucault, *History of Sexuality*, 61–62.

first published in 2003 with limited sales, went on to sell 3.5 million copies, becoming the second best-selling title of 2005.[14] When it became apparent early the following year that Frey had embellished parts of his book, disgruntled readers lodged lawsuits against Frey and the book's publishers.[15] Oprah initially defended Frey, but then invited him back on her show to answer to her and her viewers for betraying their trust.[16] The resulting televised showdown was one of the most-viewed episodes of Oprah of all time, provoking prolonged media coverage and impassioned editorials about the status of truth in public discourse.[17] The scandal over Frey's memoir has been a touchstone for subsequent controversies over 'fake memoirs'[18] which, as critics have noted, seem to strike a particular nerve: 'we feel a kind of shame at the ease with which we have been seduced, and discomfort at how naked our desire is for certain kinds of narratives to be true.'[19] The Frey/Oprah affair demonstrates how pivotal these affective responses are to the power of confession, and to maintaining its privileged relationship to truth.

Confession is a juridical procedure, a ritual that works by staging and reaffirming a normative world and by interpellating those who witness it. The aesthetic format and techniques of Oprah's show, and her Book Club's sale of inspiration drawn from experience, affirms the external dimension of confession by mandating the standards of truth by which Frey's confessions were judged and found wanting (as legitimate memoir, then as genuine regret). His public excoriation on *Oprah* demonstrates the internal affective dimension of confession by offering a ritual humiliation by which he could redeem himself. The successive confessions that we trace in this chapter, as first Frey, then Oprah, then Frey, then Oprah again struggled to outdo the other in performing the self as the arbiter of 'emotional truth,' manifest the connection between these external and internal dimensions as well as the anxiety provoked by their apparent unraveling, an anxiety that can only be meaningfully assuaged by re-inscribing the viewer in the scene as confessor. The affair demonstrates for us that confession's ongoing power as

14 Edward Wyatt, "Author is Kicked Out of Oprah's Book Club," *New York Times,* January 27, 2006, http://www.nytimes.com/2006/01/27/books/27oprah.html (accessed April 1, 2017).

15 The lawsuits, alleging breach of contract, negligent misrepresentation and consumer fraud, were eventually folded into a class-action suit and settled by Frey and his publisher Random House in 2007 for US $2.35 million.

16 CBS "James Frey and the Million Little Pieces Controversy," *The Oprah Winfrey Show,* January 26, 2006. Transcript.

17 Edward Wyatt, "Frey Says Falsehoods Improved his Tale," *New York Times,* February 2, 2006 and Edward Wyatt, "'Pieces' Editor Now Says He was Fooled by Frey," *New York Times,* February 4, 2006.

18 Motoko Rich, "A Family Tree of Literary Fakers," *New York Times,* March 8, 2008, Motoko Rich, "Tracking the Fallout of (Another) Literary Fraud," *New York Times,* March 5, 2008.

19 Daniel Mendelsohn, "But Enough About Me," *New Yorker,* January 25, 2010, 68.

public spectacle lies in its ability to enact and to stabilise the bonds of ideology and affect that undergird our 'regime of truth.'[20]

Oprah's Book Club

The power of Oprah's confessional practices was nowhere more apparent than with regard to her Book Club. Beginning in 1996, it was an immediate sensation, propelling the featured novels to overnight best-seller status, creating what *Publishers Weekly* dubbed the 'Oprah effect.'[21] As Mark Hall explains, Oprah functioned as 'a powerful literacy sponsor, persuading otherwise reluctant readers to pick up a book.'[22] This literacy sponsorship involved a reciprocal relationship between Oprah and her readers, in which Oprah offered her credibility and resources, with the promise of self-improvement and moral elevation, and in return, gained ratings and income when readers found the fulfilment they sought. Oprah's Book Club episodes were 'not about the book but what people do with books.'[23] Episodes typically began with Oprah citing an astonishing number of letters received from viewers about the chosen book, before having an appropriate cohort of participants reading their favourite quotations. The episodes were geared towards expropriation from the plot of an ethical theme and an explicit message that is taken as its 'truth.' Normative clarity was further enhanced by the website, including reading guides, background information and resources, and a discussion board.[24] If the underlying ideological message of the club was about self-mastery in the face of an excess of choice and a loss of agency, this message was most immediately confirmed by the mastery over books that it promised its readers/viewers, overcoming the indeterminacy of choice and of interpretation that had previously overwhelmed them.[25]

The powerful impact of Oprah Winfrey's Book Club manifested the twin elements that connect truth and confession, coupling the emotional satisfaction

20 Foucault, *Discipline and Punish: The Birth of the Prison,* trans. Allan Sheridan (London: Vintage Books, 1975), 23, 30.

21 Yung-Hsing Wu, "The Romance of Reading Like Oprah," in Jaime Harker and Cecilia Konchar Farr, eds. *The Oprah Affect: Critical Essays on Oprah's Book Club* (New York: SUNY Press, 2008), 76. See further, Cecilia Konchar Farr, *Reading Oprah: How Oprah's Book Club Changed the Way America Reads* (Albany: State University of New York Press, 2005) and Kathleen Rooney, *Reading with Oprah: The Book Club That Changed America* (Fayetteville: University of Arkansas Press, 2005).

22 R. Mark Hall, "The 'Oprahfication' of Literacy: Reading 'Oprah's Book Club'," *College English* 65(6) (2003): 664.

23 Kathryn Lofton, "Reading Religiously: The Ritual Practices of Oprah's Book Club," in Jaime Harker and Cecilia Konchar Farr, eds. *The Oprah Affect: Critical Essays on Oprah's Book Club* (New York: SUNY Press, 2008) 63.

24 "Oprah's Book Club," http://www.oprah.com/app/books.html (accessed April 1, 2017).

25 Wu, "The Romance of Reading Like Oprah," 81.

of surrender to predictable normative messages. To take its external, ideological orientation first: her choices confirm a very specific world-view animated by compassion on the one hand, but directed towards individual achievement and self-actualisation on the other. Ideology relies on what appears to be evidence from the real world in order to confirm and justify its social assumptions. Oprah's show was governed by a cycle of individual confession, revision, and renewal.[26] Oprah's personal *Bildungsroman*, 'a motivational, even moral, discourse of personal achievement'[27] creates 'a kind of palimpsest'[28] through which readers respond to the text. Images and scenes, carefully selected for their conformity to these assumptions, at each point tighten the bonds between ideological belief and social experience. The books and stories featured on *Oprah* shocked but never surprised. They did not undermine but rather confirmed what we already knew. 'Literature,' Jacques Derrida emphasised, 'is an *institution:* it is not given in nature or the brain but brought into being by processes that are social, legal and political, and that can be mapped historically and geographically.'[29] The fact that literature is an institution means it exists within and not external to relations of power.

Oprah's book club forms part of a tradition of female engagement with affective reading that harks back to the women's book clubs of nineteenth-century America.[30] With this history in mind, the editors of *The Oprah Affect* call Oprah's book club 'the latest manifestation of a long tradition that deploys affect, affinity, accessibility and activism in the symbiotic relationships of readers and texts.'[31] The novels and memoirs Oprah chooses are used to mirror and reflect the private stories of the misfortunate of her guests and the readers, and to transform one's experience.[32] This process of textual transference depends on inculcating reading strategies 'that are motivated mainly by a search for something to carry away,' or to 'carry-over' into non-fictional life.[33] Kathryn Lofton has examined

26 Lofton, "Reading Religiously: The Ritual Practices of Oprah's Book Club," 58.

27 A. Tolson, *Media Talk: Spoken Discourse on TV and Radio* (Edinburgh: Edinburgh University Press, 2006), at 155; see also A. Tolson, ed. *Television Talk Shows: Discourse, Performance, Spectacle* (London and Mahwah, NJ: Lawrence Erlbaum Associates, 2001).

28 Kelley Penfield Lewis, "The Trouble with Happy Endings: Conflicting Narratives in Oprah's Book Club," in Jaime Harker and Cecilia Konchar Farr, eds. *The Oprah Affect: Critical Essays on Oprah's Book Club* (New York: SUNY Press, 2008), 211.

29 Derek Attridge, "Introduction: Derrida and the Questioning of Literature," in Jacques Derrida, *Acts of Literature,* (New York: Routledge, 1992), 23.

30 Glenn Hendler, *Public Sentiments: Structures of Feeling in Nineteenth-Century American Literature* (Chapel Hill: University of North Carolina Press, 2001).

31 Jaime Harker and Cecilia Konchar Farr, "Introduction," in Jaime Harker and Ceilicia Konchar Farr, eds. *The Oprah Affect: Critical Essays on Oprah's Book Club* (New York: SUNY Press, 2008), 3.

32 Illouz, *Oprah Winfrey and the Glamour of Misery,* 144.

33 Louise Rosenblatt, *The Reader, the Text, the Poem: The Transactional Theory of the Literary Work* (Carbonville: Southern Illinois University Press, 1978); W. Booth, *The Company We Keep: An Ethics of Fiction* (Berkeley: University of California Press, 1988)

how reading was ritualised on Oprah's show as a productive discipline. Oprah's book club encourages daily practices that create comfortable circumstances, 'down time,' going 'mindless,' relaxing with a book. By apportioning leisure time and offering alternate world-views, 'reading successfully enacts the principles of Oprah's broader spiritual ambition: to encourage 'connections' and 'success' through regulatory behaviour.'[34] Yet as Lofton points out, Oprah does not practise what she preaches when it comes to her own reading. She consistently argues that books can be lessons in compassion, yet her own moral compass remains apparently unaltered by her readings. Reading is always only the confirmation to others of a relentless *prior* knowledge.[35] 'Reading books 'The Oprah Way' is to read with the problems of the reader being negotiated alongside the problems of the characters . . . is to read only with the intent to solve the *reader's* dilemmas; in the empire of Oprah, the reader is always her.'[36] Texts are treated as commodities through which the consumer may gain specific, valuable and strategic benefits.

In this context, Oprah's selections confirm a widespread conventional wisdom about being and becoming in the modern world, modelling an instrumental relationship to the world through an instrumental relationship to the text. The instrumental reader meets the instrumental author on a field of dreams that is relentlessly apolitical, relentlessly individual, relentlessly utilitarian, and relentlessly optimistic. For these reasons, Nicola Aschoff calls Oprah one of the world's best neoliberal capitalist thinkers,[37] and Janice Peck calls her a 'cultural icon for the neoliberal era.'[38] As Peck has shown, Winfrey's ideology marries the 'mind-cure theologies'[39] of the late nineteenth century, particularly resonant among white middle-class women, to the rise of industrial capitalism and a culture of consumption. The ongoing success of 'Oprah' as a phenomenon is inextricably tied to a neoliberal model of governance, with deregulation, privatisation, the rise of economic inequality, and the advent of a new petty bourgeoisie who wish to maintain the illusion of access to the American Dream. Writing about memoir in a similar vein, Leigh Gilmore argues that redemption narratives in which a narrator overcomes adversity have displaced earlier modes of life narrative that identified the systemic nature of disenfranchisement, unmasked middle-class concerns about sexual violence, linked suffering to state violence, and challenged dominant readings about truth-telling. The narratives that succeed in the current neoliberal

34 Lofton, "Reading Religiously: The Ritual Practices of Oprah's Book Club," 56.

35 *Ibid.*, 67.

36 *Ibid.*, 70.

37 Nicole Aschoff, "Oprah Winfrey: One of the World's Best Neoliberal Capitalist Thinkers," *Guardian*, May 9, 2015, https://www.theguardian.com/tv-and-radio/2015/may/09/oprah-winfrey-neoliberal-capitalist-thinkers (accessed April 1, 2017) and Nicole Aschoff, *New Prophets of Capital* (London: Verso Books, 2014).

38 Janice Peck, *Age of Oprah: Cultural Icon for the Neoliberal Era* (New York: Routledge, 2008).

39 *Ibid.*, 108.

market point away from a critique of the systemic nature of inequalities, and promote an increasingly non-specific and generic self.[40] As Aschoff explains:

> Oprah's stories, those she elicits in confessional and those that feature in her book club, powerfully resonate with the feelings of anxiety and alienation familiar under neoliberalism, but elide the role of political, economic and social structures in creating that misery. Rather than changing the world, the answer, they suggest, is to turn inwards and reconfigure ourselves to adapt to our ideological environment. In fact Oprah's rituals of transformation-through-confession are appealing precisely *because* they elide those structures and therefore make the good life seem attainable. If we just fix ourselves, we can flourish. Neoliberalism's *coup* here is that if we turn our gaze inward, and remain in our 'affect', we make no demands of the collective apparatus of the system, only of ourselves.[41]

Thus in the act of confession it is confirmed 'in this book' and 'before the many' what it takes to *be* in the world, without at any point questioning its basic social and economic framework. The ideological implications of this approach will not be lost to anyone familiar with the work of the Frankfurt School:

> Rationality is being transformed from a critical force into one of adjustment and compliance. Autonomy of reason loses its meaning in the same measure as the thoughts, feelings and actions of men are shaped by the technical requirements . . . and the subordination of thought to pre-given external standards.[42]

In particular, the book club's reliance on memoir and personal testimony brings the Good News of this ideological adjustment, compliance and subordination, from the front lines of the real world itself. If this seems to confirm our pre-given ideological world-view, it has been carefully crafted to appeal to it in the first place.

The aura of literary merit that hangs over Oprah's Book Club itself is no less ideological than aesthetic. Pierre Bourdieu's *Distinction: A Social Critique of the Judgment of Taste* offers a theoretical framework for interpreting Winfrey's judgment:

> The ideology of natural taste owes its plausibility and its effects to the fact that [. . .] it naturalizes real differences, converting differences in the mode of acquisition of culture into differences of nature; it only recognizes as legitimate the relation to culture [. . .] which least bears the visible marks of its

40 Leigh Gilmore, "American Neoconfessional: Memoir, Self-Help, and Redemption," *Biography,* 33 (4) (2010): 657.

41 Aschoff, "Oprah Winfrey: One of the World's Best Neoliberal Capitalist Thinkers."

42 Herbert Marcuse, "Some Social Implications of Technology," *The Essential Frankfurt School Reader* (New York: Bloomsbury Publishing, 1982), 146.

> genesis, which has nothing 'academic,' 'scholastic,' 'bookish,' 'affected,' or 'studied' about it, but manifests by its ease and naturalness that true culture is nature – a new mystery of immaculate conception.[43]

As Bourdieu explained, we continue to divorce the social and aesthetic, to insist that taste is 'a gift of nature,' of sensitive spirit or high intellect, but 'all cultural practices (museum visits, concert-going, reading, etc.) and preferences in literature, painting or music, are closely linked to educational level . . . and social origin.'[44] What we choose to read, and how we engage in reading as a practice, mirrors and reproduces normative social structure.

The Book Club's commitment to the relationship between truth and text constitutes an internal, affective discipline on the part of the speaking and observing subject. The intimacy of a truthful confession 'in my heart' and 'before God' constitutes the power of Oprah herself as part of the whole assemblage of disciplinary matrices that shape the modern world. How is this discourse of authority and mercy established? Oprah rhetorically identifies herself with viewers, effacing her star quality and conveying a sense of equality. She does not talk down to them, but rather assumes a shared surprise at new discoveries, 'present[ing] herself not as the informed expert but as an informed witness-participant.'[45] So successful is this strategy that many among her viewing audience treat her television persona as 'real,' as uncontaminated by the multiple forces of mediation that delivers her to them – television, cinema, magazines and internet. This imagined intimacy results in what Louann Haarman identifies as a 'parasocial' relationship 'whereby viewers relate to the media personalities as if they actually know them.'[46] Oprah's willingness to talk about her own history of sexual abuse, and her open struggles with weight, self-esteem and food, shortened this interpersonal distance further, resonating with many viewers and furthering their sense of commonality and connection.[47] (That this relationship is fictitious is demonstrated by the fact that this disclosure was always carefully managed – Oprah never spoke about her husband, for instance.)

In her relationship to her guests, Oprah is the authority to whom confession is offered – the confessor – but in relation to the audience, she is frequently in the position of confessant, and this endows her with another form of power

43 Pierre Bourdieu, *Distinction: A Social Critique of the Judgment of Taste*, trans. Richard Nice (New York: Harvard University Press, 1987), 68.

44 Bourdieu, *Distinction*, 1.

45 Jennifer Harris and Elwood Watson, "Introduction: Oprah Winfrey as Subject and Spectacle," in Jennifer Harris and Elwood Watson, eds. *The Oprah Phenomenon* (Lexington, KY: University Press of Kentucky, 2007), 5. See further, Jane M. Shattuc, *The Talking Cure: TV Talk Shows and Women*, 95–96.

46 Louann Haarman, "Performing Talk," in Andrew Tolson, ed. *Television Talk Shows: Discourse, Performance, Spectacle* (Mahwah, NJ: Lawrence Erlbaum Associates, 2001), 46, cited in Jennifer Harris and Elwood Watson, "Introduction: Oprah Winfrey as Subject and Spectacle," 3.

47 See Illouz, *Oprah Winfrey and the Glamour of Misery*, 34.

and authority, one that derives from personal experience. Her ability to move seamlessly between the two roles means she is able to embody the extremes of celebrity and intimacy, of moral authority and close confidant. And as Misha Kavka observes, live talk shows like Oprah's exploit television as a 'technology of intimacy . . . inseparable from emotional proximity, or the capacity of the camera to make me *feel* as if I am there, to make me care about the event, and to draw me into an intimate relation with those in the frame.'[48] This televisual intimacy invites viewers to 'inhabit the space of audience and celebrity simultaneously'[49] – what Jean Baudrillard terms an 'ecstasy of communication.'[50] This intimate moral bond between Oprah and her viewers[51] consolidates her transcendent authority as the arbiter of truth and feeling. The sanctity of her confessional is a necessary component, if that authority is not to be revealed to be an artifice.

Truth in crisis

Oprah's power, like Augustine's confession, relies on the production of truth in order to fully affirm both an external dimension (read: ideological conformity, including conformity to established literary norms) in which truth is related 'in a book' and 'before the many'; and an internal dimension (read: intimate abjection as a form of radical submission) in which truth is exposed 'in my heart' and 'before God'. The former truth-telling ensures that everyone knows what to think. The latter truth-telling ensures that everyone knows how to feel. It is in this context that we can best understand what was at stake in the scandal over James Frey's memoir *A Million Little Pieces,* which signalled nothing less than a crisis in the relationship between truth and confession.

After Oprah announced that her next pick for her Book Club was one she 'couldn't put down . . . a gut-wrenching memoir that is raw and it's so real,'[52] Frey appeared on an episode called "The Man Who Kept Oprah Awake at Night." Oprah hailed Frey's book as 'like nothing you've ever read before. Everybody at Harpo is reading it. When we were staying up late at night reading it, we'd come in the next morning saying, "What page are you on?"' Though she did ask Frey about a few particular events in the book, Oprah generalised the themes and content of *A Million Little Pieces* and instead focused on the affective reading experience, speaking to the audience's common feeling and reception of the book: 'I've never read a book like this. It's like you were talking to us . . . How did you decide on that style?' In emotional filmed testimonials, employees of Harpo Productions lauded the book as revelatory, with some choking back tears. When the

48 Misha Kavka, *Reality, Affect and Intimacy* (London: Palgrave Macmillan, 2008), 6.

49 Decker, *Made in America: Self-Styled Success from Horatio Alger to Oprah Winfrey,* 117.

50 Jean Baudrillard, "The Ecstasy of Communication," *The Anti-Aesthetic: Essays on Postmodern Culture.* Hal Foster, ed. (Port Townsend, WA: Bay, 1983), 126.

51 Steven Shapin, *A Social History of Truth: Civility and Science in Seventeenth-Century England* (Chicago: University of Chicago Press, 1994), 6.

52 CBS, *The Oprah Winfrey Show*, September 22, 2005.

camera then returned to a damp-eyed Oprah, she said, 'I'm crying 'cause these are all my Harpo family, and we all loved the book so much.'[53]

The book follows Frey, a drug addict seeking escape and self-medication through a veritable pharmacopoeia of reality-altering chemicals, as he makes his way through a drug rehabilitation program. *A Million Little Pieces* highlights Frey's rejection of the rigid twelve-step program used at the clinic, and ultimately attributes his recovery to his copious willpower. The book ends with Frey winning a climactic duel with a glass of bourbon on the day of his release. Frey's work thus followed the familiar contours of what Allen G. Borst calls that 'narrative form par excellence of contemporary American culture,' 'the addict-subject confession.'[54] Megan C. Brown has called contemporary American addiction memoirs like Frey's 'biopolitical guides for living,' in which 'each author teaches methods of substance abuse recovery by describing his/her deviance from norms, and illustrating possibilities for reentering the realm of the normal, the productive, the well-managed.'[55] In this way, memoirist's confessions work as a biopolitical technology, serving the broader goal of governing at a distance as subjects learn and perpetuate norms for healthy, productive citizenship.

A Million Little Pieces provided a model narrative of willpower and the resiliency of the human spirit that Oprah's audience could feel a part of, identify with, and imitate. In the episode's climactic segment, Oprah discussed how Frey inspired one viewer, Sandy, to deal with her own addiction and enter rehab. According to Oprah, Sandy's story began when she posted messages on the book club website. Oprah explained that 'Just days ago an addicted mom teetering on the edge reached out for help as she was reading *A Million Little Pieces*.' Frey responded to Sandy by offering the proverb from his book: 'Hold on.' After reading the book and receiving information about a clinic from Oprah's producers, Sandy entered rehab. Video footage shown during the segment even captured Frey visiting her at the clinic. As Borst observes, this scene is a metonymy of Oprah's self-help logic: she wants viewers to relate to the show as would addicts in recovery, and 'to look to her for a perpetual supply of motivational stories and advice for scripting a healthy and fulfilling life.'[56]

At first blush, Frey's book lived up to the label on the box. His narrative resolutely confirmed both the conventional understanding of the problems of addiction and the resources of self-actualisation needed to triumph over them. And his appearance enabled the production of emotional intimacy that consolidated both his subservience to Oprah's hieratic authority and that of her audience. He *emphasised* his honesty, saying on *Oprah* during his first appearance, 'If I was

53 CBS, "The Man Who Kept Oprah Awake at Night: A Million Little Pieces," *The Oprah Winfrey Show*, October 26, 2005. Transcript.

54 Borst, "Managing the Crisis," 148.

55 Megan C. Brown, "Learning to Live Again: Contemporary U.S. Memoir as Biopolitical Self-Care Guide," *Biography* 36 (2) (2013): 360.

56 Borst, "Managing the Crisis," 157.

going to write a book that was true, and I was going to write a book that was honest, then I was going to have to write about myself in very negative ways.' The 'raw,' 'real' truth of Frey's memoir confirmed the familiar trope of individual autonomy and likewise confirmed the familiar submission to priestly power.

But then it all fell apart. On January 8, 2006, *The Smoking Gun* released a report originally called "The Man who Conned Oprah," revealing that vast portions and key incidents in Frey's supposed memoir had no basis in fact.[57] Frey had invented many of the book's gruesome details, including a root canal without anesthetic, the amount of time he spent in prison, and his involvement in the death of a girl from his high school (represented as the tragic death of his first love). Appearing on the *Larry King* show three days later, Frey claimed that all memoirs alter minor details for literary effect. He stressed that the book was 'a subjective story,' 'one person's event' and 'an individual's perception.' 'I've acknowledged that there were embellishments in the book. I don't think it's necessarily appropriate to say I've conned anyone . . . I still stand by the essential truths of the book.' Frey repeated the phrase 'essential truth' seven times during that interview.

> As I said, the essential truth of the book, which is about drug and alcohol addiction[,] is there. I couldn't have written about what I write about if I hadn't gone through it. You know, the emotional truth is there.[58]

When Oprah called into King's live show, her version of this claim was that 'the underlying message of redemption still resonates with me.' She stressed the reality of his painful past with addiction and his status as a survivor with a message 'to save other people and allow them to save themselves.'

> If you're an addict whose life has been moved by this story, and you feel that what James went through was able to – to help you hold on a little bit longer, and you connected to that – that is real. That is real. And it's – it's irrelevant discussing, you know, what – what happened or did not happen to the police.[59]

This was a courageous defence, but it was soon to become untenable.

Frey's manuscript contained an inherent problem. An addict's confession is surely an updated version of the Cretan liar paradox.[60] On the one hand, its

57 "A Million Little Lies: Exposing James Frey's Fiction Addiction," *The Smoking Gun*, January 8, 2006, http://www.thesmokinggun.com/archive/0104061jamesfrey1.html (accessed April 1, 2017).

58 CNN "Interview with James Frey," *Larry King Live*, January 11, 2006, http://transcripts.cnn.com/TRANSCRIPTS/0601/11/lkl.01.html (accessed April 1, 2017).

59 *Ibid.*

60 One of themselves, even a prophet of their own, said, 'The Cretans are always liars. . . . This witness is true' (Titus 1: 12–13). The Liar's Paradox is the problem of a sentence asserting its own falsehood: 'This very sentence is false.' If this sentence is true, then it is false; and if it false, it is true: a paradox.

success as memoir was due to its conformity to familiar stereotypes of the addict as a degenerate, amoral, liar. But on the other hand, given how explicitly the manuscript promoted this conventional wisdom, why did it not fall foul of the same sceptical response? If Frey was really a compulsive liar, why should we believe him? Was he lying then? Is he lying now? Frey told *The Times* that he had originally 'envisioned' the book as a novel, and he and the publisher were 'in discussions after we sold it as to whether to publish it as fiction or as non-fiction.'[61] In the end, Doubleday punted for the latter.[62] When Frey appeared on CNN's *Larry King Live*,[63] he revealed that Doubleday had hoped that 'the aura of truth might give it traction.'[64] Frey's publisher was later reported as saying that Frey, in the gripping manuscript he had submitted, had described himself as 'a liar, a cheater and an addict,' and under those circumstances she did not believe she was reading 'the New Testament, where every word was avowed truth.'[65]

In the original 2003 *New York Times Review*, Janet Maslin skewered the book's use of predictable, masculine tropes and self-conscious literariness: 'Little problem,' she wrote then. 'This story is supposed to be all true.'[66] Jaime Harker points out the book's continuities with mean street, hard-boiled detective fiction (Hammet, Chandler, etc.) as well as creative non-fiction about drug addiction (Bret Easton Ellis).[67] The prose of *A Million Little Pieces* contains random capitalisations of nouns within sentences, pervasive profanity, and graphic descriptions of vomit, blood and faeces. The book proceeds through a number of conventional tropes, beginning with its opening conceit, 'waking up not knowing where you are':

> I wake to the drone of an airplane engine and the feeling of something warm dripping down my chin. I lift my hand to feel my face. My front four teeth are gone, I have a hole in my cheek, my nose is broken and my eyes are swollen nearly shut. I open them and I look around and I'm in the back of a plane and there's no one near me. I look at my clothes and my clothes are covered with a colorful mixture of spit, snot, urine, vomit and blood.

61 Edward Wyatt, "Best-Selling Memoir Draws Scrutiny" *New York Times*, January 10, 2006, http://www.nytimes.com/2006/01/10/books/10frey.html?_r=1 (accessed April 1, 2017).

62 *Ibid.*

63 CNN "Interview with James Frey," *Larry King Live*, January 11, 2006. Transcript, http://transcripts.cnn.com/TRANSCRIPTS/0601/11/lk1.01.html (accessed April 1, 2017).

64 Randy Kennedy, 'My True Story, More or Less, and Maybe Not at All.' *New York Times (Late Ed.)* January 15, 2006, s. 4 at 1, http://www.nytimes.com/2006/01/15/weekinreview/15kenn.html?pagewanted=print

65 Hilary Hylton, "Oprah v James Frey: The Sequel," Monday, July 30, 2007, http://www.time.com/time/arts/article/0,8599,1648140,00.html?cnn=yes (accessed April 1, 2017).

66 Janet Maslin, "Cry and You Cry Alone? Not if You Write About It," *New York Times*, April 21, 2003, http://query.nytimes.com/gst/fullpage.html?res=9802E3DE133AF932A15757C0A9659C8B63 (accessed April 1, 2017).

67 See Jaime Harker, "Afterword: Oprah, James Frey, and the Problem of the Literary," in Jaime Harker and Cecilia Konchar Farr, eds. *The Oprah Affect: Critical Essays on Oprah's Book Club* (New York: SUNY Press, 2008), 326.

Frey insists that going to therapy, submitting to a 'higher power,' naming alcoholism as a disease, and identifying genetic and environment 'causes' for substance abuse are simply excuses for a weak, effeminate character. Through his performance, he could become a man so formidable that even the shadowy Mafia boss is frightened of him, so tough he survives four root canals without anesthetic, so stoic that only he, of all his friends in recovery, survives. Frey's fantasy of 'Frey' is a bad guy who can throw down with anyone. 'Why be just a run-of-the-mill jackass when you can make yourself into a monster?'[68] Frey's novel is a fantasy come to life; a fantasy that Oprah and her readers naively accepted at face value.

Frey attempted to maintain an incoherent subject position: the lying-author-cum-truth-telling-narrator. He was a liar as a person, that is, in his real existence as an addict, and a truth-teller as a persona, i.e. in his unreal existence as an author. These contradictions were invisible because of the extent to which the book's narrative functioned within the mode of public confession to confirm so reassuringly *Oprah's* ideological world-view. Frey filters his own experience through the pre-existing expectations of the genre: what seems authentic is utterly dependent on the kinds of traditions commonly used to describe such experiences. This is, of course, precisely the way that both literature and ideology function, and indeed collaborate.[69] In the sappy love story in particular, Frey performs a conversion to the ideology of self-improvement through the adoption of feminine values that must have seemed a perfect choice for Oprah's therapeutic focus.[70] As one blogger put it, 'exaggeration of the power we have over our own destinies rings true to those who are looking for that kind of thing, and false to anyone who knows better.'[71]

The Frey affair erupted in the midst of the media's preoccupation with 'truthiness,' popularised after the pilot of *The Colbert Show* in October 2005, the same month Frey went on Oprah's show.[72] 2005 was later dubbed 'The Year of Truthiness.'[73] Colbert was satirising the appeal to emotion and 'gut feeling' as a rhetorical device in contemporary socio-political discourse – of 'feeling' the truth as a higher form of knowledge. We live in 'an age of truthiness,' declared Frank Rich in the *New York Times*:

> As Oprah Winfrey, the ultimate arbiter of our culture, has made clear, no one except pesky nitpickers much cares whether Mr. Frey's autobiography is true

68 Trysh Travis, "James Frey: Feelings as Facts," *The Chronicle of Higher Education* 52.22 (February 3, 2006), B5.

69 D. A. Miller, *The Novel and the Police* (Berkeley: University of California Press, 1988).

70 Harker, "Afterword: Oprah, James Frey, and the Problem of the Literary," 326.

71 Mara Naselli, "Truth as Memoir," *Identity Theory*, January 31, 2006, http://www.identitytheory.com/nonfiction/naselli_truth.php (accessed April 1, 2017).

72 Colbert applied the word to Bush's nomination of Harriet Miers to the Supreme Court and the decision to invade Iraq in 2003.

73 Monica Davey, "2005: In a Word; Truthiness," *New York Times*, December 25, 2005, http://www.nytimes.com/2005/12/25/weekinreview/2005-in-a-word.html (accessed April 1, 2017).

> or not . . . Such distinctions have long since washed away in much of our public life. What matters most now is whether a story can be sold *as* truth, preferably on television.[74]

Truthiness in short, is not the same as truth. It is rather the illusion or patina of truth, its familiarity, its reassuring texture of plausibility: its ideology. If Frey's memoir had been opposed to the forces of normalisation, then the confession of untruth would be a triumph for the status quo. But when memoirs so blatantly conform to what we want, hoax memoirs force us to look at the power of our own desire to construct the reality that mirrors it. Frey exposed Oprah to mortal peril: his duplicity exposed her credulity. She believed him because his story so perfectly satisfied what she wanted and expected to hear. The logic of ideology itself is thereby uncannily exposed. A logic to which Oprah herself appeared to be in thrall; sometimes the addict, always the pusher.

The empire strikes back

The backlash against both Frey and Oprah was considerable.[75] Tom Scocca of the *New York Observer* accused Frey of 'retreating into the language of criticism and sophistication.' Heaven forbid.

> Mr. King, the old-line interview guy, couldn't quite get it. In a baffled coda, he mused about the limits of the unreliable narrator. Were he writing his own memoir, he said, 'I know that the first famous person I interviewed, let's say, was Bobby Darin. Now, I have – that's 49 years ago. Now, maybe it was Danny Thomas, you know?' What Mr. King was getting at, in his secretly tenacious way, was that no, you can't fudge the root canal. You can't fudge the jail time. The truth that James Frey had been offering was not divisible. It was not shaded or interpreted. It was the truth of experience – of testimony: This happened, and I bear witness.[76]

Oprah was accused of succumbing to blatant subjectivism. Writing for the *New York Times*, Michiko Kakutani called Frey's assertion that the writer of a memoir was re-telling a subjective story 'cavalier.'[77] She contrasted Frey's book with

74 Frank Rich, "Truthiness 101: From Frey to Alito," *New York Times*, January 22, 2006, http://select.nytimes.com/2006/01/22/opinion/22rich.html?_r=2 (accessed April 1, 2017). See, further, Frank Rich, "Truthiness Stages a Comeback," *New York Times*, September 20, 2008, referring to John McCain's campaign for presidency.

75 Silbey observes that the ambivalence of the public and media regarding Frey's lies was a 'second scandal.' Jessica Silbey, "Criminal Performances: Film, Autobiography and Confession," *New Mexico Law Review* 37 (2007): 189.

76 Tom Scocca, "The Awful Untruth," *New York Observer*, January 22, 2006, http://www.observer.com/node/38267 (accessed November 1, 2016).

77 Michiko Kakutani, "Critic's Notebook: Bending the Truth in a Million Little Ways," *New York Times*, January 17, 2006, E1.

Oprah's next choice, Elie Wiesel's *Night,* the embodiment of 'the apprehension of memory as a sacred act.'[78] Kakutani explains that Frey's memoir lies at the intersection of our cultural obsession with the first-person singular, and the popularity of recovery movement reminisences, fuelled by talk-shows like Oprah's:

> These two phenomena yielded the so-called 'memoir of crisis' – a genre that has produced a handful of genuinely moving accounts of people struggling with illness and personal disaster but many more ridiculously exhibitionistic monologues that like to use the word 'survivor' (a word once reserved for individuals who had lived through wars or famines or the Holocaust) to describe people coping with weight problems or bad credit.
>
> . . . It creates a climate in which concepts like 'credibility' and 'perception' replace the old ideas of objective truth – a climate in which the efforts of nonfiction writers to be as truthful and accurate as possible give way to shrugs about percentage points of accountability, a climate in which Ms. Winfrey can declare that the revelation that Mr. Frey made up parts of his memoir is 'much ado about nothing.'[79]

Given Kakutani's identification of the Holocaust as a sacred place, it is indeed ironic that subsequent memoir scandals involving the Holocaust have not garnered the same level of outrage as Frey's. In *Fragments,* for example, the author continued to be accepted by Holocaust survivor groups even after it was revealed that he had invented the entire thing.[80]

Different subject matter exerts different forces on the boundary that delimits 'truth' from 'non-fiction.' But confession and truth are intrinsically related to the authority of Oprah. The Frey scandal placed in jeopardy her beliefs about individuality, autonomy, addiction, the rehabilitative powers of love, and so on. He undermined her claim to recognise and communicate the truth, that is, to be worthy of the trust placed in 'the Brand Called Oprah'[81] by her viewers. But more than this, the scandal jeopardised her own authority as confessor. The intimate vulnerability of confession confers a disciplinary power: the forgiveness of sins. But this power depends on the confession's abject and unguarded honesty, and the sincere acceptance that the confessor is entitled either to grant or to refuse her forgiveness. It is an act of mercy, desirable but freely given from on high, never the subject of a demand or an entitlement. The power differential between the two is critical.[82]

> The quality of mercy is not strained.
> It droppeth as the gentle rain from heaven

78 *Ibid.*

79 *Ibid.*

80 Blake Eskin, *A Life in Pieces: The Making and Unmaking of Binjamin Wilkomirski* (New York: W.W. Norton and Co., 2003), 107–108.

81 David Carr, "How Oprahness Trumped Truthiness," *New York Times,* January 20, 2006.

82 See Linda Meyer, *The Justice of Mercy* (Ann Arbor: University of Michigan Press, 1999).

Upon the place beneath. It is twice blessed:
It blesseth him that gives and him that takes.
'Tis mightiest in the mightiest. It becomes
The thronèd monarch better than his crown.
His sceptre shows the force of temporal power,
The attribute to awe and majesty
Wherein doth sit the dread and fear of kings,
But mercy is above this sceptred sway.
It is enthronèd in the hearts of kings.
It is an attribute to God himself.[83]

No doubt, lying to an all-powerful God is bad enough. To lie is to hide from power. Adam tried it in Eden with terrible consequences. But to ***trick*** an all-powerful God is much, much worse. There is no cowering involved. Since God is all-knowing, by definition He cannot be fooled. And if He is, then He reveals Himself as an impostor: a liar. This was the predicament in which Oprah found herself. Frey had not just sought to evade her authority, but destroyed it. Frey's lie exposed Oprah's lie. By conning the confessional genre, Frey hit in the moment of their weakness both Oprah and the many millions who had succumbed to the ecstasy of his cathartic vulnerability.

Not surprisingly, Oprah hit back hard to re-establish the hieratic authority of the confession. On January 26 she invited Frey back on the show, and, in what was described as 'a stunning switch from dismissive to disgusted,'[84] 'an extraordinary reversal of her defense,'[85] Oprah forced Frey to admit that he had indeed lied about spending time in jail, and that he had no idea whether he had two root canals without painkillers or not, despite devoting several pages to describing them in excruciating detail. Oprah then brought out Frey's publisher Nan Talese to defend her decision to classify the book as a memoir, and forced Talese to admit that she had done nothing to check the book's veracity, despite the fact that her representatives had assured Winfrey's staff that the book was indeed non-fiction and described it as 'brutally honest' in a press release. Oprah used 'I' frequently throughout the episode, thereby asserting her anger, sense of betrayal and displeasure at her predicament: 'trust and truth are key to her brand; to be placed in a position that caused her – however inadvertently – to let her audience be duped is to undermine the basis of her relationship with her viewers, a relationship of which she is fiercely protective.'[86]

83 William Shakespeare, *The Merchant of Venice,* Act IV, scene 1, ll. 173–184.

84 CBS, "Oprah Says Author "Betrayed Millions," *CBS News,* January 27, 2006, http://www.cbsnews.com/news/oprah-says-author-betrayed-millions (accessed April 1, 2017).

85 Edward Wyatt, "Author is Kicked Out of Oprah Winfrey's Book Club," *New York Times,* January 27, 2006, http://www.nytimes.com/2006/01/27/books/27oprah.html (accessed April 1, 2017).

86 Harris and Watson, "Introduction: Oprah Winfrey as Subject and Spectacle," in *The Oprah Phenomenon,* 28.

The aesthetic structure and framing of Frey's appearance on Oprah embodies Foucault's description of the ritual of confession. The episode began with footage of Frey's face in black and white, the camera sliding over it as though to suggest the slipperiness of his conduct, and the voiceover from various television commentators, extracted from the media spectacle of the previous two weeks, conveying the sense of crisis:

> Bastone: 'He has been promoting the book for two and a half years and basically has lied continuously for two and a half years.' Mr. ANDERSON COOPER: (From CNN news broadcast) 'Because the book has seemed so honest and raw, who knows what's real and what's not?'[87]

Oprah then shows footage of her call to Larry King, which quietly fades to a head shot of Oprah, looking straight into the camera as she delivers a 'confession' to her viewers:

> I regret that phone call. I left the impression that the truth does not matter, and I am deeply sorry about that, because that is not what I believe. I called in because I loved the message of this book at the time, and every day I was reading email after email from so many people who had been inspired by it, and I have to say that I allowed that to cloud my judgment. So to everyone who has challenged me on this issue of truth, you are absolutely right.[88]

Oprah thus begins the show with a confession. In a stunning role reversal, she apologises to her audience before seeking to turn the salutary performance of her humbling purification into a new beginning for her own confessional authority. The preliminary modelling of her subjugation before a higher authority becomes the grounds on which she demands the abasement of Frey before her, as an Aztec priest might purify himself before his god before engaging in an orgy of human sacrifice. When, later in the same show, Frank Rich notes how hard it is to admit you're sorry in front of millions of people, it is unclear whether he is talking about Oprah or Frey, and she does not lose the chance to affirm the sentiment. Throughout the catechism that follows, she carefully prescribes or scripts Frey's confession for him, providing him with prompts as to what to say, and approving of his liturgical recitation – 'Good.'

Oprah clearly contrasts her emotional response to the book with a more reflective and analytic 'judgment' that emerges when her vision is no longer clouded. The unreality of Frey's memoir is reproduced in the unreality of Oprah 'recanting' her endorsement of Frey's book notwithstanding her view of it as an effective literary text. When Frey tried to dissociate his real life from his book – 'if I'm

87 "*The Oprah Winfrey Show* with James Frey: Transcript," *New York Times*. January 26, 2006, http://www.nytimes.com/2006/01/26/books/oprah-transcript.html (accessed April 1, 2017).

88 *Ibid.*

talking about any of them, I talk about them not as they were in real life but as they are in the book,' Winfrey emphasised precisely the language of truth and the experience of her own deception.

> But then – OK, I read this book as a memoir, and to me, a memoir means it's the truth of your life as you know it to be and not blatant fictionalization. So when I pick up a book and it says it's a memoir, I'm thinking that that is your life. I'm not thinking that's a character. I'm thinking that that is Lily and that happened to you. And I sat on this stage back in September and I asked you, you know, lots of questions, and what you conveyed to me and, I think, to millions of other people was that that was all true. That was all true.[89]

Frey's heresy lay in undermining the truth of the *author's relationship to Oprah herself*, not to mention her viewers, rather than the truth – or truthiness – of the events in his book. On *Oprah* his book was no longer a literary text but a substantiation of lived, bodily presence: Oprah says she had to keep reminding herself that he survived: 'He's okay, he's still alive.' She would later say that, 'After turning the last page . . . You want to meet the man who lived to tell this tale.'[90]

Oprah: Why would you lie – why do you have to lie about the time you spent in jail? Why did you have to do that?

Mr. FREY: I mean, I think part of what happened with a number of the things in the book is when you go through an experience like the one I went through, you develop different coping mechanisms, and I think one of the coping mechanisms I developed was sort of this image of myself that was greater probably than – not probably, that was greater than what I actually was. In order to get through the experience of – of the addiction, I thought of myself as being tougher than I was and badder than I was, and it – it helped me cope. And when I was writing the book, I – instead of being as introspective as I should have been, I clung to that image.

Oprah: And did you cling to that image because that's how you wanted to see yourself, or did you cling to that image because that would make a better book?

Mr. FREY: Probably both.[91]

Both Oprah and Frey confess. Oprah confesses to being duped, Frey confesses to the process of lying not in what he wrote in the book but in the process of

89 *Ibid.*

90 CBS, "The Man Who Kept Oprah Awake at Night: A Million Little Pieces," *The Oprah Winfrey Show*, October 26, 2005. Transcript.

91 "*The Oprah Winfrey Show* with James Frey: Transcript," *New York Times*, January 26, 2006, http://www.nytimes.com/2006/01/26/books/oprah-transcript.html (accessed April 1, 2017).

writing itself. He reiterated this confession in his 'Note to the Reader,' released by Random House in early 2007, and included in all subsequent editions to the book. Frey identifies his 'mistake' not as presenting a false persona to the public on Oprah's show, which was the thrust of Oprah's allegation, but rather as presenting a false character *in the process of writing the book itself*:

> I made other alterations in my portrayal of myself, most of which portrayed me in ways that made me tougher and more daring and more aggressive than in reality I was, or I am. People cope with adversity in many different ways, ways that are deeply personal. I think one way people cope is by developing a skewed perception of themselves that allows them to overcome and do things they thought they couldn't do before. My mistake, and it is one I deeply regret, is *writing about the person* I created in my mind to help me cope, and not the person who went through the experience.[92]

The difference between a false character and a false confession lies at the heart of their exchange on the *Oprah Winfrey Show*, and reveals the extent to which the deception that troubled Oprah was personal to her and to her relationship with him:

Oprah: OK, I think this is interesting that you keep calling them characters, because as a reader and trusting your story and many times in the story, you say that this is my truth and that the truth matters and you know, and so as a reader, I'm believing you because it's on the book shelf as a memoir. So why, in a – as a – why didn't you just write a novel?

Mr. FREY: I don't think it is a novel. I – I don't think it's a novel. I think – I – I still think it's a memoir . . .

Oprah: No. But – but I remember when you were here the last time in the after-show, a woman stood up and said, 'After reading this book and seeing you coming through what you came through the way you did and you having the attitude that you did makes me feel that I can do it, too.' I think you presented a *false person*.[93]

On having written his account of the dental operation 'from memory,' the audience booed. Frey offered: 'you know, since that time, I've struggled with the idea of it, and . . ., ' Oprah interrupted: 'No, the lie of it. That's a lie. It's not an idea, James, that's a lie.'[94] The audience applauded.

At the climax of the show, Oprah entices him into saying the word lying, by saying it before him and then after him so the word is pronounced three times.

92 "Frey's Note to the Reader," *New York Times*, February 1, 2006, http://www.nytimes.com/2006/02/01/books/01cnd-ftex.html (accessed April 1, 2017).

93 "*The Oprah Winfrey Show* with James Frey: Transcript."

94 *Ibid.*

This re-establishment of the sanctity of the confessional relationship is framed within the importance of truth and the possibility of redemption:

Oprah: I appreciate you being here today, but – because I do believe that telling the truth can set you free . . . maybe this is the beginning of another kind of truth for you.
Mr. FREY: I'm as . . .
Oprah: I don't know.
Mr. FREY: I – I think you're absolutely right. I mean, this is obvious – this hasn't been a great day for me.
Oprah: No.
Mr. FREY: And it certainly hasn't been a great couple of weeks for me.
Oprah: Yeah.
Mr. FREY: But I think I come out of it better.
Oprah: Yeah. Yeah.
Mr. FREY: I mean, I feel like I came here and I have been honest with you. I have, you know, essentially admitted to . . .
Oprah: Lying.
Mr. FREY: . . . what I have been – to lying.
Oprah: To lying.
Mr. FREY: And I think that's . . .
Oprah: Which is not an easy thing to do.
Mr. FREY: No, it's not an easy thing to do in front of an audience full of people and a lot of others watching on TV.
Oprah: Yes.
Mr. FREY: I mean, if I come out of this experience with anything, it's being a better person and learning from my mistakes and making sure that I don't repeat them.
Oprah: We'll be right back.[95]

Her final lines to him offer a hope or promise of redemption that is tied to an assertion of the power of her own program: the fact of his having come clean on her show in front of millions of people has now unburdened him. *We'll be right back.*

Torture and truth[96]

The media had a field day with the televised showdown between Frey and Oprah. The episode was one of the highest-rated shows in Oprah's history; a full

95 *Ibid.* The transcript of the show on Oprah's website is edited to downplay her role in eliciting the word 'lying' from Frey via prompts: see "Oprah's Questions for James," Oprah.com, January 26, 2006, http://www.oprah.com/oprahshow/Oprahs-Questions-for-James (accessed April 1, 2017).
96 Page Dubois, *Torture and Truth* (London: Routledge, 1991).

transcript was published in the *New York Times.* This meta-narrative was decisive and revealing. In it, the drama was not characterised as a conversation about the limits of narrative authenticity or policing the line between fiction and non-fiction, but as the reassertion of a power relation with an explicit undertone of physical violence. 'Oprah annihilates Frey,' proclaimed Larry King.[97] Of her transformation from confessor to interrogator, Heffernan wrote, 'she turned in an uncanny performance, modulating her aggression with such finesse that she seemed to be the penitent one, and not the one with the whip hand.'[98] David Carr of the *New York Times* wrote, 'Both Mr. Frey and Ms. Talese were snapped in two like dry winter twigs'[99] and Oprah was left 'surrounded by carnage' but without 'a hair out of place.'[100] Some of the press commended Oprah. *New York Times* columnist Maureen Dowd wrote, 'It was a huge relief, after our long national slide into untruth and no consequences, into Swift boating and swift bucks, into W.'s delusion and denial, to see the Empress of Empathy icily hold someone accountable for lying,'[101] and the *Washington Post*'s Richard Cohen was so impressed by the confrontation that he crowned Winfrey 'Mensch of the Year.'[102] Others were more uneasy, perceiving Oprah's reversal and performance as a little too unnerving. Kolhatkar reported, 'Ms. Winfrey aggressively reduced Ms. Talese and Mr. Frey to puddles on the couch.'[103] Poniewozik describes,

> Oprah let him have it, with a controlled, icy rage that was gripping and frankly scary to watch. 'It is difficult for me to talk to you,' she said, 'because I really feel duped.' It got uglier from there, as Oprah laid into Frey, grilled him on plot points, prodded him to call himself a liar, then tossed the cudgel to the likes of Maureen Dowd, who in a taped bit said, 'Oprah should kick James Frey's bony, lying, nonfiction butt out of the kingdom of Oprah.'[104]

97 CNN, "Interview with Oprah Winfrey," *Larry King Live,* May 1, 2007, http://transcripts.cnn.com/TRANSCRIPTS/0705/01/lkl.01.html (accessed April 1, 2017).

98 Virginia Heffernan, "Ms Winfrey Takes a Guest to the Televised Woodshed," *New York Times Critics Notebook,* January 27, 2006, http://www.nytimes.com/2006/01/27/arts/television/27note.html?ref=books (accessed April 1, 2017).

99 David Carr, "How Oprahness Trumped Truthiness," *New York Times,* January 20, 2006, http://www.nytimes.com/2006/01/30/business/media/30carr.html?ex=1296277200&en=1c0e8843da5b43d6&ei=5088&partner=rssnyt&emc=rss (accessed April 1, 2017).

100 *Ibid.*

101 Maureen Dowd, "Oprah's Bunk Club," *New York Times,* January 28, 2006, http://query.nytimes.com/gst/fullpage.html?res=9C01E2D8113FF93BA15752C0A9609C8B63 (accessed April 1, 2017).

102 James Poniewozik, "Oprah Clarifies Her Position: Truth, Good. Embarrassing Oprah, Very Bad," *Time Magazine online* January 26, 2006, http://tunedin.blogs.time.com/2006/01/26/oprah_clarifies_her_position_t/ (accessed April 1, 2017).

103 Sheelah Kolhatkar, "Freyed Tomato," *The New York Observer,* February 5, 2006, http://www.observer.com/node/38348 (accessed April 1, 2017).

104 Poniewozik, "Oprah Clarifies her Position: Truth, Good. Embarrassing Oprah, Very Bad."

David Carr wrote about Frey's 'public abasement' by Winfrey, who 'turned on him with calculated efficiency, using him to mop up the floor and clean up her reputation at the same time.'[105] He wrote that 'the battle cry to reform the book industry was really just an effort to repair the specific damage to Ms. Winfrey's own lustrous brand' and that Winfrey had stuck by Frey 'until it was clear that it was not just his reputation taking a pounding.'[106] Hilary Frey wrote,

> it was hard to avoid thinking that Frey was being put on display not to set the record straight, but for a public flogging. More than once Oprah emphasised that this experience has 'embarrassed' her. Her revenge: shaming another person in front of a live studio audience.[107]

On his blog author Stephen King called it 'a ritual scourging' that was like 'watching Mike Tyson in his prime beating up some tank-town palooka in a grudge match where the ref refused to stop the fight.'[108]

> It was indeed amazing television. James Frey – the truculent tough guy who used to compare himself to Hemingway – now sat like a boy in detention, gloomily taking his licks from the nation's headmistress until he seemed to whimper. Sure, Mr. Frey was supposed to have been humbled already, brought low by the grievous sins he chronicled in 'A Million Little Pieces,' his best-selling creative nonfiction memoir novel of drug addiction. Oh, but that book's phony 'hitting bottom' was nothing compared to the chastening – the emasculation, really – that he received yesterday on 'The Oprah Winfrey Show.'[109]

Images of ferocious physical violence occur with stunning repetition throughout these reports: cudgels, canes, and whips, beating, castration, breaking, murdering, exsanguination and blood. Viewers witnessed not just an interview or an

105 Carr, "How Oprahness Trumped Truthiness."

106 *Ibid.*

107 Hilary Frey, "Oprah's Revenge," *Salon*, January 27, 2006, http://www.salon.com/books/feature/2006/01/27/oprah (accessed April 1, 2017); Mara Naselli, "Truth in Memoir," see also Deborah Hope, "Loose with the Truth," *The Australian*, January 25, 2008, http://www.theaustralian.news.com.au/story/0,23103214-28737,00.html?from=public_rss (accessed April 1, 2017).

108 Stephen King, "Stephen King on James Frey's 'Million Little Pieces,'" *Entertainment Weekly*, February 1, 2007 http://ew.com/article/2007/02/01/stephen-king-james-freys-million-little-pieces/ (accessed April 1, 2017).

109 Virginia Heffernan, "Ms Winfrey Takes a Guest to the Televised Woodshed," *New York Times Critics Notebook*, January 27, 2006, http://www.nytimes.com/2006/01/27/arts/television/27note.html?ref=books (accessed April 1, 2017).

interrogation but an inquisition.[110] It brings to mind not so much the rituals of confession but those of torture. The comparison is not out of place. For as Foucault and Elaine Scarry insist, the purpose of torture is not to elicit the truth but to stabilise, through the body of the accused, a disruption in the field of power.[111] The torturer doesn't want the truth; he – or she – wants the entire acceptance of the world-view of the torturer.[112] The sovereign does not want or need the truth either. He – or she – wants to demonstrate the absolute inequality of subject positions at the point where it had been challenged. Torture is not about the truth. It is about who gets to decide. It is about domination, and specifically about compelling the abject body of the victim not just to accept it but to *show* it in a public act of penitence; *l'amende honorable*. The language of torture that the media used with astonishing vehemence demonstrated the remarkable extent to which Oprah Winfrey had accomplished that goal. Frey's coerced confession 'before the many,' the viewing audience, re-established the external, public ideology he had undermined by the duplicity in his book. Even more importantly, the bodily intimacy of his confession 'before God' reinstated the internalised, disciplinary supremacy he had subverted by the duplicity in his heart. The natural order first traced by St Augustine had been restored with a vengeance.

Postscript

When Oprah was about to retire her television show in 2011, she invited a number of her feature guests back to do special episodes, and Frey was one of them. Unsurprisingly, it reportedly took several overtures and finally a personal phone call before he agreed to appear. Filmed sitting in an armchair across from him, with no audience present, Oprah reflected on the criticism she received for the interview she conducted in 2006, and apologised to Frey. She explained to him that upon rewatching the video, she noticed that she said 'I'm so embarrassed' three times, and thus realised that her ego was involved:

Oprah: I felt that I had been attacked and therefore had to defend myself. And what I realized when I looked at the tape now . . . this came *[clicks fingers]* as clear as if it was being spoken to me . . . is that what people saw was my lack of compassion. So I apologize for my lack of compassion because I am, you know, in the business of trying to get people's stories, and trying to get to what is the truth of those stories,

110 On the connection between the practices of confession and inquisition, see Peter Brooks, *Troubling Confessions: Speaking Guilt in Law and Literature* (Chicago: University of Chicago Press, 2000), 11–13.

111 Foucault, *Discipline and Punish*, Foucault, *History of Sexuality,* 59 and Elaine Scarry, *The Body in Pain* (Oxford: Oxford University Press, 1985).

112 Robert Cover, "Violence and the Word," *Yale Law Journal* 95 (1986): 1603.

but never in the history of my career . . . and I've talked to every . . . I've talked to murderers, I've talked to, you know, child molesters . . . never in any situation have I walked in to an interview and didn't have a sense of compassion for the person, and I think where my ego was involved with you was I was . . . when I looked at that tape last night my position and intention was: How dare you? How dare you? How dare you lie to me? How dare you lie to the viewers? How dare . . .? And it really was not a position of 'Let me hear your story . . . Let me hear your side', and that was what people saw . . . that was what the lashing was. The lashing was not the questioning; the lashing was the lack of compassion, and for that I apologize.

Mr. FREY: Thank you very much.

Oprah: Take a break. *[Covers her mouth with her hand. Frey reaches out his arms and Winfrey does the same and they hug.]*[113]

In this – final? – confession, Oprah shows her acute awareness that the role of confession in stabilising the 'regime of truth' turns on the complicity of the viewer or witness to the confession. In this respect, Oprah is in the position of the priest or sovereign, an agent of God whose accountability before God is a critical part of their power (think, for instance, of the crisis in Tudor England when Henry was excommunicated). The people are the witness of the relationship between the sovereign and God. In the Catholic mass, the priest carries on a dialogue with God with his back to the people. In the sovereign's public spectacles discussed by Foucault, it is the people who ratify coronations, executions and public punishments. Similarly, Oprah's audience is witness to what must be a reaffirmation of her privileged relationship with God/truth. Oprah's 'confession' that her ego was involved reflects that he had hit her where it hurt, threatening to expose it as a sham and in so doing to expose her. What embarrasses her is that her response made visible her power too manifestly, and in the process undermined her stance as one of the people. The power disparity that lies underneath confession was exposed – by her exposing him exposing her exposing him. And that visibility is what she found uncomfortable (public torture and public execution eventually suffered from the same problems). Oprah couches this discomfort, however, in terms of compassion. She is so clearly a creature of the contemporary logic of confession that she can only see herself in its light. The final lesson, then, is that no one is immune from the logic of confession, no one fails to be trapped within it, not even those who we say are powerful. Oprah is a creature of confession, subject to its bonds of ideology and of affect, just as much as her audience. That is what Foucault meant when speaking of power as a kind of instrument that is not owned by the powerful, but merely uses them.

113 "Oprah Apologizes to Author James Frey," Oprah.com, March 17, 2011, http://www.oprah.com/oprahshow/oprah-apologizes-to-author-james-frey-video.

Bibliography

Books and articles

Aschoff, Nicole. *New Prophets of Capital.* Verso Books, 2014.

Attridge, Derek. "Introduction: Derrida and the Questioning of Literature." In Jacques Derrida, *Acts of Literature,* edited by Derek Attridge, 1–32. New York: Routledge, 1992.

Baudrillard, Jean. "The Ecstasy of Communication." In *The Anti-Aesthetic: Essays on Postmodern Culture,* edited by Hal Foster, 126–134. Port Townsend, WA: Bay, 1983.

Benjamin, Walter. "The Work of Art in the Age of Its Mechanical Reproducibility," *Zeitschrift für Sozialforschung* (May 1936). In Walter Benjamin, *Selected Writings, Vol. 3–1935–38,* edited by Howard Eiland and Michael Jennings, 101–133. Cambridge, MA: Belknap Press, 2006; revised version in Walter Benjamin, *Selected Writings, Vol. 4–1938–40,* edited by Howard Eiland and Michael Jennings, 251–283. Cambridge, MA: Belknap Press, 2006.

Booth, W. *The Company We Keep: An Ethics of Fiction.* Berkeley: University of California Press, 1988.

Borst, Allan G. "Managing the Crisis: James Frey's *A Million Little Pieces* and the Addict-Subject Confession." *Cultural Critique* 75 (2010): 148–176.

Bourdieu, Pierre. *Distinction: A Social Critique of the Judgment of Taste.* Translated by Richard Nice. New York: Harvard University Press, 1987.

Brooks, Peter. *Troubling Confessions: Speaking Guilt in Law and Literature.* Chicago: University of Chicago Press, 2000.

Brown, Megan C. "Learning to Live Again: Contemporary U.S. Memoir as Biopolitical Self-Care Guide." *Biography* 36 (2) (2013): 359–375.

Cotton, Trystan T., and Kimberly Springer, *Stories of Oprah: The Oprahfication of American Culture.* Jackson: University Press of Mississippi, 2010.

Cover, Robert. "Violence and the Word." *Yale Law Journal* 95 (1986): 1601–1629.

Decker, Jeffrey Louis. *Made in America: Self-Styled Success from Horatio Alger to Oprah Winfrey.* Minneapolis: University of Minnesota Press, 1997.

Dubois, Page. *Torture and Truth.* London: Routledge, 1991.

Eskin, Blake. *A Life in Pieces: The Making and Unmaking of Binjamin Wilkomirski.* New York: W.W. Norton and Co., 2003.

Farr, Cecilia Konchar. *Reading Oprah: How Oprah's Book Club Changed the Way America Reads.* Albany: State University of New York Press, 2005.

Foucault, Michel. *Discipline and Punish: The Birth of the Prison.* Translated by Allan Sheridan. London: Vintage Books, 1975.

Foucault, Michel. *The History of Sexuality Volume 1: An Introduction.* Translated by Robert Hurley. New York: Vintage, 1990; New York, Pantheon, 1978.

Frey, James. *A Million Little Pieces.* New York: Random House, 2003.

Gilmore, Leigh. "American Neoconfessional: Memoir, Self-Help, and Redemption." *Biography,* 33(4) (2010): 657–679.

Hall, R. Mark, "The 'Oprahfication' of Literacy: Reading 'Oprah's Book Club'." *College English* 65(6) (2003): 646–667.

Harker, Jaime. "Afterword: Oprah, James Frey, and the Problem of the Literary." In *The Oprah Affect: Critical Essays on Oprah's Book Club,* edited by Jaime Harker and Cecilia Konchar Farr, 321–333. New York: SUNY Press, 2008.

Harker, Jaime and Cecilia Konchar Farr, "Introduction." In *The Oprah Affect: Critical Essays on Oprah's Book Club,* edited by Jaime Harker and Cecilia Konchar Farr, 1–12. New York: SUNY Press, 2008.

Harris, Jennifer, and Elwood Watson, "Introduction: Oprah Winfrey as Subject and Spectacle." In *The Oprah Phenomenon,* edited by Jennifer Harris and Elwood Watson, 1–31. Lexington: University Press of Kentucky, 2007.

Hendler, Glenn. *Public Sentiments: Structures of Feeling in Nineteenth-Century American Literature.* Chapel Hill: University of North Carolina Press, 2001.

Illouz, Eva. *Oprah Winfrey and the Glamour of Misery: An Essay on Popular Culture.* New York: Columbia University Press, 2003.

Illouz, Eva. *Saving the Modern Soul: Therapy, Emotions and the Culture of Self-Help.* Berkeley: University of California Press, 2008.

Kavka, Misha. *Reality, Affect and Intimacy.* London: Palgrave Macmillan, 2008.

Lewis, Kelley Penfield. "The Trouble with Happy Endings: Conflicting Narratives in Oprah's Book Club." In *The Oprah Affect: Critical Essays on Oprah's Book Club,* edited by Jaime Harker and Cecilia Konchar Farr, 211–234. New York: SUNY Press, 2008.

Lofton, Kathryn. *Oprah: The Gospel of an Icon.* Berkeley: University of California Press, 2011.

Lofton, Kathryn. "Reading Religiously: The Ritual Practices of Oprah's Book Club." In *The Oprah Affect: Critical Essays on Oprah's Book Club,* edited by Jaime Harker and Cecilia Konchar Farr, 55–72. New York: SUNY Press, 2008.

Marcuse, Herbert. "Some Social Implications of Technology." In *The Essential Frankfurt School Reader*, edited by Andrew Arato and Eike Gephardt, 138–162. New York: Bloomsbury Publishing, 1982 [1941].

Meyer, Linda. *The Justice of Mercy.* Ann Arbor: University of Michigan Press, 1999.

Miller, D. A. *The Novel and the Police.* Berkeley: University of California Press, 1988.

Peck, Janice. *Age of Oprah: Cultural Icon for the Neoliberal Era.* New York: Routledge, 2008.

Peck, Janice. "The Secrets of Her Success: Oprah Winfrey and the Seductions of Self-Transformation." *Journal of Communication Inquiry* 34(1) (2010): 7–14.

Priest, Patricia Joyner. *Public Intimacies: Talk Show Participants and Tell-All TV.* Cresskill, NJ: Hampton Press, 1997.

Rooney, Kathleen. *Reading with Oprah: The Book Club That Changed America.* Fayetteville: University of Arkansas Press, 2005.

Rosenblatt, Louise. *The Reader, the Text, the Poem: The Transactional Theory of the Literary Work.* Carbonville: Southern Illinois University Press, 1978.

Saint Augustine of Hippo. *Confessions* Book X, Chapter 1. Harmondsworth: Penguin Books, 1961.

Scarry, Elaine *The Body in Pain.* Oxford: Oxford University Press, 1985.

Shakespeare, William. *The Merchant of Venice.*

Shapin, Steven. *A Social History of Truth: Civility and Science in Seventeenth-Century England.* Chicago: University of Chicago Press, 1994.

Shattuc, Jane M. *The Talking Cure: TV Talk Shows and Women.* New York: Routledge, 1997.

Silbey, Jessica. "Criminal Performances: Film, Autobiography and Confession." *New Mexico Law Review* 37 (2007): 189–243.

Thomsen, Steven R., and Harper Anderson, "Using the Rhetoric of Atonement to Analyse Lance Armstrong's Failed Attempt at Redeeming his Public Image." *Journal of Sports Media* 10(1) (2015): 79–99.

Tolson, A. *Media Talk: Spoken Discourse on TV and Radio.* Edinburgh: Edinburgh University Press, 2006.

Tolson, A., ed. *Television Talk Shows: Discourse, Performance, Spectacle.* London and Mahwah, NJ: Lawrence Erlbaum Associates, 2001.

Travis, Trysh "James Frey: Feelings as Facts." *The Chronicle of Higher Education* 52(22) (3 February 2006), B5.

White, Mimi. *Tele-Advising: Therapeutic Discourse in American Television.* Chapel Hill: University of North Carolina Press, 1992.

Wilson, Sherryl. *Oprah, Celebrity and Formations of Self.* New York: Palgrave Macmillan, 2003.

Wu, Yung-Hsing. "The Romance of Reading Like Oprah." In *The Oprah Affect: Critical Essays on Oprah's Book Club,* edited by Jaime Harker and Cecilia Konchar Farr, 73–87. New York: SUNY Press, 2008.

Newspaper articles

"A Million Little Lies: Exposing James Frey's Fiction Addiction," *The Smoking Gun,* January 8, 2006, http://www.thesmokinggun.com/archive/0104061jamesfrey1.html (accessed April 1, 2017).

Aschoff, Nicole, "Oprah Winfrey: One of the World's Best Neoliberal Capitalist Thinkers," *The Guardian,* May 9, 2015,. http://www.theguardian.com/tv-and-radio/2015/may/09/oprah-winfrey-neoliberal-capitalist-thinkers (accessed April 1, 2017).

Carr, David. "How Oprahness Trumped Truthiness," *New York Times,* January 30, 2006, http://www.nytimes.com/2006/01/30/business/media/30carr.html?ex=1296277200&en=1c0e8843da5b43d6&ei=5088&partner=rssnyt&emc=rss (accessed April 1, 2017).

Davey, Monica. "2005: In a Word; Truthiness," *New York Times,* December 25, 2005, http://www.nytimes.com/2005/12/25/weekinreview/2005-in-a-word.html (accessed April 1, 2017).

Dowd, Maureen. "Oprah's Bunk Club," *New York Times,* January 28, 2006, http://query.nytimes.com/gst/fullpage.html?res=9C01E2D8113FF93BA15752C0A9609C8B63 (accessed April 1, 2017).

Frey, Hilary. "Oprah's Revenge," *Salon,* January 27, 2006, http://www.salon.com/books/feature/2006/01/27/oprah/ (accessed April 1, 2017).

Heffernan, Virginia. "Ms Winfrey Takes a Guest to the Televised Woodshed," *New York Times Critics Notebook,* January 27, 2006, http://www.nytimes.com/2006/01/27/arts/television/27note.html?ref=books (accessed April 1, 2017).

Heffernan, Virginia. "Ms Winfrey Takes a Guest to the Televised Woodshed," *New York Times Critics Notebook,* January 27, 2006, http://www.nytimes.com/2006/01/27/arts/television/27note.html?ref=books (accessed April 1, 2017).

Hope, Deborah. "Loose with the Truth," *The Australian,* January 25, 2008, http://www.theaustralian.news.com.au/story/0,23103214-28737,00.html?from=public_rss (accessed April 1, 2017).

Hylton, Hilary. "Oprah v James Frey: The Sequel," *Time*, July 30, 2007, http://www.time.com/time/arts/article/0,8599,1648140,00.html?cnn=yes

Kakutani, Michiko. "Critic's Notebook: Bending the Truth in a Million Little Ways," *New York Times*, January 17, 2006, E1.

Kennedy, Randy, "My True Story, More or Less, and Maybe not at All," *New York Times (Late Ed.)*, January 15, 2006, http://www.nytimes.com/2006/01/15/weekinreview/15kenn.html?pagewanted=print (accessed April 1, 2017).

King, Stephen. "Stephen King on James Frey's 'Million Little Pieces,'" *Entertainment Weekly*, February 1, 2007, http://ew.com/article/2007/02/01/stephen-king-james-freys-million-little-pieces/ (accessed April 1, 2017).

Kolhatkar, Sheelah. "Freyed Tomato," *The New York Observer*, February 5, 2006, http://www.observer.com/node/38348 (accessed April 1, 2017).

Maslin, Janet, "Cry and You Cry Alone? Not if You Write About It," *New York Times*, April 21, 2003, http://query.nytimes.com/gst/fullpage.html?res=9802E3DE133AF932A15757C0A9659C8B63 (accessed April 1, 2017).

Mendelsohn, Daniel. "But Enough About Me," *New Yorker*, January 25, 2010.

Naselli, Mara. "Truth as Memoir," *Identity Theory*, January 31, 2006, http://www.identitytheory.com/nonfiction/naselli_truth.php (accessed April 1, 2017).

Poniewozik, James. "Oprah Clarifies Her Position: Truth, Good. Embarrassing Oprah, Very Bad," *Time Magazine online*, January 26, 2006, http://tunedin.blogs.time.com/2006/01/26/oprah_clarifies_her_position_t

Rich, Frank. "Truthiness 101: From Frey to Alito," *New York Times*, January 22, 2006, http://select.nytimes.com/2006/01/22/opinion/22rich.html?_r=2 (accessed April 1, 2017).

Rich, Frank. "Truthiness Stages a Comeback," *New York Times*, September 20, 2008.

Rich, Motoko. "A Family Tree of Literary Fakers," *New York Times*, March 8, 2008.

Rich, Motoko. "Tracking the Fallout of (Another) Literary Fraud," *New York Times*, March 5, 2008.

Scocca, Tom. "The Awful Untruth," *The New York Observer*, January 22, 2006, http://www.observer.com/node/38267 (accessed April 1, 2017).

Wyatt, Edward. "Author is Kicked Out of Oprah Winfrey's Book Club," *New York Times*, January 27, 2006, http://www.nytimes.com/2006/01/27/books/27oprah.html (accessed April 1, 2017).

Wyatt, Edward. "Best-Selling Memoir Draws Scrutiny," *New York Times*, January 10, 2006, http://www.nytimes.com/2006/01/10/books/10frey.html?_r=1 (accessed April 1, 2017).

Wyatt, Edward. "Frey Says Falsehoods Improved his Tale" *New York Times*, February 2, 2006.

Wyatt, Edward. "'Pieces' Editor Now Says He was Fooled by Frey," *New York Times*, February 4, 2006.

Television episodes

CBS, *The Oprah Winfrey Show*. September 22, 2005. Transcript.

CBS, "The Man Who Kept Oprah Awake at Night: A Million Little Pieces." *The Oprah Winfrey Show*. October 26, 2005. Transcript.

CBS, "James Frey and the Million Little Pieces Controversy," *The Oprah Winfrey Show*, January 26, 2006. Transcript, http://www.nytimes.com/2006/01/26/books/oprah-transcript.html (accessed April 1, 2017).

CNN, "Interview with James Frey," *Larry King Live,* January 11, 2006, http://transcripts.cnn.com/TRANSCRIPTS/0601/11/lkl.01.html (accessed April 1, 2017).

CNN, "Interview with Oprah Winfrey," *Larry King Live,* May 1, 2007, http://transcripts.cnn.com/TRANSCRIPTS/0705/01/lkl.01.html (accessed April 1, 2017).

Websites

"Oprah Apologises to Author James Frey," Oprah.com, March 17, 2011, http://www.oprah.com/oprahshow/oprah-apologizes-to-author-james-frey-video (accessed April 1, 2017).

"Oprah's Book Club," Oprah.com, *http://www.oprah.com/app/books.html* (accessed April 1, 2017).

"Oprah's Questions for James," Oprah.com, January 26, 2006, *http://www.oprah.com/oprahshow/Oprahs-Questions-for-James* (accessed April 1, 2017).

Part III

Scenes of legality

Chapter 9

Legal unconsciousness: tragedy and melodrama in the wake of terror

*Bonnie Honig**

> Trauma: "a memory that one cannot integrate into one's own experience, and . . . a catastrophic knowledge that one cannot communicate to others."
>
> Cathy Caruth[1]

If, as Geoffrey Nowell-Smith, says, "melodrama is the inheritor of many tragic concerns,"[2] then scholars of law, culture, and humanities have good reason to take melodrama seriously. Until now, tragedy has been the legal studies genre par excellence, and with good reason. As the classicist Jean-Pierre Vernant pointed out, tragedy is the genre that first explored the formation of subjectivity by law and plumbed the depths of law's demands.[3] Melodrama, by contrast, seems to be focused on affect, not law, even though crime, violence, and the limits of legalism are often this genre's topics and targets. I will argue in this chapter, via an exploration of two legal-political melodramas, Rainer Werner Fassbinder's contribution to the 1978 omnibus film *Germany in Autumn* and Lars von Trier's *Dogville* (2003), in favor of melodrama's relevance to law, culture and humanities scholarship. I assess the value of these films as sites of critical engagement with law by subjecting them to some of the tests of political efficacy proposed by Jacques Rancière in his critique of the so-called "turn to ethics." In turn, I offer a

* For comments on this paper, I am grateful to the editors of this volume, the other contributors who attended the conference from which the papers here are drawn, and Lori Marso, for "breaking the waves."

1 For Caruth, testimony is a response to what resists narration. See Cathy Caruth and Thomas Keenan, "'The AIDS Crisis is Not Over': A Conversation with Gregg Bordowitz, Douglas Crimp, and Laura Pinsky" (1991), in *Trauma: Explorations in Memory*, ed. Cathy Caruth (Baltimore, MD: Johns Hopkins University Press, 1995), 256.

2 Geoffrey Nowell-Smith, "Dossier on Melodrama: Minnelli and Melodrama," *Screen* 18(2) (1977): 114.

3 Jean-Pierre Vernant and Pierre Vidal-Naquet, "Intimations of the Will in Greek Tragedy," in *Myth and Tragedy in Ancient Greece* (New York: Zone Books, 1988), 63. On Vernant and literature, see Kevin Crotty, *Law's Interior: Legal and Literary Constructions of the Self* (Ithaca, NY: Cornell University Press, 2001), 100 and passim.

critique of that critique, which rejects melodrama as an ethico-political dead end. Instead, I argue, melodrama is a site of critical intensification and exploration of legal unconsciousness.

Melodrama and the limits of tragedy in three waves

Melodrama is the genre that explores, and tries to work through, the impasses into which we are thrust by law and other powerful forces of normativity, habit, or convention. One way to appreciate melodrama's potential for law, culture and humanities scholars is by comparing its entry into the field with the impact of the third wave of feminist scholarship on feminist theory.[4]

In feminist scholarship, the first wave is referential. It asks: "Where are the women?" while tracking their absence. Here one response is to rectify by way of inclusion. Thus, when first-wave feminists objected to the exclusively male "canon," many political theorists began teaching Mary Wollstonecraft, Christine de Pisan, and Simone de Beauvoir in courses on history of political thought. The focus was often still on the same basic political theory issues (justice, inequality, sovereignty, and so on), but once these "timeless" questions were pursued in relation to texts authored by women as well as men, written by authors with concerns about gender, sexuality, and the demands of justice in the "private realm," the new texts began to have an effect on the questions, and on age-old assumptions. For example, justice and equality became thinkable as norms for the household and not just for the state. Similarly, what we might call the first wave in law, culture, and humanities was also initially referential. New texts, novels, were read by legal scholars but the ostensible aim was not to rethink law; it was to track its meanderings. An example of such first-wave legal scholarship might be Wigmore's "A List of Legal Novels," which appeared in the *Illinois Law Review*, 1908.

In feminist scholarship, the second wave names a shift from women as the focus to the feminine, partly in response to the recognition that not all women represent feminist aims (this was once referred to as the Maggie Thatcher problem) and to awareness that patriarchal societies police not just women but also femininity (for example, in men as well). Second-wave feminists ask about the constitution of subjectivity and/as gender/sexuality. The corollary in law, culture, and humanities scholarship is the move to legal consciousness, which looks not, narrowly and referentially, at positive law or jurisprudence, but rather, more broadly, at the constitution of subjectivity as legal subjectivity and at law's productivity in every sphere. Legal consciousness scholars in the domain of

4 I think the analogy between the waves of feminist and legal scholarship may have been first suggested to me by Bill MacNeil. I developed it in 2013 for a presentation to the American Bar Foundation called "That 70's Show."

culture and humanities focus on how subjects conceive of themselves as legal or rights-bearing subjects in literature and film. Here, law moves from jurisprudence to consciousness but still carries a jurisprudential trace, since legal consciousness scholarship tends to focus specifically on subjects' self-understanding as rights-bearing subjects.

In the third wave of feminist scholarship (which does not necessarily succeed the other two, but may be contemporaneous with them; indeed many authors' work – most obviously that of de Beauvoir – qualifies as belonging to more than one "wave"), the feminine is seen as always in relations of sameness or difference to other terms and powers, first and most obviously, masculinity, but also race, gender, heteronormativity and more. This third wave is more focused on the affective and social construction of the terms or the phenomena it aims to investigate. Similarly, we might say, the third wave of law, culture and humanities which, as in feminist scholarship, co-exists alongside the other two and is not their successor, is interested in the constitution of legal subjectivity as part of the broader (to borrow the phrase from Ravit Reichman) affective life of law.[5] If the second wave follows the work of law in subjective consciousness, the third wave moves from a focus on legal consciousness to legal *un*consciousness. We move from being (more or less articulate) carriers of law's norms to being inhabited by law's terrors. Consequently, instead of the second-wave project of looking for law in the actions and opinions of legal subjects, the third-wave perspective invites a focus on impasse. Law's power may be more evident in silence rather than speech; collapse rather than agency may testify to law's diffuse agencies. Even as we trace its effects, the thing we trace – law – has become ambiguous, even imperceptible. It is not jurisprudence (law on the books), it is not the statements of the authorized, it is not what people think it is. Well, it is all of these, but it is also a force that moves through us and exerts force upon us in nameless and multiple ways.

Impasse, silence, affect, and collapse; these are traits of melodrama. Melodrama intensifies the elements of tragedy in which law and subjectification normally find representation by way of speech, rectitude, principle, agency, and discernment, but also reach their limit. Melodrama, we might say, takes up the remains of tragedy and turns them into a genre of its own. For example, in the classical drama most beloved by law, culture, and humanities scholars, Sophocles' Antigone speaks (loudly, often, and at length, as Creon complains) and in so doing represents (il)legality. Melodrama directs attention to her sister, Ismene, and homes in on her sense of impasse, as she struggles to enter into law(lessness), but fails. The tragic orientation offers heroic agency, even if thwarted, melodrama offers (im)passivity, and calls attention to forms of agency that are less obvious than the traditionally heroic: iterative, subversive, or conspiratorial. In the end, a melodramatic approach to the play also alters our sense of Antigone, herself, who

5 Ravit Reichman, *The Affective Life of Law: Legal Modernism and the Literary Imagination* (Stanford, CA: Stanford University Press, 2009).

can also be seen as a conspiratorial rather than solitary heroic actor.[6] Genre frames her: tragedy in one way, melodrama in another. Given its tendency to promote a focus on heroic actors thwarted by law(lessness), it is no wonder tragedy is the genre of choice for most scholars of law and politics. But this is so at some cost, for melodrama's third-wave orientation to legal unconscious may be the domain in which law's power is most forceful even if not always most manifest.

Tragedy and melodrama as politics versus ethics in the work of Jacques Rancière

The idea that melodrama is a genre of law and politics is not widely shared.[7] Jacques Rancière's well-known critique of the "turn to ethics" is also, I would argue, a critique of melodrama, and this in spite of the fact that the low culture genre fits with Rancière's preference for what he calls cinema of the everyday.[8]

By contrast with my own characterization of Sophocles' Antigone above, Rancière sees Antigone as emblematic of the ethical turn of 20th-century philosophy, in particular, the indistinction of ethics. The ethical turn results from 20th-century French philosophers' fascination since World War II with "catastrophe," the "unthinkable," and the "unrepresentable," which leads, Rancière argues, to an ethical focus on witnessing, testimony, or fidelity to the event. Its proponents abandon political action and contestatory division in favor of some abstract right of the other (Lyotard), messianism (Agamben), or mourning of catastrophe (Antigone).[9]

6 See my *Antigone, Interrupted* (Cambridge: Cambridge University Press, 2013) for a consideration of the merits of approaching Antigone herself through a melodramatic lens.

7 See Elisabeth R. Anker, *Orgies of Feeling Melodrama and the Politics of Freedom* (Durham, NC: Duke University Press, 2014).

8 Jacques Rancière, "From One Image to Another? Deleuze and the Ages of Cinema," in Jacques Rancière, *Film Fables*. translated by E. Battista (Oxford and New York: Berg, 2006), 107–123.

9 Rancière here has in mind figures like Levinas, Blanchot, Lyotard, and Agamben. He also allies Hannah Arendt with this group, which means it is a capacious group. Rancière's critique of the turn to ethics is also in effect a critique of trauma studies and so it is a bit surprising to find he dovetails with Dominick LaCapra (a historian and scholar of trauma) with regard to Agamben's work. (Thanks to Anna Terweil for research assistance with LaCapra's work.) Rancière and LaCapra differ on several things (they have different assessments of the film, *Shoah*, for example), but both light on the same detail in Giorgio Agamben's writing, and both recoil from it for similar reasons: Agamben claims that in ordinary soccer matches today, "in the normalcy of everyday life" (*Remnants of Auschwitz: The Witness and the Archive*, New York: Zone Books, 2000, 26), there is a repetition of "the routine yet surreal soccer match in Auschwitz between the SS and Jewish members of the Sonderkommando" (quoted in Dominick LaCapra, *History in Transit: Experience, Identity, Critical Theory* (Ithaca, NY: Cornell University Press, 2004), 178). Agamben warns that "(i)f we do not succeed in understanding that match, in stopping it, there will never be hope" (*Remnants of Auschwitz*, 26). Focusing on the stopping and letting pass the part about "understanding," LaCapra "objects to the shrill yet leveling logic in Agamben's exclamation" (*History in Transit*, 178), a trait he also identifies with those who act out rather than work through trauma.

Those who ontologize suffering, casting vulnerability as common to the human, for example, do not instantiate equality (as they may hope). Rather, they disable efforts to mobilize to overcome inequality, Rancière argues, as he takes Sophocles' tragedy to represent the problem: "The trauma that is summarized in *Antigone*," Rancière says, "is without beginning or end."[10] And so Rancière recommends a move away from Antigone, preferring the puzzle-solving Oedipus to his eternally lamenting daughter/sister. With this move, Rancière is, in aesthetic terms, recommending a return to tragedy as conflict and away from tragedy as suffering. For Rancière: Oedipus offers "clash," Antigone only "miasma."

Rancière never refers to melodrama by name but that genre seems to capture most of the traits of modern film and philosophy that Rancière associates with the ethical turn, affiliates with tragedy as suffering, and brands deleterious to politics. Indeed, distinguishing tragedy and melodrama helps make sense of Rancière's proclaimed preference for Brecht's *St. Joan of the Stockyards*, which depicts a clash between two rights, over Lars von Trier's *Dogville,* which – Rancière argues – is animated by the problem of suffering caused by evil and not by a "system of domination that could be understood and destroyed" through clash. In *St. Joan*, Rancière argues, politics divides morality into two, creating a conflict that can be mediated or resolved, albeit with violence. In *Dogville*, by contrast, the dramatic center shifts from conflict to disease and there is no room for politics. In *Dogville*, the good heroine's suffering does not "depend on any system of domination that could be understood and destroyed." Instead the solution is the destruction of evil people.[11] Rancière's critique is aimed at films that move from a still emancipatory framework to a catastrophic realm of infinite justice, evil, or redemption;

Rancière objects as well, seeing here evidence of how "all differences are erased in the global situation," whose law seems to be "the accomplishment of an ontological destiny that leaves no room for political dissension and expects salvation only from an improbable ontological revolution" (Rancière, "The Ethical Turn of Aesthetics and Politics," *Critical Horizons* 7(1) (2006): 10). LaCapra and Rancière converge in their criticism of those who catastrophize politics and ontologize suffering: "The postapocalyptic Auschwitz-now-everywhere hyperbole obviates" judgment, LaCapra says (*History in Transit*, 178). And Rancière argues that it undermines action: when Agamben aligns everyday power with the Nazi genocide and says "the camp is the *nomos* of modernity" (Jacques Rancière, *Dissensus: on Politics and Aesthetics* (London: Continuum, 2010), 192), he makes political action or analysis difficult, at best, and renders impossible the future-oriented perspective on which political emancipation depends. Still, LaCapra worries that if we refuse Agamben's leveling logic we may be "condemned to hopeless complacency and business as usual" (*History in Transit*, 178).

10 Rancière, "The Ethical Turn of Aesthetics and Politics," 5.

11 Indeed, this is the crux of the matter for Rancière: "Previously, encounters between heterogeneous elements were meant to underline contradictions of a world marked by exploitation and question the place of art and its institutions in this conflicted world. Today the same gathering is stated as the positive operation of an art that has been put in charge [not in question] of the functions of archiving and bearing witness to a common world" (Rancière, "The Ethical Turn of Aesthetics and Politics," 11). In sum, art is now in the service of consensus creation. (Rancière notes a similar slide in Goddard's films from a collage of clash to collage of fusion, which Rancière indicts but does not analyze).

from the realm of action to the realm of mourning or suffering; from clash to hyperbole.

I have some sympathies with this view, having myself argued elsewhere – analyzing the impact of the *Antigone* on social movement politics – that all too often the important politics of lamentation slips into a lamentation of politics.[12] But, I part from Rancière with regard to *Dogville,* which strikes me as an exceedingly political film. In my view, the film presents not a problem of human nature, *per se*, but a critique of the corrupting effects of dependence. Three times in the film, the problem of autonomy is posed and three times in the film, the voluntary relinquishment of autonomy is criticized. First, at the beginning we are told that the people of Dogville gave up democracy because they no longer "felt the democratic need;" second, we are told that though the townspeople had never needed anyone to do their work for them, they soon get used to Grace (Nicole Kidman), a recently arrived stranger, providing free labor and, as they do so, their self-sufficiency wanes and their lack of neighborliness, once merely reserve, now becomes active malice; finally in the film's denouement, Grace says, significantly, but also comically (she is here reiterating the townspeople's bromides), "some things you have to do yourself." When the film closes with Depression-era photos of impoverished people, it makes clear that it aims at a system of domination that is not really invisible.[13] Like the violence that occurs in the Brechtian, open-plan, unwalled homes of the people of Dogville, the system's injustices can be seen if we just stop averting our gaze.[14]

Germany in Autumn: tragedy, catastrophe, melodrama

The move from clash to suffering, emancipation to catastrophe, is not just the route taken by the so-called ethical turn. It is also a genre move from tragedy to melodrama. Rancière discusses catastrophe in terms that call melodrama to mind (fusion, indistinction, hyperbole), but catastrophe and melodrama are not the same thing. It is important to distinguish them and we are helped in so doing by a unique film that I see as a contribution to the third wave of law, culture, and humanities scholarship: the omnibus film, *Germany in Autumn* (1978), which

12 Honig, *Antigone, Interrupted,* Chapter One.

13 See the fine essay by Paul Apostolidis, "'Young Americans': Rancière and Bowie in *Dogville*," in *Breaking the Rules: Gender, Power, and Politics in the Films of Lars von Trier*, ed. Bonnie Honig and Lori Marso, *Theory & Event* 18(2) (2015).

14 Rancière similarly distinguishes *Mystic River* from his preferred scenario of the falsely accused, first given cinematic expression by Alfred Hitchcock and Fritz Lang, Rancière says. Hitchcock, Lang *and* Eastwood all explore the plight of the unjustly accused but only in Eastwood's *Mystic River* (spoiler alert!) is that sad fellow murdered, and with impunity at that. In the films of Hitchcock and Lang, justice is possible, Rancière argues, but not in *Mystic River.*

invites exploration of the political and legal merits of different genres and forms of emplotment.[15]

Germany in Autumn is a New Left Cinema film made by several West German directors and organized by Alexander Kluge in response to the hot autumn of 1977, a season of political uncertainty in West Germany amid Red Army Faction (RAF) kidnappings and murders, a violent airplane hijacking, the development of enhanced state counter-terror measures such as widespread wiretapping, search and seizure, new hotlines for people anonymously to inform on 'suspicious' neighbors, and the turn from diplomacy and negotiation to the use of special forces to rescue hijacked hostages.[16]

The film's various vignettes employ different techniques, genres, and film strategies. But some are more dominant than others. One powerful strategy of the film is to emplot the events of the day as classical tragedy in which the element of clash is central. Another strategy is that of 'catastrophe,' a mode of ethical witnessing and fidelity to the event, which rejects such narration or emplotment as a recuperative ruse and leaves us with what Agamben in *Remnants of Auschwitz* treats as the raw matter of direct testimony.[17] For Agamben, poetry is one instance of such testimony. Its parallel in *Germany in Autumn* is documentary footage, which looks and feels raw. A salient moment is the film's closing line uttered at the RAF funerals, which declares suicide as the last option of those who see no options. Its rawness, itself an aestheticization of the catastrophe approach, underwrites its seeming authenticity.

We might think of melodrama as the genre of catastrophe, its aestheticized form, but this is the difference between them: catastrophe despairs of meaningful narration and treats emplotment as a kind of betrayal, while melodrama self-consciously aestheticizes, providing a genre-frame through which to explore despair, precisely by making affect the center of its concerns, indulging in hyperbole, depicting speechlessness, and aestheticizing collapse. Director Rainer Werner Fassbinder's contribution to *Germany in Autumn* does all of this, depicting law as the source of despair and the force of law as the condition of miasma. Where conflictual tragedy's apparatus of clash depicts political action by lawful or lawless subjects possessed of legal consciousness, Fassbinder's melodrama depicts the legal unconscious that is constituted thereby, haunted in the 'hot autumn' by state terror, emergency powers, and paranoid politics. This is in the context

15 I discuss the film in detail and treat it as a reception of Sophocles' *Antigone*, in *Antigone, Interrupted*, on which some of the following paragraphs draw.

16 In addition to Kluge, the other contributing directors are: Heinrich Böll, Hans Peter Cloos, Rainer Werner Fassbinder, Alexander Kluge, Maxmiliane Mainka, Edgar Reitz, Katja Rupé, Volker Schlöndorff, Peter Schubert and Bernhard Sinkel.

17 In one of the film's sequences by Böll and Schlöndorff, discussed below, Antigone is designated a terrorist as well. Here, though, the concern is not (as in Rancière) that Antigone will stymie action with her indistinction but rather that she might ignite action, generate violence, or inflame popular sentiment.

of a larger film in which events are framed in classically tragic terms and the focus is on legal consciousness: the film's *central* gaze is on the sense of injustice caused by police brutality, for example, rather than the feelings of despair and impotence caused by uncertainty about Germany's Nazi past and its incomplete democratic transformation; the film's central focus is on the raised revolutionary fist in a crowd, rather than on the isolated depressive at home; the preferred clash is over big ideas and not a fight between lovers. The tension in the film – between tragedy and melodrama – caused by Fassbinder's embedding of a melodramatic sequence in an otherwise classically tragic structured film is cast, notes film historian Thomas Elsaesser, as a tension between two Antigones: between a traditional Antigonean frame and one that is "antigonising."[18] The former Elsaesser attributes to Alexander Kluge, who organized the final film, the latter to Fassbinder, who, Elsaesser says, is struggling to break out of Kluge's imposition of form. It is, however, better to think not in terms of form and resistance, but rather in terms of a directorial agon in which alternative forms contend with each other over which is able best to respond to the political challenges of the day.

The Antigonean frame of *Germany in Autumn* can be seen in its several revisitations of the themes of Sophocles' *Antigone*, in particular the politics of burial, with its focus on the debate at the time regarding whether to bury three RAF prisoners – Gudrun Ensslin, Andreas Baader and Jan-Carl Raspe – who were said to have committed suicide in prison. The movie opens with documentary footage of the official, honorific funeral of Hanns-Martin Schleyer, a German industrialist (Chairman of the German Federation of Industry and a Director of Daimler Benz) and former Nazi, who was kidnapped and murdered by the RAF in 1977. The movie closes with the hotly contested funeral a short while later of the three RAF members. "Hotly contested" means there were public objections to allowing the bodies of Baader, Raspe, and Ensslin to be buried in any cemetery and calls were made to dispose of their bodies in the sewers. These terrorists, it was said, had crossed the line from human to animal and could be treated like refuse. The two funerals, of Schleyer and the RAF members, coded by *Germany in Autumn* as official versus transgressive, state-approved versus state-policed, are made central to the story of the hot autumn. This framing of the film echoes unmistakably the plot of Sophocles' *Antigone*, in which Antigone's two dead brothers are given disparate treatment by Creon, their uncle and new ruler of Thebes: Eteocles buried as a hero, Polynices left out to rot, then later buried hastily and without fuss in a makeshift way.

Germany in Autumn makes the reference to *Antigone* most explicit in a comic-tragic sequence, written by Heinrich Böll and directed by Volker Schlöndorff, which the film carries at its moral center. This sequence depicts a Broadcast Commission Meeting debating whether to show a film version of Sophocles' *Antigone*

18 Thomas Elsaesser, "Antigone Agonistes: Urban Guerilla or Guerilla Urbanism?" *Rouge* 4 (2004), http://www.rouge.com.au/4/antigone.html (accessed April 1, 2017).

as part of a television series called *Youth Meets the Ancient Classics.* With the German public in the middle of a debate about whether or how to bury the bodies of three RAF members, all three said to have committed suicide and one of them a woman, this ancient play about burial, resistance, and suicide, which features women acting politically in transgressive ways, seems to anticipate the 1970s political scene, so much so that one of the board members suspects the director has altered the ancient script to inflame the events of the day: "Is that really Sophocles' ending?" he asks, only to be reassured that yes, it is. The television executives decide that "it is not a good time for Antigone," and the executives leave the room.[19] Then onto the television screens pops the play's messenger who describes in tight close-up how Haemon tried and failed to kill his father, Creon, and then killed himself. This unviewed scene, shown to an empty room in a seeming error of broadcasting, calls the film viewer's attention to the parricide (Schleyer) and filial suicide (Baader and Raspe) at the center of current events.

The tragic prism of father–son clash, a politics of generational succession punctuated by the lamentation and resistance of Antigone figures, is also everywhere in *Germany in Autumn.* The film opens with a scene of paternal bequest: a letter, written by Hanns-Martin Schleyer to his son the night before he is killed by the RAF, is read aloud. The letter signs off "dein fati," interpellating the viewer into the position of the son, as it warns of doom if the constitutional state cannot learn how to deal with terrorism.[20] Later, the film features yet another important père/fils pairing: the son is the Mayor of Stuttgart, who uses his executive power of decision to clear the way, against public opinion, for Ensslin's family to arrange her burial, along with Baader and Raspe. The mayor, who makes "a quick decision and clean choice" (as he himself puts it in the film) to allow for

19 Quoted in Martin Blumenthal-Barby, "*Germany in Autumn*: The Return of the Human," *Discourse: Journal for Theoretical Studies in Media and Culture* 29(1) (2007): 143. "Ultimately they decide not to scrap the film but to 'put it on ice until quieter times' – the exact opposite strategy as that undertaken by the makers of *Germany in Autumn*": Evan Kindley, "Germany in Autumn," *notcoming.com,* June 9, 2010, http://www.notcoming.com/reviews/germanyinautumn, (accessed April 1, 2017).

20 Schleyer also laments his betrayal by the state which failed to rescue or redeem him from his captors. That betrayal is backgrounded for those in the know by the open (if denied) secret of Schleyer's service in the SS during the war. The real betrayal, for Schleyer, is the regime change. For others, of course, it is the fact that regime change from German Reich to constitutional democracy was unaccompanied by elite change. As Elsaesser says (in "Antigone Agonistes"), Schleyer in his letter "implicitly accus[es] the Government of having sacrificed him out of clearly political calculations." He adds in a note: "The sense of official hypocrisy – strongly felt by the members of the Schleyer family at the funeral itself – was also alluded to by the Federal President Walter Scheel, who in his funeral oration said: "the face of terrorism makes us blanch. But we ourselves may have to look more often into the mirror.' " Schleyer denied his Nazi past, but as Elsaesser puts it, "behind [his] Biedermann appearance the RAF wanted to expose the fervent SS officer he strenuously denied ever having been." In captivity, Schleyer was apparently several times interrogated by his guards as to his Nazi past. Photos of him in SS uniform circulated in the left-wing press.

the burial, is named . . . Rommel.[21] The father is Field-Marshall Erwin Rommel, Hitler's general, a point underlined by documentary film footage showing the mayor as a young boy standing near the coffin of his famous father, who obeyed orders to commit suicide so that Hitler could host a state funeral to celebrate a national hero.[22]

Thomas Elsaesser argues that the father–son framing depoliticizes: Kluge cast the 1970s "German protest movement [as] anti-authoritarian," as merely "caught in the ruses of patriarchy . . ." rather than as egalitarian.[23] Tragic conflict is overtaken and diminished by mere psychological need. Ironically, however, it is one of the film's most domestic and seemingly psychological sequences, Fassbinder's, that Elsaesser brilliantly finds most promisingly anti-authoritarian and vastly preferable to the classically Antigonean rhythms of resistance and lamentation promoted by the film's director, Kluge, and others, like Schlöndorff and Böll. The Antigonean option seduces with its symmetry, Elsaesser points out, and symmetry is not mere innocent form: "symmetry, balance and repetition' set up 'their narrative to achieve almost 'classical' closure." They "master the German past" by "letting it metaphorically slide into a master narrative of fathers and sons."[24]

By contrast, Elsaesser argues, Fassbinder's sequence is "antigonising." It prizes the singular power of the event over the domesticating power of the frame. Fassbinder makes clear that "neither such doubling for the sake of structure, nor the proliferation of situations alluding to the classical Antigone can 'domesticate' the

21 The Desert Fox; and in a further doubling, as Miriam Hansen notes, the German rescuers of the hostages from Mogadishu were hailed in a British newspaper as "desert foxes."

22 Rommel was suspected of plotting against Hitler and so, arguably, Rommel senior could be cast not just in the role of Nazi father to democratic, if decisive, mayor (son) but also as parricidal son who, Haemon-like, commits suicide when his attempted violence against his father (Hitler) fails.

23 ". . . feature from which the women's movement had to extricate itself, perhaps by countering this 'Hamletization' [or oedipalization, surely] of German post-war history with its own (agonising) 'Antigonising'?" I find Elsaesser's critique of the limits of the father–son frame very useful but see no reason why this problem should be cast as necessary just for the women's movement to work through.

24 Elsaesser here cites Charles Maier, *The Unmasterable Past.* For Elsaesser, the emplotment of political conflict as tragic Oedipal rivalries of fathers and sons yields not saving revelations (contra Rancière) but only unwelcome repetitions, the eternal return of the same. Elsaesser points in particular to the mid-1990s television film, *Todespiel*, which recuperates the story of the hot autumn twenty years after Kluge's *Germany in Autumn*, this time depicting the official leaders of 1970s West Germany as well prepared for their role to defend the state from attack precisely by their experience as (de-Nazified) Wehrmacht soldiers in the Second World War. The very traits that at midcentury were seen as evidence of the incipient authoritarianism of the would-be democratic state, are twenty years later co-opted, rescripted (in the way perhaps called *for* by Schleyer in his letter to his son) as the necessary and laudable ingredients of its success in defending itself against terrorist violence. Kluge invites this problematic *Aufhebung*, Elsaesser argues, by trying to master events with his Oedipal frame rather than aestheticize them in their sublime singularity.

fantasmatic power emanating from the events."[25] That fantasmatic power finds expression, in Fassbinder's sequence, when he shows himself

> alternately naked and wrapped in an untidy bathrobe, restless and sweating, in his sombre Munich apartment, frantic about the news blackout, cynically incredulous about the Stammheim [RAF] suicides, in fear of possible police-raids and house-searches, on the verge of a nervous breakdown, finally collapsing on the floor in a fit of uncontrollable hysterical weeping.[26]

Elsaesser refers to this as " 'a body too much': violent, obese, naked, grossly material. Fassbinder assaults the viewer," exhibits the body that is not buried, and demands "an Antigone to mark the site where mourning has not taken place."[27] And when he interrogates his mother at length about her views on Germany's response to terrorism, seeking to elicit from beneath her good German citizenship a longing for authoritarianism, Fassbinder makes "the primary incestuous mother-son bond so over-explicit that it effectively de-Oedipalizes the lineage from (guilty) father to (guilty) son." And so, in sum, says Elsaesser, "Fassbinder's self-display is an act of resistance, and a double Antigone gesture, partly directed at the film that Alexander Kluge has bound him into."[28] It is important for Elsaesser that Fassbinder's gesture is antigonising, *not* Antigonean, since the latter would just be a different way of being tragic.

The ties to *Antigone*, so strong in Kluge's film, seem weak in the Fassbinder sequence, however, too weak even to support Elsaesser's neologism – *antigonising*. There are some parallels noted by Elsaesser, but there is in Fassbinder's sequence, after all, no corpse, no sister, no suicide, no civil disobedience, just emotionalism, petty brutality, personal collapse and a lot of frustration. Fassbinder, who rages at everyone he encounters, polices the borders of his apartment, and ends collapsed in a heap on the floor, is at least as much Creon as Antigone, perhaps even more so.

On *closer* examination, however, it turns out there are some telling connections between Sophocles' play and Fassbinder's film sequence: most important,

25 Elsaesser, "Antigone Agonistes."

26 Ibid.

27 Ibid.

28 Ibid. Fassbinder's "body too much" rendering of Antigone is echoed in more recent attention to Antigone's corporeality in Deleuzean vein and by way of melodramatic devices: in a reading of Hertmans' Antigone, Christel Stalpaert says: "Hertmans looks for the tension between personal, corporeal memory, collective memory, and 'public' images of cruelty to actualize Greek tragedies. He does not look for catharsis within a classical dramatic aesthetic, but for a painful and embarrassing actualization "without catharsis, so that in the end," he says, "you do not know which way to go with your emotions" (Hertmans, quoted in Sels, n.p.). You are thrown out of kilter and are overwhelmed with images and voices of disgust and suffering" ("The Mind Taken Hostage: Antigone's Corporeal Memory in *Mind the Gap*," in *Mosaic*, 41(3): 149). One could definitely describe the effect of *Dogville* in the same way.

Fassbinder's sequence begins with him on the telephone frantically trying to retract something he just said in an interview, to the effect that if his films contribute to the destruction of conventional marriage that is fine with him. This is an Antigonean sentiment, uttered boldly: anti-conjugal, anti-heteronormative. Fassbinder's effort to retract it, however, is rather unheroic – small. With this opening, surely, Fassbinder calls attention immediately to the curious genre of his sequence. It will not make tragic heroes of the RAF and villains of Germany's public figures, nor vice versa. It will not replay the old heroic, tragic scripts. With the tight shots of his face as he sweats and tries to take back his words but finds he cannot, Fassbinder announces with his images that he also wants to reject tragedy: this is melodrama.

Elsaesser, the author of a canonical essay on melodrama in the 1970s, never mentions melodrama here.[29] But it seems hard to avoid. Melodrama, as Peter Brooks explains, is anti-grandiose; the genre levels. It "generally ends in resignation," with characters "emerg[ing] as lesser human beings for having become wise and acquiescent to the ways of the world."[30] Fassbinder's sequence features virtually all the traits of melodrama listed by Brooks: hyperbole (Fassbinder shouts and storms and collapses), externalization of inner/psychic violence (he sweats and vomits and collapses), acting out (he hectors his mother and berates and roughs up his lover, Armin), a sense of being overwhelmed by outside forces (he expresses his felt impotence in the face of news blackouts and state power several times on the telephone to his ex-wife in Paris), paranoia (he expects his apartment to be searched at any moment by the police or invaded by spies and he acts accordingly), a *mise-en-scène* of confinement (he seems never to leave the apartment), and a move from the big city to a small town (the sequence opens with him arriving from Paris and he says more than once that he wishes he could go back to Paris but he needs to finish his work first) with the attendant biases and prejudices a big city dweller expects to find among rural counterparts (Armin in the apartment repeatedly expresses small-minded political views).[31] The anti-grandiosity of melodrama is evident as well in its granting of a central place to members of the lower orders, servants, criminals, workers, queers, women – another marked departure from tragedy.[32]

29 See Thomas Elsaesser, "Tales of Sound and Fury: Observations on the Family Melodrama" (1971) in *Film Genre Reader III*, ed. Barry Keith Grant (Austin: University of Texas Press, 2003), 366–395.

30 Peter Brooks, *The Melodramatic Imagination*, *The Melodramatic Imagination: Balzac, Henry James, Melodrama, and the Mode of Excess* (New Haven, CT: Yale University Press, 1976), 77.

31 Dissonant music that is either atonal or in some way at odds with the scene depicted is the only one of Brooks' listed traits *not* in Fassbinder's sequence.

32 Melodrama need not be counterposed to tragedy. Carolyn Williams suggests a continuity between tragedy and melodrama (here echoing Elsaesser) especially with regard to themes of freedom and necessity when she notes that melodrama "insistently concentrates on the implacable force of social relations and the consequences of deviating from their conventions of normalization" ("Moving Pictures: George Eliot and Melodrama," in *Compassion: The Culture and Politics of an Emotion,* ed. Lauren Berlant (New York and London: Routledge

Fassbinder explored melodrama in many of his films (especially during his Sirkean 1970s) but in *Germany in Autumn* he makes clear the challenge melodrama poses to tragedy as a genre. Reorienting the tragic gaze from action to affect, elites to servants, and high political conflicts to low household drama, melodrama puts law on trial. Brooks does not call particular attention to that trait of the genre, but Fassbinder does. His paranoia increases when he hears police sirens, and he invokes the rule of law's norms and values even as he wonders skeptically about official state claims exonerating prison guards from implication in the deaths of Ensslin, Baader, and Raspe. He craves constitutionalism but cannot rise to the call of citizenship.

Perhaps with Fassbinder in mind, Kluge airs a subtle critique (unnoted by Elsaesser) of melodrama as politically useless or stifling when he records one of the RAF eulogies: "If you are truly outraged, you won't shout but will consider what to do." Fassbinder in his sequence shouts for thirty minutes straight and ends in a pile on the floor, infant-like, wrapped in the arms of his battered lover, collapsed into drug use, rage, paranoia and abuse under pressure of events in the hot autumn of 1977. Doesn't Fassbinder's sequence make clear that melodrama is anti-political: debilitating and nothing but a self-consuming artifact? That is, even if Elsaesser is right, and there is something anti-tragic (and anti-Kluge) at work in Fassbinder's sequence, how political is a sequence that depicts Fassbinder at home, alone, and indistinct, seemingly unable to leave his apartment much less offer a serious political alternative to events that frighten and enrage him? All the problems of the day meld into one long narcissistic journey for this protagonist who seems never to go out.

Might this be precisely the point, however? This melodramatic self-absorption and collapse is Fassbinder's dramatization of the effects on citizens of the state's expansion of its power. He gives expression to their affective responses to heightened political pressures and new forms of violence. He enacts the call to the rule of law repeatedly in his discussion with his mother, not as a sober principled or reasoned (shall we say, academic) conclusion to a dispassionate argument about the Rechtstaat, but as the only recourse for those caught in an overheated political crisis in which all parties and institutions, including the state, are acting in ways that are affectively charged.

The laws of melodrama

The outcome seems to be no better in von Trier's *Dogville,* where the violence in the end is turned outward, rather than inward.[33] But, like Fassbinder, von Trier

(2004), 115). In Fassbinder, of course, the state and not society is the locus of implacability, though conventional social mores are also present as *bêtes noires.*

33 Rancière notes the film caused a scandal at Cannes, where the Film Festival jury "reproached it for its lack of humanism" (*Dissensus,* 186). But, I would argue, the problem may well have been its genre infidelity which is mistakable for want of humanism. That is, such a charge is

too does not just depict the situation, he comments on it, and invites us to do so as well. Fassbinder takes the politics of the day and turns them into household drama, showing them playing out in 1978 in a queer household, and interrogating his mother not his father about what she is doing now, politically, and, by implication, about what she had done earlier, during the war. Von Trier, for his part, powerfully intensifies and ironizes the melodramatic genre's effects when, using chalk lines for a set, he dispenses with the walls of the domestic sphere but nonetheless retains their melodramatic effects: the sense of suffocation, isolation, suffering, and the crimes of non-intervention are intensified.

Fassbinder does not model political agency for those seeking to act; and von Trier's Grace does seem only able to lurch from overdrawn Christian forgiveness to catastrophic vengeance. This is what troubles Rancière about the von Trier film. But moving from plot to genre, we may find something more intriguingly political going on. Melodrama explores the psychic drama of dis-identification that is actually essential to Rancière's politics. His best example is the identification of French protesters with murdered Algerians, massacred at night in Paris, in 1962, their bodies thrown into the Seine.[34] Similarly, for Fassbinder, as Elsaesser shows, the problem is how to greet the turmoil of terrorism in a way that owns the incomplete dis-identification with Germany's Nazi past. Tragedy, the genre of clash, may seem more 'political' or action-oriented than melodrama, but tragedy (in Kluge's hands) lacks the characteristic play of dis-identification and equality at the core of Rancière's own political project. True, in Rancière, such dis-identification is willed and enacted successfully, powerfully, whereas in melodrama it is depicted as a painful struggle that may devolve merely into violence. But the willed and enacted dis-identification lauded by Rancière is often a product of long and painful struggle, and melodrama, in exhibiting its violence, does not catastrophize – or it does not necessarily do that – but realizes, gives reality to, the difficulty.

In his politics and aesthetics, Rancière has pursued what we might call a Dionysian communism that cherishes pleasure, play, and leisure and prizes representations of those aspects of work life. Fassbinder's melodrama may represent the reality principle that always threatens to interrupt such Dionysian pleasure. But surely these cannot be separated out: the frenzy is driven by the thrill of its proximity to that which may interrupt its pleasures. This is Fassbinder's domain: we see him throughout the sequence "trying to work" but unable to do so because he's distracted by events of the day and by the paranoia they generate in him.[35]

less likely to be directed at a film like *Bonnie and Clyde* because the fact that it is consistent with its genre all the way through seems to make its violence meaningful rather than wanton, and this is true even when what it depicts is wanton violence.

34 As I note in *Democracy and the Foreigner*, this is referred to as "crossing over" by Zora Neale Hurston, in her reading of Moses, the Egyptian.

35 Fassbinder's sequence, said the *New York Times* reviewer when the film first came out, is "photographed and acted with such intense self-absorption that it has the effect of

Still, paranoia can be a democratic virtue. Kluge arguably gives in to resignation when he closes *Germany in Autumn* with the sad, catastrophizing, voiced-over observation that suicide is the last resort of those who see no other options. Fassbinder, for his part, expresses deep doubts about the official claim of suicide. Melodrama is the genre of suspicion and its mode of interrogation is to suspect everywhere abuses of power. It illustrates what happens when subjects are isolated from each other, torn out of the in-between that Hannah Arendt said was the necessary condition of common sense, reality, and truth.[36] This isolation, Fassbinder explains in his sequence, is not a personal preference, but a product of law. The result of such isolation is a legal unconsciousness that lacks access to reality (which is necessarily intersubjective, in Arendt's terms). Fassbinder's sequence testifies to the politically traumatic effects of a legal regime in which neighbors are encouraged to report on each other and private homes are subject to police invasion at any moment, especially when this is all done in the name of something that is universally supported: the rule of law.

What Fassbinder achieves by combating the seeming universal and necessary tragic emplotment of social and political conflict goes beyond even this, however. He exhibits the inner affective life of law, the way in which law and lawful lawlessness (emergency powers) consume those who live in their ambit. When Fassbinder goes from leather-jacketed cosmopolitan to bathrobed, housebound lover to full frontal nudity in his sequence – from powerful male to paranoid coward to, finally, a mushy mess of a vulnerable man weeping on the floor – this has everything to do with law.

The same can be said of Nicole Kidman's Grace in von Trier's film, whose collapse mirrors Fassbinder's, but in reverse trajectory. He begins in a leather jacket, she ends with a machine gun in her hand. He treats Armin and his mother aggressively until he finally collapses. Grace bears the aggressions of others to the point of abject collapse, and only then finds her way to aggression. When Grace cedes her own autonomy and enters, first into the town's grateful service and then into subservience, she habituates the townspeople into unaccustomed forms of dependence that are seductive, and dangerous. The violence she visits upon them at the end of the film can be seen as the vivid realization of their own fear of their increasingly addictive dependence upon, and exploitation of, her. The terrible ending of the film is, then, an expression of the town's legal unconsciousness.

Moreover, both films explore the dis-identification of their central characters with conventional gender norms. Grace trades feminine abjection for aggression.

transforming narcissism into a higher form of commitment." In *Public Things: Democracy in Disrepair*, I discuss in detail von Trier's interest in the incessant demand for incessant work, a feature that drives the protagonist to submission, rage, and vengeance in *Dogville*, and to melancholy and then a kind of playful joy in *Melancholia*.

36 Hannah Arendt, *The Origins of Totalitarianism* (New York: Harcourt Brace Jovanovich, 1973), 473–474.

Fassbinder trades male aggression for abjection. For neither one is this progress – psychologically or politically. But in both films, we find an exploration of the conditions under which these seem like the only two options. This does not amount to an embrace of the options but rather to a critique of the conditions that give rise to them and this is one of the several contributions melodrama might make to the study of law, culture, and humanities.

Bibliography

Agamben, Giorgio. *Remnants of Auschwitz: The Witness and the Archive.* Translated by Daniel Heller-Roazen. New York: Zone Books, 2000.

Anker, Elisabeth R. *Orgies of Feeling Melodrama and the Politics of Freedom.* Durham, NC: Duke University Press, 2014.

Apostolidis, Paul. "'Young Americans': Rancière and Bowie in *Dogville*," in *Breaking the Rules: Gender, Power, and Politics in the Films of Lars von Trier*, ed. Bonnie Honig and Lori Marso, *Theory & Event* 18(2) (2015).

Arendt, Hannah. *The Origins of Totalitarianism.* New York: Harcourt Brace Jovanovich, 1973.

Blumenthal-Barby, Martin. "*Germany in Autumn*: The Return of the Human," *Discourse: Journal for Theoretical Studies in Media and Culture* 29(1) (2007): 140–168.

Brooks, Peter. *The Melodramatic Imagination, The Melodramatic Imagination: Balzac, Henry James, Melodrama, and the Mode of Excess.* New Haven, CT: Yale University Press, 1976.

Caruth, Cathy and Thomas Keenan. "'The AIDS Crisis is Not Over': A Conversation with Gregg Bordowitz, Douglas Crimp, and Laura Pinsky" (1991). In *Trauma: Explorations in Memory*, edited by Cathy Caruth, 256–272. Baltimore, MD: Johns Hopkins University Press, 1995.

Crotty, Kevin. *Law's Interior: Legal and Literary Constructions of the Self.* Ithaca, NY: Cornell University Press, 2001.

Elsaesser, Thomas. "Antigone Agonistes: Urban Guerilla or Guerilla Urbanism?" *Rouge* 4 (2004), http://www.rouge.com.au/4/antigone.html

Elsaesser, Thomas. "Tales of Sound and Fury: Observations on the Family Melodrama" (1971). In *Film Genre Reader III*, edited by Barry Keith Grant, 366–395. Austin: University of Texas Press, 2003.

Honig, Bonnie. *Antigone, Interrupted.* Cambridge: Cambridge University Press, 2013.

Honig, Bonnie. *Democracy and the Foreigner.* Princeton, NJ: Princeton University Press, 2001.

Honig, Bonnie. *Public Things: Democracy in Disrepair.* New York: Fordham University Press, 2017.

Kindley, Evan. "Germany in Autumn," notcoming.com, June 9, 2010, http://www.notcoming.com/reviews/germanyinautumn (accessed April 1, 2017).

LaCapra, Dominick. *History in Transit: Experience, Identity, Critical Theory.* Ithaca, NY, and London: Cornell University Press, 2004.

Maier, Charles. *The Unmasterable Past: History, Holocaust, and German National Identity.* With a new preface. Cambridge, MA: Harvard University Press, 1997.

Nowell-Smith, Geoffrey. "Dossier on Melodrama: Minnelli and Melodrama." *Screen* 18(2) (1977): 113–118.

Rancière, Jacques. *Dissensus: on Politics and Aesthetics*. Edited and translated by Steven Corcoran. London: Continuum, 2010.

Rancière, Jacques. "The Ethical Turn of Aesthetics and Politics." *Critical Horizons* 7(1) (2006): 1–20.

Rancière, Jacques. "From one Image to Another? Deleuze and the Ages of Cinema." In *Film Fables*, translated by E. Battista, 107–123. Oxford and New York: Berg, 2006.

Reichman, Ravit. *The Affective Life of Law: Legal Modernism and the Literary Imagination*. Stanford, CA: Stanford University Press, 2009.

Stalpaert, Christel. "The Mind Taken Hostage: Antigone's Corporeal Memory in *Mind the Gap*." *Mosaic* 41(3): 137–152.

Vernant, Jean-Pierre, and Pierre Vidal-Naquet, "Intimations of the Will in Greek Tragedy." In *Myth and Tragedy in Ancient Greece*, 49–84. New York: Zone Books, 1988.

Williams, Carolyn. "Moving Pictures: George Eliot and Melodrama." In *Compassion: The Culture and Politics of an Emotion*, edited by Lauren Berlant, 105–144. New York and London: Routledge, 2004.

Chapter 10

Mephistopheles in Hamsterdam: carnival and the state of exception in HBO's *The Wire*

Edwin Bikundo

Realism: *The Wire* as Greek tragedy and anti-Christian morality tale

What does lawlessness look like? Is it the *absence* of law or the exact *opposite* of law? This chapter examines how the suspension of legality is represented in HBO's critically acclaimed television series *The Wire*. A state of emergency was declared in Baltimore after violent riots broke out in West Baltimore following the death of one Freddie Gray in police custody on 19 April 2015.[1] A week after the death David Simon – credited as the Creator-Writer-Producer of *The Wire* – asked 'those claiming the right to violence in Freddie Gray's name . . . to cease', '[t]urn around' and [g]o home' in an open letter published on his personal blog and in an interview.[2] This overtly political critique and foray of art into life where reality and its representation begin to coincide did not seem unusual in the show's context, as we shall see below.

The Wire initially ran for five seasons from 2 June 2002 to 6 January 2008.[3] Right from the opening theme, Tom Waits' 'Way Down in the Hole', the viewer is exhorted to keep the devil down in the hole and walk with Jesus to safeguard their soul. That clear and seemingly unambiguous invocation of Christian morality is in constant tension with the Greek tragedy that instead unfolds in the narrative from the first scene of the first episode in the first series or 'Episode 01 The Target' in HBO's nomenclature.[4] In it, a young man responds to Baltimore Homicide Detective Jimmy McNulty (Dominic West) querying as to why they would let someone place bets in a game even when

1 Daniel Kreps, "Baltimore: State of Emergency Declared Amid Protests, Riots", *Rolling Stone*, April 28, 2015, http://www.rollingstone.com/culture/news/baltimore-state-of-emergency-declared-amid-protests-riots-20150428

2 David Simon, "Baltimore", *The Audacity of Despair*, April 27, 2015, http://davidsimon.com/baltimore/; see also http://www.slate.com/articles/arts/culturebox/2015/08/david_simon_interview_the_wire_creator_on_his_new_series_freddie_gray_ta.html

3 HBO, "The Wire, Episodes", http://www.hbo.com/the-wire/episodes/index.html

4 David Simon, "The Target", *The Wire*, Season 1, Episode 1, Directed by Clark Johnson (HBO, 2002); see also http://www.hbo.com/the-wire/episodes/1/01-the-target/synopsis.html

he (the deceased victim of a shooting) would invariably steal the pot of money staked and run with it by saying simply: 'This is America, man'. Such an ethic (if indeed it is one) does not recognise any necessary link between crime and punishment, which is precisely that which the policeman's question presupposes. This scene, which provides the viewer with their first experience of *The Wire*, has even greater significance in its framing of the series, as is it is not entirely fictional but actually happened in real life. Indeed many of the characters in *The Wire* are based on actual people or composites of actual people. Furthermore, many of the actors are the actual people upon whom the series is based. For instance, the real-life Defense Attorney Billy Murphy, who was Freddie Gray's family lawyer, appears as a character named Billy Murphy who acts as a Defense Attorney based on his real-life self.[5]

Consequently, *The Wire* is radically different from the typical police procedural show mainly because of its realism. It both *presents* and *represents* Baltimore and its denizens. Not only do the actual individuals upon whom characters are based have cameo appearances but even the abandoned row-houses filmed as the backdrop to 'Hamsterdam' (a corruption of 'Amsterdam' – a set of so-called free zones where the drug trade is not just tolerated by the police but is actively encouraged by them) are exactly as they appear without embellishment. At least one actor – Snoop Pearson playing a character of the same name – was involved in the drug trade before *and after* playing a role in the show as a drug gang enforcer. Ironically, Melvin Douglas, the actor cast as the Deacon (a church figure involved in a number of community projects), was in real life a drug trafficker and the inspiration for one of the main drug bosses in the series. Furthermore, the show routinely used Baltimorean non-actors to fill minor roles.

This lends the show a feeling of gritty authenticity at the price of blurring the lines between fiction and reality. So much so that David Simon himself is uncomfortable with no distinction being drawn between being interviewed as the creator of *The Wire* and being interviewed as himself.[6] Simon, formerly a Baltimore *Sun* newspaper reporter based the show on his book 'Homicide', which was made into an NBC cop series of the same name.[7] His primary writing partner, Ed Burns – a former Baltimore homicide detective – is one of Simon's sources. Simon even gives numerous small parts to his former colleagues in the Baltimore *Sun*.[8] As Simon puts it 'these are faces you don't see on television, the faces

5 CBS Baltimore, "Freddie Gray Family Atty: BPD's Essential Personnel 'Old, White Guys that are Racist to the Core'", *CBS Baltimore*, July 12, 2016, http://baltimore.cbslocal.com/2016/07/12/freddie-gray-billy-murphy-baltimore-police-department/

6 Isaac Chotiner, "Everything is Not The Wire: David Simon Would Like You to Stop Trying to Understand What's Going on in Baltimore by Quoting His TV Show", *Slate*, August 12, 2015, http://www.slate.com/articles/arts/culturebox/2015/08/david_simon_interview_the_wire_creator_on_his_new_series_freddie_gray_ta.html

7 Margaret Talbot, "Stealing Life: The Crusader behind 'The Wire'", *The New Yorker*, October 22, 2007, http://www.newyorker.com/magazine/2007/10/22/stealing-life

8 Talbot, "Stealing Life".

and voices of the real city'.[9] Furthermore, 'You can't make this shit up'.[10] He describes this use of supposedly more 'real' actors and faces as reflecting his own concern with authenticity:

> I'm the kind of person who, when I'm writing, cares above all about whether the people I'm writing about will recognize themselves. I'm not thinking about the general reader. My greatest fear is that the people in the world I'm writing about will read it and say, 'Nah, there's nothing there.'

No less than then US President Barack Obama said of the show that it is: 'one of the greatest, not just television shows, but pieces of art in the last couple of decades', when he spoke with Simon about how the show had showcased the impact of the criminal justice system on Baltimore.[11] As we shall see below the quasi- realism of the series is a key plank of the show's unique subversion of the cop show genre. As Guy Debord put it and the creators of *The Wire* would probably agree: 'In societies where modern conditions of production prevail, all life presents itself as an immense accumulation of spectacles. Everything that was directly lived has moved away into representation'.[12]

Like many of the subsequent episodes the very first has a signature line from one of the characters that is taken as representative of the episode's themes. In this instance, it is McNulty's 'When it's not your turn'.[13] He speaks this to his colleague Detective William 'The Bunk' Moreland (based on the real-life Rick Requer)[14] to criticise him for taking a homicide case that he could well have avoided.

The opposition to conventional morality in the lines above sketches out the tension in the series between pantheistic pagan and monotheistic Christian worldviews in the following ways. The ostensibly 'good guys' in the show display a Christian morality. They are constrained within linear time where good supposedly triumphs over evil in the end but are placed in an irredeemably pagan world (with circular time, where jealous and petty gods act irrationally). Indeed, McNulty does not just open the initial scene of the first season he also closes the last scene of the final season. What is more, the models used in *The Wire* to create mortal protagonists that are doomed to their fate were the Greek playwrights Aeschylus, Sophocles, Euripides.[15] However pagan the show may be, though, it is

9 Talbot, "Stealing Life".
10 Talbot, "Stealing Life".
11 Daniel Kreps, "Watch Barack Obama and 'The Wire' Creator Talk Criminal Justice Reform", *Rolling Stone*, March 17, 2015, http://www.rollingstone.com/tv/videos/watch-barack-obama-and-the-wire-creator-talk-criminal-justice-reform-20150327
12 Guy Debord, *The Society of the Spectacle,* trans. Fredy Perlman (Detroit: Black and Red, 1977), 1.
13 David Simon, "The Target", *The Wire,* Season 1, Episode 1.
14 David Simon, *Homicide: A Year on the Killing Streets* (First Owl Books, 2006), 4th edn, 641.
15 Nick Hornby, "David Simon, interview by Nick Hornby", *The Believer Magazine,* August 2007, http://www.believermag.com/issues/200708/?read=interview_simon

pagan with a Christian or, perhaps better, Anti-Christian sensibility. As a character in the fifth season puts it 'At the Baltimore *Sun*, God still resides in the details'.[16] This of course inverts the usual saying, which places the devil, not God, in the details and is a clue to the ethical universe the characters inhabit.

The narrative arc of the specific phenomenon addressed by this chapter (that of Hamsterdam) can be sketched out by lines from characters in the show as follows. Police Major Bunny Colvin (Robert Wisdom) says early on in a faux-ironic manner that in order to keep crime statistics low and please his bosses 'I think I'm gonna legalize drugs'. To which, unable to take him seriously, his colleagues (just as he calculated) laugh. Following this, Detective Shakima Greggs (Sonja Sohn) stumbles onto Colvin's scheme and works out that 'You legalized drugs and you didn't tell the bosses!'. Later on when Colvin is explaining to his bosses the tactical deployments he has done to effect a real drop in crime, Deputy Commissioner Rawls (John Doman) cuts him off and says somewhat perceptively 'He's legalized drugs!' Crucially for this chapter's argument, the character of the Deacon (played by Melvin Williams) surveys the physical manifestation of Colvin's actions and tells him that 'that place is Hell'. This idea of 'legalizing' drugs through the forbearance from law enforcement as leading to hellish conditions (and how that is presented) is what gives the present chapter its basis and impetus. The impetus is to say – despite the views of the characters – that drugs are not really legalised just because drug laws are not enforced for a time in a specific place. Further, the surface appeal of desisting from law enforcement shows how the road to hell is not only paved with good intentions but the promise of good in exchange for evil is necessarily Faustian.

Each of the five seasons of *The Wire* begins with a fresh look at the city of Baltimore from a different perspective. Season 1 looks at the drug-affected neighbourhoods, season 2 shifts to connect to crime in the city port, season 3 (the focus of this chapter) examines City Hall as a site for politics, season 4 looks at the school system and season 5 looks at the press. The cycle impliedly begins again at the end of the fifth season, which has a mock serial killer, a mock funeral for McNulty, and even a mock resurrection for a homeless man preceding the rebirth of stock characters like McNulty himself as well as Omar (Michael Kenneth Williams) – a robber who preys exclusively on drug dealers and who happens to be President Obama's favourite character in the show.[17]

Simon self-consciously seeds various pagan signatures throughout the work. He, for instance, puts in the mouth of one of the characters Police Commissioner Burrell that 'this is Baltimore, gentlemen, the gods will not save you'. Further, the classically pagan themes of circularity of time as renewal, pantheism and irrationality with no redemption can be identified in examples too many to exhaustively list out. Only a representative few will be examined here. David

16 Talbot, "Stealing Life".
17 Kreps, "Watch Barack Obama and 'The Wire' Creator".

Simon himself describes *The Wire* as self-consciously Greek tragedy.[18] He stated in an interview that:

> The drama that I reread before I started *The Wire* was Greek drama in which fated and doomed protagonists are confronted by a system that is indifferent to their heroism, to their individuality, to their morality. The police department is the god, the drug trade is the god, the school system is the god, city hall is the god, the election is the god. Capitalism is the ultimate god in *The Wire*. Capitalism is Zeus.[19]

He further elaborated the Pantheistic theme of social institutions as gods:

> The Wire is a Greek tragedy in which the postmodern institutions are the Olympian forces. It's the police department, or the drug economy, or the political structures, or the school administration, or the macroeconomic forces that are throwing the lightning bolts and hitting people in the ass for no decent reason. In this drama, the institutions always prove larger, and those characters with hubris enough to challenge the postmodern construct of American empire are invariably mocked, marginalized, or crushed, a drama in which postmodern institutions trump individuality and morality and justice seems different in some ways, I think.[20]

Unlike the usual television fare, here there is no clear distinguishing between good and evil. Each season is structured to present 'multiple points of view and giving equal screen time to "the good guys" and "the bad guys" ', so both sides are shown to have all shades of humanity – there are no clear-cut heroes or villains.[21] The drug trade and the police department subtly mirror each other.[22] The show departs from the kind of Christian morality that would envision an omnipotent God by not granting even 'Yahweh himself that kind of unbridled, interventionist authority' that is expected from an all-powerful deity.[23] Its politics of dissent are inescapable:

> It is perhaps the only storytelling on television that overtly suggests that our political and economic and social constructs are no longer viable, that our leadership has failed us relentlessly, and that no, we are not going to be all right.[24]

18 Chris Love, "Greek Gods in Baltimore: Greek Tragedy and The Wire", *Criticism* 52 (3–4) (2010): 487, DOI: 10.1353/crt.2010.0052.

19 Eric Ducker, "The Left Behind: Inside The Wire's World of Alienation and Asshole God", *The Fader*, December 8, 2006, http://www.thefader.com/2006/12/08/listening-in-part-iv/#ixzz2PjqAwXdS

20 Hornby, "David Simon, Interview".

21 Theresa Clifford, "A Greek Tragedy on the Streets of Baltimore", *Spiked,* April 25, 2007, http://www.spiked-online.com/site/article/3131/

22 Talbot, "Stealing Life".

23 Hornby, "David Simon, Interview".

24 Talbot, "Stealing Life".

After contextualising Paganism in an overall Anti-Christian framework the rest of this chapter expounds on the emancipatory potential of the Carnival aspect of the Third Season of *The Wire* and concludes on the Faustian bargain that is outlined and proffered within it. In order to do this, the analysis links Ancient Greek myths to Ancient Greek politics via the work of Italian philosopher Giorgio Agamben. The first volume in Agamben's series of the same name, *Homo Sacer*, concludes in enunciating three theses: first that the original political relation is the 'ban' or exclusion of 'bare life' from the polis or political sphere. This banning is made possible through the 'state of exception', as the situation whereby the sovereign decides on the meta-legal applicability of the law itself and not merely whether a certain act is legal or illegal. Consequently, the second thesis is that the fundamental activity of sovereign power is the production of bare life. The third thesis is that it is currently not the city but rather 'the camp', that is, the fundamental global bio-political paradigm.[25] Each of these theses will be examined in the analysis of *The Wire* and Hamsterdam demonstrated below.

'As if' but only for a moment: carnival and flirting with the state of exception

Hamsterdam is supposedly modelled upon its Dutch near-namesake where drugs are at least by repute legal. It has its beginnings in the third season of *The Wire*, right in the middle of the series. The trajectory of its development is mapped below through direct quotations from Season 3. In Hamsterdam, the police first ignore, then countenance, subsequently aid and by the end actually participate in drug deals and cover up serious crimes. The drug dealers on their part initially ignore, are then intrigued by and finally participate enthusiastically in Hamsterdam – even to the point of solving murders for the police. This carnivalesque drama pitting cops-as-drug-dealers and drug-dealers-as-cops somehow makes sense in the topsy-turvy context of Hamsterdam.

Agamben explicitly identifies the carnival as the state of suspended law or exception in which 'criminal behaviour is considered licit or, in any case, not punishable'.[26] This is a period when the prevailing social order is temporarily subverted.[27] This is clearly seen in Hamsterdam with the police and drug dealers mingling cooperatively both in keeping order as well as investigating crimes but also in distributing and selling drugs. Agamben's most well-known paradigms are the 'homo sacer', being who can be killed but not sacrificed, and the 'state of exception', where the law is 'in force without significance'.[28] These two paradigms are notable in their usefulness to explaining the phenomenon of Hamsterdam as

25 Giorgio Agamben, *Homo Sacer: Sovereign Power and Bare Life* (Stanford, CA: Stanford University Press, 1998), at 181.
26 Giorgio Agamben, *State of Exception* (Chicago: University of Chicago Press 2005), at 71.
27 Agamben, State *of Exception*, at 71.
28 Agamben, *Homo Sacer: Sovereign Power and Bare Life*, at 8 and 51 respectively.

a paradigmatically exceptional occurrence and its denizens as beings who may be killed, but whose deaths cannot be sacrifices. Which is to say their lives are outside the protection of law without being independent of the force of law.

Hamsterdam's key elements include white flags that mark the boundary between inside and outside. This demarcation includes within it relatively vacant and boarded up houses. This desertion minimises the harm that would otherwise occur were the sites to be occupied, vibrant neighbourhoods. Indeed the stated aim of Hamsterdam is precisely to salvage the other neighbourhoods. Most importantly for present purposes, however, is that inside the defined zones there is freedom from arrest and prosecution. However, the police do not repeal the law – they would have neither the power nor the authority to achieve that. They simply abstain from enforcing it, even though it remains in force. Which is to say the law remains in force without – at least for a certain time and place, i.e. temporarily – bearing any significance.[29] Outside the zones, however, the normal enforcement of the law carries on. Indeed, it is intensified. This is crucial because that strict demarcation between inside and outside is buttressed by the threat and promise of intensified violence if the drug dealers are not compliant to the distinction. To make this zonal planning work, the police use mid-level drug managers – not the so-called 'hoppers' or middling participants that lack the necessary influence, nor the bosses who are too powerful to listen to any such proposal, no matter how tempting. As Colvin explains it to his deputy, the middle managers have just enough power to pull it off, but not so much that they can ignore the threats of violence and resist the blandishments of freely trading drugs. The question is, do the police desist from policing in Hamsterdam? Not quite. What they *do* do is abstain from violent force as long as violence is not present. The police also go further than this to actually transport customers to the zones and even collect informal taxes to contribute to sporting amenities. Moreover, governance broadly speaking is further present in the form of public medical personnel who take advantage of the scene of opportunities for intensified governmentality.

To begin with Agamben's first thesis, that the original political relation is the ban – exclusion of bare life from the political sphere – the first inkling of a move to a different policing paradigm occurs in Episode 4 of the season (29 in the overall series), where Major Colvin tells a public gathering (in effect, a political meeting based on the city as paradigm) that he can offer no ready solutions to the city's drug problem. In his words: 'Truth is, I can't promise you it's gonna get better':

> We can't lock up the thousands that are out on those corners. There's no place to put them if we could . . . This here is the world we've got, and it's time that all of us had the good sense to at least admit that much.[30]

29 Agamben, *Homo Sacer: Sovereign Power and Bare Life*, at 51.

30 David Simon, "Amsterdam", *The Wire,* Season 3, Episode 4 (29 overall). Directed by Ernest Dickerson (HBO, 2004); see also http://www.hbo.com/the-wire/episodes/3/29-amsterdam/synopsis.html

He gives up on any utopian notions of progress and instead counsels to settle for whatever is feasible in the circumstances. This sets the stage for the shift from a policing model based on the city with its democratic and everlasting progress to one modelled on the camp whose foundation is predicated upon an exceptional situation.[31]

Following Colvin's edict, the police under his command publicise the so-called free zones among the street dealers, strongly urging them to move in order to avoid police harassment. The dealers take their time coming around to the idea of a radically different legal order to what they are used to. One clearly confused and uncomfortable drug dealer says 'Look: We grind [sell drugs], and y'all try to stop it. That's how we do. Why you got to go and fuck with the program?' Sergeant Carver (Seth Gilliam) explains the situation with eloquent directness and simplicity: 'We're coming back tomorrow and when we do, everybody wears bracelets [handcuffs] – unless you people move your shit down to Vincent Street, down where the houses are all vacant. You do that and we don't give a shit'. 'Vincent Street is like Switzerland. Or Amsterdam', explains another policeman. 'The fuck is that?' inquires one of the dealers clearly requiring an explanation for an area where the police tolerate what would otherwise be illicit behaviour.[32] It has to be noted, however, that this is the police promising to ignore criminal behaviour without either in fact or in law suspending the illegality of such behaviours. Again, the law remains in force but is – at least for a time – without significance in not being enforced. The transformation of the free zones or Hamsterdam to a state of exception is thus functionally complete and only the drug dealers' initial inertia prevents it from being operationalised because their consent is absolutely essential, otherwise the police edict remains a dead letter and the ban not effective.

In Episode 30, when the police do bring round a group of suspicious mid-level dealers, they find no customers in the free zone and as a consequence the police themselves have to bus some in. This action by the police clearly goes beyond ignoring crime to actually participating in it. Moreover, Colvin is very explicit on the consequences of non-compliance:

> I swear to God, I have over 200 sworn personnel and I will free them all up to brutalize every one of you they can. If you're on a corner in my district, it will not be just a humble or a loitering charge. It will be some Biblical shit that happens to you on the way into that jail wagon. You understand? We will not be playing by any rules that you recognize.[33]

Here, Colvin takes up the mantle of the sovereign because he unilaterally excludes the dealers from the protection of the law. That is to say, he treats them as bare life denuded from the protections of law while still (or better even more)

31 Agamben, *Homo Sacer: Sovereign Power and Bare Life*, at 170.

32 David Simon, "Amsterdam", *The Wire*, Season 3, Episode 4.

33 David Simon, "Straight and True", *The Wire*, Season 3, Episode 5 (30 overall). Directed by Dan Attias (HBO, 2004); see also http://www.hbo.com/the-wire/episodes/3/30-straight-and-true/synopsis.html

subjected to its strictures. Thus Agamben's second thesis that the fundamental activity of the sovereign is to produce bare life is seemingly demonstrated by this stage. Hamsterdam is the camp and the drug dealers are treated as *homo sacer*.

This trajectory of the camp and producing bare life carries on. By Episode 31, the police have successfully created a free zone on Vincent Street in a deserted neighbourhood in West Baltimore. When Carver informs Colvin that some dealers remain resistant to moving their business to the free zones, Colvin urges his police to use anything short of deadly violence to ensure compliance: 'bang them senseless. Anything you need to do, you do. Up to a body that can't walk itself out of an emergency room, I will back you and your men'.[34] Following this promise of immunity, the police proceed to go along with confiscating and destroying their property, harassing, intimidating, and even physically assaulting any dealers they find outside the safe zones.[35]

It can now be pointed out that although Colvin takes up the mantle of the sovereign he is emphatically not one as a matter of either fact or law. But this does not make his made-up authority any less effective. In effect, he counterfeits the office necessary to carry out his plans and it works at least for a while. This confirms another argument of Agamben's from elsewhere in the *Homo Sacer* series that "the term 'office'":

> is more efficacious than the law because it cannot be transgressed, only counterfeited. It is more real than being because it consists only in the operation by means of which it is realized. It is more effective than any ordinary human action because it acts *ex opere operato,* independently of the qualities of the subject who officiates it.[36]

Colvin successfully counterfeits the use of his office to act effectively even though he has no actual authority to do what he did. The law was no barrier to the efficacy of his actions, which were effective merely because he carried them out. They did, however, retain the colour of law and in that sense were not ordinary human actions that any thug off the street, for instance, could do on his own.

Inevitably, other police inadvertently stumble onto the unusual arrangement. Detectives Greggs, Sydnor and McNulty from a special investigative unit observe mid-level drug dealer Bodie and his cohort on a suspected drug run. When stopped and duly found holding a sizeable quantity of drugs, the dealers are outraged. This is because they are, from their perspective, following police instructions and heading for Hamsterdam and are, or at any rate should be, untouchable.

34 David Simon, "Home Coming", *The Wire,* Season 3, Episode 6 (31 overall). Directed by Leslie Libman (HBO, 2004); see also http://www.hbo.com/the-wire/episodes/3/31-homecoming/synopsis.html

35 David Simon, "Home Coming", *The Wire,* Season 3, Episode 6.

36 Giorgio Agamben, *Opus Dei: An Archaeology of Duty* (Stanford: Stanford University Press, 2013) pxii.

In Bodie's words: 'Yo, Officer, we got immunity from y'all. We goin' to the free zone'. McNulty and his fellow detectives have no idea what the dealers are talking about until Major Colvin shows up. Colvin implores the detectives to keep the discovery secret from the downtown police bosses:

> I know it hurts your heads to think about it, but before you decide to lose your minds over this, you might take a moment and ride past some of my drug corners. Empty. All of them. And district-wide, my crime is down five percent.

This is when Greggs realises the enormity of the situation: 'You legalized drugs and you didn't tell the bosses'. Colvin's justifies this by saying 'I'm just trying to save what's left of my district if I can. And the longer I have before I have to brief the bosses about this . . .'. The detectives agree to keeping their discovery secret as it greatly assists them with their own investigations.[37]

By Episode 33, Hamsterdam is a scene of flourishing criminality under controlled laboratory conditions – not just drugs but prostitution and common crime, including robbery. Drug dealers themselves fall victim and let Carver know: 'Can't you ever get a motherfucking police 'round here when you need one?' They are disappointed in the police: 'You say it's gonna be like the Valley of Eden up in here', one says.[38] This evocation of the promise of paradise betrayed is important. Taking it all in, the Deacon is as appalled as he is mystified: 'What in God's name did you do here?'[39] The Deacon rips Colvin for creating Hamsterdam, saying: 'No offense, but you're like the blind man and the elephant. It's a lot bigger than what you got your hand on, you just can't see it'. Colvin responds with: 'See what?' The Deacon's answer is:

> A great village of pain, and you're the mayor. Where's your drinking water? Where's your toilets? Your heat, your electricity? Where's the needle truck? The condom distribution? The drug treatment intake? Half these people are dyin' on their feet, and the other half's gonna catch what's killin' them.

Colvin tries to explain all that away in a sort of lay theodicy: 'Look, they ain't no worse off when they was all over the map. Now they just in one place, is all', The deacon responds in the same theological vein with: 'And that place is hell'.[40] Hell is quite apposite, because when detective McNulty is confronted with an accusation that he sought Colvin's help to bypass the chain of command, he

37 David Simon, "Back Burners", *The Wire,* Season 3, Episode 7 (32 overall). Directed by Tim Van Patten (HBO, 2004); see also http://www.hbo.com/the-wire/episodes/3/32-back-burners/synopsis.html

38 David Simon, "Moral Midgetry", *The Wire,* Season 3, Episode 8 (33 overall). Directed by Agnieszka Holland (HBO, 2004); see also http://www.hbo.com/the-wire/episodes/3/33-moral-midgetry/synopsis.html

39 David Simon, "Moral Midgetry", *The Wire,* Season 3, Episode 8.

40 David Simon, "Moral Midgetry", *The Wire,* Season 3, Episode 8.

responds that he would have gone to 'the devil himself' to get his way. It is a characterisation that fits because the Deacon identifies Colvin as in charge of the hellish Hamsterdam and McNulty approximates him with the devil, each of them independent of the other. Agamben turns to the question of hell in *Kingdom and Glory*, where he states that: 'The principle according to which the government of the world will cease with the Last Judgment has only one important exception in Christian theology. It is the case of hell.'[41] For him, hell is the only place where government survives for eternity, only moreover in a penitentiary form. Which is to say the demons, remain as 'eternal executioners of divine justice.'[42] When Colvin gives up on Utopia, he settles for dealing with the world as it is which, for him, means with no hope of redemption only an endless cycle of policing and crime and more policing and more crime – eternal governance in all but name, which as noted above is a distinguishing feature of hell.[43]

At a meeting of police commanders at headquarters, Bunny Colvin attempts to justify the Western District's ensuing and dramatic crime drop while keeping secret exactly how it was engineered: 'Through the effective use of resources, an increased police presence and an intensive reach out into the community we've been able to have a significant impact on those areas to the effect of a 12 percent decrease overall'. Rawls his boss is sceptical: 'Seriously, Bunny. I already got the City Council asking questions about the 8 percent. We want to please the mayor, not go to jail behind this shit.' Colvin's wry reply is: 'Sometimes, the gods listen, sir'.[44] This deferential reference to the mayor brings us to Agamben's third and final thesis that it is currently not the city but rather 'the camp' that is the fundamental global bio-political paradigm.

Episode 34 finds a young black teenager dead in Hamsterdam. Sergeant Carver moves the body out of Hamsterdam to prevent detectives assigned to the case from discovering Hamsterdam. When Colvin arrives on the scene, he insists to Carver that he'll take the blame for tampering with the scene of the crime. Colvin tells the Hamsterdam dealers that:

> What I'm sayin' is, come tomorrow, if I don't have a shooter in bracelets, the Hamsterdam thing is over, finished. It's back to the corners for all of us and fuck y'all any way we can. You hear me? It was good while it lasted. For y'all it was cash on the barrel and no one needs no bail money. For me, I had clean corners damn near everywhere I looked. But that's all gone tomorrow unless y'all bring me my shooter.[45]

41 Giorgio Agamben, *The Kingdom and the Glory: for a Theological Genealogy of Economy and Government (Homo Sacer II, 2)* (Stanford, CA: Stanford University Press, 2011), 163.

42 Agamben, *The Kingdom and the Glory,* 164.

43 Agamben, *The Kingdom and the Glory,* 164.

44 David Simon, "Moral Midgetry", *The Wire,* Season 3, Episode 8 (33 overall).

45 David Simon, "Slapstick", *The Wire,* Season 3, Episode 9 (34 overall). Directed by Agnieszka Holland (HBO, 2004); see also http://www.hbo.com/the-wire/episodes/3/34-slapstick/synopsis.html

When a senior gangster Stringer Bell (Idris Elba) learns about the threat to Hamsterdam he organises for the killer to, incredibly, turn himself in at the Western District headquarters.[46] The carnival is now complete, the police act as criminals and the criminals in turn now act as police.

A local reporter discovers Hamsterdam in Episode 35 and Colvin lies to him: 'Command is well aware of the situation'. In a desperate bid to keep the lid on Hamsterdam, Colvin convinces the reporter that prosecution of the dealers will begin soon, and implores him to sit on the story for a couple of weeks:

> Bottom line is that if you start throwing calls right now, everyone is gonna shit blue thinking we got a leak. They might come up on the case early, not get all they could out of the work we did down here.

The reporter agrees to give Colvin a week in exchange for the exclusive.[47]

Colvin finally faces the music at a meeting of police commanders at headquarters. He shows a variety of photographs of former drug corners, now clean and empty of vice. He now explains explicitly and in detail the tactical decisions that led to the creation of Hamsterdam without referencing the strategic aims that led him to this. He demonstrates the consequential result of a dramatic drop in felony incidents in his district as following a set of small decisions – leaving the devil as it were in the details. The enormity of the situation gradually dawns on his commander Rawls ahead of the rest of his colleagues in the department: 'Don't you see what he' s done. He legalized drugs!'

Following the revelation, Colvin offers to sacrifice himself to protect his men unaware of what exactly the amount of sacrifice shall be. He is careful to explain that it is he, not his men, who are guilty:

> What I did, I did knowingly and on my own. My men had nothin' to do with it. They thought it was all part of an elaborate trap. So if you need me to fall on that sword, I'm good with that.

Rawls, as furious as he is, is also grudgingly impressed with Colvin's outrageous scheme:

> Bunny, you cocksucker, I got to give it to you, a brilliant idea. Insane and illegal, but stone fuckin' brilliant nonetheless. After all my puttin' my foot up people's asses to get the numbers down, he comes along and in one stroke, gets a 14 fuckin' percent decrease. Fuckin' shame it's gonna end our careers, but still.

As a parting shot, Colvin hands the Police Commissioner Burrell a stack of letters from community associations, ministers, business people, citizens: 'All positive',

46 David Simon, "Slapstick", *The Wire,* Season 3, Episode 9.

47 David Simon, "Reformation", *The Wire,* Season 3, Episode 10 (35 overall). Directed by Agnieszka Holland (HBO, 2004); see also http://www.hbo.com/the-wire/episodes/3/35-reformation/synopsis.html

Colvin says. 'Happy the dealers aren't on their corners any more'. Oh, and one more thing, he adds as he exits: 'A Sun reporter is aware of my deployments. I told him a major investigation was pending and he agreed to delay his article'.

Later, Commissioner Burrell reports to an incredulous Mayor Royce what Colvin has been up to: 'He did it without our knowledge', Burrell is quick to reassure. He tries to convince the Mayor that they can make it disappear, explain it away as 'some sort of new initiative to trap high end drug dealers', but Mayor Royce (Glynn Turman) is having none of it. 'I trusted you, Erv', he says to Burrell. 'You let me down. This goes wrong, no tellin' the damage. On this, you walk point'.[48] The mayor is seriously considering sacrificing the Commissioner.

Episode 36 portrays an indecisive Mayor Royce poised like Faust, as it were, between his good and evil angels. His political advisors urge him to shut Hamsterdam down immediately while the public health officials argue that it is like a life-size Petri dish that has given them unprecedented access to an at-risk population, an ideal site of bio-political governance. The Mayor is intrigued by the drop in violent crime and is inclined to explore ways to extend the experiment without spending political capital: 'A 14% decline in felonies citywide and I might be untouchable on this. We need to see if there's some way to keep this thing going without calling it what it is'.[49] A fearful Burrell, observing and misinterpreting the inaction fears that he's being set up and goes to Royce's rival (and subsequent mayor) Councilman Carcetti (Aiden Gillen) with the story, hoping Carcetti will use it against the Mayor. Burrell explains himself to Carcetti: 'I spin Royce before he spins me'.[50]

Episode 37 shows Burrell at the Mayor's office, he will not self-sacrificially take the blame for Hamsterdam as he is asked to do. What he proposes instead is the sacrifice and scapegoating of Colvin: 'I put what I can on crazy-ass Bunny Colvin and I take the hit. And if Carcetti or Gray holds hearings, I'm a wall between them and you. In which case, I'm your commissioner for a full five-year term'. Once this is agreed, the police come down on Hamsterdam on the ground and in the air in scenes carefully choreographed for the press (to the strains of Wagner's *Die Walküre*) and shut it down. Colvin learns that Burrell's personal intervention has ensured that the university security job that he had expected to retire is withdrawn. Furthermore, Colvin is demoted to lieutenant and his pension drastically cut as a consequence.[51] Colvin assents to all this punishment and humiliation to protect his men from official reprisals whom he led astray in the first place. This sacrifice calls for an analysis of of whether Colvin's actions are Faustian or Mephistophelean nature.

48 David Simon, "Reformation", *The Wire,* Season 3, Episode 10.

49 David Simon, "Middle Ground", *The Wire,* Season 3, Episode 11 (36 overall). Directed by Joe Chappelle (HBO, 2004); see also http://www.hbo.com/the-wire/episodes/3/36-middle-ground/synopsis.html.

50 David Simon, "Middle Ground", *The Wire,* Season 3, Episode 11.

51 David Simon, "Mission Accomplished", *The Wire,* Season 3, Episode 12 (37 overall). Directed Ernest Dickerson (HBO, 2004); see also http://www.hbo.com/the-wire/episodes/3/37-mission-accomplished/synopsis.html

Is Bunny Colvin Faust or Mephistopheles?

Bunny Colvin sacrifices himself for the sake of his men in a scene modelled on, or rather parodying him as a Christlike figure. Now that the chapter has outlined the narrative of Hamsterdam and connected it to Agamben's analyses of *homo sacer*, the state of exception, the camp, the office and the carnival, this section will address three specific themes. First, the nature of Colvin as a scapegoat/faux Christ-figure. Second, that inauthentic or counterfeit Christ-likeness and its connection to the Faustian pact. Third, the section will look at the nature of profanation as carnivalisation, particularly in its latent tendency to subvert the law.

The Wire's presentation of Hamsterdam and Colvin's experiment seems, initially, to present a way of dealing differently and in a positive manner with the drug trade. And there, at first glance, appears to be a tragic nature to its end. However, what the analysis has demonstrated is that such a temporary state of exception is always just that – temporary – it is not a final or permanent solution. This is connected too to how *The Wire*'s literalism temptingly makes us believe its make-believe is real.

As is clear above, there are broad hints strewn throughout the dialogue that Colvin is not as angelic as he presents, though. When the devil does God's work this can only be explained if not justified through a rationalisation for why there is evil in the world – a theodicy. Which is to say with an all-powerful God even the devil would of necessity have to do God's bidding – literally, doing God's work. This is all providentially part of the plan. However, when mortal humans have dealings with the devil (as McNulty and Royce both did with Colvin in their various ways) those are generally referred to as Faustian pacts, the proverbial selling one's soul to the devil.

Named after the legendary German figure of Dr Faust as its most famous or infamous example, the ambiguity of the deal between man and devil is also apparent in the two most famous literary examples of the genre. In Marlowe's version, Faust is – as might be expected – damned, whereas in Goethe's version he is – rather disconcertingly, to anyone with an ethical frame of mind – redeemed. Importantly for this chapter's argument is that when Goethe's Faust asks Mephistopheles 'Who are you then?' the response is 'Part of that force which would Do ever evil, and does ever good.'[52] This is a very patent theodicy.

According to Mikhail Bakhtin, the image of Faust originated in the atmosphere of carnival legends.[53] Agamben too explicitly identifies the carnival as the state of suspended law or exception in which 'criminal behaviour is considered licit or, in any case, not punishable'.[54] This is a period when the prevailing

52 Johann Wolfgang von Goethe, *Faust: A Tragedy: Interpretive Notes, Contexts, Modern Criticism* (2nd edn) (New York: W.W. Norton 2001), 36.

53 Mikhail Bakhtin, *Problems of Dostoevsky's Poetics* (New York: Ardis, 1973), 109.

54 Agamben, *State of Exception*, 71.

social order is temporarily subverted.[55] That subversion is clearly seen in Hamsterdam with the police and drug dealers mingling and cooperating in law breaking and law enforcement. While drug dealers keep order and investigate crime the police enable, are complicit in and participate in serious criminal activity. Colvin in essence reduces crime only by desisting from policing. If a temporary desisting from policing can reduce crime, surely this brings into question more than merely the effectiveness or utility of policing but its very purpose. Colvin takes the place of the sovereign but he still remains human. Nevertheless, his unauthorised action remains effective which gives the actual sovereign, in this instance the Mayor, paralysed by the temptations of the situation. There is a clear difference between God/the sovereign 'dealing', as it were, with the devil than deals between humans and the devil. The first is necessary and permanent, while the second is temporary as well as contingent on desire and sacrifice. The first is theodicy, while the second is merely sin. This is why Colvin while presenting and presented as a Christlike figure is in actual fact an anti-Christian-figure.

Is there a way out of the Faustian bargain? Agamben teases out a possible solution. For him, we are like humans in limbo abandoned in the absence of God. This means we have no destiny and are therefore indifferent to redemption and, as such, embody that life that is merely human and not sacred which can therefore still survive the end of the politico-theological machine.[56] Agamben thus calls for profanation as a solution.[57] Profanation itself is a species of carnivalisation given both its ambivalence and its turning of concepts into their opposites. We can therefore render inoperative any activity directed towards a Faustian pact in order to open it to a new use – a new use that does not abolish the old one but only exposes and disarms it.[58] Profanation is a kind of 'play' or neutralisation, which is distinct from secularisation, which is a form of repression.[59] Agamben expresses it thus: 'we must always wrest from the apparatuses – from all apparatuses – the possibility of use that they have captured. The profanation of the unprofanable is the political task of the coming generation.'[60]

Both secularisation and profanation are political operations but in opposed ways. The first guarantees the exercise of power by carrying it back to a sacred model; the second deactivates the apparatuses of power and returns to common use the spaces that power had seized. Agamben names the *real* state of exception

55 Agamben, *State of Exception*, 71.

56 Giorgio Agamben, *The Coming Community*, *Theory Out of Bounds v. 1*. (Minneapolis: University of Minnesota Press, 1993), 5–7.

57 Giorgio Agamben, *Profanations*, trans. Jeff Fort (New York: Zone Books, 2007).

58 Alex Murray and Jessica Whyte, *The Agamben Dictionary* (Edinburgh: Edinburgh University Press, 2011), 107.

59 Agamben, *Profanations*, 77.

60 Agamben, *Profanations*, 92.

as 'The Messianic Kingdom', in which 'the Law will return to its new form'.[61] That distinguishes it from the *declared* state of exception such as in Hamsterdam:

> The difference between the state of exception in which we now live and the *real* state of exception is that in the former the law is in force without signifying anything, and, in the latter, the law neither signifies anything nor is it in force . . . This is why Agamben believes that the state of exception in which we now live can be transgressed only by an even more radical state of exception; the state of exception where the law is returned to its originary meaninglessness; to a medley of letter without any order.[62]

The point is that Colvin did not have the *authority* to legalise drugs but by virtue of the office he held he had the *power* to do so. By the same token, the realism of *The Wire* can obscure the fact that it is literally not real.[63] This is why Bunny Colvin's temporary subversion of the law in Hamsterdam is a false hope that makes him a false messiah, a parody of salvation. His activities can be laid bare as a series of temptations to the public, the police, the politicians and the drug dealers, all of whom for a time succumb with no tangible improvement to their lot, but yet at great cost. It is an excellent and timely critique of politics broadly speaking, but the reason why it is successful is because it is great television and not because it is good or even authentic politics.

Bibliography

Books and articles

Agamben, Giorgio. *Homo Sacer: Sovereign Power and Bare Life*. Stanford, CA: Stanford University Press, 1998.

Agamben, Giorgio. *Opus Dei: An Archaeology of Duty*. Stanford, CA: Stanford University Press, 2013.

Agamben, Giorgio. *Potentialities: Collected Essays in Philosophy*, translated by Daniel Heller-Roazen. Stanford, CA: Stanford University Press, 1999.

Agamben, Giorgio. *Profanations*, translated by Jeff Fort. New York: Zone Books, 2007.

Agamben, Giorgio. *State of Exception*. Chicago: University of Chicago Press, 2005.

Agamben, Giorgio. *The Coming Community*, *Theory Out of Bounds v. 1*. Minneapolis: University of Minnesota Press, 1993.

61 Giorgio Agamben, *Potentialities: Collected Essays in Philosophy*, trans. Daniel Heller-Roazen (Stanford, CA: Stanford University Press, 1999), 167.

62 Signe Larsen, "Agamben: The Messianic Kingdom", *Critical Legal Thinking*, February 1, 2016, http://criticallegalthinking.com/2016/02/01/agamben-messianic-kingdom/#_edn2

63 David Simon "I'm David Simon, Creator of HBO's The Wire", *Reddit*, September 7, 2016, https://www.reddit.com/r/IAmA/comments/51lz1y/im_david_simon_creator_of_hbos_the_wire_the/

Agamben, Giorgio. *The Kingdom and the Glory: For a Theological Genealogy of Economy and Government (Homo Sacer II, 2)*. Stanford, CA: Stanford University Press, 2011.

Bakhtin, Mikhail. *Problems of Dostoevsky's Poetics*. New York: Ardis, 1973.

Debord, Guy. *The Society of the Spectacle*, translated by Fredy Perlman. Detroit, MI: Black and Red, 1977.

Goethe, Johann Wolfgang von, *Faust: A Tragedy: Interpretive Notes, Contexts, Modern Criticism* (2nd edn). New York: W.W. Norton, 2001.

Love, Chris. "Greek Gods in Baltimore: Greek Tragedy and The Wire". *Criticism* 52 (3–4), 2010.

Murray, Alex and Whyte, Jessica. *The Agamben Dictionary*. Edinburgh: Edinburgh University Press, 2011.

Simon, David. *Homicide: A Year on the Killing Streets*. First Owl Books, 2006. 4th edition.

Newspaper articles, magazines and websites

CBS Baltimore. "Freddie Gray Family Atty: BPD's Essential Personnel 'Old, White Guys that are Racist to the Core' ". *CBS Baltimore*. July 12, 2016, http://baltimore.cbslocal.com/2016/07/12/freddie-gray-billy-murphy-baltimore-police-department/

Chotiner, Isaac. "Everything is Not The Wire: David Simon Would Like You To Stop Trying to Understand What's Going on in Baltimore by Quoting His TV Show". *Slate*. August 12, 2015, http://www.slate.com/articles/arts/culturebox/2015/08/david_simon_interview_the_wire_creator_on_his_new_series_freddie_gray_ta.html

Clifford, Theresa. "A Greek Tragedy on the Streets of Baltimore". *Spiked*. 25 April, 2007, http://www.spiked-online.com/site/article/3131/

Ducker, Eric. "The Left Behind: Inside The Wire's World of Alienation and Asshole God". *The Fader*. December 8, 2006, http://www.thefader.com/2006/12/08/listening-in-part-iv/#ixzz2PjqAwXdS

HBO. "The Wire, Episodes", http://www.hbo.com/the-wire/episodes/index.html

Hornby, Nick. "David Simon, interview by Nick Hornby". *The Believer Magazine*. August, 2007, http://www.believermag.com/issues/200708/?read=interview_simon

Kreps, Daniel. "Baltimore: State of Emergency Declared Amid Protests, Riots". *Rolling Stone*. April 28, 2015, http://www.rollingstone.com/culture/news/baltimore-state-of-emergency-declared-amid-protests-riots-20150428

Kreps, Daniel. "Watch Barack Obama and 'The Wire' Creator Talk Criminal Justice Reform". *Rolling Stone*. March 17, 2015, http://www.rollingstone.com/tv/videos/watch-barack-obama-and-the-wire-creator-talk-criminal-justice-reform-20150327

Larsen, Signe. "Agamben: The Messianic Kingdom". *Critical Legal Thinking*. February 1, 2016, http://criticallegalthinking.com/2016/02/01/agamben-messianic-kingdom/#_edn2

Simon, David. "Baltimore", *The Audacity of Despair*. April 27, 2015, http://davidsimon.com/baltimore/

Simon, David. "I'm David Simon, Creator of HBO's The Wire". *Reddit*. September 7, 2016, https://www.reddit.com/r/IAmA/comments/51lz1y/im_david_simon_creator_of_hbos_the_wire_the/

Talbot, Margaret. "Stealing Life: The Crusader behind 'the Wire'". *The New Yorker*. October 22, 2007, http://www.newyorker.com/magazine/2007/10/22/stealing-life

Television episodes

Simon, David. "Amsterdam", *The Wire,* Season 3, Episode 4. Directed by Ernest Dickerson. HBO, 2004.
Simon, David. "Back Burners", *The Wire,* Season 3, Episode 7. Directed by Tim Van Patten. HBO, 2004.
Simon, David. "Home Coming", *The Wire,* Season 3, Episode 6. Directed by Leslie Libman. HBO, 2004.
Simon, David. "Middle Ground", *The Wire,* Season 3, Episode 11. Directed by Joe Chappelle. HBO, 2004.
Simon, David. "Mission Accomplished", *The Wire,* Season 3, Episode 12. Directed Ernest Dickerson. HBO, 2004.
Simon, David. "Moral Midgetry", *The Wire,* Season 3, Episode 8. Directed by Agnieszka Holland. HBO, 2004.
Simon, David. "Reformation", *The Wire,* Season 3, Episode 10. Directed by Christine Moore. HBO, 2004.
Simon, David. "Slapstick" *The Wire,* Season 3, Episode 9. Directed by Agnieszka Holland. HBO, 2004.
Simon, David. "Straight and True", *The Wire,* Season 3, Episode 5. Directed by Dan Attias. HBO, 2004.
Simon, David. "The Target", *The Wire,* Season 1, Episode 1. Directed by Clark Johnson. HBO, 2002.

Chapter 11

Intercultural cinema and the (re)envisioning of law: exploring life, death and law in *Atanarjuat* and *Before Tomorrow*

Rebecca Johnson

Introduction: contesting Canadian narratives of 'The North'

The Canadian national narrative has been marked by the North. Indeed our national anthem refers to Canada as 'our True North strong and free.' The trope of a snow-covered landscape and the character required to survive in it is common in Canadian literature and film. For Canadians (and by this, I mean 'settler Canadians'), the North is imagined as central to who we are, and this despite the fact that the vast majority of our population lives within 500 miles of our southern border. Of the many indigenous peoples inhabiting the continent, the Inuit have been of particular interest. The Canadian national archives are full of documentation of the North and the Inuit in particular – photographic, cinematic, and descriptive. Indeed, the Inuit may well be the most-photographed people on earth. Robert J. Flaherty's epic silent film *Nanook of the North* (1922) is a founding example of this fascination with a hostile but beautiful North and the nomadic peoples who survive in its climate.[1]

However, while at some level Canadians all share the cold, and some imagined sense of what that cold means about who we are, and indeed a sense that the inuksuk is a piece of 'Canadian' iconography, we do not share a robust sense or understanding of the history of the North. For decades, stories of encounters between settlers and the Inuit were documented primarily through settler eyes, eyes that were all too often blind to the political, social and legal orders that were present at the time of contact, and which persist into the present.[2] The history

1 There is a long history of filmic portrayal of the Inuit as mobile happy-go-lucky people who could best be trained for repetitive jobs. See also *Qallunaat!: Why White People are Funny*, directed by Mark Sandiford (National Film Board of Canada, 2006), and *Martha of the North*, directed by Marquise Lepage (National Film Board of Canada, 2008).

2 Hester Lessard, Rebecca Johnson and Jeremy Webber, eds, *Storied Communities: Narratives of Contact and Arrival in Constituting Political Community* (Vancouver: UBC Press, 2010); John L. Steckley, *White Lies About the Inuit* (Peterborough, ON: Broadview Press, 2008; Hugh Brody, *The Other Side of Eden: Hunters, Farmers, and the Shaping of the World* (Vancouver: Douglas & McIntyre 2001). For a very readable account of this phenomenon of

of colonial contacts between the Canadian state and the Inuit has been more complicated (and fraught) than is captured in the image of the happy-go-lucky Eskimo, or of Inuit sculpture. A full account of the encounter between Canada's North and its South involves difficult accounts of forced relocations, the killing of sled dogs, projects of renaming, removal of children to residential schools, the spread of tuberculosis and other settler diseases, loss of language, and more.[3]

The past 25 years, however, have witnessed what might be called a revolution of Inuit activism, and political mobilization.[4] In 1993, the Federal government entered into the Nunavut Land Claims Agreement, the largest indigenous land claim in Canadian history (an agreement involving land, money and self-government). The agreement involved the creation of a new territory for the Inuit peoples of the central and eastern Arctic. Nunavut, a word in Inuktitut meaning 'our land,' is 1.9 million square kilometers, nearly one fifth of Canada.[5] In a territory larger than Europe, there are less than 33,000 people, 85% of which are Inuktitut.

For those interested in legality, there is much to explore in the ways this newest territory draws conventional, traditional and modern together in its legislative action. The government of Nunavut runs on a consensus basis, rather than the party system, which is the conventional approach to politics in Canada.[6] The consensus approach in this blended system is a modern adaptation of old and new, more in keeping with Inuit ways of organizing and decision-making. Education has been a large part of the Nunavut Land Claims Agreement, with the federal government taking on obligations with respect to funding both educational and employment plans for Inuit.[7]

---

denial in North America as a whole, see Thomas King, *The Inconvenient Indian: A Curious Account of Native People in North America* (Toronto: Anchor Canada, 2012).

3 Frank J. Tester and Peter Kulchyski, *Tammarniit (Mistakes): Inuit Relocation in the Eastern Arctic, 1939–63* (Vancouver: UBC Press, 1994). Melanie McGrath, *The Long Exile: a Tale of Inuit Betrayal and Survival in the High Arctic* (New York: Vintage Books, 2006); Alan Marcus, *Relocating Eden: The Image and Politics of Inuit Exile in the Canadian Arctic* (Dartmouth, NH: University Press of New England, 1995); Paulette, Regan, *Unsettling the Settler Within: Indian Residential Schools, Truth Telling, and Reconciliation in Canada* (Vancouver: UBC Press, 2010); Canada – Royal Commission on Aboriginal Peoples, *Report of the Royal Commission on Aboriginal Peoples* (Canada, 1996); The Truth and Reconciliation Commission of Canada, *Honouring the Truth, Reconciling for the Future: Summary of the Final Report of the Truth and Reconciliation Commission of Canada* (Canada, 2015).

4 For a cinematic exploration of this history, see the film *Arctic Defenders*, directed by John Walker (Unikkaat Defenders Productions, 2013), http://www.arcticdefenders.ca

5 http://www.polarnet.ca/polarnet/nunavut.htm

6 http://www.gov.nu.ca/node/924

7 See for example, the recent settlement of ongoing litigation between the federal government and the Inuit (represented by the NTI, the corporate body that represents the Inuit in the land claims agreements. In May of 2015, the federal government agreed to pay an additional $255 million, which is directed to education for Inuit. Note, there is currently no University in the North, which means that most Inuit must travel south in order to seek higher education: http://www.jfklaw.ca/implementation-matters-the-2015-nunavut-land-claim-agreement-settlement.

Political and legal mobilizations have been accompanied by significant action in the cultural arena. Nunavut has experienced an explosion in media cultural production with the founding of the Inuit Broadcasting Corporation (the first native language television network in North America) and several Inuktitut film companies, the most well known of which is Igloolik Isuma. In many ways, this taking up of the cinematic media is a natural extension, since the Inuit have a rich and deep tradition of storytelling. Throughout Canadian history, there have been frequent articulations of the position that the Inuit have a rich culture, but it is often accompanied by the articulation that they have no 'law'. The claim in this chapter is that this is of course untrue. Indeed, the assertion here is that the rich practice of Inuit storytelling is not simply 'culture,' but is also a site of 'law'[8] (a claim that is also made throughout this collection).

In this chapter, I explore the envisioning of legality in the context of Inuit storytelling, using two films from the Igloolik Isuma Trilogy, *Atanarjuat: The Fast Runner*, directed by Zacharias Kunuk (Igloolik Isuma Productions, 2001), and *Before Tomorrow*, directed by Marie-Hélène Cousineau and Madeline Ivalu (Igloolik Isuma Productions, 2008). The trilogy is a group of movies filmed in the North, with Inuit actors, in Inuktitut, telling Inuit stories from within an Inuit world-view. The most well known in the trilogy is the first film, *Atanarjuat,* the cinematic retelling of a famous Inuit legend. The second film, *The Journals of Knud Rasmussen,* directed by Zacharias Kunuk and Norman Cohn (Igloolik Isuma Productions, 2006), is a portrayal of the life of Avva, a great Inuit shaman, and his daughter Apak, drawn on extracts from the journals of Danish explorer and anthropologist Knud Rasmussen during the Fifth Thule Expedition (1921–24), but told from the perspective of the Inuit.[9] *Before Tomorrow* completes the trilogy by moving explicitly into the world of fiction, taking Danish writer Jørn Riel's novel *Før Morgendagen* (1975) and re-telling it as a piece of Inuit storytelling.

I begin with my own experiences with the film *Atanarjuat,* in the space of what Laura Marks refers to as the intercultural cinematic encounter,[10] in order to situate the argument that such films can help us to think otherwise about both legality and the envisioning of law. I offer a few comments on methodological

Significantly, the settlement of the agreement involved a commitment to working in partnership to implement the obligations of the land claims (working in partnership being another important principle of Inuit law).

8 For a fuller exploration of this point, see Rebecca Johnson and Lori Groft, "Learning Indigenous Law: Reflections on Working with Western Inuit Stories," *Lakehead Law Journal* 2(2) (2017): 117–144.

9 For a wonderfully rich collection of articles engaging with this film, see Gillian Robinson, editor, *The Journals of Knud Rasmussen: A Sense of Memory and High-Definition Inuit Storytelling.* (Montreal: Isuma Distribution International, 2008).

10 Laura Marks, *The Skin of the Film: Intercultural Cinema, Embodiment and the Senses* (Durham, NC: Duke University Press, 2000).

resources that can support explorations of law envisioned, and then I turn to *Before Tomorrow*, to further extend the argument in the context of a modern fiction that draws in traditional Inuit law (stories) to envision a living law.

Encountering *Atanarjuat*: law envisioned in intercultural cinema

In 2001, I moved from Fredericton, New Brunswick (Canada's east coast, in Mi'ig maw territory) to Victoria (Canada's west coast, in Salish territory). Though Victoria is in the far south of Canada, over the years the Law School had built and developed a series of connections to the Arctic: as part of the University of Victoria Law's Co-op Program, a regular stream of our law students had gone North to spend a work term working in Iqaluit, often with Maliiganik Tukisiiniakvik (the Legal Services Board). Extending this experience, in 2001, the University of Victoria had entered into a partnership to establish the Akitsiraq Law School Program, where a four-year law degree would be delivered to Inuit students in Iqaluit, the capital of Nunavut.[11]

That year, I offered the law-and-film class that I had been teaching in Fredericton. As usual, students were invited to choose their own filmic text for their research paper. And also as usual, many students chose texts that were relatively current. Given the significant Northern focus around the law school, it was no surprise to have a number of students write on *Atanarjuat*. *Atanarjuat* was the first ever feature film to be written, directed and acted entirely in Inuktitut. It is also currently listed first on the list of 'Top Canadian Films of All Time'.[12] The movie gripped popular imagination, with critics speaking of the 'timeless' tale of an Inuit community from 2,000 years ago. The story involved love, adultery, murder and vengeance. The story itself was understandable within the Western tradition in ways that resonated with some standard Western tropes.[13] On

11 Rather than drawing Inuit students to the South, law professors (drawn from a number of schools across the country) were sent North, so that Inuit students were able to study law at home with the support of family and community, in a program that was tailored to the legal context of Nunavut, and which included instruction in Inuktitut, and the active participation of Inuit elders: http://communications.uvic.ca/releases/release.php?display=back&id=70. See Serena Ableson, "Bringing Legal Education to the Canadian Arctic: the Development of the Akitsiraq Law School and the Challenges for Providing Library Services to a Nontraditional Law School," 34 *International Journal of Legal Information* 34(1) (2006): Article 4. Available at: http://scholarship.law.cornell.edu/ijli/vol34/iss1/4

12 https://en.wikipedia.org/wiki/Top_10_Canadian_Films_of_All_Time#2015_list

13 See, for example, Anthony G. Amsterdam and Jerome Bruner, *Minding the Law: How Courts Rely on Storytelling, and How Their Stories Change the Ways We Understand the Law – and Ourselves* (Cambridge, MA: Harvard University Press, 2000). They provide a compelling argument concerning the operation of, for example, the western tropes of love and infidelity in the story of Arthur, Guinevere and Lancelot.

the personal front, I had the experience of seeing the movie and loving it while being simultaneously conscious of the ways in which the film seemed to give and require things of me that were different from what was required of me by films from genres with which I had greater familiarity.[14]

For one thing, I found the time/space of the film to be quite unexpected. Things moved at a very different (slower) pace. The cinematography was stunning in its expanse, with hours spent in confronting a very different colour palette of light and snow. There were also challenges of translation. I don't mean simply the need to read subtitles, nor the fact that the filmmakers actively chose to leave certain portions of the film untranslated.[15] It was rather that, as Pooja Parmar points out, the 'translation of unfamiliar stories narrated in unfamiliar languages into a familiar language does not automatically lead to comprehension of lifeworlds.'[16] The non-verbal register of the film was rich, in ways that left me uncertain that I fully understood the characters. I found myself consciously wondering about the social/legal register that was underpinning the story being told. Something different seemed to be going on.

This sense was affirmed when several of the students in my class had returned home having watched *Atanarjuat* in the North, and pointed out that audiences there had seemed to read the film quite differently.[17] Students noted, for instance, that Inuit friends had suggested that Atanarjuat was himself implicated in the wrongdoings that had been done. This was not intuitively obvious to me at the time. I gradually came to appreciate more fully, through discussion with others, the ways in which my reading of the film might be shifted (and enriched) through a better understanding of the social and legal order out of which the story emerged.[18] For one thing, the story itself was a familiar one within the Inuit community, as an ancient story, with currency within the Inuit

14 On the commonality of this response among cultural outsiders, see Shari Hunhdorf, "Atanarjuat, the Fast Runner: Culture, History and Politics in Inuit Media". *American Anthropologist* 105(4) (2003): 822–826.

15 For a lovely exploration of this point, see Sophie McCall, "'I Can Only Sing This Song to Someone Who Understands It': Community Filmmaking and the Politics of Partial Translation in *Atanarjuat, the Fast Runner*". *Essays on Canadian Writing* 83 (2004): 19–46.

16 Pooja Parmar, *Indigeneity and Legal Pluralism in India* (New York: Cambridge University Press, 2015), 12–13. I quite agree with Pooja Parmar's comments on the utility of the concept of translation, particularly when working with intercultural cinema, which requires its audience to be active translators: "The concept of translation is a useful one to understand the practices and processes that enable both the creation as well as the destruction of meanings as people inhabiting one normative universe receive, interpret, reorder, and re-resent claims that arise in and are informed by legal cultures different from their own" (at 12–13). Here, she too emphasizes the importance of non-verbal modes of communication for those seeking to understand human beings living a different life (at 17).

17 In particular, I am grateful for the insights of Jessica Lot Thompson.

18 For an elaboration of the life contexts in which the narrative of the story is embedded, see Michael Robert Evans, *The Fast Runner: Filming the Legend of Atanarjuat* (Lincoln, NE and London: University of Nebraska Press, 2010).

community as a source of Inuit legal principles, as a source of law.[19] While it was possible for a North American student to read this film as a story of love triumphant and vengeance delivered, it seemed that many in the Inuit audiences understood the story differently. For Inuit audiences, the film was thick with traditional Inuit justice principles: respect for others, the duty to care, collective responsibility and accountability.[20] From inside these principles, the simple (western archetypal) story of heroes and villains, love and revenge, is disrupted. Law is envisioned not simply as an outcome, but as the context in which all action takes place.

In an open letter on Traditional Inuit justice principles, Robert Kilpatrick said,

> Justice to our ancestors' way of thinking was not a system of law enforcement. Justice was not something that was handed out by the court, Crown attorney, or police. The elders tell us that justice was something far more exciting. It was an attitude – a state of mind.[21]

I began to understand that the story was about this 'state of mind,' where attention was not on 'judging' in the way most common in Western film.[22] In *Atanarjuat*, from the perspective of many Inuit audiences, the story was about practices of decision-making, caring for, and taking responsibility for the health of the family and community.

This approach makes the ending of the film all the more interesting as a form of law envisioned. Inuit audiences (unlike Southern ones) would have been aware of the many versions of the Atanarjuat legend. While the various tellings differ in some ways, they all end with Atanarjuat killing his rival Oki. In producing the film, the directors worked with a number of elders, seeking to combine elements from different accounts of the stories. One significant adaptation was

19 Several versions of it are recorded in Neil Christopher, Noel McDermott and Louise Flaherty, eds. *Unikkaaqtuat: an Introduction to Inuit Myths and Legends* (Toronto: Inhabit Media, 2011).

20 For a rich elaboration of Inuit *qaujimajatuqangit* (traditional knowledge and law), see the five-volume series, *Interviewing Inuit Elders,* Jarich Oosten, Frederic Laugrand and Wim Rasing, eds. For an introduction to the series, see Paul Groarke, "Review Essay: Legal Volumes from the Arctic College's *Interviewing Inuit Elders* Series". *Osgoode Hall Law Journal* 47 (2009): 787–805.

21 Mr Justice Robert Kilpatrick, Senior Judge, Nunavut Court of Justice, "An Open Letter to the Citizens of Nunavut on the Importance of Traditional Justice Values in the 21st Century," May 6, 2011, http://www.nucj.ca/phocadownloadpap/TJV_EnglishA.pdf (accessed October 22, 2015).

22 For an argument about the significance of trial movies in western popular culture (suggesting that trials are movie-like to begin with, and that many movies are trial-like to begin with), see Carol Clover, "Law and the Order of Popular Culture," in *Law in the Domains of Culture*, edited by Austin Sarat and T. R. Kearns (Ann Arbor: University of Michigan Press, 1998): 97–119.

the decision to end the film without a killing, but instead with the banishment of the offenders. In making this choice, both elders and filmmakers actively worked with the story to envision Inuit law operating in the modern context. At a time when Inuit communities have suffered the devastating impacts of the colonial encounter, and where communities live with the devastation of intra-community and inter-generational violence, the film makes a legal argument that it is crucial to break the cycle of violence in a new way. It argues that the communities need additional strategies, which seek to keep people safe without killing. That is, it envisions new ways of thinking about (legal) strategies to end a cycle of violence.

Working with *Atanarjuat*, I began to better understand how the film was not simply 'showing' or 'representing' the law of the past. The film was envisioning both life and law in a particular way, inviting its audience to experience that life/law, and consider the need for the community to disrupt certain patterns of vengeance present in the older stories. Justice is rendered visually in ways that could encourage an audience to imagine themselves occupying the legal order in which such an argument would make sense. Law is placed into space, time and movement. The story performed its legal argument, invited a shift in the justice 'state of mind'. The film performs Inuit identity and law in a ways that, as Shari Huhndorf put it, 'provides a sense of continuity with the past and responds to changing circumstances.'[23]

As I spent time with the film, I found myself thinking more about its invitation and its challenge. One of the great challenges of settler society has always been the limit of its own legal imagination, a tendency to understand its laws as universal and to project them onto others in a particular colonial fashion. In exploring intercultural cinema, it would be important to accept that there may be different ways of conceptualizing and living 'law'.[24] For certain, I could see that it was possible for different audiences to see and enjoy and make use of the film without having at all the same experience (indeed, my own experience of the film shifted drastically as I began learning more about Inuit histories, stories and law). Of course, this is on some levels simply a truism: people have different experiences of seeing the same film.[25] But I could also see how this film was a powerful tool that could make space for audiences to do some of the work crucial to Indigenous-Settler reconciliation, and to

23 Huhndorf, at 825.

24 On the challenges in translating concepts of 'law' from Inuktitut to English and back again, see Marian Aupilaarjuk, Marie Tulimaaq, Akisu Joamie, Emile Imaruittuq, and Lucassie Nutaraaluk. *Interviewing Inuit Elders, Vol 2: Perspectives on Traditional Law*, edited by Jarich Oosten, Frederic Laugrand and Wim Rasing (Iqaluit: Nunavut Arctic College, 1999), 1–8.

25 The point was nicely made by Frank Tomasulo, in "'I'll See It When I Believe It': Rodney King and the Prison-House of Video". In *The Persistence of History: Cinema, Television, and the Modern Event*, edited by Vivian Sobchack (New York: Routledge, 1996), 69–88. On film as evidence in the courtroom, see, for example, Jessica Silbey, "Persuasive Visions: Film and Memory," *Law, Culture and the Humanities* 10(1) (2014): 24–42.

laying the foundation for more egalitarian intercultural encounters in a world of legal pluralism.[26]

Tools for working with law envisioned

Certainly, there are resources for doing this 're-imagining' work within Western traditions – there is a significant body of law-and-literature scholarship focusing on the legal imaginary, and a rich and expanding literature exploring these questions in the context of law and film. In the context of intercultural encounters, I take particular inspiration from James Boyd White's work on justice as 'translation'.[27] He operates with the premise that law is less a set of rules than an imaginative and intellectual activity, a way of imagining a shared history.[28] White's framework takes as a given the importance of learning how to *live* within a language, a culture, a legal order. This invitation to inhabit a world *imagined* is at the heart of using the filmic text as an 'other' way of envisioning law.[29] Film (like literature) works with narrative. But it also can draw on sound and vision in ways that can create the context for particularly embodied imaginative encounter.[30] This is not to saw that a film can *make* a viewer *feel* in a particular way, but is simply to acknowledge that it does invite the viewer to an experience that engages multiple sensory sites of judgement.[31] Film (and television, for that matter) invites the reader to imagine what it would be to inhabit the world it describes, drawing on narrative, sight, sound, and the magic of editing.

How can film help us inhabit another site of law? Laura Marks' work on haptic visuality in the context of intercultural cinema (fourth-world cinema) is useful in this context. Haptic visuality is tactile, kinaesthetic, and proprioceptive; the eyes

26 This observation was part of the grounding for the development at our law school of a course in Inuit Law and Film. For a discussion of the course, see Rebecca Johnson, "Reimagining 'the Truth North Strong and Free': Reflections on Going to the Movies with James Boyd White". In *Living in a Law Transformed: Encounters with the Works of James Boyd White*, edited by Julen Etxabe and Gary Watt (Ann Arbor, MI: Maize Books, 2014), 258–283.

27 White, James Boyd. *Justice as Translation: An Essay in Cultural and Legal Criticism* (Chicago: University of Chicago Press, 1990).

28 James Boyd White, *From Expectation to Experience: Essays on Law and Legal Education* (Ann Arbor: University of Michigan Press, 1999), ix.

29 For a succinct elaboration of different ways one might approach questions of law and film, see Orit Kamir, "Why 'Law-and-Film' and What Does It Actually Mean?: A Perspective". *Continuum: Journal of Media and Cultural Studies* 19(2) (2005): 255–278.

30 For an elaboration of this point, see Rebecca Johnson and Ruth Buchanan, "Getting the *Insider*'s Story Out: What Popular Film Can Tell Us About Legal Method's Dirty Secrets," *Windsor Yearbook of Access to Justice* 20 (2001): 87–110; and Ruth Buchanan and Rebecca Johnson, "Strange Encounters: Exploring Law and Film in the Affective Register," *Studies in Law, Politics, and Society* 46 (2009): 33–60.

31 For example, sound and sight are arguably two different registers of accessing 'truth'. See Mary Ann Doane, "Ideology and the Practice of Sound Editing and Mixing," in *The Cinematic Apparatus*, edited by Teresa de Lauretis and Stephen Heath (New York: St Martin's Press, 1980), 47–60.

operate more as organs of touch than as organs of optical mastery. Haptic cinema does not invite us to identify with a figure, so much as engage a bodily relationship between viewer and image: it asks us to be present with the image.[32] Intercultural films like *Atanarjuat*, Marks notes, are rich with haptic qualities, with encouragements to feel. But the cinematic choices of intercultural cinema are ones that may require more work of western audiences. Indeed, she says, 'haptic visuality implies making oneself vulnerable to the image, reversing the relation of mastery that characterizes optical viewing.'[33] Rather than having our eyes directed in their focus, we are given many scenes where we are asked to spend time in observation, time to let our eyes wander over the spaces to see. Extensive close-ups give us a sense of intimacy, without much in the way of direction. This is not the observation of the ethnographic film (showing us 'how' things are done, though there is certainly significant attention to authenticity). It is rather an invitation to be immersed in a different 'sensorium,' to bring one's own memories of touch, sound, and smell to the experience of making sense of haptic images.

Of course, a viewer's own sense memories may draw them into an image in a powerful way, but it may also involve moments of bafflement. As Marks notes, 'bafflement in the face of the representation of unfamiliar sense experiences is an aspect of intercultural relations that is unavoidable and salutary: it provides the ground of respect for cultural differences that must precede intercultural learning.'[34] The haptic in these films creates the conditions for new stories: 'when verbal and visual representation is saturated, meanings seep into bodily and other dense, seemingly silent registers.'[35]

In this second part of the chapter, I turn to a closer exploration of the place of story and haptic perception in my own efforts to better understand how intercultural cinema opens space for the work of decolonization. How can film in general offer a way for viewers to begin to inhabit Inuit ways of doing law? What can be learned from the film *Before Tomorrow*?

Before Tomorrow: truthful fictions, and the envisioning of Inuit law

While *Atanarjuat* is the telling of an Inuit legend (a legend that can properly be understood as a traditional legal text), *Before Tomorrow* is firmly within the realm of fiction. Indeed, here, the Inuit filmmakers have claimed the right commonly held by other directors: to take a story from another culture, and re-tell it from within their own cultural context. The film is based on Jørn Riel's novel *Før Morgendagen*, which focuses tightly on the relationship between a grandmother and her grandson. In an interview about the book, Riel recounts an experience from

32 Marks, at 164.
33 Marks, at 185.
34 Marks, at 239.
35 Marks, at 5.

when he was a tracker in Greenland.[36] On a winter hunting trip, he came upon a cave on a remote island, a cave in which were the skeletal remains of an old woman, and a child of 8 or 10 years. How, he wondered, had these two come to die in this place, their bodies left unattended and unburied? Why had they not been picked up by their community? He speculated that the entire family must have been dead. Knowing that the population in northeast Greenland had disappeared suddenly over a century before, he speculated that there must have been a plague. And so, he wrote a novel, imagining the grandmother and child, their entire community wiped out, asking how they might have come to be alone on an island, and how they might have faced the prospect of being the last living human beings?

While the film is explicitly within the domain of fiction (and thus, arguably, far from the world of obvious legality), it is within the category of stories that one might refer to as truthful fictions.[37] The novel was adapted by Arnait Video Productions (an Inuit women's film collective) and set in the Nunavik region of Northern Quebec, which itself was historically marked by the decimation of Inuit communities through contact with southern diseases. In *Before Tomorrow*, the grandmother Ninioq (played by Madeline Piujuq Ivalu) and her grandson Maniq (played by Paul-Dylan Ivalu, her grandson in real life) are dropped off on a remote island, where, every year, the family dries the fish gathered in the summer, for use through the winter. They bring with them Ninioq's elderly friend Kuutujuk (played by Mary Qulitalik). Kuutujuk, who is very frail, wants to spend her last months in the company of her good friend, and she dies soon after their arrival on the island. Ninioq and Maniq spend the time on the island working. As winter approaches, they wait for their family to return to pick them up. Eventually, as the fall approaches, they make their way back, only to find that the entire community is dead from smallpox, the after-effect of an encounter with outsiders (white men). Ninioq and Maniq return to the island where the food has been cached, and attempt to survive the winter, the only two people left from their community. Near the end, wolves attack them, eating their food, and injuring Ninioq. She is left to confront her choice: to die and leave her grandson alone as the sole surviving person in the world as she knows it, or to end his life as well.

In the North American film tradition, there are genres of film dealing with apocalyptical moments, with the death of not simply a single person (after all, death does come to each), but with larger tragedies, those that put the continuity of a people at risk, that eradicate communities, or humanity itself: disaster films

36 https://www.isuma.tv/arnaitvideo/interview-jorn-riel-author-morgendagen-tomorrow

37 For a helpful exploration of the power of truthful fictions, see David Dow, "Fictional Documentaries and Truthful Fictions: The Death Penalty in Recent American Film". *Constitutional Commentary* 17(3) (2000): 511–553. Arguably, these insights are deeply embedded in the vast majority of indigenous legal orders, which do in fact embed the most powerful of their truths (and legal procedures, protocols, and principles) in story. See Val Napoleon and Hadley Friedland, "An Inside Job: Engaging with Indigenous Legal Traditions Through Stories" *McGill Law Journal* 61(4) (2016): 725–754.

(*Titanic*, *Poseidon Adventure*, *Towering Inferno*) explore interactions between nature and human intervention that lead to large scale tragedy; science fiction (*Omega Man*, *Alien*, *Scanner*, *The Matrix*) imagines apocalyptic errors that place mankind on the verge of eradication, through an alien species, or indeed through technology gone horribly wrong. *Before Tomorrow* can be read against a trajectory of apocalyptic/holocaust narratives. It can be read as a story of 'the end of times'. And yet, *Before Tomorrow*, in its Inuit storytelling mode, is in some ways different from other films in this genre.

The opening moments of the film provide us with one set of framing questions. Against a background that seems to be a slow swirl of smoke, or of ink in water, we hear the McGarrigle Sisters song (original music for the movie) 'Why Must We Die?' We begin to see faces emerge from the smoke, and then fade away. We are already being introduced to the faces of those we will meet and lose throughout the film, for death comes to every character seen in this movie. But the invitation from this movie is not to focus on the deaths. The focus of the film seems to be more directly on life and relationships. Though the song asks 'Why must we die?,' the film itself seems to ask rather 'How might we live?' and 'In what ways might these stories of dying inform our ways of living?' 'How are these, the dead, made part of the world in which we live?' 'What Laws govern us as we confront the inevitability of life which encounters death?'

In what follows, I will signpost two particular pieces of Inuit law which are envisioned in the film. Each takes the form of a unikkaaqtuat (story), a story that embeds, embodies, and constitutes legal community. In each case, we are positioned as the audience for the story. In each case, the recounting is filmed in a way that is rich with haptic visuality. The first occurs at the beginning, and the second at the halfway mark of the film. Together, these two pieces of law structure a rich space for us to imagine living deeply within another legal order.

The first story: 'The Raven and the Whale'

Against the foreshadowing of the film's opening credits, the first scene begins with a long sustained shot of two figures walking across the snowy tundra, the sound of snow crunching, and breathing. While the figures are too far away to be recognizable, the one behind wears an amauti (an Inuit outer coat that is generally worn by a woman, the hood of which is designed so that it could carry a child).[38] The smaller one in front carries a walking stick and a bag. The relation

38 Note, amautik can also be worn by men. Gendering (whether of people, names, clothing or tools) in the north is another interesting subject. See, for example, Bernard Saladin D'Anglure, "From Foetus to Shaman: The Construction of an Inuit Third Sex," in *Amerindian Rebirth: Reincarnation Belief among North American Indians and Inuit*, edited by Antonia Mills and Richard Slobodin (Toronto: University of Toronto Press, 1994), 82–106.

between the two characters crystallizes as we hear a young voice speak (in Inuktitut), with the subtitle 'Grandmother, tell me a story.' The line spoken ('Grandmother, tell me a story') is the signal that we are being told a story (this is akin to 'once upon a time').[39] In reply, we hear an older voice begin to speak:

> One time, a raven flew over a beach. Suddenly a bowhead whale surfaced and swallowed it whole. Inside the whale it was very dark, like a cave. In the distance, the raven saw the flickering light of an oil lamp.

At this point, we visually shift from the tundra, and are drawn into a dark cave-like space (a space that echoes the words we have heard). In close-up, we have the face of an old Inuit woman centred in the screen, the storyteller, Ninioq. She continues to tell the tale. 'A girl was trying desperately to keep the light from dying'. The shot cuts to a close-up of the traditional inuit stone lamp, the qulliq, a thin line of flame flickering along its edge.[40] As the camera focuses our field of vision on the flickering flames, she continues speaking. At the same time, a series of shot/reverse-shot techniques enables us (as viewers) to join her in the cave, and watch the face of the young boy to whom she is telling the story. Again, we have a close-up on his face, the light from the flickering lamp drawing him out of the darkness in which they both sit. In this intimate space, the story continues:

> The raven heard the girl's voice: you must be faithful to me. Promise never to touch this light. The Raven promised, I'll never touch it! But when the girl returned to her work the raven forgot his promise and touched the lamp. And when the light went out the girl fell over, dead. The Raven realized his terrible mistake. The girl had taken possession of the raven's soul. And when the light went out, so did the raven's heart. That's the end of my story.

39 See notes to the story "The Ptarmigan," in Neil Christopher, Noel McDermott and Louise Flaherty, eds. *Unikkaaqtuat: an Introduction to Inuit Myths and Legends* (Toronto: Inhabit Media, 2011), 73. See also the comments of Alexina Kublu (Language Commissioner for Nunavut) in Saullu Nakasuk, Hervé Paniaq, Elisapee Ootoova and Pauloosie Angmaalik, *Interviewing Inuit Elders, Vol 1: Introduction*, edited by Jarich Oosten and Frédéric Laugrand (Iqaluit: Nunavut Arctic College, 1999), at 188. As Kublu says, the English phrase, "Grandmother, tell a once-upon-a-time story" is, in Inuktitut, "anaanattiaq unikkaaqtualaurit". This is also the first line of the story "The Ptarmigan and the Snowbunting," which Alexina Kublu translates as "Irngutarjuapiga nauk? ("Where is my dear grandchild?").

40 The lamp is a crescent-shaped cup carved from soapstone. It is filled with oil from seal blubber. Arctic cotton grass or moss is used as a wick (drawn to the edge with a tool, the height to the flame to be managed by the (usually woman) person tending it. It provides light, heat, is for cooking, etc. The level of flame can also be regulated to provide significant or minimal heat and light. For a discussion of the qulliq, and other aspects of Inuit material culture, see John Bennett and Susan Rowley, eds. *Uqalurait: An Oral History of Nunavut* (Montreal and Kingston: McGill-Queen's University Press, 2004).

The story is thus told in this setting, with many pauses, and time for us to focus on the faces and their expressions, both in the speaking and the listening. The telling of the story already pulls us into a space of story time, situating us as listeners, and inviting us to feel (in a haptic sense) the sound of crunching snow, the warmth of the lamp, the feel of fur. We are left to think about the story, a story that places us (like the raven? like the girl?) in the belly of the whale.

The end of Ninioq's story (of the Raven and the Whale) is the beginning of the cinematic story. For immediately after the telling, we move in flashback of sorts to an earlier season: we move from winter to summer. With a second McGariggle Sisters song, the grandmother's voice sends us to the past, as friends and relatives come to visit.[41] Cinematically, we have a beautiful shot from under the water, looking up to the sky, as a large boat (perhaps in the shape of a whale) passes overhead. The extended scenes of the umik and kayait travelling across the water are captivating in a strongly haptic ways (or, as students in the course put it, 'immersive'). We are treated to the landscape of the North during the summer, a time when families travel to visit with each other. The scene unfolds, as we move to open space, to a rich community full of people, tents, children, visitors, play, food, laughter and sharing. Over a meal of shared seal, the group listens to an old man, Kukik, tell of an encounter with strangers (whalers), who have strange and marvellous tools (knifes, barrels, needles), who drink a liquid that burns and makes them more friendly, and who are willing to engage in trade (one metal needle for one night with one of the women.)[42]

In this moment in the fiction, the story lays out all the elements of the histories known to have come: traders who come with steel, with needles, with alcohol. The scene is set up as a piece of foreshadowing: we may, as viewers, suspect what will come to pass, but we see also that the community sees Kukik's story of the strangers as fantastical – something to laugh over, and not yet something to fear. The film maintains a focus on the Inuit community, with the strange traders mentioned but never seen. As viewers, the film again visually positions us as part of the community, sitting on the ground, sharing food, and laughter. But we are also left with a sense of unease, given the opening story. We are left thinking about how to link this story of strangers to the story of the Raven and the Whale.

Keavy Martin, in her quite exceptional work on Inuit literature, emphasizes the centrality of adaptation and transformation to Inuit stories, stories which aim to entertain and to assist in problem solving: to offer strategies and resources,

41 There are only two pieces of extra-diegetic music in this film, the two songs we hear in the first minutes of the film. Indeed, the film deprives us of almost any extra-digetic sound. What songs we hear after this are sung with no accompaniment. The sounds we hear (if amplified) are nearly always strictly diegetic. We have to listen in a quite different way than is currently common in Western film.

42 For a historical account of the relations between Inuit and whalers, see Nancy Wachowich *et al.*, *Saqiyuk: Stories from the Lives of Three Inuit Women* (Montreal and Kingston: McGill-Queen's University Press, 1999), 113–122. Apphia Agalakti Awa (the grandmother) speaks of the fear Inuit women had of whalers, and of the possibilities of trade.

something captured in the word *qanuqtuurniq*, which is a quality of resourcefulness in problem solving.[43] And so, given the centrality of adaptation, it is again unsurprising that a story like 'The Raven and the Whale' appears in a number of variants in published form. As recounted in *Before Tomorrow,* Raven is said to be only forgetful or careless. In several versions of the tale, Raven is portrayed as arrogant, selfish and stupid.[44] In these versions, Raven kills the girl/whale through his greed/curiosity, and he later brags to the people that it was through his great prowess as a hunter that the whale was killed. There is yet another version of this story which focuses on grief and healing, in the context of the journey that takes each person to death.[45] In this version, Raven's desire for the girl leads to the death of the Whale, which leads Raven to cry the first tears, and sing the first song of grief and healing.

In Inuit storytelling (as in most stories) the telling links the storyteller and the person being spoken to with the story itself. The story adapts itself to the situation. And so it is here. *Before Tomorrow* begins with a tale that will carry the resonances of multiple accounts, pointing in the direction of curiosity, foolishness, greed, lust, life, death, grief, sorrow, and healing. On one level of course, the film does use the story of the Raven and the Whale to invite its audience to think about Canada's encounters with the Inuit, and the place of curiosity and death in those encounters. Cole Harris has pointed to settler Canada's wilful blindness with respect to histories of disease among indigenous peoples.[46] So from one perspective, the film might be seen as using the story of the Raven and the Whale to explore colonial history. For in this story, Raven's great sins are curiosity, desire, and denial. Raven is the beneficiary of the whale's hospitality, makes a promise, and yet, through his ignorance, brings death to the girl.

But the story also is set within an Inuit cosmological world, one in which humans and animals are linked and related. In the story as recounted in *Before Tomorrow*, it is not simply that Raven has killed the girl/whale, but is also that Raven's own heart has died. The story asks us to consider the ways in which it is

43 See Keavy Martin, *Stories in a New Skin: Approaches to Inuit Literature* (Winnipeg: University of Manitoba Press, 2012), 3.

44 See Susie Tiktalik, 'The Raven and the Whale,' in Herbert T. Schwarz, *Elik, and Other Stories of the MacKenzie Eskimos* (Toronto: McClelland and Stewart, 1970), 43. Two versions of the story appear in Knud Rasmussen, *The Alaskan Eskimos as Described in the Posthumous Notes of Dr. Knud Rasmussen / by H. Ostermann ; Edited after the Latter's Death with the Assistance of E. Holtved ; Translated from the Danish by W.E. Calvert* (Copenhagen: Gyldendal, 1952), 24–26, and 172.

45 http://www.youtube.com/watch?v=fUx5_inL-4k, http://www.youtube.com/watch?v=3Lkur3PmQvo

46 Cole Harris, "Voices of Disaster: Smallpox around the Strait of Georgia in 1782". *Ethnohistory* 41(4) (1994): 591–626. See also Corinne Hodgson, "The Social and Political Implications of Tuberculosis among Native Canadians," *Canadian Review of Sociology and Anthropology* 19 (1982): 50; Ebba Olofsson, Tara L. Holton and Imaapik "Jacob" Partridge, "Negotiating Identities: Inuit Tuberculosis Evacuees in the 1940s–1950s," *Etudes/Inuit/Studies* 32(2) (2008): 127–149.

not simply that others have been harmed, but also that we, like Raven, may have not understood the ways in which we are connected, and the ways in which our own lives are linked to the heart of the Whale.

Against the backdrop of these two stories (the Raven and the Whale, and Kukik's seemingly fantastical tale of strangers with sharp blades and needles), Ninioq, Maniq and Kuutujuk head off to the island to dry fish. The next 20 minutes of the film seem to pull us out of the forward driving movement of narrative, and instead embed us firmly in the sensorium of daily life. There is very little in the way of conversation. In some ways, the film seems almost ethnographic in its attention on the practices of life: old women tending a lamp, a boy gathering berries with his grandmother, caring for an old woman as she is dying, Maniq practising with his bow and arrow, watching the sky, the sound of footsteps and the wind. There are long passages with no conversation, and no 'action'. But the time is rich with haptic visuality. You listen, and watch, feel fall in the air, see and hear the geese flying. We are shown not the harshness of living from the land, but rather the beauty of the land, its resources, its landscapes and its skies. We watch Maniq practise with a harpoon, and catch his first seal. We see Ninioq shelter her beloved grandson both literally and metaphorically.[47] What conversation there is involves the Ninioq singing to Maniq, working alongside him, comforting him, sharing memories of the past and hopes for the future. We watch as Maniq becomes capable and self-reliant. This self-reliance is not centred on separation or autonomy from others. Rather Maniq's ability to be self-reliant is shown at each juncture to involve his increasing capacity to care for others and not only for himself (the sharing of berries, the bringing of water, the killing of a seal).

Finally, Ninioq's increasing disquiet over the non-arrival of their family leads them to return to the camp on their own, and to the horrifying discovery of their entire community dead in their tents, covered by sores. Ninioq finds a piece of skin holding a number of metal sewing needles, and weeps, 'Needles from strangers! They brought this sickness to everybody'. She stops Maniq from entering the tents to see the bodies, she gathers supplies, and the two of them return by kayak to the island (where food for the winter has been cached). They arrive in a storm, a storm of epic proportions, one which has blown down and ripped apart their tents. She calls out into this gale, 'When will this nightmare end? Where are all the people?'

In the midst of this storm they seek shelter in a cave, the same cave we inhabited in the movie's opening scene. And here, we see Ninioq sheltering her grandson, who is asleep against her chest, as she sits upright, with her back to the wall. In a voiceover, with a close-up on her unmoving face, we hear the words, 'Husband, I was so tired. I needed help for our grandson. I was so tired. How could he live without parents or companionship?'[48] And so, at the midpoint of the movie, we have this second question ('How could he live?'), a counterpart to the question

47 http://www.cbc.ca/news/arts/film/story/2009/03/12/f-before-tomorrow-review.html

48 At several points in the film, we hear Ninioq speaking (sometimes in her mind, sometimes aloud) to her dead husband.

posed at the beginning ('Why must we die?'). And this second question leads us to our second law envisioned.

The second story: 'The Ptarmigan and the Snow Bunting'

The close shot on the grandmother and sleeping child switches to a shot of the clouds moving across the moon in a black sky. The blackness gradually fades to white, and we are faced with a bright sunlit snowy tundra. In a sustained shot, we watch the wind blowing the snow across the open space. And then, the shot resolves, and visually we are returned to the first shot of the movie, with Maniq and Ninioq walking across the tundra. This time it is she who speaks first, saying, 'Are you going to keep asking me to tell you more stories?' She laughs, and adds 'Of course you are.'

We return again to the cave of our opening scene, where the grandmother and grandson are again sitting on the floor, surrounded by skins, the qulliq providing a sense of flickering light and warmth. This time, the story is the very well-known tale, 'The Ptarmigan and the Snowbunting'.[49] Ninioq begins her story by drawing a little piece of shell out from a bag, saying, 'look, a ptarmigan'. She puts the shell into his hands, watching him hold it, and corrects him on how to hold it just right, to see in it the shape of the bird. As he holds the shell in his hands, she continues, in a close-up, with a smile, saying:

> 'I have heard that they haven't always been ptarmigans. There was an old woman and her grandson who were all alone, maybe like us? When the grandson went to bed he asked his grandmother to tell a story. The grandmother responded by saying, "I don't have any stories, get comfortable and go to sleep!" But the child insisted and started to cry, "Grandmother tell me a story . . ."'

Ninioq pretends to be the whining child, and laughs at her own voice, then continues: 'Finally the grandmother started to speak.' At this point, the English subtitles become vague, and it is clear that the translation is only partial at best. The English subtitles read 'story . . . story . . . baby lemmings . . . having no fur . . . arms folded in . . . start falling . . . feels ticklish . . .' As her voice gets slower, she suddenly reaches in, grabs her grandson and tickles him. As the two of them laugh, she continues her story:

> 'The grandson was so startled, he shouted "TEEOOK!" and flew off. He turned into a snow bunting and flew away right out the air hole. The grandmother looked all around and said "Grandson, where did you go?" Again

49 Three different versions of it are recorded in Christopher, *Unikkaaqtuat*. This story can be listened to online on the CBC radio series *Ideas*, with Paul Kennedy, focusing on indigenous legends, read by Imalaiu Imnuquuk and David Sirquois, http://www.cbc.ca/aboriginal/2008/11/inuit-legends-ii-legends-of-the-eastern-arctic.html, (accessed October 22, 2015), http://www.cbc.ca/video/news/audioplayer.html?clipid=1449050829 (see minute 46:30).

> and again, "Where are you?" Then she cried so much, and she wiped her eyes so much, that her eyes turned red, but she couldn't find him. Finally, she puts her needles into her boots. Then she took her oil lamp wick and hung it around her neck. That's the collar filled with seeds around the ptarmigan's neck. And then she went, Ap-ap-ap-ap-ap! And flew off to join her grandson.'

Again, she laughs. After a moment, she continues, this time giving her interpretation of the story: 'He was so startled he turned into a snow bunting! She went flying right out after him! Too bad!' She smiles again. 'But it must have been all right as long as they were together again. That's the end of that story.' We return to a close-up shot of the light flickering in the qulliq.

And so, we have been told a story of a grandmother and grandchild, a story of transformation. On one level, this can be read as a creation story, about the origin of two animals. Like many Inuit stories, it also emphasizes the relations between people and animals, the ability of both animals and people to put on 'new skins'. As with many stories, 'The Ptarmigan and the Snowbunting' has multiple functions. It can function as a cautionary tale that explains what happens when children do not listen to their elders (and demand too many stories!).[50] Despite being a cautionary tale, it is one that was frequently told. This story, which Alexina Kublu (Language Commissioner for Nunavut) translates as 'Irngutarjuapiga nauk?' ('Where is my dear grandchild?') is a story 'easily prompted whenever anyone says to somebody who is known to be a storyteller "unikkaaqtualarit" "tell us a story" '.[51] Kublu recounts: 'This is one story that stopped me from asking my oldest brother Serapie to tell me stories because with "ah tu tu tu tu tu" someone ended up being tickled (usually it was me).'

Elder Pelagie Owljoot positions the story as a legend not simply for children, but also to remind parents about how to handle children.[52] In particular, she says, it is a story that seeks also to teach young mothers how to work with young children, to ensure they do not scare or frighten them, that they do not speak too loudly, or startle young ones. Indeed, in the context of widespread concern by elders that younger Inuit are culturally deficient (or that there are challenges in the transfer of cultural knowledge),[53] the character of Ninioq is teaching in the way that elders traditionally have taught: by modelling. So what then is Ninioq modelling in this

50 Christopher, *Unikkaqtuat* at 75.

51 Christopher, *Unikkaqtuat*, at 152.

52 Pelagie Owlijoot, in consultation with the Language and Culture Committee of Nunavut Arctic College. *Guidelines for Working with Inuit Elders* (Iqualuit: Nunavut Arctic College, 2008).

53 Frédéric Laugrand and Jarich Oosten, "Transfer of Inuit Qaujimajatuqangit in Modern Inuit Society". *Études/Inuit/Studies* 33(1–2) (2009): 115–152; Jarich Oosten and Frederic B. Laugrand, eds, *Surviving in Different Worlds: Transferring Inuit Traditions from Elders to Youth* (Iqaluit: Nunavut Arctic College, 2012).

context? So much of what we see focuses on the relationship of grandmother and grandson, on practices of caring for children.[54] It seems significant that this second story is told once we (like the characters) have seen the awful death of their entire community. They are alone in the world. How is the story functioning here? What does it help us envision? It is a story that speaks to the world in which the two find themselves. If this is a cautionary story about the risks of frightening a child, are we seeing Ninioq interact with Maniq in line with the story's moral? That is, in telling the story, is she taking care *not* to scare him? In her interactions with her grandson in the later part of the film, she focuses on helping him plan for the future, remember the past, and enjoy the time they have with each other. But is this simply an effort to distract Maniq from what lies ahead, or is the story in this context doing more? Is she also preparing him to think about transformations that might have happened? Is she indeed giving him tools for what may lie ahead?

This scene is one rich in the haptic qualities that Marks alerts us to. As with the opening scene, as viewers, we are drawn into a space of physical presence. And, as Marks reminds us, 'meaning is conveyed through physical presence as well as through intellectual signification.'[55] We are drawn closely into intimate space with both Ninioq and Maniq. The close-ups and angles ensure that, as she puts the shell into Maniq's hands, she also puts the story into his hands, inviting both Maniq and the viewer to hold the shell/story, to shift its angles, to reveal there something otherwise not visible.

We thus have another story, told in a context where the story is again adapted to the situation. The story is then followed in some ways by a performance of the story's law. In the second half of the film, the two continue to live. The film demonstrates the reality of a land that is marked by a particular relationship of life and death, scarcity and plenitude, sorrow and joy, light and dark and of the unavoidable connection of living and dying. The passing and the return of seasons. There is a priority placed on the importance of being able to work hard to share, and to participate in a tradition of non-judgement, of watching and learning. There is a moment in the second half of the movie, sitting in the cave with his grandmother, playing with a toy sled, that Maniq asks his grandmother the question, 'Why did those strangers hurt our family?' But the question is not answered. Or rather, she answers him in a way consistent with Inuit traditional practices: to speak only of things one knows oneself.[56] She replies, 'I do not know. I never knew these people. Maybe some day you will find out.'

54 For an elaboration of these practices, see Naqi Ekho and Uqsuaralik, *Interviewing Inuit Elders, Vol 3: Childrearing Practices,* edited by Jean Briggs (Iqaluit: Nunavut Arctic College, 2000).

55 Marks, at 121.

56 For a full discussion of this imperative to speak only of what one knows through one's own experience, see Saullu Nakasuk, Hervé Paniaq, Elisapee Ootoova and Pauloosie Angmaalik, *Interviewing Inuit Elders, Vol 1: Introduction*, edited by Jarich Oosten and Frédéric Laugrand (Iqaluit: Nunavut Arctic College, 1999).

The question is, in some ways, left for the viewers: will we be in a position to find out why? And what would the why tell us? Would the 'why' (from curiosity, greed, selfishness or error) change the conditions in which the living continue to live? The strangers never make an appearance in the film, and the question is not answered. Rather, after the telling of the second story, the film again returns us to the business of living. We watch Ninioq at night singing her favourite songs to help her grandson fall asleep. We see Maniq cleaning furs by sliding down hills while sitting on them. We see Ninioq repairing ripped skins using the (fatal) metal needles. Maniq plays with his puppies, giving them names, playing with a toy sled (qamautiq), asking his grandmother to make a whip (for a dog team) so he can learn to use it during the winter.

And, unfortunately, yet another tragedy comes. And it is not at the hands of strangers, but of the world in which they live. For while the island is safe from animals in the summer, once the winter comes and the ice forms, it is accessible. We see the arrival of a pack of wolves. Ninioq manages to get Maniq hidden beneath a qayaq, but the food cache is taken, and she is badly wounded. And so, with the departure of the wolves, Ninioq and Maniq return to the cave; Maniq does what he can to care for his grandmother, to seek food outside in the darkness of the long winter nights. When he speaks of his fear of the darkness outside the cave, she comforts him, saying:

> 'Dear little one, don't be scared. The light is friends with the dark. I love you. You don't have to be afraid of the dark. We are going through hard times right now but we will survive. And when we go to that beautiful place we will have lots of stories to tell. Maybe we have to talk all the time. Even though we were alone we did a lot: our tent blew away, our relatives passed away, you caught your first seal. We found this cave to make a safe home indoors. We could have been stranded outdoors with no shelter. We told so many stories, and planned a happier future. I love you so much. You are so able now. You learned so much. You are able now, and I love you my little one.'

She continues speaking lots of little love words to him, touching his hair and face as he falls asleep. Only then, after a close-up on the sleeping child, do we return to a close up on her. Again, with Maniq sleeping, Ninioq's fears come out and she again speaks to her dead husband. At the beginning of the second section, she had posed the question, 'How can a child live, without family or community?' Now, she calls out 'Husband! Help me'. For the first time in the film, we have a moment of extra-diegetic sound, signalling something new. And here, we hear the sound of an old man's voice calling back to her, providing an answer to her question: 'No child can live alone'.

In the final moments of the movie, we watch the wounded Ninioq arranging things in the cave, placing objects and items in order as Maniq sleeps under the warmth of his furs. Again, this scene is shot in a way that makes us feel physically present, that holds us in slow-moving time, as Ninioq makes what we already sense to be 'final preparations' of a sort. There will be no one who will come to prepare their bodies. We are held in this close-up sensorium as she takes a comb, and runs it though her hair, (painfully) pulling it back into an orderly braid. She then crawls to the mouth of the cave, and removes the skin that was functioning as a door. Snow and wind are visible outside. She returns to sit by the sleeping child, and re-sings the song that he had asked her to sing to him in the first half of the movie. She sings the entire song, seated in front of the qulliq, which occupies the centre bottom of the screen. There are no edits or cuts in the film to enable a space of escape or relief for the viewer: we sit with her through the singing. Her laboured breathing is audible, as is the wind outside. Indeed, there is no respite by extra-diegetic music or noise. The soundscape again holds us in the present and in close proximity to Ninioq. As the song proceeds, we feel the temperature in the cave dropping, as steam increasingly comes from her mouth as she sings. The lyrics of the song ('When will you come home? When you hear me sing this song?') evoke the story of the Ptarmigan and the Snowbunting, with the grandmother calling out for the return of her grandchild.

And then, Ninioq slowly begins to put out the flames in the qulliq. This is not the rapid blowing out of a candle, but a deliberate and orderly process (60 seconds) of tapping out the flames, dimming the qulliq until only a single tiny flame burns at the centre. She waits a moment, and then slides the fur skins off her sleeping grandchild, exposing his naked torso, and then puts out the last flame. She then slides off her own parka and lays down beside her grandson, so that they both have only legs covered, and torsos exposed. We listen to her breath inhaling and exhaling, and then the screen goes dark. Gradually, the McGarrigle Sisters' song of the beginning returns. This time, the song lyrics 'Why Must We Die?' are accompanied by light- and colour-filled (slow motion) images of the community from the opening scenes, but scenes we have not seen until now: scenes of all those who have appeared in the film, in moments of eating, play, games, laughter. We end not with the darkness of the cave, but images of life.

Conclusion: envisioning Inuit law – reading ourselves into the story

We begin and end the movie with the story of the Raven and the Whale in our minds – with the extinguishing of the flame. Though it is tempting to view the film through western eyes as an epic tragedy, *Before Tomorrow* in some ways resists this reading; it focuses on the shape of life as the grandmother and the grandson continue forward, living in the world. He continues to ask for, and she continues to tell stories of law, stories that speak about transitions and change, and loss and possibly return. The relations seem to affirm the importance of continuing forward with the work of living, raising the puppy, playing with toys, speaking of a whip, and speaking of successes and all they have accomplished, planning for the future, enjoying each other's company, singing, talking, telling stories, sharing food. What we see is not fatalistic acceptance of death. Rather there is engagement in a way that makes visible an Inuit cosmological understanding of the world: a world in which it makes sense that the grandmother would continue to speak to her dead husband, one in which it makes sense that a child might turn into a snow bunting, that the night would be friends with the day. A life in which death is something that will arrive, that it may bring with it grief or sorrow, but that it is not a final end.

We have seen Inuit law embedded throughout this film. It emerges in story, but is also embedded and envisioned in its characters. Judgements and decisions are made about things that must be done and things that should not be done. The law is not focused on an outsider judging someone else's performance; it is a judgement made on looking and watching. This view of the law is a challenge for the west. We see law in things that are written on tablets of stone. Not law as written in practices, in stories and on the land itself. Like in many Inuit stories, there is more than one law in the story and more than one way to have the story make sense and to use it. Just as Ninioq put the piece of shell into Maniq's hand when she told him her story, the story has been put into our hand. We, like Maniq, have been asked to do the work of thinking through and with the story; of becoming capable in the business of living life against a horizon of events that may arrive, both expected and unexpected, produced through strangers or the world around us.

But this film is an invitation to linger longer within the community, to feel and experience its rhythms, to watch its practice of life, and practices of community and to rethink how we understand its law or law's function in the context of this terrain, this landscape and this people. It is a film that foregrounds relations of love and care, work and community.

As western viewers, it is unavoidable that we come to film with the lenses of our own analysis. The western view is to engage in the questions of who is guilty and what are they guilty of. A person can go to this film and come away thinking about the interaction of settler and Inuit societies, and the devastating impact that occurred through carelessness or accident. That is one of the possible readings. But that reading does not feel like the film's centre. The film invites us, through its deployment of both story and haptic visuality, to experience ways of living, rather than ways of dying. And it asks us to engage in different practices of memory, of holding the past up, and of asking what it might take for the heart of the raven and the heart of the whale to be restored. If Edward Said is right to remind us that tales of the past are invariably tales of the present,[57] then one of the questions might be what the film invites us to imagine or feel now. In its envisioning of law, the film asks us to consider our relations with others and the world around us, and to work at living the practices that can help give new shape to our daily lives in the now that is always before tomorrow.

57 Edward Saïd, *Culture and Imperialism* (New York: Vintage Books, 1994), 14.

Bibliography

Books and articles

Ableson, Serena. "Bringing Legal Education to the Canadian Arctic: the Development of the Akitsiraq Law School and the Challenges for Providing Library Services to a Nontraditional Law School." *International Journal of Legal Information* 34(1) (2006): Article 4.

Amsterdam, Anthony G., and Jerome Bruner. *Minding the Law: How Courts Rely on Storytelling, and How Their Stories Change the Ways We Understand the Law – and Ourselves.* Cambridge, MA: Harvard University Press, 2000.

Aupilaarjuk, Marian, Marie Tulimaaq, Akisu Joamie, Emile Imaruittuq, and Lucassie Nutaraaluk. *Interviewing Inuit Elders, Vol 2: Perspectives on Traditional Law.* Edited by Jarich Oosten, Frederic Laugrand, and Wim Rasing. Iqaluit: Nunavut Arctic College, 1999.

Bennett, John, and Susan Rowley, eds. *Uqalurait: An Oral History of Nunavut.* Montreal and Kingston: McGill-Queen's University Press, 2004.

Brody, Hugh. *The Other Side of Eden: Hunters, Farmers, and the Shaping of the World.* New York: Anchor Books, 2001.

Buchanan, Ruth, and Rebecca Johnson. "Strange Encounters: Exploring Law and Film in the Affective Register." *Studies in Law, Politics, and Society* 46 (2009): 33–60.

Canada – Royal Commission on Aboriginal Peoples. *Report of the Royal Commission on Aboriginal Peoples.* Canada, 1996.

Canada – The Truth and Reconciliation Commission of Canada. *Honouring the Truth, Reconciling for the Future: Summary of the Final Report of the Truth and Reconciliation Commission of Canada.* Canada, 2015.

Christopher, Neil, Noel McDermott, and Louise Flaherty, eds. *Unikkaaqtuat: an Introduction to Inuit Myths and Legends.* Toronto: Inhabit Media, 2011.

Clover, Carol. "Law and the Order of Popular Culture." In *Law in the Domains of Culture,* edited by Austin Sarat and T. R. Kearns, 97–119. Ann Arbor: University of Michigan Press, 1998.

D'Anglure, Bernard Saladin. "From Foetus to Shaman: The Construction of an Inuit Third Sex." In *Amerindian Rebirth: Reincarnation Belief among North American Indians and Inuit,* edited by Antonia Mills and Richard Slobodin, 82–106. Toronto: University of Toronto Press, 1994.

Doane, Mary Ann. "Ideology and the Practice of Sound Editing and Mixing." In *The Cinematic Apparatus,* edited by Teresa de Lauretis and Stephen Heath, 47–60. New York: St Martin's Press, 1980.

Evans, Michael Robert. *The Fast Runner: Filming the Legend of Atanarjuat.* Lincoln and London: University of Nebraska Press, 2010.

Ekho, Naqi, and Uqsuaralik. *Interviewing Inuit Elders, Vol 3: Childrearing Practices.* Edited by Jean Briggs. Iqaluit: Nunavut Arctic College, 2000.

Groarke, Paul. "Review Essay: Legal Volumes from the Arctic College's *Interviewing Inuit Elders* Series." *Osgoode Hall Law Journal* 47 (2009): 787–805.

Harris, Cole. "Voices of Disaster: Smallpox around the Strait of Georgia in 1782." *Ethnohistory* 41(4) (1994): 591–626.

Hodgson, Corinne. "The Social and Political Implications of Tuberculosis among Native Canadians." *Canadian Review of Sociology and Anthropology* 19 (1982): 502–512.

Hunhdorf, Shari. "Atanarjuat, the Fast Runner: Culture, History and Politics in Inuit Media." *American Anthropologist* 105(4) (2003): 822–826.

Johnson, Rebecca, and Ruth Buchanan. "Getting the *Insider*'s Story Out: What Popular Film Can Tell Us About Legal Method's Dirty Secrets." *Windsor Yearbook of Access to Justice* 20 (2001): 87–110

Johnson, Rebecca, and Lori Groft. "Learning Indigenous Law: Reflections on Working with Western Inuit Stories." *Lakehead Law Journal* 2(2) (2017): 117–144.

Johnson, Rebecca. "Reimagining 'The Truth North Strong and Free': Reflections on Going to the Movies with James Boyd White." In *Living in a Law Transformed: Encounters with the Works of James Boyd White.* Edited by Julen Etxabe and Gary Watt, 258–283. Ann Arbor, MI: Maize Books, 2014.

Kamir, Orit. "Why 'Law-and-Film' and What Does It Actually Mean?: A Perspective." *Continuum: Journal of Media and Cultural Studies* 19(2) (2005): 255–278.

Kilpatrick, Mr. Justice Robert. "An Open Letter to the Citizens of Nunavut on the Importance of Traditional Justice Values in the 21st Century," May 6, 2011, http://docslide.us/documents/justice-robert-kilpatrick-open-letter-to-citizens-of-nunavut.html (accessed October 22, 2015).

King, Thomas. *The Inconvenient Indian: A Curious Account of Native People in North America.* Toronto: Anchor Canada, 2012.

Lessard, Hester, Rebecca Johnson, and Jeremy Webber, eds. *Storied Communities: Narratives of Contact and Arrival in Constituting Political Community.* Vancouver: UBC Press, 2010.

Marcus, Alan. *Relocating Eden: The Image and Politics of Inuit Exile in the Canadian Arctic.* Dartmouth, NH: University Press of New England, 1995.

Marks, Laura. *The Skin of the Film: Intercultural Cinema, Embodiment and the Senses.* Durham, NC: Duke University Press, 2000.

Martin, Keavy. *Stories in a New Skin: Approaches to Inuit Literature.* Winnipeg: University of Manitoba Press, 2012.

McCall, Sophie. "'I Can Only Sing This Song to Someone Who Understands It': Community Filmmaking and the Politics of Partial Translation in *Atanarjuat, the Fast Runner.*" *Essays on Canadian Writing* 83 (2004): 19–46.

McGrath, Melanie. *The Long Exile: a Tale of Inuit Betrayal and Survival in the High Arctic.* New York: Vintage Books, 2006.

Nakasuk, Saullu, Hervé Paniaq, Elisapee Ootoova, and Pauloosie Angmaalik. *Interviewing Inuit Elders, Vol 1: Introduction.* Edited by Jarich Oosten and Frédéric Laugrand. Iqaluit: Nunavut Arctic College, 1999.

Napoleon, Val and Hadley Friedland. "An Inside Job: Engaging with Indigenous Legal Traditions Through Stories." *McGill Law Journal* 61(4) (2016): 725–754.

Olofsson, Ebba, Tara L. Holton, and Imaapik 'Jacob' Partridge. "Negotiating Identities: Inuit Tuberculosis Evacuees in the 1940s–1950s." *Etudes/Inuit/Studies* 32(2) (2008): 127–149.

Oosten, Jarich, and Frederic B. Laugrand. *Surviving in Different Worlds: Transferring Inuit Traditions from Elders to Youth.* Iqaluit: Nunavut Arctic College, 2012.

Owlijoot, Pelagie, in consultation with the Language and Culture committee of Nunavut Arctic College. *Guidelines for Working with Inuit Elders.* Iqualuit: Nunavut Arctic College, 2008.

Parmar, Pooja. *Indigeneity and Legal Pluralism in India.* New York: Cambridge University Press, 2015.

Rasmussen, Knud. *The Alaskan Eskimos, as Described in the Posthumous Notes of Dr. Knud Rasmussen/by H. Ostermann ; Edited after the Latter's Death with the Assistance of E. Holtved; Translated from the Danish by W.E. Calvert.* Copenhagen: Gyldendal, 1952.

Rasmussen, Knud. *Intellectual Culture of the Iglulik Eskimos.* Report of the Fifth Thule Expedition 1921–24: The Danish Expedition to Arctic North America in Charge of Knud Rasmussen. Vol. Volume VII, No.1, Copenhagen: Glydendalske Boghandel Nordisk Forlag, 1929.

Regan, Paulette. *Unsettling the Settler Within: Indian Residential Schools, Truth Telling, and Reconciliation in Canada.* Vancouver: UBC Press, 2010.

Riel, Jørn. *Før Morgendagen.* Copenhagen: Lademann, 1975.

Robinson, Gillian, ed. *The Journals of Knud Rasmussen: A Sense of Memory and High-Definition Inuit Storytelling.* Montreal: Isuma Distribution International, 2008.

Saïd, Edward. *Culture and Imperialism.* New York: Vintage Books, 1994.

Silbey, Jessica. "Persuasive Visions: Film and Memory." *Law, Culture and the Humanities* 10(1) (2014): 24–42.

Steckley, John L. *White Lies About the Inuit.* Peterborough, ON: Broadview Press, 2008.

Tester, Frank J., and Peter Kulchyski. *Tammarniit (Mistakes): Inuit Relocation in the Eastern Arctic, 1939–63.* Vancouver: UBC Press, 1994.

Wachowich, Nancy *et al.*, *Saqiyuk: Stories From the Lives of Three Inuit Women.* Montreal and Kingston: McGill-Queen's University Press, 1999.

White, James Boyd. *From Expectation to Experience: Essays on Law and Legal Education.* Ann Arbor: University of Michigan Press, 1999.

White, James Boyd. *Justice as Translation: An Essay in Cultural and Legal Criticism.* Chicago: University of Chicago Press, 1990.

Films

Arctic Defenders, directed by John Walker (Unikkaat Defenders Productions, 2013).

Atanarjuat: The Fast Runner, directed by Zacharias Kunuk (Igloolik Isuma Productions, 2001).

Before Tomorrow, directed by Marie-Helene Cousineau and Madeline Ivalu (Igloolik Isuma Productions, 2008).

The Journals of Knud Rasmussen, directed by Zacharias Kunuk and Norman Cohn (Igloolik Isuma Productions, 2006).

Martha of the North, directed by Marquise Lepage (National Film Board of Canada, 2008).

Nanook of the North, directed by Robert J. Flaherty (1922).

Qallunaat!: Why White People are Funny, directed by Mark Sandiford (National Film Board of Canada, 2006).

Index

Note: page numbers in italics indicate figures.

For Product Safety Concerns and Information please contact our EU representative GPSR@taylorandfrancis.com
Taylor & Francis Verlag GmbH, Kaufingerstraße 24, 80331 München, Germany

www.ingramcontent.com/pod-product-compliance
Ingram Content Group UK Ltd.
Pitfield, Milton Keynes, MK11 3LW, UK
UKHW021301190926
475701UK00009B/432
9780367232566